1898-1954

AMERICA'S RISE
TO WORLD POWER

HARPER ✦ TORCHBOOKS

*A reference-list of Harper Torchbooks, classified
by subjects, is printed at the end of this volume.*

THE NEW AMERICAN NATION SERIES

Edited by HENRY STEELE COMMAGER *and*

RICHARD B. MORRIS

David B. Quinn	DISCOVERY AND EXPLORATION.*
Wallace Notestein	THE ENGLISH PEOPLE ON THE EVE OF COLONIZATION, 1603-1630. TB/3006.
Charles Gibson	SPAIN IN AMERICA. TB/3077
Mason Wade	FRANCE IN AMERICA.*
Wilcomb E. Washburn	THE INDIANS IN AMERICA*
John E. Pomfret	FOUNDING THE ENGLISH COLONIES.*
Wesley Frank Craven	GROWTH OF THE ENGLISH COLONIES, 1660-1710.*
Jack P. Greene	THE ENGLISH COLONIES IN THE EIGHTEENTH CENTURY.*
Louis B. Wright	THE CULTURAL LIFE OF THE AMERICAN COLONIES, 1607-1763. TB/3005.
Lawrence Henry Gipson	THE COMING OF THE REVOLUTION, 1763-1775. TB/3007.
John Richard Alden	THE AMERICAN REVOLUTION, 1775-1783. TB/3011.
Richard B. Morris	CONFEDERATION AND CONSTITUTION.*
Henry S. Commager	CONSTITUTIONAL DEVELOPMENT, 1789-1835.*
John C. Miller	THE FEDERALIST ERA, 1789-1801. TB/3027.
Marshall Smelser	THE JEFFERSONIAN ERA.*
George Dangerfield	THE AWAKENING OF AMERICAN NATIONALISM, 1815-1828. TB/3061.
Francis S. Philbrick	THE RISE OF THE WEST, 1754-1830. TB/3067.
Glydon G. Van Deusen	THE JACKSONIAN ERA, 1828-1848. TB/3028.
Clement Eaton	THE GROWTH OF SOUTHERN CIVILIZATION, 1790-1860. TB/3040.
Louis Filler	THE CRUSADE AGAINST SLAVERY, 1830-1860. TB/3029.
Russel B. Nye	THE CULTURAL LIFE OF THE NEW NATION, 1776-1830. TB/3026.
Frederick Rudolph	CULTURAL DEVELOPMENT, 1830-1860.*
Bernard Schwartz	AMERICAN CONSTITUTIONAL HISTORY, 1835-1877*
Ray A. Billington	THE FAR WESTERN FRONTIER, 1830-1860. TB/3012.
David M. Potter	THE COMING OF THE CIVIL WAR.*
Richard Current	THE CIVIL WAR, 1860-1865.*
Frank E. Vandiver	THE CONFEDERACY.*
David Donald	RECONSTRUCTION.*
John A. Garraty	HAYES TO HARRISON, 1877-1890.*
Harold U. Faulkner	POLITICS, REFORM AND EXPANSION, 1890-1900. TB/3020.
Foster Rhea Dulles	AMERICA'S RISE TO WORLD POWER, 1898-1954. TB/3021.
John W. Ward	CULTURAL HISTORY, 1860-1900.*
Rodman Paul	THE FAR WEST AND THE GREAT PLAINS.*
George E. Mowry	THE ERA OF THEODORE ROOSEVELT, 1900-1912. TB/3022.
Arthur S. Link	WOODROW WILSON AND THE PROGRESSIVE ERA, 1910-1917. TB/3023.
Arthur S. Link	WORLD WAR I.*
Loren P. Beth	CONSTITUTIONAL HISTORY, 1877-1917.*
Max Lerner	AMERICAN CULTURE IN THE TWENTIETH CENTURY.*
Paul Murphy	THE CONSTITUTION IN CRISIS TIMES, 1918-1965*
John D. Hicks	REPUBLICAN ASCENDANCY, 1921-1933. TB/3041.
William E. Leuchtenburg	FRANKLIN D. ROOSEVELT AND THE NEW DEAL, 1932-1940. TB/3025.
John Hope Franklin	THE NEW SOUTH *
A. Russell Buchanan	THE UNITED STATES AND WORLD WAR II, Volume I. TB/3044.
A. Russell Buchanan	THE UNITED STATES AND WORLD WAR II, Volume II. TB/3045.
Alfred B. Rollins, Jr.	POST WORLD WAR II—Domestic Affairs.
Kenneth W. Thompson	AMERICAN FOREIGN POLICY SINCE 1945*
Clifford Lord	STATISTICAL VOLUME.*

* *In preparation*

1898-1954

AMERICA'S RISE TO WORLD POWER

BY FOSTER RHEA DULLES

HARPER TORCHBOOKS ❧

HARPER & ROW, *Publishers*

The University Library

New York

Once Again to Marion

Contents

EDITORS' INTRODUCTION   xiii

PREFACE   xvii

1. THE TRADITION OF ISOLATION   1

2. AMERICA LOOKS OUTWARD   21

3. IMPERIALIST ADVENTURE   40

4. A NEW WORLD ROLE   59

5. THE IMPACT OF WAR   87

6. THE GREAT RETREAT   108

7. GIANT OF THE WESTERN WORLD   128

8. THE IDEAL AND THE REAL   144

9. THE MIRAGE OF NEUTRALITY   167

10. CHALLENGE AND RESPONSE   187

11. THE SEARCH FOR PEACE   208

12. COLD WAR   221

13. BROADENING TENSION   246

14. MID-CENTURY   262

      BIBLIOGRAPHY   283

      INDEX   303

Illustrations

*These photographs, grouped in a separate section,
will be found following page 138*

1. ALFRED THAYER MAHAN

2. HENRY CABOT LODGE

3. JOHN HAY

4. PRESIDENT MCKINLEY and VICE PRESIDENT THEODORE
   ROOSEVELT

5. ELIHU ROOT

6. PHILANDER C. KNOX

7. WILLIAM JENNINGS BRYAN

8. ROBERT LANSING

9. The "Big Four" at the Paris Peace Conference

10. Premier Clemenceau inviting the Germans to sign the Treaty
    of Versailles

11. CHARLES EVANS HUGHES

12. Signing the Kellogg-Briand Anti-War Treaty

13. PRESIDENT HOOVER with FRANK B. KELLOGG and HENRY L.
    STIMSON

14. SENATORS HIRAM JOHNSON, ARTHUR VANDENBERG and WIL-
    LIAM E. BORAH

15. PRESIDENT ROOSEVELT and SECRETARY HULL

16. President Roosevelt signing the declaration of war on Japan

17. Signing of the Four Power Pact in Moscow

18. President Roosevelt and Prime Minister Churchill at Casablanca

19. Premier Stalin, President Roosevelt and Prime Minister Churchill at Teheran

20. Generalissimo Chiang Kai-shek, President Roosevelt, Prime Minister Churchill and Madam Chiang Kai-shek at Cairo

21. Prime Minister Churchill, President Roosevelt and Premier Stalin at Yalta

22. Prime Minister Attlee, President Truman and Premier Stalin at Potsdam

23. JAMES F. BYRNES

24. GEORGE C. MARSHALL

25. President Truman, Secretary of State Stettinius and Field Marshal Smuts at the San Francisco Conference

26. PRESIDENT TRUMAN and SECRETARY OF STATE DEAN ACHESON

27. Signing the Japanese-American Security Pact

28. The "Big Three" meet German Chancellor Konrad Adenauer in Bonn preparatory to signing the Allied-Germany Peace Contract

29. Secretary of State John Foster Dulles and Mutual Security Administrator Harold E. Stassen report to President Eisenhower

30. Korean prisoners of war

31. Red Chinese Premier Chou En-lai at the Geneva Conference

32. President Eisenhower bids Sir Winston Churchill good-by

Maps

THE AMERICAN ADVANCE INTO THE PACIFIC   57

MIDDLE AMERICA AND THE CARIBBEAN   75

THE SUBMARINE ENTERS MODERN WAR   94

PEACE BY INSULATION   190

ZONES OF OCCUPATION IN GERMANY   224

RIO TREATY SECURITY ZONE   238

NATO COUNTRIES   243

THE JAPANESE PEACE SETTLEMENT   269

THE GLOBAL COMMITMENTS OF THE UNITED STATES   278

Editors' Introduction

IMPERIALISM and world power are familiar and perhaps essential aspects of modern nationalism. Some nations may be said to be born to power; others achieve power, or try to. Of the United States alone can it truly be said that power has been thrust upon her, and with the United States, alone of major nations, the problem of power has been not to circumscribe it but to enlarge it, to implement it, and to make it self-conscious and responsible.

Thus the story that Mr. Dulles has to tell in this sweeping account of the rise of America to world power, while in some respects analogous to the history of other modern empires, is in important respects unique. As Mr. Dulles makes clear in his opening chapter, the instinct of the American people was for isolation, and if that isolation was never as deep as some politicians assume it was perhaps deeper than some scholars realize, for it was rooted not only in geography, economy and history, but in emotion. How, notwithstanding history, tradition, and emotion, Americans found themselves involved first with the fragments of the Spanish Empire in America, then in Pacific and Asiatic adventures, and finally in Europe, and how, through advance and retreat and advance they responded, is the central theme of Mr. Dulles's book.

In the light of the American past, it was no wonder that the transition from the romanticized isolation and exaggerated security of the nineteenth century to the implacable involvements and the harsh responsibilities of the twenties was accompanied by soul-searching and turbulence. It is no wonder that during this sixty-year period Americans were pulled back and forth by the strains and pressures of tradition and of reality; that the venture into the Pacific in the nineties was

greeted by a clamorous demand for withdrawal; that the comfortable
neutrality of the early years of the First World War gave way to the
seeming necessities of involvement and that this, in turn, was followed
by disillusion and retreat; that the cataclysmic crises of the thirties
and forties led irresistibly to a second and greater involvement. What
is, perhaps, wonderful is that all of these prodigious decisions were
made by public opinion, for American foreign policy, more fully than
that of any other major power, was a public policy formulated by
democratic processes. What is impressive is that the ultimate decisions
were dictated not by greed for territory, for trade, for power, or for any
of the more ostentatious traditional rewards of imperialism, but rather
by a willingness to accept—or at least an unwillingness to escape—responsibility. Americans seem to have known by instinct what most Old
World nations have found it difficult to learn, that power is a burden,
not a prize, and that its rewards are not material.

Mr. Dulles's book presents what future historians will probably
record as a unified chapter of American history: the emergence from
isolation in the nineties; a half century of debate and involvement; the
tremendous climax of the Second World War; the fateful commitments
to world organization and world leadership; the dramatic and irre-
versible change in the whole character of the problem of power precipitated by the invention of the absolute weapon. This sixty-year period
—all within the lifetime of men still active in public affairs—saw the
beginning and end of the greatest debate in the history of American
foreign policy, and the most momentous in its consequences. The
.echoes still resound along the dusty corridors of politics, to be sure, but
the issue of involvement and responsibility is no longer debatable, only
the tactics and the strategy.

Mr. Dulles has not attempted to add yet another to the almost
countless studies of tactics and strategy that pour from our presses in
an endless stream. He has attempted, rather, to provide the historical
background upon the basis of which judgment and policies can be
formed. What he gives us is not argument but analysis, not politics but
history. And in an area bristling with controversy he has written with
impartiality; on a subject clamorously current he has maintained historical perspective; confronted by the temptation to cover the whole
broad and intricate field of American foreign affairs over a sixty-year
period he has avoided the irrelevant and the trivial and held to the
central theme—America's Rise to World Power.

This volume is one of the New American Nation Series, a comprehensive co-operative survey of the history of the area now embraced in the United States from the days of discovery to the mid-twentieth century. Since the publication by the House of Harper of the American Nation Series, half a century ago, the scope of history has been immensely broadened, many new approaches explored and some developed. The time has now come for a judicious reappraisal of the new history, a cautious application of the new techniques of investigation and presentation, and a large-scale effort to achieve a synthesis of new findings with the familiar facts and to present the whole in attractive literary form.

To this task the New American Nation Series is dedicated. Each volume is part of a carefully planned whole and fitted to the other volumes in the series; at the same time each volume is designed to be complete in itself. From time to time, doubtless, the same series of events and the same actors will be presented from different points of view. Thus the ten or twelve volumes that will explore twentieth-century American history chronologically will expand many of the suggestions, fill in many of the details, and illuminate many of the episodes merely touched on in this volume. The forthcoming volume on constitutional history can be trusted to deal with the constitutional problems raised by world power, and the cultural history volume with some of the cultural implications of the shift from isolation to internationalism. That all this may result in some overlapping is inevitable, but it has seemed to the editors that repetition is less regrettable than omission, and that something is to be gained by looking at the same material from different and independent points of view.

HENRY STEELE COMMAGER
RICHARD BRANDON MORRIS

Preface

I N THE introduction to his penetrating study *The United States as
a World Power*, first published in 1908, Archibald Cary Coolidge
wrote: "No one can be more conscious than the author of this volume
how far it is from carrying out the too ambitious promise of its title."
In having the audacity to bring out a book under so similar a title a
momentous half century later, the present writer must strongly emphasize, pointedly underscore, a comparable disclaimer of even attempting
to tell the full story of America's rise to world power.

The growth and development of the American nation are after all
the general topic of the series of which this book is only a single volume. The purpose of this unit is obviously more limited. It is concerned only with those developments in the field of foreign policy
which mark the gradual emergence of the United States as a great
power. If there may be said to be an underlying theme in the treatment
and interpretation of such developments, it centers about the continuing conflict since the close of the nineteenth century between those
forces in our national life making for an assumption of the responsibilities of world power and those which have always sought the avoidance of such obligations.

This contest between responsible internationalism and what is called
isolationism has been of great significance in the exercise of the power
implicit in America's world position. The term isolationism, however,
has always been misleading. Among modern nations only the Japan of
pre-treaty days, through her rigorous exclusion of foreigners and prohi-
bition of all overseas trade or travel by her own subjects, has pursued

a truly isolationist policy. The United States has never turned away from the world in this sense. Its isolationism has gone no further than an assertion of complete independence and a refusal to accept any foreign political commitments which might infringe upon the nation's full freedom of action. Even within these limitations, however, the isolationist spirit has consistently warred against the acknowledgment of international obligations, and it provides a significant key to the foreign policy followed by the United States until very recent days.

To write of America's rise to world power from this point of view necessitates a highly selective treatment of the vast mass of available material. Nothing could be more difficult than the problems of omission and emphasis. It is the author's hope, however, that his approach may throw some light on those historical developments that account for the present world position of the United States, and help to provide a basis for a better understanding of the immense problems with which the nation today finds itself confronted.

In the preparation of this manuscript a grant-in-aid from Ohio State University made available the services of two research assistants, James P. Thomas and Gerald E. Ridinger. The author would like to express his appreciation for their very real help. He is also indebted to his colleagues at Ohio State, to many of his students for suggestions while the book was in progress, to Professor Henry Graff of Columbia University, and most importantly to the editors of this series, Professors Henry Steele Commager and Richard B. Morris, for their generous aid in the final preparation of the manuscript for publication. His daughter, Sally Dulles, did much of the typing and as on many previous occasions his wife, Marion Dulles, bore up nobly under the strain of having her husband write a book, and helped inestimably in reading and stylistically correcting it.

Ohio State University   FOSTER RHEA DULLES

AMERICA'S RISE
TO WORLD POWER

CHAPTER 1

The Tradition of Isolation

AMERICA'S rise to world power is a consequence of the nation's geographic position, natural resources, and dynamic energy. For the first century and more of national history, however, continental expansion and internal developments largely absorbed the energies of the American people. Every dictate of public interest emphasized the importance of avoiding all entanglements that might involve the young Republic in foreign rivalries and foreign wars. Only with the twentieth century did a rapidly contracting world, impending shifts in the European balance of power, and the growth of American economic and industrial strength create a situation that made impossible a continued aloofness from international affairs.

In spite of these changing conditions, there has been from the formation of the Republic an underlying continuity in the purposes governing the determination of foreign policy. They have included first and foremost a basic concern with safeguarding national security; second, a constant preoccupation with the promotion of foreign trade; and finally, a sense of national mission in encouraging the cause of freedom throughout the world. If the needs of national security generally sustained the doctrine of nonintervention in foreign affairs throughout the greater part of the nineteenth century, economic ambition and humanitarian sympathy for other peoples at times exercised a strong counterforce. Nevertheless the United States during these years was able to promote its trade without political entanglements, and helped to advance the cause of freedom, as the American people devoutly believed, through precept and example rather than interference with other nations' concerns.

When the changed world of the twentieth century undermined the bases of this independent foreign policy, the United States was confronted with problems—and potential dangers—that demanded a new approach. It could no longer live entirely to itself; it was unable to escape the larger role thrust upon it by the processes of history. Every move toward the assumption of the responsibilities of a great power, however, was combated by the tradition of that policy of aloofness and wholly independent action which in other circumstances had appeared to serve the nation so well. This tradition, which by the close of the nineteenth century became popularly designated as isolationism, had a tremendous emotional force. It continued to exercise a powerful influence long after the conditions that fostered and justified it had ceased to exist.

The idea that the United States should avoid all foreign political commitments stems from the earliest days of the Republic. It was, indeed, a corollary of the independence movement itself. Well before either Washington or Jefferson gave their famous advice to their countrymen about the dangers of becoming involved in what the latter termed "entangling alliances," John Adams had given a similar warning. "We should separate ourselves," he wrote in 1776, "as far as possible and as long as possible, from all European politics and wars." [1]

The policy so encouraged in the eighteenth century did not then have a negative connotation. It symbolized a further projection of the revolutionary doctrines of the Declaration of Independence. The nation's leaders were determined to establish their country's complete freedom, not only from political control by Great Britain, but from any sort of dependence on foreign countries. The colonies had been— and they recognized the fact—a part of the Atlantic Community. Again and again they had been drawn in spite of themselves into Europe's continuing power conflicts. In the light of this experience there was a general belief in the 1780's that unless every possible precaution was taken, the still weak and struggling United States would become "little better than puppets, danced on the wires of the cabinets of Europe." [2]

It is true that the new nation concluded a wartime alliance with

[1] Charles F. Adams (ed.), *The Works of John Adams* (10 vols., Boston, 1856), II, 505.
[2] *Ibid.*, I, 200.

France, and for a time sought membership in the Armed Neutrality League sponsored by Russia, but these were temporary measures dictated by immediate political expediency. A determined opposition to any such European ties soon asserted itself. "The true interest of these states," read a resolution of the Continental Congress adopted in 1783, "requires that they should be as little as possible entangled in the politics and controversies of European nations." [3]

This policy statement in no way implied isolationism in the sense of complete withdrawal from the outside world. There was no more possibility in the 1780's than in subsequent years of severing the cultural and economic ties that bound the United States to Europe. The urgent needs of the country placed a tremendous emphasis upon the importance of commercial treaties, recognized by Jefferson no less than by Hamilton, and on all other practical measures to promote foreign trade with Europe, Asia, and Africa. The practical wisdom of the founders of the Republic, however, caused them to stress above everything else the imperative necessity for the new country to stand on its own feet. They were convinced that nothing was more important than to avoid any foreign commitment if the United States was to achieve the national unity so essential for independence. John Adams reported a conversation with the Swedish ambassador in London in 1784 in which that diplomat expressed what was indeed the American point of view: " 'Sir,' said he, 'I take it for granted that you will have sense enough to see us in Europe cut each other's throats with a philosophic tranquility.' " [4]

Washington's Farewell Address, set against the circumstances of the time, clearly reveals that what the first President had in mind was freedom of action rather than complete isolation. He particularly feared foreign meddling in the affairs of the United States, and the disruptive influence of a popular attachment on the part of its citizens to any European power. He pointedly emphasized that the Old World had a set of primary interests, to which Americans had none or a very remote relation, and logically asked: "Why forego the advantages of so peculiar a situation? Why quit our own to stand upon foreign ground? Why, by interweaving our destiny with that of any part of

[3] Gaillard Hunt (ed.), *Journals of the Continental Congress, 1774–1789* (34 vols., Washington, 1922), XXIV, 394.

[4] Adams, *Works*, VIII, 178.

Europe, entangle our peace and prosperity in the toils of European ambition, rivalship, interest, humor or caprice?" [5]

Washington realized that changing conditions might make a change in policy advisable; he also accepted the possibility of "temporary alliances for extraordinary emergencies." Moreover Hamilton, who had no small part in writing the Farewell Address and whose views so obviously coincided with those of the President, stated in the *Federalist* that he saw nothing "absurd or impractical in the idea of a league or alliance between independent nations for certain defined purposes." [6] What Washington opposed was "permanent alliances" that would have limited or curtailed an independence not yet fully established. What he insisted upon was establishment by the United States of "command of its own fortunes."

This policy was overwhelmingly approved throughout the Republic. For once politics stopped at the water's edge. Madison and Jefferson, as well as Adams and Hamilton, added the weight of their experience and wisdom to Washington's advice. When Jefferson enunciated his program—"Peace, commerce and honest friendship with all nations—entangling alliances with none"—it could be said, as when he penned the Declaration of Independence, that it was an expression of the American mind. [7]

The United States was to find it difficult to maintain the neutrality in European wars that Washington first proclaimed. Its interest in trade and commerce demanded vigorous efforts to safeguard American rights in a warring world. Hamilton urged a navy sufficiently strong "to dictate the terms of connection between the old and the new world," and Jefferson declared that "we ought to begin a naval power, if we mean to carry on our own commerce." [8] During the first quarter century of its national existence, the young Republic became engaged in a naval war with France, dispatched two expeditions against the Barbary pirates, and fought Great Britain in the War of 1812. On each of these occasions, however, it acted independently. Every care was

[5] James D. Richardson (ed.), *A Compilation of the Messages and Papers of the Presidents, 1789–1902* (10 vols., Washington, 1904), I, 222–223.

[6] John C. Hamilton (ed.), *The Federalist. A Commentary on the Constitution of the United States* (Philadelphia, 1875), Number 15, p. 142.

[7] *Messages of the Presidents*, I, 323.

[8] *The Federalist*, Number 11, p. 120; Jefferson to Monroe, November 11, 1784, quoted in Dumas Malone, *Jefferson and the Rights of Man* (Boston, 1951), p. 27.

taken to see that these developments did not involve the country in matters that were solely of foreign concern, or entangle the United States in the European balance of power. To win recognition of America's rights as an independent nation, and establish upon a firm basis the trade and commerce so necessary to make independence a reality, remained the primary goal of foreign policy.

The idea of a broader responsibility toward the community of nations incompatible with a rigid policy of nonintervention first found expression in the years immediately following the War of 1812. A friendly reception was accorded in some quarters to the proposal for American membership in the Holy Alliance which Alexander I had established with the professed purpose of promoting world-wide peace.[9] As Secretary of State, however, John Quincy Adams rejected the advice of overenthusiastic pacifist societies urging this step. With a tactful reference to American devotion to the cause of peace, he instructed the American minister in St. Petersburg to decline the formal invitation for membership in the Alliance tendered by the Russian Czar in 1819: "The political system of the United States, is . . . essentially extra-European. To stand in firm and cautious independence of all entanglement in the European system has been a cardinal point of their policy under every administration of their government from the peace of 1783 to this day." [10]

Events on the Continent soon caused an abrupt change in the popular attitude toward the Holy Alliance. The measures taken by the European monarchs to stamp out every sign of democratic tendencies in such countries as Spain, Portugal, Naples and Greece appeared to be convincing evidence that the real aim of Alexander I was to suppress liberalism under the guise of upholding peace. Popular sympathy for the Holy Alliance was transformed into active hostility. Proposals for American intervention in European affairs of quite a different character than membership in this league began to be heard. Convinced that "in the perfection of the scheme of the 'holy alliance,' we must anticipate the extinction of civil and religious liberty," many Americans would have had the United States forthrightly declare its

[9] Merle Curti, *The American Peace Crusade* (Durham, N. C., 1929), p. 27; J. Fred Rippy, *America and the Strife of Europe* (Chicago, 1928), p. 46.

[10] Worthington C. Ford (ed.), *The Writings of John Quincy Adams* (7 vols., New York, 1917), VII, 49.

opposition to the Alliance and its sympathy for the people whose freedom Alexander was attempting to stamp out.[11]

The drive behind this movement was inspired by the conception of America's destined role in spreading abroad the light of freedom. Indeed, the vision of this country as a potentially great power whose beneficent influence would help to extend to all peoples the blessings of justice, liberty and peace already had a long history. Jonathan Edwards had thought of America as "the glorious renovator of the world"; John Adams envisaged the settlement of the country as "the opening of a grand scheme and design in Providence for the illumination and emancipation of the slavish part of mankind all over the earth"; Washington had declared that "the preservation of the sacred fire of liberty" was staked "on the experiment intrusted to the hands of the American people"; and Jefferson believed that the "last hope of human liberty in this world rests on us." From such idealistic sources, strengthened by the belief that whenever reaction triumphed America's own liberties were endangered, stemmed the conviction that the United States could never be completely neutral where freedom was at stake.[12]

Popular emotions were especially aroused in the early 1820's in behalf of Greece. This little country, valiantly struggling against the oppressive rule of the Turks, was believed to face the loss of liberties already won through possible intervention by the Holy Alliance in the name of law and order. Resolutions upholding the Greek cause were debated on the floor of Congress and President Monroe for a time contemplated extending recognition to the rebels.[13]

Once again it was John Quincy Adams, refusing to be carried away by emotional fervor, who stood out most emphatically against any intervention in European affairs. Wherever the standard of freedom was unfurled, he declared in a ringing Independence Day oration in 1821, there lay the sympathies of America—"But she goes not abroad in search of monsters to destroy. She is the well-wisher to the freedom

[11] *Niles' Weekly Register,* XXV (Sept. 6, 1823), 2, quoted in Foster Rhea Dulles, *The Road to Teheran: the Story of Russia and America, 1781–1943* (Princeton, 1945), p. 41.

[12] Quoted in Merle Curti, *The Growth of American Thought* (New York, 1943), p. 49; *Messages of the Presidents,* I, 53; Jefferson to Duane, March 28, 1811, in Paul L. Ford (ed.), *The Writings of Thomas Jefferson* (10 vols., New York, 1898), X, 313.

[13] Edward Mead Earle, "American Interest in the Greek Cause," *American Historical Review,* XXXIII (Oct., 1927), 44–63.

and independence of all. She is the champion and vindicator only of her own." Enlisting under the banners of foreign independence, he warned, would involve America "in all the wars of interest and intrigue, of individual avarice, envy, and ambition, which assume the colors and usurp the standard of freedom. The fundamental maxim of her policy would insensibly change from liberty to force." [14]

The issue continued to agitate the country. The President expressed sympathy for the Greek cause in his message to Congress in 1823, and a year later Daniel Webster introduced a resolution in the House attacking the Holy Alliance and calling for the appointment of an American commissioner to Greece. He declared that the great political question of the day was the contest between absolute and regulated governments. What interest had the United States in resisting autocracy in Europe? "The thunder, it may be said, rolls at a distance. The wide Atlantic is between us and danger; and however others may suffer, *we* shall remain safe." Webster deplored this limited view. As one of the nations interested in the preservation of a system of national law and order, the United States had a duty over and beyond any immediate or direct concern to support religious and civil liberty wherever it was threatened. While he did not talk war, he urged the exercise of the utmost moral pressure in support of the principles in which Americans believed.[15]

Among others John Randolph took the floor to oppose what he thought a complete change in traditional policy. Any such crusade in defense of liberty, he declared, would conjure and beguile the nation out "of the high way of Heaven . . . into all the disastrous conflicts arising from the policies of European Powers." He summoned Americans to adhere to the advice of Washington and Jefferson against entangling alliances—"for to entangling alliances we must come if you once embark in projects such as this." His views were some years later echoed by Henry Clay. This country's contribution to freedom, Clay asserted, was to keep the "lamp burning brightly on this western shore as a light to all nations" rather than to hazard "its utter extinction amid the ruins of fallen or falling republics in Europe." [16]

[14] *Niles' Weekly Register*, XX (July 21, 1821), 326 ff., quoted in Edward Howland Tatum, Jr., *The United States and Europe, 1815–1823* (Berkeley, Cal., 1936), p. 244.

[15] Quoted in Marion M. Miller (ed.), *Great Debates in American History* (14 vols., New York, 1913), II, 255, 258.

[16] *Ibid.*, II, 259, 264; Calvin Colton (ed.), *The Works of Henry Clay* (10 vols., New York, 1904), III, 224.

American policy never reached the point of actually considering the abandonment of the rule of nonintervention in order to combat the European designs of the Holy Alliance. Randolph rather than Webster reflected public opinion. In the meantime, however, a far more severe test of our traditional policy had arisen, involving the whole question of the relationship between the Old World and the New.

This was the proposal made in 1823 by George Canning, British Foreign Secretary, for a joint protest by England and the United States against any move on the part of the Holy Alliance to aid Spain in suppressing the newly won independence of the Latin American republics. President Monroe seriously contemplated accepting this proposal, and was strengthened in his resolve by the well-known advice of Madison and Jefferson.

The latter took occasion to emphasize in his letter to Monroe two fundamental maxims—that the United States should not become entangled in European broils, and that it should never suffer Europe to meddle with cisatlantic affairs. While Europe was laboring to become the domicile of despotism, America should endeavor to make this hemisphere the domicile of freedom. Nevertheless Jefferson thought that Canning's proposal was an exception to any general rule of standing aloof from political connections. England was the one nation that could most effectively interfere with the United States, and she now offered to lead, aid, and accompany us. "By acceding to her proposition," Jefferson wrote Monroe, "we detach her from the band of despots, bring her mighty weight into the scale of free government, and emancipate a continent at one stroke." [17]

While the elder statesmen were thus prepared to concede the advantages, under such special circumstances, of cooperating with England, John Quincy Adams stuck resolutely to his more nationalistic position. He had already warned Czarist Russia that the American continents were no longer subjects for any new European colonial establishments; he was ready to oppose with equal vigor any European interference with the New World governments that had declared their independence. Shrewdly realizing that such a policy would in any event have the support of England, because her own interests coincided with those of the United States, he insisted that in taking a stand against the Holy Alliance, "it would be more candid, as well as more digni-

[17] Andrew A. Lipscomb (ed.), *The Writings of Thomas Jefferson* (20 vols., Washington, 1903), XV, 477.

fied, to avow our principles explicitly to Russia and France, than to come in as a cock-boat in the wake of the British man-of-war." [18]

The Monroe Doctrine, as enunciated in December, 1823, conformed to the ideas of Adams rather than the advice of Jefferson and Madison. It upheld the freedom of action for which Washington and Jefferson himself had originally called, implicitly emphasized national security, and set forth the concept of the two spheres as determining American policy. President Monroe, that is, warned the European powers—including England—that the United States would consider any attempt on their part to extend their system to the Western Hemisphere as "dangerous to our peace and safety." And as a corollary to this statement, he made it clear that for its part the United States had no intention of interfering in the affairs of Europe.[19]

This national policy as developed during the early years of the Republic did not mean that the United States was not deeply concerned with developments abroad. It could not be otherwise while engaged in the negotiations with European powers that were to add Louisiana, Florida, and Oregon to the Union. Nor could isolationism be really said to characterize an attitude so increasingly affected by the concept of Manifest Destiny as to lead to the gradual extension of national boundaries to the Pacific. What American policy actually meant—and it was strengthened and reinforced by continental expansion—was nonentanglement in solely European matters and unimpaired freedom in the pursuit of national aims and aspirations.

When John Quincy Adams became President, he stressed this "great rule of conduct" in foreign relations. It was further affirmed by Andrew Jackson. Van Buren declared his opposition to all alliances; Tyler in turn expressed his determination to abstain from European politics; and Polk directly quoted the historic phrase "peace with all nations, entangling alliances with none." Repeating his predecessor's statement, Fillmore pointedly added that the intent of the United States was "to teach by example and show by our success, moderation and justice the blessings of self-government and the advantages of free institutions." [20]

A tradition, based upon the practical needs of the nation and the existing realities of the international balance of power, had been firmly

[18] Charles F. Adams (ed.), *Memoirs of John Quincy Adams* (12 vols., Philadelphia, 1874–77), VI, 179.

[19] *Messages of the Presidents*, II, 209, 218.

[20] *Ibid.*, II, 337; III, 3, 603; IV, 197, 633; V, 177.

established in the public mind. The American people were determined that their country should remain "in command of its own fortunes."

Popular feeling in this highly nationalistic era was carried away by the tremendous promise of continental expansion and what appeared to be the glorious future of the thriving young Republic. John Adams had originally urged an independent policy, at least in part, as a means of freeing the American mind from any fear or self-diffidence, any excessive admiration of foreigners.[21] In the 1830's and 1840's such diffidence was hard to discover. The belief was well-nigh universal that the United States was so strong, so vigorous, so dynamic—so morally superior—that it could ignore all other countries. Had not the original settlers "shaken off the dust of Babylon" in founding the colonies? [22] There was nothing more natural than for their descendants to turn their backs upon the Old World monarchies from whose rivalries and wars every successive stream of immigrants was attempting to escape.

Jefferson's scorn for the jealousies, complicated alliances, and reactionary governments of Europe had led him to wish that there was "an ocean of fire between us and the old world." Timothy Dwight rejoiced that America was as far as it was "from Europe's mischiefs and Europe's woes." The barbarities of the Old World left behind, wrote William Cullen Bryant:

> Here the free spirit of mankind, at length,
> Throws its last fetters off . . .[23]

Foreign visitors during these years were astounded by the nation's self-confidence and this easy dismissal of Europe. The faith of the American people in their republican institutions appeared illimitable. There was absolute certainty in the great future stretching ahead for the New World as compared with what was believed to be the inevitable decline and decadence of the Old World. Caught up in the excitement of a westward movement that was step by step bringing about the conquest of the continent, no bounds were placed upon the ulti-

[21] John Adams, *Works*, VIII, 144.

[22] The phrase is Increase Mather's, quoted in Max Savelle, "Colonial Origins of American Diplomatic Principles," *Pacific Historical Review,* III (1934), 335.

[23] Lipscomb, *Writings of Jefferson*, IX, 385; Thomas A. Bailey, *The Man in the Street, the Impact of American Public Opinion on American Foreign Policy* (New York, 1948), p. 244; Henry C. Sturges (ed.), *The Poetical Works of William Cullen Bryant* (New York, 1919), *"The Ages,"* p. 20.

mate extension of American power and influence. Whatever vestiges of a colonial complex may still have affected the attitude of the sophisticated toward European culture, the common people never doubted a glorious destiny for their country.[24]

An English traveler, William Baxter, on one occasion was discussing what he considered to be the mission of the United States and Great Britain to civilize the globe. " 'Two nations!' broke in a little sharp featured man," Baxter recorded. " 'Guess there's only one, stranger; goin' to annex that island of yours one of these fine days;—don't know how little Vic will like that, but got to do it, no mistake about that.' " And then there was the somewhat similar interruption to a general conversation reported by Alexander Mackay: " 'I know'd it,' said a long Yankee from Maine; 'we're born to whip universal nature. The Europeans can't hold a candle to us already.' " [25]

In his official capacity as Secretary of State, Daniel Webster was in 1850 to express much the same spirit when he arrogantly told the Austro-Hungarian chargé that in comparison with the immense regions over which the power of the Republic held sway, the possessions of the House of Hapsburg "are but as a patch on the earth's surface." [26]

Such quotations might be multiplied indefinitely. The great role of the United States as the exemplar of liberty—for it was invariably liberty that was most heavily stressed—was the theme of hundreds of Independence Day orations. Flamboyant, grandiloquent, self-assertive, they reflected the naïve bumptiousness of a young nation, inordinately proud of what it believed to be its innate superiority over the peoples of Europe, and superbly sure that the principles for which it stood would in time rule the entire world. For all the extravagance of such orations, they were an expression of the American spirit no less confidently reflected in Emerson's characterization of America as "a beacon lighting for all the world the paths of human destiny," and in Walt Whitman's summation of the pioneer spirit:

[24] See Albert K. Weinberg, *Manifest Destiny: A Study of National Expansion* (Baltimore, 1935), pp. 72–130.

[25] William Baxter, *America and the Americans* (London, 1885), p. 104; Alexander Mackay, *The Western World* (London, 1850), quoted in Allan Nevins (ed.), *America Through British Eyes* (New York, 1948), p. 247.

[26] Webster to Hülsemann, Dec. 21, 1850, *Senate Executive Document 9*, 31st Congress, 2nd Session, p. 7, quoted in Thomas A. Bailey, *A Diplomatic History of the American People* (New York, 1940), p. 286.

Have the elder races halted?
Do they droop and end their lesson,
Wearied over there beyond the seas?
We take up the task eternal.[27]

In the 1850's, their independent and self-confident spirit intensified by the successes of the Mexican War, many Americans began to find continental boundaries too confining. A new sense of Manifest Destiny called for overseas expansion—in the Caribbean and in the Pacific. At the same time, the suppression of revolutionary movements in Europe once again gave rise to the idea of extending American support to all peoples struggling for liberty.

The stamping out of rebellion in Hungary and the visit of the patriot Louis Kossuth to the United States in 1851 awoke the liveliest concern. Kossuth's cause was made a symbol of freedom. A group known as "Young America" campaigned zealously for active alliance with European republicanism,[28] and a debate in the Senate found William H. Seward and Lewis Cass insisting that the United States should speak out in defense of liberty, without fear of offending foreign powers. There was nothing contrary to the principles enunciated by Washington and Jefferson, they argued, in seeking to exert at least a moral influence on European affairs.

Senator Robert F. Stockton of New Jersey further developed this thesis. It was not Washington's idea, he declared, that the United States should always be neutral. "We chose to nurse the infant Hercules, until he should be able to encounter, upon more equal terms, the monsters he was destined to overthrow." That time had now arrived, Stockton concluded, and today "we acknowledge no superiors." If he was still thinking perhaps of no more than an official declaration of American sympathy for the European revolutionaries, at least one member of the Senate was ready to go further. To prevent interference by one nation with the freedom of another, said Senator Isaac P. Walker of Wisconsin, "the country must interpose both her *moral and physical power.*" [29]

Such views were still strongly opposed, and by no one more vigor-

[27] For an interesting treatment of "the American dream" see Robert E. Spiller (ed.), *Literary History of the United States* (3 vols., New York, 1949); I, 192–215.

[28] Merle Curti, "'Young America,'" *American Historical Review*, XXXII (Oct., 1926), 34–55.

[29] *Congressional Globe*, 32nd Congress, 1st Session (Dec. 12, 1851), 51; (Dec. 16, 1851), 105.

ously than by Charles Sumner. Intervention of any sort in Europe, he declared in a speech on December 10, 1851, "would open vials of perplexities and ills which I trust our country will never be called upon to affront." Then, using for perhaps the first time in public debate the term that was to become so familiar, he continued:

I inculcate no frigid isolation. God forbid that we should ever close our ears to the cry of distress, or cease to swell with indignation at the steps of tyranny! In the wisdom of Washington we find perpetual counsel. Like Washington, in his eloquent words to the Minister of the French Directory, I would offer sympathy and God-speed to all, in every land, who struggle for Human Rights; but, sternly as Washington on another occasion, against every pressure, against all popular appeals, against all solicitations, against all blandishments, I would uphold the peaceful neutrality of the country.[30]

John C. Calhoun had already spoken out against any idea of breaking with past tradition. It was a sad delusion, he told the Senate, to believe that it was the mission of the United States to spread civil and religious liberty over all the globe. To preserve liberty, it was necessary to adopt a course of moderation and justice toward all nations, to avoid war whenever it could be avoided, and to let the natural forces in operation in this country continue to work: "By pursuing such a course we may succeed in combining greatness and liberty—the highest possible greatness with the largest measure of liberty—and do more to extend liberty by our example over this continent and the world generally, than would be done by a thousand victories." [31]

The concern for European republicanism, which caused some trepidation on the part of foreign envoys to the United States even though the course recommended by Sumner and Calhoun was to prevail, ran parallel with that upsurge of imperialistic fervor which more directly challenged stay-at-home traditions. The expansionists of this period called most vociferously for the annexation of Cuba, but there was also in many quarters a keen interest, as one observer reported, in "grasping the magnificent purse of the commerce of the Pacific." [32]

[30] *Charles Sumner; His Complete Works* (20 vols., Boston, 1900), III, 178–179. It is intriguing, although perhaps without significance, that the sentence in which "isolation" was incorporated was omitted from the report on the speech in the *Congressional Globe*.

[31] R. K. Crallé (ed.), *The Works of John C. Calhoun* (6 vols., New York, 1867), IV, 420, quoted in Ralph Henry Gabriel, *The Course of American Democratic Thought* (New York, 1940), pp. 107–108.

[32] Edmund Burke to Franklin Pierce, June 14, 1852, quoted in Curti, " 'Young America,' " p. 45.

After the Democratic victory in the election of 1852, President Pierce sounded what seemed to be a new and challenging note in foreign policy. His administration was not to be controlled "by any timid forebodings of evil from expansion." While recognizing that the United States had heretofore been independent of European political complications, he also went much further than any of his predecessors in admitting that there were necessarily close ties between Europe and America. In 1854 he said in terms that were to have even greater relevancy a century later: ". . . As a nation we are reminded that whatever interrupts the peace or checks the prosperity of any part of Christendom tends more or less to involve our own." [33]

An important motive behind the interventionist suggestion that the United States should take a more active part in world affairs was always the encouragement of trade and commerce. Such considerations had even entered into the movement in support of European republicanism. "What, speak of isolation!" Senator Pierre Soulé of Louisiana had cried out when opposition was expressed to any gesture in behalf of Hungarian independence. "Have you no markets to secure for the surplus of your future wealth?" [34]

Economic factors were far more important in the drive for a bolder assertion of American influence and power in the Pacific. The opportunities for commercial expansion, founded on great expectations in the future exploitation of the markets of China and Japan, had long since been wrapped in glittering promise. Trade with Asia had again and again been stressed in public debate as an argument in favor of the acquisition of California and Oregon.[35] Just as commercial interest had supplemented liberal sympathy for European revolutionaries, however, so did idealism reinforce arguments for expansion across the wide reaches of the Western Ocean. The United States would carry abroad "science, liberal principles in government, and the true religion." Thomas Hart Benton believed that America should "wake up and reanimate the torpid body of Asia. . . . The moral and intellectual superiority of the White race will do the rest; and thus the youngest people, and the newest land, will become the reviver and regenerator of the oldest." [36]

[33] *Messages of the Presidents,* V, 198, 199, 273.

[34] *Congressional Globe,* 32nd Congress, 1st Session (Mar. 22, 1852), Appendix, 349 ff., quoted in Curti, " 'Young America,' " p. 39.

[35] Foster Rhea Dulles, *America in the Pacific* (Boston, 1932), pp. 29–46.

[36] Quoted in Gabriel, *American Democratic Thought,* pp. 343–344.

Under the impact of these expansive forces, the 1850's witnessed a series of important moves extending American influence to the shores of Asia—the expedition led by Commodore Perry for the opening up of Japan, protracted negotiations and active intervention in China for the promotion of trade and commerce, and signature of an abortive treaty of annexation with the Kingdom of Hawaii. The imperialist-minded Perry would have gone further. In dispatches from the China seas he urged—though unsuccessfully—establishment of "a foothold in this quarter of the globe, as a measure of positive necessity to the sustainment of our maritime rights in the east." [37]

There was already evident, in the middle of the nineteenth century, an apparent willingness on the part of some Americans to compensate for aloofness toward Europe through a more active policy in Asia. America had turned her back on the Old World. Its troubled rivalries represented only complications and dangers from which the United States was determined to be free. And there could be no denial that Great Britain controlled the Atlantic. Once the young Republic had stretched out to the Pacific shore, however, the horizons of a further world where the European powers were not so deeply entrenched dazzled ambition. The dictates of national security—to prevent England from "belting us about with her kingly powers"—commercial and business opportunity, and even the idea of national mission seemed to encourage expansion in this part of the globe, whereas everything counseled against involvement in the tinderbox of European politics. The advocates of such a program accepted the Pacific as an untrammeled outlet for the dynamic energy of the American people—and on its further shores were the great nations of Asia, with all their incalculable riches.

The Orient appeared, indeed, to have a strange and wonderful fascination. Thomas Hart Benton declared that whatever power controlled the Asiatic trade was destined to world dominance. In no instance had such trade, he said, "failed to carry the nation or people which possessed it, to the highest pinnacle of wealth and power, and with it the highest attainments of letters, arts, and science." [38]

Senator Seward, who became Lincoln's Secretary of State, was the

[37] Perry was especially interested in Formosa, the Bonin Islands, and the Ryukyus. *Senate Executive Document 34*, 33rd Congress, 2nd Session, p. 81, quoted in Dulles, *America in the Pacific*, p. 73.

[38] Quoted in Henry Nash Smith, *Virgin Land* (Cambridge, 1950), pp. 28–29; see entire chap., "Passage to India."

foremost proponent of Pacific expansion. He was convinced that European commerce, politics, thought, and action were sinking in relative importance, and in an often-quoted phrase declared that "the Pacific Ocean, its shores, its islands, and the vast regions beyond will become the chief theater of events in the world's great hereafter." Here lay America's future. Anticipating Alfred Thayer Mahan's theory of sea power, Seward further insisted that "the nation must command the empire of the seas, which alone is real empire." [39]

In spite of Seward's enthusiasm, there were to be no further developments in mid-century expansionism. The interplay of domestic politics, overshadowed by the dread fear of impending civil war, blocked any move along these ambitious lines. The proposals for the extension of American power in the Caribbean through the acquisition of Cuba came to nothing, the annexation treaty with Hawaii was dropped, and further advance in eastern Asia lost popular support. When Buchanan took office in 1857, he affirmed the policy of nonintervention in the affairs of other nations with renewed emphasis: "To avoid entangling alliances has been a maxim of our policy ever since the days of Washington and its wisdom no one will attempt to dispute." [40]

During the Civil War the United States was confronted with a threat to the policy already known as the Monroe Doctrine that awoke deep concern. Napoleon III set up with the aid of French arms a Mexican Empire under the Archduke Maximilian of Austria. Not until the war was over did Secretary of State Seward feel able to exercise any real pressure to thwart this mad adventure, but in 1866 he took so strong a stand that the French Emperor felt obliged to withdraw all support from the already crumbling regime of his protégé. At no time did Seward officially mention the Monroe Doctrine. Nevertheless the lesson was not lost upon the chancellories of Europe; it was borne home that the United States was determined to safeguard its interests in the Western Hemisphere. [41]

About this same time efforts were made to revive the imperialist spirit of the 1850's with demands voiced for further territorial acqui-

[39] George E. Baker (ed.), *The Works of William H. Seward* (5 vols., Boston, 1884), I, 249–250. See also Tyler Dennett, "Seward's Far Eastern Policy," *American Historical Review*, XXVIII (Oct., 1922), 45–62.

[40] *Messages of the Presidents*, V, 435.

[41] Dexter Perkins, *The Monroe Doctrine, 1867–1907* (Baltimore, 1937), pp. 547–548.

sitions both on the continent and among the islands in the Pacific and the Caribbean. There were those who looked forward to the ultimate absorption of Canada within the Union, and wartime difficulties with Great Britain had done nothing to dampen this historic ambition in expansionist circles. In his annual message to Congress in December, 1868, President Johnson stated: "Comprehensive national policy would seem to sanction the acquisition and incorporation into our Federal Union of the several adjacent continental and insular communities as speedily as it can be done peacefully, lawfully, and without any violation of national justice, faith or honor." [42]

The American people, however, were uninterested. Negotiations for the settlement of Anglo-American disputes thrust Canada into the background and island possessions awoke no popular appeal. Seward succeeded almost singlehandedly in bringing about the purchase of Alaska, but all his other schemes—the acquisition of the Danish West Indies, the Dominican Republic, the Hawaiian Islands, some sort of a foothold in China—foundered on the rock of public apathy. Nor was President Grant any more successful when he too urged the annexation of the Dominican Republic. He assured Congress that its people were yearning to embrace American liberty, but a treaty negotiated in 1869 was rejected. [43]

All arguments that expansion was both an opportunity and a duty failed to convince the country that it should embark on what Senator James A. Bayard, Jr., of Delaware, called "the vast and trackless seas of imperialism." The domestic problems growing out of the war absorbed popular attention. As Seward ruefully admitted, the public refused to dismiss them in order "to entertain the higher, but more remote, questions of national extension." [44]

The opposition to any close ties with Europe was also reinforced in this period. France had appealed in 1863 for American cooperation in a move to bring pressure on Russia to induce her to deal more leniently with rebels in Poland. In refusing this request, Seward fell back on the advice of the founders of the Republic. He admitted that Washington had thought that the time might come when the United States should play a more active role in foreign affairs. He stated that there

[42] *Messages of the Presidents,* VI, 688.
[43] See Theodore Clarke Smith, "Expansion After the Civil War, 1865–71," *Political Science Quarterly,* XVI (Sept., 1901), 412–436.
[44] Frederick W. Seward, *William H. Seward at Washington, as Senator and Secretary of State* (3 vols., New York, 1891), III, 383.

had been frequent occasions "which presented seductions to a departure from what, superficially viewed, seemed a course of isolation and indifference." Nevertheless, Seward said, the avoidance of all such temptation was still sound doctrine: "Our policy of non-intervention, straight, absolute and peculiar as it may seem to other nations, has become a traditional one, which could not be abandoned without the most urgent occasion, amounting to a manifest necessity." [45]

If a desire to maintain Russian friendship during the Civil War may in part have motivated this answer, no such political consideration could have affected Seward's attitude five years later in avoiding such an apparently innocuous foreign engagement as American adherence to the Geneva Convention establishing the International Red Cross. He declared on this occasion that it had always been deemed questionable, if not unwise, for the United States to become a party to any instrument to which there were many parties and "nothing but the most urgent necessity should lead to a departure from this rule." [46]

The reasons for this renewed emphasis upon isolationism, which was to become increasingly accentuated in the next few years, are not difficult to discover. The America of post-Civil War years was launched on the great era of industrial development. National attention and national energy were primarily absorbed in the development of industry and the settlement of the West. Moreover, to an even greater degree than in the years before the war, a sense of security and potential power made events in other parts of the world seem of only the most remote concern. As President Johnson again pointed out, the geographic position, territory, and production of the country made it "singularly independent of the varying policy of foreign powers and protect us against every temptation to 'entangling alliances.'" [47]

Popular interest in foreign affairs sank to the lowest ebb in all American history—in comparison with either pre-Civil War days or the twentieth century. Henry Cabot Lodge wrote that they filled "but a slight place in American politics, and excite generally only a languid interest," and Henry Adams later observed that the "Secretary of State exists only to recognize the existence of a world which Congress

---

[45] Department of State, *Diplomatic Correspondence, 1862–63*, Part II, pp. 737–739, quoted in Charles A. Beard and G. H. E. Smith, *The Idea of National Interest* (New York, 1934), pp. 361–62.

[46] Quoted in Foster Rhea Dulles, *The American Red Cross* (New York, 1950), p. 10.

[47] *Messages of the Presidents*, VI, 366.

would rather ignore." The New York *Sun* even suggested abolition of the diplomatic service on the ground that it had outlived its usefulness. "It is a costly humbug and sham," this paper said. "It is a nurse of snobs. It spoils a few Americans every year, and does no good to anybody." While these quotations undoubtedly give an exaggerated picture, for Americans were always concerned with what went on in the world, they reflect the general popular attitude toward diplomacy.[48]

Although the spirit of self-confidence and self-sufficiency was not as naïve as it had been in the 1840's, the conviction that Americans were inherently superior to any other people had in no way altered. It was inculcated through school textbooks. "The United States are the freest, most enlightened, and powerful government on earth," one of them stated, adding with a nice note of condescension that the people of Germany were "intelligent," and in France "the better classes are refined and cultivated." [49] Here such different figures as William Jennings Bryan and Andrew Carnegie could find a common meeting ground. "Behold a republic increasing in population, in wealth, in strength and in influence, solving the problems of civilization . . ." cried the Great Commoner. "The old nations of the earth creep on at a snail's pace; the Republic thunders past with the rush of the express," echoed the exuberant steelmaster. ". . . America already leads the civilized world." [50]

The influence of the immigrants, as in earlier periods, greatly strengthened the popular attitude toward nonentanglement in European affairs. America symbolized liberty, opportunity, and peace; Europe stood for suppression, poverty, military conscription, and war. "I will speak of Americanism as the great representative of the reformatory age, as the great champion of the dignity of human nature, as the great repository of the last hopes of suffering mankind," Carl Schurz, the German-born Republican political leader, exclaimed.[51] It

[48] Henry Cabot Lodge, *George Washington* (2 vols., Boston, 1889), II, 129; Henry Adams, *The Education of Henry Adams* (Modern Library edition, New York, 1931), p. 422; *Public Opinion*, VI (Feb. 9, 1889), 367.

[49] James Cruikshank, *The Primary Geography* (New York, 1867), quoted in Mark Sullivan, *Our Times—The United States: 1900–1925* (6 vols., New York, 1926–35), II, 62–63.

[50] William Jennings Bryan and Mary Baird Bryan, *The Memoirs of William Jennings Bryan* (Philadelphia, 1925), 500–501; Andrew Carnegie, *Triumphant Democracy, or Fifty Years' March of The Republic* (New York, 1886), p. 1.

[51] Carl Schurz, "True Americanism," a speech delivered in Boston, Apr. 18.

was the voice of countless new Americans who rejected the Europe from which they had fled, and would at all costs have kept America uncontaminated from the evils of foreign association.

Of immense importance in further building up the feeling of self-reliance and security that persuaded the American people they could safely ignore all other countries was the belief that the great wheat-growing areas of the Midwest had become the granary of all the world and made Europe entirely dependent on America. What has been characterized as "the myth of the garden" created the illusion that, here within continental boundaries, could be finally realized the great dream of American empire which had stirred the imagination since colonial days.[52] Manifest Destiny did not seem to call for overseas expansion as there arose on the western plains a new agricultural Eden. To safeguard the future, it was only necessary to raise protective barriers that would enable the American people to go their own way, free of all foreign distractions and insulated from all alien influences.

This complex of forces operative in the post-Civil War decades—the tradition of nonintervention, a basic sense of security, the feeling of national superiority—appeared to emphasize more strongly than ever the wisdom of a foreign policy that so studiously avoided all foreign·commitments or overseas adventure. The popular view was clearly expressed in President Cleveland's inaugural in 1885:

The genius of our institutions, the needs of our people in their home life, and the attention which is demanded for the settlement and development of the resources of our vast territory dictate the scrupulous avoidance of any departure from that foreign policy commended by the history, the traditions, and the prosperity of our Republic. It is the policy of independence, favored by our position and defended by our known love of justice and by our power. It is the policy of peace suitable to our interests. It is the policy of neutrality, rejecting any share in foreign broils and ambitions upon other continents and repelling their intrusion here. It is the policy of Monroe and of Washington and Jefferson—"Peace, commerce, and honest friendship with all nations; entangling alliances with none." [53]

This was the summation of isolationist doctrine.

1859, quoted in Willard Thorp, Merle Curti, and Carlos Baker, *American Issues—the Social Record* (Philadelphia, 1941), p. 336.

[52] This concept of "the garden of the world," and the extent to which inferences drawn from such a myth may constitute "the core of what we call isolationism," is brilliantly developed in Smith, *Virgin Land,* especially pp. 184–188.

[53] *Messages of the Presidents,* VIII, 301.

CHAPTER 2

America Looks Outward

IN MANY respects Cleveland's vigorous statement on foreign policy was the swan song of an older era. Forces were stirring that were to bring about a sharp break with the traditions of the past. The United States was soon to find itself launched on a new role in world affairs, and in casting off old moorings the American people were confronted with uncertainties and confusions that were to endure into the long future.

A first sign of a changing attitude toward the nation's position in the world was a revival during the 1890's of earlier imperialistic ambitions. The expansion to which this led was opposed as a repudiation of the doctrines laid down by the founders of the Republic; it was defended as a necessary move in support of these same principles. Over against the arguments of those who maintained that overseas bases would inevitably entangle the United States in the affairs of other countries was advanced the theory that only through such defensive outposts could the nation effectively safeguard its traditional freedom of action. The facts of expansion were more conclusive than all such discussion. As a world power, America could no longer escape the interweaving of her destiny with that of other nations.

A number of closely related factors provided the impetus for the overseas extension of national boundaries. The virtual completion of western settlement and the closing of the frontier combined with the widespread agrarian distress of the 1890's to create a different attitude toward the future potentialities of inland empire than the optimistic outlook of earlier decades. As impoverished farmers suffered the recurrent scourges of drought, dust storms, and insect plagues, as well as the downward swing of grain prices, the myth of the garden was shattered. It again seemed necessary, as it had for a time in the 1850's, to look beyond ocean barriers to realize the full destiny of the United States. In a world in which the mounting rivalry of the European nations for foreign colonies and overseas spheres of influence foreshadowed dangerous shifts in the existing balance of power, the American people felt that in the interests of their own well-being and ultimate safety they could not stand aside. Moreover, immediate economic need was said to point toward the desirability of overseas expansion. The tremendous growth of industry gave rise to a widely held belief that new markets were essential to absorb the surplus of domestic manufactures. Something had to be done, the expansionists declared, to prevent such markets from falling under the control or domination of European trade rivals. And finally, the reinvigoration of earlier concepts of the nation's destined role in spreading abroad republican or democratic principles served notably to strengthen the demands of both political and economic ambition.

James Bryce, the most acute British observer of the American scene, suggested in a friendly warning that the main though perhaps little-realized motive in the minds of many expansionists resulted from the notion "that it is a fine thing for a great country to have vast territories, and to see marked as her own, on the map of the world, dominions beyond her natural borders." [1] Yet it was something more than this. As they had formerly operated in favor of abstention from world affairs, so now the assumed dictates of national security, the interests of trade and commerce, and the historic belief in a national mission were working together to set the United States on an entirely new course.

Its world position could hardly have been more dramatically changed than it was during the brief two decades between 1885 and 1905. A Navy that had been inconsequential, ranking below that of Chile, rose to third place among those of the major nations and was soon to be second. With the annexation of Puerto Rico, establishment of a protectorate over Cuba, and the seizure of Panama, complete control was established over the Caribbean and the approaches to an isthmian canal. The occupation of Hawaii and Guam, Samoa and the Philippines, extended the frontier to the western Pacific, while the

[1] James Bryce, "The Policy of Annexation for America," *Forum*, XXIV (Dec., 1897), 392.

pronouncement of the Open Door policy in China and mediation in the Russo-Japanese war further enhanced American influence in the affairs of eastern Asia. Before the period drew to a close, a new note was struck in relations with Europe. American participation in the Algeciras Conference, involving a Franco-German dispute over rights in Morocco, showed a concern over the continental balance of power foreshadowing still further foreign involvements.

Addressing Congress in 1902, Theodore Roosevelt expounded ideas that had found no place in Cleveland's message less than twenty years earlier:

As a people we have played a great part in the world, and we are bent upon making our future even larger than the past . . . Our place must be great among the nations. We may either fail greatly or succeed greatly; but we cannot avoid the endeavor from which either great failure or great success must come. Even if we would, we cannot play a small part. If we should try, all that would follow would be that we should play a large part ignobly or shamefully.[2]

The first concrete evidence of a renewed interest in overseas expansion was a series of moves to build up American strength in the Pacific. If it was to be left to Captain Mahan to develop most persuasively the arguments for sea power, they were consciously or unconsciously given practical application through our tightening bonds with Samoa and Hawaii. President Harrison, coming into office in 1889, looked with grave concern on foreign intrigues in these islands. He was determined to secure American communications with the Far East and block any other power from Pacific domination.

His administration also showed a growing interest in an isthmian canal, for which Nicaragua was at this time believed to be the logical site, and in the general extension of American influence in the Caribbean. It went on record as considering a canal under the exclusive control of the United States "a matter of highest concern." Moreover it was as protection for such a canal that Secretary of State Blaine took a page out of Seward's book in trying to lease naval bases in Santo Domingo and Haiti, and considering the purchase of the Danish West Indies.[3]

While Blaine himself was especially concerned with promoting the

[2] James D. Richardson (ed.), *A Compilation of the Messages and Papers of the Presidents, 1789–1902* (10 vols., Washington, 1904), X, 511.

[3] *Ibid.*, IX, 189; Alice Felt Tyler, *The Foreign Policy of James G. Blaine* (Minneapolis, 1927), pp. 91–98.

commercial interests of the United States throughout South America, the canal project was closely tied in with the expansion of American power in the Pacific. It was insistently argued that this interocean link, if adequately safeguarded•by naval bases, would assure the United States a controlling influence in that part of the world. It could be done, a contributor to the *Forum* declared in 1887, "without departing too far from our republican tendencies of a small army and navy, and without involving ourselves too much in international complications." [4] The isles of the Pacific and the great potential markets of eastern Asia were once again arousing the popular imagination.

Interest in Samoa led to the establishment, in 1889, of a tripartite protectorate over those islands, shared by Germany and Great Britain. Although interpreted by its critics, if not its supporters, as a first departure from the doctrine of no entangling alliances, its importance may easily be exaggerated. Samoa was far away, of relatively little strategic or commercial value, and American commitments were strictly limited. The strength of old traditions was clearly demonstrated, however, by the charge that in concluding the Samoan treaty the United States had invited the risks and dangers of foreign entanglement against which the founders of the Republic had so wisely warned. [5]

New ties with Hawaii brought up the same issue. A step toward the annexation first contemplated in mid-century had been taken when the United States leased Pearl Harbor as a naval station in 1887. In the face of vigorous protests by England and France, for these two nations were scheming for establishment of a joint protectorate over Hawaii somewhat similar to that set up in Samoa, the United States refused to admit any foreign restraint whatsoever upon its Hawaiian policy. "We planted a Gibraltar in the heart of the Pacific," Senator John T. Morgan of Alabama would later state, "which is stronger and better and more useful than the Gibraltar that commands the Mediterranean sea." [6] The idea of sharing such a vital base with any other power, especially Great Britain, at once aroused alarm even among

[4] H. C. Taylor, "The Control of the Pacific," *Forum*, III (June, 1887), 441.

[5] See George H. Ryden, *The Foreign Policy of the United States in Relation to Samoa* (New Haven, 1933). That James G. Blaine's interest in Samoa was actually very slight is suggested in Tyler, *Foreign Policy of Blaine*, pp. 232–233, 368.

[6] *Congressional Record*, 53rd Congress, 2nd Session (July 2, 1894), p. 7062. An admirable account of relations with Hawaii is in J. W. Pratt, *Expansionists of 1898* (Baltimore, 1936).

those who opposed the idea of annexation. Pearl Harbor was repeatedly said to be the key to the Pacific. Its complete control, far from violating the established principles of American foreign policy, was considered by expansionist congressmen as a necessary projection of the Monroe Doctrine.

Cleveland was convinced that Hawaii fell within the American sphere of influence. Disclaiming any idea of interference with the islands' autonomy, he insisted in 1886 that "the intimacy of our relations with Hawaii should be emphasized." [7] Developments that might have been foreseen were soon to follow upon such an ambiguous program. Seven years after Cleveland's statement, a revolutionary uprising engineered by the islands' American residents, and supported by official representatives of the United States, provided an opportunity for annexation which the outgoing Harrison Administration was quick to seize. The "American solution" of Hawaii's future so long envisaged by Pacific expansionists appeared to be at hand.

It was once again delayed. Before the Senate could act upon the annexation treaty, quickly concluded by the United States and the Hawaiian Provisional Government, the administration in Washington changed. Cleveland, re-elected in 1892, was back in office. He may have been willing to stress the intimacy of Hawaiian-American relations, but he immediately withdrew this pact from Senate consideration. And soon thereafter he took occasion to condemn the protectorate over Samoa. Although he recognized the importance of preventing other nations from establishing control over such island bases in the Pacific, he still believed, in the words of an earlier message, that the "acquisition of new and distant territory or the incorporation of remote interests with our own" could not be reconciled with "the tenets of a line of precedents from Washington's day, which proscribe entangling alliances with foreign states." [8]

There were political implications in Cleveland's stand, over and beyond his own stubborn opposition to overseas possessions. The Republicans had become the party of imperialism. While their platform in 1892 had reaffirmed adherence to the principle of no entangling alliances, it had also called for "the achievement of the manifest destiny of the Republic in its broadest sense." [9] Had it not been for the return of the Democrats to power, expansion might well have taken

[7] *Messages of the Presidents,* VIII, 500.
[8] *Ibid.,* VIII, 327.
[9] Kirk H. Porter, *National Party Platforms* (New York, 1924), p. 175.

place even before the Spanish-American War. In February, 1893, a reporter of the Washington *Star* wrote: "There is very good reason for believing that if he [Harrison] had been re-elected, an aggressive foreign policy would have been the most marked feature of his administration and that the end of another four years would have found this country in possession of strong points of advantage, from a naval point of view, in the South Atlantic and in the Pacific . . ." [10]

This is mere conjecture. Nevertheless the expansionist drive was steadily gaining momentum, and for all his anti-imperialism Cleveland ironically enough was soon to stimulate the spirit underlying it even more than had his predecessor. This was a result of his belligerent insistence, in 1895, that England accept arbitration in her dispute with Venezuela over the boundary of British Guiana. Neither expansion nor an entangling alliance were immediately involved. Cleveland was no more than reaffirming the principle that the Western Hemisphere was an exclusive sphere of American influence. Nevertheless the note which his Secretary of State, Richard Olney, dispatched to England, and his own subsequent message to Congress on the issue, had a tremendous influence in arousing the nation to a new realization of the role that the United States might play in world affairs. More than that, it encouraged a jingoism that was deeply to affect later policy toward Spain.

The position taken by Olney in first calling Great Britain to account was that any dispute involving the boundary of Venezuela directly affected the United States under the terms of the Monroe Doctrine. He maintained that this country could not stand aside while the rights of Venezuela were assailed, and was wholly warranted in insisting that the entire issue be submitted to arbitration. The tone of Olney's note was harsh and peremptory—he would later state that "only words the equivalent of blows" could make any impression upon England—and he did not hesitate to give the broadest possible interpretation, regardless of historical validity, to the scope of American interests in Latin America.

The United States had a primary interest in the cause of self-government, Olney further stated, and it was one for which its people "might not impossibly be wrought up to an active propaganda." Generally they were content—"the age of the crusades had passed"—to assert such interest only when their own security and welfare de-

[10] Washington *Star,* Feb. 1, 1893, quoted in Pratt, *Expansionsits of 1898,* pp. 32–33.

manded it. The latter considerations ruled, Olney implied, wherever liberty was threatened in the New World. The warning to Great Britain against any intervention in the affairs of the Western Hemisphere was then heavily emphasized in the following passage: "Today the United States is practically sovereign on this continent, and its fiat is law upon the subjects to which it confines its interposition . . . Its infinite resources combined with its isolated position render it master of the situation and practically invulnerable as against any or all other powers." [11]

When England then denied that the dispute over the Venezuela boundary in any way involved the Monroe Doctrine and rejected the demand that the issue be arbitrated, Cleveland took an even firmer stand. On December 17, 1895, he called upon Congress to set up a commission of investigation and advised that, after its report had been made, the United States should be prepared to resist by all the means in its power any attempt by Great Britain to exercise jurisdiction over territory that "we have determined of right belongs to Venezuela." [12]

Congress and the greater part of the nation's press wildly applauded Cleveland's belligerent message and for a time there was talk of war. Fortunately, more realistic counsels prevailed on both sides of the Atlantic. England agreed to accept arbitration and further negotiations were conducted in a friendly atmosphere that marked the beginning of a new era in Anglo-American relations. However, the deeper significance of this crisis over Venezuela, precipitated by Cleveland, was most clearly expressed by Captain Mahan: "It indicates as I believe and hope, the awakening of our countrymen to the fact that we must come out of our isolation, which a hundred years ago was wise and imperative, and take our share in the turmoil of the world." [13]

About this same time, another development reflected and intensified the new stirring of national power. The United States was building a modern Navy. From the 1880's on, indeed, the demand for a bigger Navy ran· hand in hand with that for a more vigorous foreign policy. "What do the nations of the earth care about your moral power after

[11] Olney to Bayard, June 20, 1895, *Papers Relating to the Foreign Relations of the United States, 1895* (Washington, 1896), I, 558.

[12] *Ibid.*, I, 545. See also Allan Nevins, *Grover Cleveland* (New York, 1932), Chap. XXIV; A. L. P. Dennis, *Adventures in American Diplomacy, 1896–1906* (New York, 1928), Chap. II.

[13] Letter of Jan. 10, 1896, quoted in William E. Livezey, *Mahan on Sea Power* (Norman, Okla., 1947), p. 109.

you leave your own shores?" asked Senator Charles W. Jones of
Florida. And Representative Washington C. Whitthorne of Tennessee,
anticipating Mahan, again pointed out that those nations which in
past history had attained "the highest rank in dominion, power and
civilization" were invariably nations with "powerful navies and commercial marine." [14]

The actual start on new construction was rather slow. Congress
authorized four steel vessels (equipped, however, with sail as well as
steam power) early in the 1880's, and additional construction during
this decade included a number of armored cruisers. But these vessels
were for coastal defense only. "It is no part of our policy," President
Arthur had announced, "to create and maintain a navy able to cope
with that of the other great powers of the world." [15] It was not until
1890 that a Naval Policy Board, especially appointed by Secretary
Tracy to study naval requirements, first stressed the need for a fighting
fleet that would be strong enough to protect the highways of commerce. It was no longer practical for the United States to think solely
in terms of coastal defense, this report stated, for there were already
indications that its isolation "will soon cease." The Policy Board declared that the conception of a European balance of power now had
world application. The United States should be ready to uphold the
Monroe Doctrine as well as to repel possible invasion of its own territory. [16]

The misgivings of a public still reluctant to accept this interpretation of America's changing world role—or to acknowledge possible
threats to national security—compelled the big-Navy advocates to
move cautiously. The new vessels for which appropriations were made
in 1890 were officially identified as "sea-going coastline battleships" in
a neat attempt to reconcile the contradictory concepts of isolation and
world power. Nevertheless there appeared to be steadily increasing
popular support for a fleet that would be able to safeguard American
interests in all parts of the world rather than remain tied to home
ports. By the close of the century, successive appropriations had pro-

[14] *Congressional Record*, XV, 48th Congress, 1st Session (Feb. 27, 1884),
p. 1421; X, 46th Congress, 2nd Session (Apr. 14, 1880), Appendix, p. 143. See
Robert Seager II, "Ten Years Before Mahan: The Unofficial Case for the New
Navy, 1880–1890," *Mississippi Valley Historical Review*, XL (Dec., 1953), 491–
512.

[15] *Messages of the Presidents*, VIII, 181.

[16] *Naval Policy Board Report, 1890, Senate Executive Document 43*, 51st
Congress, 1st Session, V, 4.

vided a formidable array of seventeen battleships, six armored cruisers, and three monitors, together with protected cruisers, gunboats, and other small craft, in comparison with the handful of obsolescent, almost unarmed, wooden ships that had made up the Navy in 1880.[17]

Even before the Spanish-American War there was a glowing pride in this new fleet which led the martial-minded to welcome any test of its effectiveness, if not actually to seek out such a trial. Representative Champ Clark of Missouri appeared ready for all comers. "Now that we are the most puissant nation on the globe," he declared grandiloquently, ". . . the American Republic . . . warns Europe, Asia, and Africa to keep their hands off the Western Hemisphere on the penalty of being thrashed within an inch of their lives." [18]

In spite of Samoa and Hawaii, the Venezuela incident, and the agitation for a big Navy, foreign policy issues were by no means a dominant preoccupation during the early 1890's. The people as a whole were more deeply absorbed in the problems of economic depression, agrarian revolt, embittered labor disputes, and the excitement and hysteria of Populism. Yet there was evidence on every hand of a growing interest in the larger part America might take in international affairs. To some extent this interest reflected an attempt to escape from domestic ills. The frustrating and divisive problems that the nation faced, so far as its internal economy was concerned, encouraged the popular demand for a."vigorous" foreign policy as something upon which all elements in the population could agree. There was a close and continuing relationship between domestic discontent and the jingoism so evident at the time of the Venezuelan crisis, and between the later Populist demands for Free Silver and Free Cuba.[19] Magazine articles, newspaper editorials, congressional debates, and public speeches, in sharp contrast with the apathy of the previous decade, again and again reverted to the theme of extending commercial and political interests beyond their traditional boundaries.

[17] See Harold and Margaret Sprout, *The Rise of American Naval Power, 1776–1918* (Princeton, 1939), pp. 209 ff.; and George T. Davis, *A Navy Second to None* (New York, 1940), pp. 40 ff., 168.

[18] Theodore Roosevelt to Spring-Rice, Apr. 14, 1889, in Elting E. Morison (ed.), *The Letters of Theodore Roosevelt* (8 vols., Cambridge, Mass., 1951–54), I, 157; *Congressional Record*, XXXI, 55th Congress, 2nd Session (Jan. 20, 1898), p. 794.

[19] See Richard Hofstadter, "Manifest Destiny and the Philippines," in Daniel Aaron, *America in Crisis* (New York, 1952), pp. 173 ff.

One important factor in awakening this interest in overseas expansion was the sense of racial superiority derived from the evolutionary theories set forth by Charles Darwin, and popularized in this country by such men as the philosopher John Fiske and the political scientist John W. Burgess. The idea of survival of the fittest in the biological struggle for existence was carried over to the competition of racial groups. The Anglo-Saxon people, it was maintained, had demonstrated their superior fitness, especially in government, and were fated to extend their rule over those people less fortunately endowed. There could be no question that ultimately they would produce a civilization grander than anything the world had ever known.

Fiske firmly believed that because of the superiority of their institutions and the growth of their power, the Anglo-Saxons were bound to lead the world. Having already spread out over two hemispheres, he declared, they could not fail "to keep that sovereignty of the sea and that commercial supremacy" first acquired in the settlement of America. Burgess was convinced that Anglo-Saxons were uniquely endowed with the capacity for establishing national states, were foreordained to carry political institutions to all parts of the world, and consequently "must have a colonial policy." [20]

Even more assertive in the development of such ideas was Josiah Strong, a prominent Congregational minister and enthusiastic evangelist. His widely read and widely quoted *Our Country*, going through scores of successive cheap editions, had a pervasive influence. The Anglo-Saxon, Strong wrote, held in his hands the destinies of mankind, and the United States was "to become the home of this race, the principal seat of his power, the great center of his influence." [21]

Strong's starting point was his concern with world evangelization, reflecting the powerful missionary impulses of this generation in American life. He was convinced that such evangelization was the bounden duty of the Anglo-Saxon people. With their two great ideals of spiritual Christianity and civil liberty, they had risen by a process of natural selection to world pre-eminence. Strong saw the race spreading out from its principal seat in North America over the earth—moving down upon Mexico, down upon Central and South America, out upon the islands of the sea, over upon Africa and beyond. "And

[20] John Fiske, "Manifest Destiny," *Harper's Magazine*, LXX (March 1885), 578–590; John W. Burgess, *Political Science and Comparative Constitutional Law* (2 vols., Boston, 1891), I, 45.

[21] Josiah Strong, *Our Country* (New York, 1885), p. 165.

can any one doubt," he asked rhetorically, "that the result of this competition of races will be the 'survival of the fittest'?" [22]

It was the unique task of the United States, Strong further believed, to make certain that this expansion spread abroad American national ideals. The introduction to *Our Country* stated in succinct summary its author's views, ". . . As goes America, so goes the world." [23] Here, in terms embodying the new theory of evolution, was the old and recurrent theme of America as the regenerator of all mankind.

When *Our Country* was first published in 1885, there was still little thought of extending American territory overseas. The program of world evangelization, especially emphasized in the case of the peoples of Asia, was nevertheless to give important support to the economic and political forces later working for expansion. Religious groups throughout the nation gradually united behind the "imperialism of righteousness." In 1900, Strong published another little book, entitled *Expansion under New World Conditions,* in which he staunchly upheld this concept: "It is time to dismiss 'the craven fear of being great,' to recognize the place in the world which God has given us and to accept the responsibilities which it devolves upon us in behalf of Christian civilization." [24]

The widely held views on the racial superiority of the Anglo-Saxon people and on their colonizing genius were of immense importance in the 1890's. They served to build up a popular belief that non-Caucasians were totally unfit to play an independent role in modern civilization. It was not chance that such ideas, applied to the peoples of Asia, coincided with a renewed emphasis throughout the South on racial discrimination and "Jim Crow" legislation.[25]

Moreover, the idea of Anglo-Saxon superiority blinded even the thoughtful to the possibility of an awakening among the colored races which might some day lead them to challenge the domination of the white race. Many writers of the 1890's foresaw the effect upon the international balance of power of the gradual decline of British strength, appreciated the significance of the rise of Germany, and

[22] *Ibid.,* pp. 160–161, 175. The author's only doubt of the country's destiny, apparently, was whether the race might not be "devitalized by alcohol and tobacco." *Ibid.,* p. 178.

[23] *Ibid.,* p. vii.

[24] Josiah Strong, *Expansion under New World Conditions* (New York, 1900), p. 295.

[25] Richard Hofstadter, *Social Darwinism in American Thought* (Philadelphia, 1945), pp. 146–173.

even pointed to a possible future collision between America and Russia. Very rarely, however, does one find the suggestion that an ultimate consequence of colonialism might well be a reinvigoration of the subject people of Asia and their assertion of the right to independence and self-government.

The comfortable premise of racial superiority was generally assumed in support of each successive step toward American overseas expansion. Publicists repeatedly pictured the United States as standing guard over western civilization. They urged the annexation of new territory in the Caribbean, in the Pacific, and off the coasts of Asia, not only in the national interest, but in behalf of the welfare of the world.

Among the advocates of expansion in the 1890's, Alfred Thayer Mahan was perhaps the most influential, both through the effect upon public thinking of his books, innumerable articles, and letters to newspapers and because of his close association with men in a position to put his ideas into effect.[26] His historical studies on the influence of sea power, with the realization that new forces were invading "that little corner" which had previously made up the world of the United States, convinced him that "no nation, certainly no great nation, should henceforth maintain the policy of isolation." And once persuaded that the United States could not live unto itself, Mahan preached this broader point of view in and out of season—"whether they will or no, Americans must now begin to look outward." [27]

He was primarily concerned with naval power as the means to achieve national greatness, and in elaborating his ideas developed an ambitious program of mercantile imperialism. Accepting the thesis that a growing volume of industrial production demanded new foreign markets to maintain a healthy economy, Mahan insisted that in the face of existing imperialistic rivalries the United States had to be prepared to safeguard its commercial interests throughout the entire world. This meant a strong and powerful Navy, for only that nation which commanded the seas was in a position of real power, and such

[26] Mahan's articles for this period are conveniently available in Alfred Thayer Mahan, *The Interest of America in Sea Power, Present and Future* (Boston, 1897). See also Livezey, *Mahan on Sea Power,* and W. D. Puleston, *Mahan* (New Haven, 1939).

[27] Livezey, *Mahan on Sea Power,* pp. 77–78; Mahan, *The Interest of America in Sea Power,* p. 21.

a Navy in turn had to have overseas bases to operate effectively away from its home ports.

These ideas, although not altogether new, had directly influenced the Naval Policy Board report in 1890—the same year in which Mahan published his first important magazine article—and they were to have a steadily broadening impact. Mahan was not content, however, with building up naval strength. He emphasized the need for a foreign policy clearly breaking with the past in every respect. His arguments brought together, logically and persuasively, the several factors supporting an emergent imperialism: the "aggressive restlessness" underlying the struggle for survival among the great powers, the consequent necessity for the United States to build up predominant economic and political strength, and the moral responsibility of the nation to maintain a position which would enable it to uphold law and justice in an international society.[28]

Mahan strongly advocated the construction of an isthmian canal and American dominance in the Caribbean; he enthusiastically supported the principle of exclusive control over both Samoa and Hawaii. These, however, were only preliminary steps. He wrote in 1893: "The annexation, even, of Hawaii would be no mere sporadic effort, irrational because disconnected from an adequate motive, but a first-fruit and a token that the nation in its evolution has aroused itself to the necessity of carrying its life—that has been the happiness of those under its influence—beyond the borders which have heretofore sufficed for its activities." [29]

In his vision of a new and dynamic America, building up political and economic power throughout the world, Mahan outran the views of many other contemporary imperialists. While they sought to reconcile expansion with the traditional policy of the past, in that a stronger United States could continue to go its own way and effectively safeguard its freedom of action, Mahan candidly recognized that this was impossible. The United States, he wrote in 1894, would be led "to cast aside the policy of isolation which befitted her infancy" and assume commitments, heretofore unwise, in carrying forward the nation's "inevitable task, and appointed lot in the work of upholding the common interests of civilization." [30]

---

[28] *Ibid.*, pp. 3–27, 137–172.
[29] *Ibid.*, p. 49.
[30] Alfred Thayer Mahan and Captain Lord Charles Beresford, "Possibilities

The course he proposed, as elaborated somewhat later, was an "implicit admission of entanglement in that net known as 'world politics.' " The challenging rise of Germany, already an ominous development on the European scene, and a recognized community of interests between Great Britain and the United States in part growing out of the threat to both nations of German imperialism, seemed to point to the advisability of a closer Anglo-Saxon accord. The friction with Germany over the Samoa issue, and recurrent fears of Germany attempting intervention in the affairs of Latin America, had strengthened not only Mahan's ideas along such lines, but those of many other Americans. For while there was still rivalry between England and the United States, the fundamental importance of their common bonds of race and language, of the basic similarity of their aims and aspirations, was becoming ever more widely recognized.

There were numerous proposals for an actual alliance. Mahan was not ready to go this far, doubting that such an alliance would receive popular support, but he strongly urged "accordant relations" with Great Britain as a means of presenting united resistance to any further manifestations of German imperialism.[31] The caution he displayed in not wanting to move too fast was based upon the sound premise that "in our country national policy, if it is to be steadfast and consistent, must be identical with public conviction." [32]

One of the most influential converts to Mahan's basic thesis was Henry Cabot Lodge. Throughout the 1890's, in both current periodicals and on the floor of Congress, the Massachusetts senator stressed the vital importance of naval expansion—"it is the seapower that is essential to the greatness of every great people"—and, further echoing Mahan's views, he repeatedly declared that with the conquest of the continent "the American people had begun to turn their eyes to those interests of the United States which lie beyond our borders and yet so near our doors." Lodge called for a Nicaraguan canal, annexation of Hawaii, and the maintenance of American influence in Samoa. He favored the purchase of the Danish West Indies and even suggested

---

of an Anglo-American Reunion," *North American Review*, CLIX (Nov., 1894), 558.

[31] Alfred Thayer Mahan, *The Interest of America in International Conditions* (Boston, 1910), pp. 118, 115, 36. For a comprehensive study of German-American relations, see Alfred Vagts, *Deutschland und die Vereinigten Staaten in der Weltpolitik* (New York, 1935).

[32] Mahan and Beresford, "Possibilities of an Anglo-American Reunion," p. 556.

that of Greenland. He looked confidently toward American dominance in the Caribbean, if not further south, and the ultimate annexation of Cuba. In an article for the *Forum*, published in March, 1895, he wrote: "The great nations are rapidly absorbing for their future expansion and their present defense all the waste places of the earth. It is a movement which makes for civilization and the advancement of the race. As one of the great nations of the world the United States must not fall out of the line of march." [33]

In one significant respect, however, Lodge differed with Mahan. While believing that the United States had to emerge from the isolation of the past, he continued to oppose any entanglement in world politics. In a traditional sense he maintained an "isolationist" rather than an "internationalist" position. He held that while "the citadel of our power and greatness as a "nation" lay within the United States itself, there were nevertheless "outworks essential to the defense of that citadel which must neither be neglected nor abandoned." With such outworks and a powerful Navy, the United States would be strong enough to guard the Western Hemisphere, would have no need for alliances, and would retain its historic freedom of action. Lodge urged this policy upon American statesmen "if they would prove themselves worthy inheritors of the principles of Washington and Adams." [34]

Another enthusiastic disciple of Mahan and a close associate of Lodge was the young Theodore Roosevelt. He too accepted without hesitation the complete Mahanite doctrine of America's need for a big Navy and overseas bases. The importance of driving all European powers—including England—out of the Western Hemisphere became almost an obsession. Roosevelt repeatedly insisted on the advisability of annexing Hawaii and building a Nicaraguan canal, impulsively writing Mahan on one occasion that if he could have his way, he would "hoist our flag over the island [Hawaii], leaving all details for after action." Addressing the Naval War College, he called for a big Navy—"peace is a goddess only when she comes girt with sword on thigh"—and expressed a new conception of how foreign policy might be conducted in stating that "the diplomat is the servant, not the master of the soldier." [35]

[33] *Congressional Record*, XXVII, 53rd Congress, 3rd Session (Mar. 2, 1895), pp. 3084–86. Henry Cabot Lodge, "Our Blundering Foreign Policy," *Forum*, XIX (Mar., 1895), 8–17.

[34] *Ibid.*, p. 16.

[35] Roosevelt to W. A. Chanler, Dec. 23, 1897, and to F. C. Moore, Feb. 9,

When he became Assistant Secretary of the Navy, Roosevelt could exercise more direct pressure. He was constantly promoting his ideas, as revealed in his correspondence, through talks with Secretary of the Navy Long and President McKinley.[36] How close were the ties linking Mahan, Lodge, and Roosevelt in their common conviction of the need for asserting American power is revealed in a letter which Roosevelt wrote Mahan on May 3, 1897. After expressing his desire to throw Spain entirely out of the Caribbean, he added: "I need not say that this letter must be strictly private. I speak to you with the greatest freedom, for I sympathize with your views, and I have precisely the same idea of patriotism, and of belief in and love for our country. But to no one else excepting Lodge do I talk like this.[37]

In the growing volume of articles dealing with foreign policy, there was sometimes a sharp note of dissent. In his warning against imperialism, in which he acknowledged he differed with his "valued friends" Captain Mahan and Theodore Roosevelt, Bryce insisted that the United States did not need colonies. They were not always a source of strength, he declared, and their acquisition would be "a complete departure from the maxims—approved by long experience—of the illustrious founders of the Republic." Carl Schurz, the German-American leader and as stubborn an anti-imperialist as Cleveland, vigorously attacked the new Manifest Destiny and the whole idea of overseas expansion. William Graham Sumner, political scientist and sociologist, stoutly declared that the annexation of overseas territory ran directly counter to the principles laid down in the 1780's, which were to avoid high politics, the balance of power, and what Franklin had termed the "pest of glory." [38]

Nor did Mahan's mercantile imperialism arouse any enthusiasm at this time in commercial circles. While the attitude of the nation's dom-

---

1898, *Letters of Theodore Roosevelt,* I, 746–747, 771–772; Roosevelt to Mahan, May 3, 1897, *ibid.,* I, 607; Naval War College Speech, June 2, 1897, quoted in Henry F. Pringle, *Theodore Roosevelt* (New York, 1931), p. 172.

[36] See, for example, Roosevelt to Mahan, June 9, 1897, *Letters of Theodore Roosevelt,* I, 622; Roosevelt to Lodge, Sept. 15, 1897, *ibid.,* I, 676; Roosevelt to Lodge, Sept. 21, 1897, *ibid.,* I, 685.

[37] Roosevelt to Mahan, May 3, 1897, *ibid.,* I, 608.

[38] Bryce, "The Policy of Annexation for America," p. 395; Carl Schurz, "Manifest Destiny," *Harper's Magazine,* LXXXVII (Oct. 1893), 737–746; William Graham Sumner, "The Fallacy of Territorial Extension," *Forum,* XXI (June, 1896), 418.

inant business interests was later to change, when overseas expansion held out the immediate promise of new markets and trade opportunities, it was definitely anti-imperialist until after the outbreak of war with Spain. Two of the more important journals representing the business community, the *Journal of Commerce* and the *Commercial and Financial Chronicle*, were originally opposed to both the annexation of Hawaii and American control of a Nicaraguan canal. The idea that the United States needed the canal to defend the islands, and the islands to defend the canal, seemed absurd to the former newspaper. In September, 1897, it declared that there was "no excuse whatever in our commercial or our political interests" for running the risk of such dangerous complications.[39]

The voice of these skeptics, however, was almost drowned out in the steady barrage of expansionist propaganda in the mid-1890's. The editorial notes appearing in the *Review of Reviews* constantly dwelt on the expansionist theme. Echoing Seward's prophecy of half a century earlier, the Pacific was said to be "the theater of great events in the coming century," and Americans were called upon to renew their faith "in the old American doctrine of our 'manifest destiny.' " The *Literary Digest* gave much space to articles by Mahan and other likeminded writers. In August, 1897, it reported that the Trans-Mississippi Congress, presided over by William Jennings Bryan, had approved resolutions for the annexation of Hawaii, construction of the Nicaragua canal as an American enterprise, and recognition of the independence of Cuba.[40] The *Forum* was also highly receptive to articles favoring a more expansive foreign policy. It published a number by John R. Proctor, chairman of the Civil Service Commission and friend of Roosevelt, which especially stressed the importance of American domination of the Pacific.

This latter publicist also drew attention, as early as 1897, to what he believed to be a danger to American interests in eastern Asia from Russian imperialism. "Now, the expanding empire of the Slav," he wrote, "threatens to absorb the descendants of the Mongols, and to establish an empire more powerful than the all-conquering empire of Genghis Khan." Proctor was prepared to accept imperialism as a clearcut alternative to isolationism. He proposed a series of treaties with

[39] *Journal of Commerce*, Sept. 8, 1897, quoted in Pratt, *Expansionists of 1898*, p. 255.

[40] *Review of Reviews*, XVII (Feb., 1898), 143; *Literary Digest*, XV (Aug. 7, 1897), 428.

Great Britain, the Netherlands, and Japan setting up a Monroe Doctrine for the North Pacific and the islands of the Indian Ocean.[41]

On the eve of war with Spain, an editorial in the *Overland Monthly,* published in San Francisco, frankly called for abandonment of the tradition stemming from Washington's Farewell Address. The subjugation of the continent had been sufficient to keep the American people busy at home for a century, it said, but now that the continent was subdued, "we are looking for fresh worlds to conquer." The editorial stressed as had so many earlier articles "the colonizing instinct" of the Anglo-Saxon race, and warned conservatives that, whether they liked it or not, this instinct could not be denied.[42]

The Washington *Post* interpreted in much the same way the temper of the nation. "A new consciousness seems to have come upon us—the consciousness of strength—and with it a new appetite, the yearning to show our strength." There was no avoiding our destiny, the *Post* continued, for the taste of empire was in the mouth of the people—"it means an imperial policy, the Republic renascent, taking her place with the armed nations." [43]

When the policies so urgently promoted by the expansionists of the 1890's were finally put into effect, the explanation repeatedly advanced was that the nation had been swept along by forces beyond its control. "No man, no party," John Hay said, "can fight with any chance of final success against a cosmic tendency." [44] And Mahan wrote, with what might appear to be undue modesty, "No man nor group of men can pretend to have guided and governed our people in the adoption of a new policy, the acceptance of which has been rather instinctive— I would prefer to say inspired—than reasoned." [45] Senator Albert J. Beveridge of Indiana spoke simply of "the unseen hand of God."

[41] John R. Proctor, "Hawaii and the Changing Front of the World," *Forum,* XXIV (Sept., 1897), 38; "Isolation or Imperialism," *ibid.,* XXVI (Sept., 1898), 14–26.

[42] *Overland Monthly,* XXXI (Feb., 1898), 177–178.

[43] Washington *Post,* June 14, 1898, quoted in Albert K. Weinberg, *Manifest Destiny* (Baltimore, 1935), p. 289.

[44] Tyler Dennett, *John Hay* (New York, 1933), p. 278.

[45] Mahan, "The Growth of Our National Feeling," *World's Work,* III (Feb., 1902), 1764. This statement may be compared, however, with an earlier comment. "Reflection and discussion, voice and pen," he wrote in 1900, "had broken up the fallow ground left untilled by the generations which succeeded the fathers of the republic." "The Problem of Asia," *Harper's Magazine,* C (Mar., 1900), 538.

There would seem to be some reason to question this interpretation of the startling events that at the close of the nineteenth century created an American empire. While the United States could not remain aloof from world affairs in view of its inherent power and a shrinking globe, this did not mean it had to embark on territorial expansion overseas. The forces making for such a move were very powerful, representing as they did what seemed to be the demands of national security, commercial advantage, and an obligation to spread abroad American principles. Nevertheless they might not have carried the day had it not been for the insistent propaganda of the expansionists themselves. Their skillful appeal to popular emotions was of decisive importance in creating public support for imperialism.

The motives of the expansionists greatly differed. Josiah Strong was carried away by evangelical fervor; Mahan was absorbed in a dream of national power for its own sake; Lodge was intrigued with the political possibilities of imperialism; and Roosevelt perhaps transferred to national policy his own propensity for martial activity and exciting adventure. The imperialists were alike, however, in urging action that they felt would build up the influence and prestige of their country. And this emphasis helps to explain the indifferent attitude of spokesmen of the industrial interests whose power was all important in domestic matters. The original imperialists, in spite of Mahan's mercantile theories, were not primarily concerned with economic advantage. They tended to be highly scornful of the business civilization epitomized by the McKinley administration. They wished to see the United States become something more than a nation of tradesmen and manufacturers, and Roosevelt is found favoring even war to give the people "something to think of which isn't material gain." [46] When they urged overseas expansion, they were thinking primarily in terms of national honor and national glory.

The stage thus appeared set, as the 1890's drew to a close, for some active, positive manifestation of the imperialistic spirit that was itself an expression of the new-found power of the United States. There was needed only a catalytic agent to precipitate the reaction. This was provided by war with Spain.

[46] Roosevelt to W. W. Kimball, Nov. 19, 1897, *Letters of Theodore Roosevelt*, I, 717; Pringle, *Theodore Roosevelt*, pp. 408–409.

CHAPTER 3

Imperialist Adventure

THE SPANISH-AMERICAN War was an epochal turning point in American history. Intervention in the revolutionary situation that had developed in Cuba gave the imperial-minded the opportunity they were seeking. In emphasizing the position of the United States as a world power, it created a demand for action as a world power—and in 1898 that meant imperialism.

While the forces making for the war itself drew much of their strength from the same sources that had given rise to the imperialist spirit of the day, the immediate cause for hostilities was not expansionist ambition. It was primarily an emotional response on the part of the American public to the plight of a colonial people struggling for freedom against foreign rule. Heretofore the United States had gone no further than to try to exercise a moral influence in support of the principles for which it stood. Where liberty was assailed and peace endangered so close to American shores, in a neighboring country with which American ties had long been exceedingly close, there was a mounting popular feeling that the nation could not stand aside. It is true that excitement was whipped up by a conscienceless "yellow press" whose owners were first and last interested in the circulation gains to be made through lurid atrocity stories. Nevertheless the unhappy lot of the Cubans instinctively appealed to the deepest humanitarian and liberty-loving instincts of the American people.

The crisis with Spain had been long in the making. No sooner had rebellion broken out in Cuba in February, 1895, than American interest was engaged and the press began to express sympathy for the revolutionaries. Nevertheless Cleveland refused to be swept away by any jingoistic outburst, even when Congress passed a resolution favoring recognition of Cuban belligerency. He resolutely stood his ground in the face of popular clamor. For a time interest in the rebellion then gave way to the more immediate excitement of the noisy battle over free silver in the presidential campaign of 1896, but once the Republicans were returned to power with the election of McKinley, the issue again surged to the front.

While the new President was a man of peace no less than his predecessor, his position became increasingly difficult as popular feeling continued to be inflamed by the crass sensationalism of newspaper reporting on conditions in Cuba. The prevailing excitement was then further heightened by the Spanish minister's inept blunder in writing a letter in which he referred to McKinley as "weak and a bidder for the admiration of the crowd," but the most telling incident in arousing the war fever was the sinking of the *Maine* in Havana harbor. When word was received on February 15, 1898, of this disaster to one of the nation's prized new battleships, there was a hysterical demand for immediate intervention in the Cuban struggle. Although American representations in Madrid appeared to be on the point of persuading the Spanish government to grant an armistice to the Cuban rebels, public opinion was not assuaged. The unhappy President, overwhelmed by the political pressures under which he was laboring, finally felt that he had no alternative other than to give in to them. In spite of Spain's virtual capitulation to his diplomatic demands, he went before Congress on April 11 and asked authority to use the Army and Navy to end hostilities in Cuba. This was war.[1]

In their martial enthusiasm, the American people took up arms to redress the wrongs inflicted on the Cuban people and to defend the national honor against a challenge to peace and justice, symbolized by the sinking of the *Maine*, that a proud nation could not ignore. But the expansionists, for long in favor of Cuban intervention for more

[1] The view once held that economic factors played a decisive part in bringing about war with Spain has been substantially modified, in no small part owing to the studies of Julius W. Pratt, especially his *Expansionists of 1898* (Baltimore, 1936). In 1924 Harold U. Faulkner wrote that the "great cause for the war" was the fact that the United States was "sufficiently advanced for financial imperialism." *American Economic History* (New York, 1924), pp. 624–625. Twenty-seven years later this same writer stated that "the point of view taken by certain economic historians that the United States went to war with Spain primarily for economic reasons seems not warranted by the evidence . . ." *The Decline of Laissez Faire*, Vol. VII in *The Economic History of the United States* (New York, 1951), p. 15.

practical reasons, were quick to seize upon the opportunities war afforded to build up national power and acquire possessions in both the Caribbean and the Pacific. While the idealistic impulses behind American action led to the adoption of a self-denying ordinance in which the United States disclaimed any intention to annex Cuba, nothing was said in this resolution about the rest of Spain's colonies. There were no barriers to prevent a war undertaken to free Cuba from being utilized to acquire other overseas bases or dependencies.

In these circumstances, the dramatic news that Commodore George Dewey had overwhelmed the Spanish fleet at Manila Bay on May 1, 1898, at once excited the nation. The presence at this juncture of an American fleet off the Philippines was due to an unusual series of events in which the jingoistic Theodore Roosevelt had played no small part. In his zeal for a war to drive Spain out of the Western Hemisphere, Roosevelt had not overlooked the fact that there were also Spanish possessions in the Pacific. As Assistant Secretary of the Navy, he had been instrumental in the appointment of Commodore Dewey to the command of the Asiatic Squadron and in the dispatch of orders calling upon him in the event of hostilities with Spain promptly to begin "offensive operations" in the Philippines.[2]

It little mattered to the general public, however, how American forces happened to find themselves in such a distant and unexpected theater of war. A new note had been sounded on the Pacific shores, cried an exuberant member of Congress—"a note that has echoed and re-echoed around the world." The Philippines immediately became the great prize. "They must be ours," Senator Lodge enthusiastically wrote Henry White. ". . . We hold the other side of the Pacific, and the value to this country is almost beyond imagination." From Theodore Roosevelt, about to sail for Cuba with the Rough Riders, came an importunate letter insisting that there should be no talk of peace until there was assurance that "we get Porto Rico and the Philippines as well as secure the independence of Cuba."[3]

Newspaper after newspaper took up the refrain of empire. "The guns of Dewey at Manila have changed the destiny of the United

[2] George Dewey, *Autobiography* (New York, 1913), p. 179.

[3] Senator Sulzer, June 14, 1898, in Marion M. Miller (ed.), *Great Debates in American History* (14 vols., New York, 1913), III, 211; Lodge to White, May 4, 1898, quoted in Allan Nevins, *Henry White—Thirty Years of Diplomacy* (New York, 1930), p. 136; Roosevelt to Lodge, June 12, 1898, in Elting E. Morison, *The Letters of Theodore Roosevelt* (8 vols., Cambridge, Mass., 1951–54), II, 840.

States," exclaimed the Washington *Post*. ". . . We are face to face with a strange destiny and must accept its responsibilities. An imperial policy!" "Our war in aid of Cuba has assumed undreamed of dimensions," the Philadelphia *Record* declared; ". . . willy nilly we have entered upon our career as a world power." [4]

The first definite move toward imperialism was not the acquisition of a Spanish colony but the annexation of Hawaii. The drive to take over this Pacific outpost had already been renewed and, as the Philippines so surprisingly swung into the national orbit, it gathered great momentum as a war measure, and supposedly a necessary one. Yet even now Hawaiian annexation was not universally approved. Although it had become a declared objective of administration policy— "We need Hawaii just as much and a good deal more than we did California," McKinley told his Secretary. "It is manifest destiny." [5]— overseas possessions of any sort still seemed a startling innovation to the general public. The congressional and popular debate on Hawaii in the summer of 1898 brought out all the old arguments revolving about the world role of the United States. [6]

Thus the advocates of annexation argued that the control of Hawaii was essential for the promotion of trade and commerce. American inaction would encourage the growth of foreign influence in the islands and there could be no further delay in fulfilling what was at once a national mission and national destiny. Hardly a speaker in Congress failed to cite the reasons for annexation so persuasively advanced by Captain Mahan in his elaboration of the importance of American control of the Pacific. [7]

The opponents of annexation were unconvinced by arguments for naval supremacy, commercial advantage, or fulfillment of a moral obligation. The "unconquerable Anglo-Saxon lust for land" came in for caustic criticism and Manifest Destiny was dismissed by one

[4] Washington *Post*, June 3, 1898; *Literary Digest*, XVI (May 14, 1898), 573.
[5] Charles S. Olcott, *William McKinley* (2 vols., Boston, 1916), I, 379.
[6] For debates see *Congressional Record*, XXI, 55th Congress, 2nd Session (1898), pp. 5570 ff., 5973 ff., 6140 ff., 6693 ff., but more conveniently, Miller, *Great Debates*, III, 190 ff. See also Thomas A. Bailey, "The United States and Hawaii during the Spanish-American War," *American Historical Review*, XXXVI (Apr., 1931), 552–560.
[7] ". . . It is upon Captain Mahan more than any other single person," one commentator later wrote, "that the nation relied in its annexation of Hawaii." Wallace Rice, "Some Current Fallacies of Captain Mahan," *The Dial*, XXVIII (Mar. 16, 1900), 199.

speaker as nothing more than "the specious plea of every robber and freebooter since the world began." Once the United States started on a course of colonial expansion, it was sternly insisted, the way would be open for the disintegration of the Republic. The anti-annexationists again pleaded with Congress to recall the advice of Washington and Jefferson. Colonialism could only mean that the United States would become a party to every European quarrel over foreign territories, one representative stated, and no longer would "our ancient peace abide with us." [8]

The position taken by George F. Hoar, Republican senator from Maine, has a special interest. He favored the annexation of Hawaii, but entirely on the grounds of national defense. The islands lay within a line drawn from the Aleutians to the southern tip of California, Hoar pointed out, and in the event of possible war with Japan, their possession by the United States would be vital to American security. "I believe that this is a contest," Hoar stated, "to be settled now peacefully or to be settled hereafter by force between America and Asia." He was nevertheless opposed to imperialism *per se*. If Hawaiian annexation were the first step in the acquisition of dominion over barbarous archipelagoes in distant seas, or of involvement in European rivalries in eastern Asia, Senator Hoar declared, he would have none of it—"then let us resist this thing in the beginning, and let us resist it to the death." However he had convinced himself, after much meditation, he told the Senate, that "the fear of imperialism is needless alarm." [9]

Senator Hoar was wrong. The annexation of Hawaii, finally brought about through a joint congressional resolution approved by the President on July 7, 1898, set up a powerful precedent for the acquisition of other overseas territory. It broke the pattern of the past. It gave solid encouragement to the imperialists who believed, with Mahan, that Hawaii was but a first token that the nation was prepared to carry its life beyond the borders which had heretofore sufficed for its activities. As the annexation resolution made its way through Congress, Lodge was confidently able to report to Roosevelt that there was every indication that the McKinley administration was "fully committed to the large policy that we both desire," and that "the whole

---

[8] Miller, *Great Debates*, III, 207–208.

[9] *Ibid.*, III, 237 ff. In recalling this speech in his memoirs, Senator Hoar omitted the sentence ending with the phrase "the fear of imperialism is needless alarm." George F. Hoar, *Autobiography of Seventy Years* (2 vols., New York, 1903), II, 311.

policy of annexation is growing rapidly under the irresistible pressure of events." [10]

If this pressure of events was irresistible, it was not for want of the continued efforts of the proponents of expansion to give it the desired direction. They had not only had their hand in initiating naval operations in the Pacific, but behind the scenes continued to exercise all possible pressure upon the President to persuade him to adopt their views. They played skillfully upon the emotions of a public all too ready to be convinced that where once the flag had been raised it should not be hauled down. "We see already," wrote Walter Hines Page on May 9, 1898, "the beginnings of an 'Imperial' party . . ." [11]

Lodge did not need Roosevelt's insistent urging to make sure that there was no talk of peace until "we get Porto Rico and the Philippines." He was doing everything he could along just this line. For a time Mahan appeared somewhat hesitant about keeping the more distant islands. In spite of his expansionist ambitions, he was not certain of their benefits from the point of view of naval strategy. He did believe that Luzon and at least one of the Ladrones should be retained, however, and soon accepted the broader view that all the Philippines should be in American hands. [12]

On one occasion Lodge and Mahan spent the evening with Secretary of State Day. After discussing Philippine annexation for two hours, they were greatly heartened by Day's statement that "we could not escape our destiny there." A few weeks later, after an interview with McKinley, Lodge further reported to the anxious Roosevelt that encouraging progress had been made even though the President was still "a little timid about it." He had himself seen "the *Sun* people," Lodge added, and they were going to use their very considerable influence with the President "in the right direction." There were also letters to Henry White in London urging him to impress upon Ambassador Hay, who Lodge expected would be one of the peace commissioners, the importance of keeping at least Manila and Luzon. [13]

[10] Lodge to Roosevelt, May 24 and June 15, *Selections from the Correspondence of Theodore Roosevelt and Henry Cabot Lodge* (2 vols., New York, 1925), I, 300, 310.

[11] B. J. Hendrick, *The Training of an American; The Earlier Life and Letters of Walter H. Page* (Boston, 1928), pp. 264–265.

[12] Mahan to Lodge, July 27, 1898, quoted in William E. Livezey, *Mahan on Sea Power* (Norman, Okla., 1947), p. 182. He was later to write that possession of the Philippines was "a proposition . . . entirely unexpected and novel." Alfred T. Mahan, *The Problem of Asia* (Boston, 1905), p. 8.

[13] Lodge to Roosevelt, June 24 and July 12, 1898, *Correspondence of Roose-*

A new and exuberant imperialist ally was Albert J. Beveridge, soon to be elected senator from Indiana. It was his ambition to be "the forming and the shaping mind which is to mark out our foreign policy," [14] and while he never quite attained this role, he unquestionably exercised a very real influence in marshaling popular support for overseas expansion. No public figure of the day was more convinced of the civilizing mission of the Anglo-Saxon race and the manifest destiny of the United States to become a dominant world power.

Two days after the outbreak of war, Beveridge told an astounded Boston audience that "the Philippines are logically our first target," and from the first reports of Dewey's victory acquisition of the entire archipelago had no more ardent champion. Vigorously attacking those who he believed were trying to make political advantage of the "prejudice of the people in favor of the old Washington dictum about isolation," he called upon the country to seize this opportunity for commercial and strategic advantage. "The Philippines not contiguous?" he asked. "Our navy will make them contiguous." There could be no question of the significance of what was taking place: "It is God's great purpose made manifest in the instincts of our race, whose present phase is our personal profit, but whose far-off end is the redemption of the world and the Christianization of mankind." [15]

For all their concern with national power for its own sake, the expansionists had never neglected commercial advantage in promoting their program, and in the summer of 1898 they finally began to win support from business leaders. If the latter had originally paid little attention to Mahan's exposition of mercantile imperialism, turning a deaf ear to earlier summons to overseas adventure for the sake of trade, new developments at home and abroad were causing a sharp shift in their attitude. In the growing conviction that new outlets had to be found for American goods if the national economy were to prosper, both manufacturers and exporters looked more and more avidly toward

---

velt and Lodge, I, 313, 323–324; Lodge to White, Sept. 23, 1898; Nevins, *Henry White,* p. 137. It is perhaps a temptation to exaggerate the influence of Roosevelt and Lodge in their vehement promotion of imperialism. A. W. Griswold has written, however: ". . . American diplomacy in the Far East in particular would, for the next fifty years, bear the stamp of these two personalities." *The Far Eastern Policy of the United States* (New York, 1938), p. 10.

[14] Beveridge to George W. Perkins, May 3, 1898, quoted in Claude G. Bowers, *Beveridge and the Progressive Era* (New York, 1932), p. 71.

[15] *Ibid.,* pp. 68–70, 71, 75–76.

what were believed to be the tremendous potentialities of the Far Eastern market. And at this very time the European powers appeared to be closing the door to American trade in China through the establishment of exclusive spheres of influence and the seizure of Chinese territory.

In such circumstances, the Philippines seemed to offer the United States an opportunity to secure a foothold in eastern Asia that would counteract these developments by establishing a strategic base for American commercial operations in China. The business community swung over to the imperialist camp. There was wide endorsement for Lodge's statement that Manila was the great prize "and the thing which will give us the Eastern trade," and for Beveridge's declaration that "the trade of the world must and shall be ours." [16]

The *Journal of Commerce,* so strongly opposed to annexationist ideas during the mid-1890's, was convinced by 1898 of the need for a more active China policy, and after the battle of Manila Bay it became frankly imperialistic. Failure to retain the Philippines, the *Journal* insisted, "would be an act of inconceivable folly." Their acquisition was necessary to establish an impregnable defense position in the Pacific, and the nation could not "calculate upon another opportunity if this be neglected." [17]

The *Wall Street Journal* believed that the United States should retain at least enough interest in the Philippines to assure a coaling station or naval base in Asiatic waters in view of the possible effects of "the breaking up of China." The *American Banker* stated that the chance to expand in the Pacific, just as Europe appeared to be moving toward a division of China, was "a coincidence which has a providential air." [18]

This change in the attitude of the business community is perhaps most graphically revealed in the altered views of Mark Hanna. As the spokesman for American industry in the high councils of the Republican party, he had opposed war with Spain and overseas expansion as threatening the economic stability the country was enjoying after the depression days of the early 1890's. There is the story of an incensed Theodore Roosevelt shaking his fist in Hanna's face and shouting, "we will have this war for the freedom of Cuba in spite of the timidity of

[16] Lodge to Roosevelt, August 15, 1898, *Correspondence of Roosevelt and Lodge,* I, 337; Bowers, *Beveridge and the Progressive Era,* p. 169.

[17] *Journal of Commerce and Commercial Bulletin,* Jan. 12, 1898.

[18] *Wall Street Journal,* May 5, 1898, and *American Banker,* May 11, 1898, quoted in Pratt, *Expansionists of 1898,* pp. 268–269.

the commercial interests." [19] When the war gave a new impetus to prosperity, however, Hanna began to change his mind about the possible benefits from an imperialistic policy. At first somewhat undecided about the Philippines, *The New York Times* quoting him in midsummer, 1898, as going no further than to say "we at least want a foothold on those islands," he was ultimately convinced that possession of them all was necessary. And only one argument appeared to him completely valid—the position of the Philippines in relation to China: "If it is commercialism to want possession of a strategic point giving the American people an opportunity to maintain a foothold in the markets of that great Eastern country, for God's sake let's have commercialism." [20]

Other Americans, dazzled by the vision of empire but reluctant to confess to economic or prestige motives, once more found their justification for an expansionist policy in the obligation of the United States to assume its share of the civilizing mission of the Anglo-Saxon race. Rudyard Kipling's stirring call to "take up the White Man's burden" was to fall on responsive ears.[21] The "imperialism of righteousness" had a tremendous popular appeal and the religious press of the country, with few exceptions, came out forthrightly in favor of expansion on the grounds of duty and responsibility. The *Churchman* was for a time critical of the whole idea of Philippine annexation, but before the close of 1898 it too had fallen in line: "Woe to any nation brought to pass where it is called to guide a weaker people's future which hesitates for fear its own interests will be entangled and its own future imperilled by the discharge of an unmistakable duty." [22]

The moralistic approach to expansion was governed not only by the traditional idea of America's role in spreading abroad her own principles of civil and religious liberty but also by the immediate opportunity for evangelization in the Philippines. The difficulty of reconciling a commitment to freedom with the imposition of colonial controls was easily met. It was maintained that the Filipinos were

[19] Henry F. Pringle, *Theodore Roosevelt* (New York, 1931), p. 179.

[20] *The New York Times,* July 31, 1898, and Oct. 20, 1900, quoted in Foster Rhea Dulles, *America in the Pacific* (Boston, 1932), pp. 230, 227–228.

[21] This poem was first published in the United States in *McClure's Magazine,* XXI (Feb., 1899), 291. Roosevelt sent advance sheets to Lodge, commenting, "rather poor poetry, but good sense from the expansionist standpoint." Lodge replied: "I like it. I think it is better poetry than you say, apart from the sense of the views." Roosevelt to Lodge, Jan. 12, 1899; Lodge to Roosevelt, Jan. 14, 1899, *Correspondence of Roosevelt and Lodge,* I, 384, 385.

[22] *Literary Digest,* XVII (Sept. 3, 1898), 290; *Churchman,* LXXVIII (Nov. 19, 1898), 727–728.

eager for the blessings which American rule represented. "Did we need their consent to perform a great act for humanity?" McKinley was later to ask. "We had it in every aspiration of their minds, in every hope of their hearts." [23] Even when they showed something less than enthusiasm for exchanging the yoke of Spain for that of the United States, the argument was turned to suggest that they needed only a period of tutelage in order to appreciate the larger freedom that would be actually theirs under American laws and institutions.

With imperialist orators declaiming upon national prestige and power, the business journals talking of the needs of trade and commerce, and the religious papers emphasizing duty and obligation, there seemed to be little question of where the country was heading. Although political partisanship sometimes drew a line between Republican enthusiasm and Democratic skepticism, a *Literary Digest* survey of newspaper opinion early in September found an overwhelming majority of nationwide papers favoring either retention of all the Philippines or at least establishment of a naval base. Only a half dozen proposed American withdrawal. [24]

Still, it was not the newspapers nor the imperialist orators who were charged with making decisions on foreign policy. The war once won, it was the responsibility of the President to draw up the peace terms to be offered Spain. It was his function within the nation's constitutional framework to present a program that the American people as a whole, acting through Congress, could then either accept or reject.

On taking office McKinley had given various assurances that there would be no "jingo nonsense" about his administration. [25] Nevertheless he had bowed to popular clamor on the issue of war with Spain; and he was now to be won over completely to the new spirit of imperialism. Within his own official family there were counteracting forces. The pressure of the imperial party was balanced by a more hesitant Cabinet. Nevertheless the President early cast his lot with the expansionists, and he thenceforth helped create imperialist sentiment quite as much as he followed it.

He lost no time in ordering troops to the Philippines and Ladrones to secure the fruits of Dewey's victory at Manila Bay—a move which

[23] *Congressional Record*, XXXII, 55th Congress, 3rd Session (Feb. 27, 1899), p. 2518.

[24] *Literary Digest*, XVII (Sept. 10, 1898), 307–308.

[25] C. M. Fuess, *Carl Schurz, Reformer* (New York, 1932), p. 349.

Lodge logically interpreted as assuring his conversion to "the large policy." He was thus directly responsible for an involvement in Philippine affairs which could have been avoided by the immediate withdrawal of the American fleet.[26]

Early in June, on the evidence of messages from Secretary Day to Ambassador Hay in London, he was still thinking of retaining only a single port in the Philippines and the island of Guam, in addition to Puerto Rico. Yet when possible armistice terms were discussed in the Cabinet a month later, with differences of opinion developing over whether anything more than a naval base should be retained in the Philippines, McKinley's attitude had already changed.[27] He had made the significant decision that, as a condition of any armistice, the United States would hold Manila pending conclusion of a treaty that would determine the control, disposition, and government of the islands as a whole. The instructions he then gave his peace commissioners on September 16 were still far from definitive, but they marked a further forward step. The "march of events rules and over-rules human action," the President said, and the United States could not escape the duties imposed upon it by the Ruler of Nations. It would be impossible to "accept less than the cession in full right and sovereignty of the island of Luzon." [28]

Nor was this, of course, the end. A nationwide tour in October in which his imperialistic speeches were widely acclaimed, a joint statement from the peace commissioners that if Luzon were to be retained the practicalities of the situation stressed the need for holding the other islands, and a growing threat of foreign complications finally convinced McKinley that either all the Philippines should be taken or none of them. "The latter is wholly inadmissible," the Secretary of State cabled the peace commissioners in behalf of the President, "and the former must therefore be required." [29]

[26] This decision was made even before official reports had been received of Dewey's victory. State Department, *Correspondence Relating to the War with Spain* (2 vols., Washington, 1902), II, 635. Later McKinley was reported to have said, "If old Dewey had just sailed away when he smashed the Spanish fleet, what a lot of trouble he would have saved us." H. H. Kohlsaat, *From McKinley to Harding* (New York, 1923), p. 68.

[27] Olcott, *William McKinley*, II, 63, 69.

[28] Day to Hay, June 3, 1898, *Hay Papers*, quoted in A. L. P. Dennis, *Adventures in American Diplomacy, 1896–1906* (New York, 1928), p. 99; *Papers Relating to the Foreign Relations of the United States, 1898* (Washington, 1901), pp. 821, 907–908.

[29] *Foreign Relations, 1898*, p. 935.

Some time later the President told a group of visiting clergymen how he had reached his final decision:

The truth is I didn't want the Philippines, and when they came to us, as a gift from the gods, I did not know what to do with them. When the Spanish War broke out, Dewey was at Hongkong, and I ordered him to go to Manila and to capture or destroy the Spanish fleet. . . . But that was as far as I thought then.

. . . I thought first we would take only Manila; then Luzon; then other islands, perhaps, also. I walked the floor of the White House night after night until midnight; and I am not ashamed to tell you, gentlemen, that I went down on my knees and prayed Almighty God for light and guidance more than one night. And one night it came to me this way—I don't know how it was, but it came: (1) That we could not give them back to Spain—that would be cowardly and dishonorable; (2) that we could not turn them over to France or Germany—our commercial rivals in the Orient—that would be bad business and discreditable; (3) that we could not leave them to themselves—they were unfit for self-government—and they would soon have anarchy and misrule over there worse than Spain's was; and (4) that there was nothing left for us to do but to take them all, and to educate the Filipinos, and uplift and civilize and Christianize them, and by God's grace to do the best we could by them. . . And then I went to bed, and went to sleep, and slept soundly, and the next morning I sent for the chief engineer of the War Department (our map-maker) and I told him to put the Philippines on the map of the United States . . . and there they are, and there they will stay while I am President! [30]

Whatever may be said of the President's vision in the night, the treaty of peace incorporated his major conclusions. Spain was required to relinquish her sovereignty over Cuba, and to cede the Philippines, Guam, and Puerto Rico. In recognition of the somewhat dubious aspect of its claims upon the Philippines, the United States paid an award of $20,000,000 on their account. The war had driven Spain from the Western Hemisphere and from the Pacific; the United States had become a colonial power.

The cession of the Philippines was of course the most important feature of the treaty. One other line of action McKinley might have taken: the establishment of a protectorate over the islands, with a pledge to grant and defend their independence once their people had established a stable government. Such a program, however, would have involved the United States quite as much in the power politics of the

[30] Quoted from the *Christian Advocate*, Jan. 22, 1903, in Olcott, *William McKinley*, II, 109–111.

Pacific as annexation—without what were expected to be annexation's benefits. A protectorate was indeed frequently suggested, but with the country so imperialist-minded it had little popular support and no appeal for the President.[31]

McKinley was unquestionably conforming to what had become predominant sentiment in adopting a policy that first embraced the annexation of Hawaii, then the acquisition of Puerto Rico, Guam, and the Philippines, and was soon to add Samoa to our Pacific possessions. Nevertheless the country was by no means unanimous in its willingness to expand national boundaries overseas. The treaty with Spain caused a renewal of the debate that had been initiated with the annexation of Hawaii—a debate that was to continue for another two years with gathering intensity.

The imperialists held almost every advantage. Theirs was the positive, active policy which reflected the new sense of power of the American people, and the compelling idea that to surrender wartime gains was somehow to impair the national prestige established by trial of arms. The stand taken by the anti-imperialists was necessarily a more negative one. They appealed to the past, to tradition, to the Constitution—to the well-tried principles of a century of experience. It was not, however, the risks of foreign entanglement growing out of overseas expansion that most alarmed them. It was the violation of republican principles in seeking to establish rule over an alien people. They condemned any colonial policy as a repudiation of the basic tenets of American democracy. Emphasizing the national commitment to liberty which had been advanced as justifying intervention in Cuba, they lost no opportunity to stress the irony of having a war to overthrow Spanish colonialism lead to the creation of an American empire.

In the political arena there was no more determined foe of imperialism than Senator Hoar. The annexation of Hawaii was one thing, he stated, but that of the Philippines was quite another; and he categorically denied that the United States had any right, in law or conscience, to govern a subject people. To do so, he told the Senate, would be "descending from the ancient path of republican liberty which the fathers trod down into this modern swamp and cesspool of imperialism." [32]

---

[31] This was, indeed, the proposal in the Democratic platform of 1900—independence with "protection from outside interference."

[32] *Congressional Record,* XXXII, 55th Congress, 3rd Session (Jan. 9, 1899), pp. 493–503.

His colleague Senator Lodge took the lead in defending the new colonial policy. He drew upon all the arguments that had already been used so effectively in winning support for the annexation of Hawaii, and in addition emphasized the duty of the United States to fulfill the obligations that devolved upon it as a result of victory over Spain. In words that should have returned to plague him twenty years later, he further stated that to hold back now from approving the treaty with Spain would be a repudiation of the President, and in such a matter this repudiation was "the humiliation of the United States in the eyes of civilized mankind and brands us as a people incapable of great affairs or of taking rank where we belong, as one of the greatest of the great world powers." Ratify the treaty and accept the cession of the Philippines, Lodge insisted, and he was confident that the nation would successfully carry out "a great, a difficult, a noble task." [33]

The fight in the Senate was a hard one. Partisanship played its usual role, but it was an extremely tangled situation and Republican and Democratic lines were often crossed. The intervention of William Jennings Bryan, strongly anti-imperialist but convinced that the treaty should be ratified and the issue of Philippine independence then submitted to the people, had a decisive influence in swinging a number of Democratic votes to the treaty's support. Nevertheless it was not until the last minute that the administration forces were assured of the backing necessary to uphold their policy. Then, on February 6, 1899, the peace treaty was approved by a slim margin of two votes. Even more significant of the division of opinion was the rejection, by the casting vote of the Vice-President, of a proposed Senate resolution definitely promising the Filipinos their independence. [34]

Although American possession of the islands had by this act become an accomplished fact, future policy toward the Filipinos was still undecided. The anti-imperialists were determined to keep up their fight. Their position, moreover, appeared to be dramatically vindicated

[33] *Ibid.*, pp. 958–960.

[34] For Lodge's account, Lodge to Roosevelt, Feb. 9, 1899, *Correspondence of Roosevelt and Lodge*, I, 391–392. In respect to the controversy over William Jennings Bryan's role in swinging Democratic support to the treaty, W. S. Holt, *Treaties Defeated by the Senate* (Baltimore, 1933), p. 174; and M. E. Curti, "Bryan and World Peace," *Smith College Studies in History*, XVI (Northampton, 1931), 122. For analysis of votes, see Garel A. Grunder and William E. Livezey, *The Philippines and the United States* (Norman, Okla., 1951), pp. 46–47.

when on the very eve of the Senate's action—although not apparently affecting it—insurrection broke out in the Philippines. The United States found itself fighting a war, which was to cost more both in lives and money than the entire war against Spain, to compel the Filipinos to accept the blessings being imposed on them. Two successive missions endeavored to persuade them to acknowledge American rule, offering them a large measure of self-government, but in meeting the challenge of insurrection the McKinley Administration stood firmly on the ground that "the supremacy of the United States must and will be enforced throughout every part of the Archipelago." [35]

The imperialists themselves were appalled by this new situation. They generally agreed, however, that American authority had to be established; the flag could not be lowered. William Howard Taft, appointed to head the second Philippine Commission, told McKinley that he could not approve American policy, and for himself did not want the Philippines. "Neither do I," a disillusioned President is said to have replied, "but that isn't the question. We've got them." [36]

If the imperialists were shaken, the anti-imperialists found their worst forebodings confirmed. They renewed their assaults on administration policy. A number of anti-imperialist leagues had been formed the previous year and they were now drawn into a national association. Congress and the public were bombarded with denunciations of the military action to suppress Filipino revolt, and with resolutions calling for immediate recognition of the independence for which the islanders were fighting. Included in the anti-imperialist ranks were Senator Hoar and Carl Schurz, Republicans; such otherwise incompatible Democratic leaders as Cleveland and Bryan; the industrialist Andrew Carnegie and labor leader Samuel Gompers; and almost all the foremost writers of the day.[37] Finley Peter Dunne was caustic in his criticism; Mark Twain wrote his angry pamphlet "To a Person Sitting in Darkness," and William Vaughn Moody his moving "Ode in Time of Hesitation":

> Tempt not our weakness, our cupidity!
> For save we let the island men go free,

[35] *Senate Document 208*, 56th Congress, 1st Session, p. 151.
[36] Olcott, *William McKinley*, II, 175.
[37] Fred H. Harrington, "The Anti-Imperialist Movement in the United States, 1898–1900," *Mississippi Valley Historical Review*, XXII (Sept., 1935), 211–230; "Literary Aspects of American Anti-Imperialism, 1898–1900," *New England Quarterly*, X (Dec., 1937), 650–667.

Those baffled and dislaureled ghosts
Will curse us from the lamentable coasts
Where walk the frustrate dead . . .
O ye who lead,
Take heed!
Blindness we may forgive, but baseness we will smite.[38]

There was no real cohesion in the anti-imperialist forces, however, and it was still the past fighting against what many Americans considered the future. The infinitely beguiling vision of empire was given perhaps most eloquent expression when Beveridge rose to make his maiden speech in the Senate on January 9, 1900. Moral obligation and commercial opportunity could not have been more skillfully blended, but the note emphasized even more strongly was national influence and prestige. In line with the tradition of which Seward had been such an ardent spokesman half a century earlier, Beveridge believed that the Pacific would be all important in the twentieth century and the scene of any future world conflicts: "The power that rules the Pacific, therefore, is the Power that rules the world. And, with the Philippines, that Power is and will forever be the American Republic." [39]

It was magnificent oratory—"ye could waltz to it," the irrepressible Mr. Dooley commented—but this did not prevent Senator Hoar from rising on the floor of the Senate to challenge quietly, even sadly, this concept of American destiny: "I heard much calculated to excite the imagination of youth seeking wealth or of youth charmed by the dream of empire. But the words Right, Justice, Duty, Freedom, were absent, my young friend must permit me to say, from that eloquent speech." [40]

As the presidential campaign of 1900 approached, the whole issue became deeply enmeshed in politics. The Republicans officially accepted overseas expansion. Their platform called for the suppression of insurrection in the Philippines in order to assure America's destiny in the Pacific. The Democrats, bluntly stating that "no nation can long endure half republic and half empire," not only called for Philippine independence but declared that imperialism was the paramount issue

[38] From *Poems* (Boston, Houghton Mifflin, 1901). Reprinted by permission of the publisher.

[39] *Congressional Record*, XXXIII, 56th Congress, 1st Session (Jan. 9, 1900), p. 704.

[40] *Ibid.*, p. 712. See also Frederick H. Gillett, *George Frisbie Hoar* (Boston, 1934), pp. 257–263.

of the campaign.[41] Nor were the two presidential candidates any less forthright in their views. Nominated by the Republicans to succeed himself, McKinley insisted that the Philippines should be retained, while Bryan, named by the Democrats, was no less emphatic that they should be given independence.

In spite of these clear-cut positions, however, the campaign obscured rather than clarified what was really at stake. For all the efforts of the Democrats to make imperialism the paramount issue, the Republicans maneuvered to evade it as much as possible. They concentrated their fire on the old free silver question, personified by Bryan's candidacy, and above all else emphasized the prosperity which the country was enjoying under the McKinley administration. "There is only one issue in this campaign, my friends," Mark Hanna stated, "and that is, let well enough alone." [42]

There was no real mandate for imperialism in McKinley's emphatic victory. The vote was rather a general endorsement of Republican policies, which in 1900 were most effectively promoted as assuring the American people "a full dinner pail." For all the excitement and controversy over events in the Philippines, popular attention had already reverted to domestic affairs. Yet the fact remains that at least by default—as would happen twenty years later when the verdict was in a sense reversed by the rejection of membership in the League of Nations—the American people gave the stamp of their approval to a breaking away from traditional restraints and to a broad extension of national power and influence.

There remained only one question: could the new overseas possessions be governed by Congress within the terms of a Constitution maintaining a republican form of government? This issue the Supreme Court met and successfully resolved in the so-called Insular Cases. An almost mystical theory was evolved. The new possessions were said to be territory appurtenant and belonging to the United States but not a part of the United States. Their inhabitants, so long as such territories remained "unincorporated," were not entitled to all the rights and privileges of American citizens, but only to such fundamental rights as were derived from natural law. While such rights included those relating to the protection of life, liberty, and property, they did not neces-

[41] Kirk H. Porter, *National Party Platforms* (New York, 1924), pp. 234, 211–212.

[42] *Public Opinion,* XXIX (Nov. 8, 1900), 584. See T. A. Bailey, "Was the Election of 1900 a Mandate on Imperialism?" *Mississippi Valley Historical Review,* XXIV (June, 1937), 43–52.

sarily embrace the constitutional provision that all duties, imposts, and excises should be uniform throughout the United States. The Constitution, that is, did not altogether follow the flag: it would be possible, most significantly, to apply special duties on Puerto Rican or Philippine imports.[43]

The Insular decisions were an expedient escape from a situation for which the Constitution made no provision, and they clearly reflected the conversion of the Supreme Court to overseas extension. "A false step at this time," Justice Brown stated, "might be fatal to the development of what Chief Justice Marshall called the American Empire."[44] Commenting on the key decision, the *World's Work* neatly summarized what had happened: "Public opinion expressed at the polls, Congressional action, and now the decision of the Supreme Court have established the policy of expansion."[45]

Although the United States appeared to have succumbed in 1900 to a natural temptation—or perhaps "cosmic tendency"—to demonstrate its power and build up its trade through colonialism, the victory of the imperialists was not to prove as long-lived as contemporary developments suggested. The nation did not actually carry through the program on which it had started so confidently. Neither what is sometimes called the economic imperialism of subsequent American policy in the Far East and Latin America nor the seizure of the Panama Canal Zone and purchase of the Virgin Islands invalidates the fundamental fact that the first half of the twentieth century witnessed a gradual retreat rather than further advance from the position taken in 1900. The American people came to regret the exuberant enthusiasm of imperialist adventure and to doubt the wisdom of Asiatic possessions.

Even among some of the expansionists of that day there were misgivings. William Allen White accepted imperialism—"This is what fate holds for the chosen people. It is so written . . . It is to be." Nevertheless he would add: "And yet thousands of people cannot help longing for the old order. They cannot help but feel that something good has gone . . . this deepening of responsibilities brings a hardship with it and a loss of the old-time individual freedom."[46] Mr. Dooley

[43] The key case in these decisions was Downes *v.* Bidwell, 182 *United States Reports* 244 (1901).
[44] *Ibid.*, 286–287, 386.
[45] *World's Work*, II (July, 1901), 903.
[46] Walter Johnson, *William Allen White's America* (New York, 1947), p. 111.

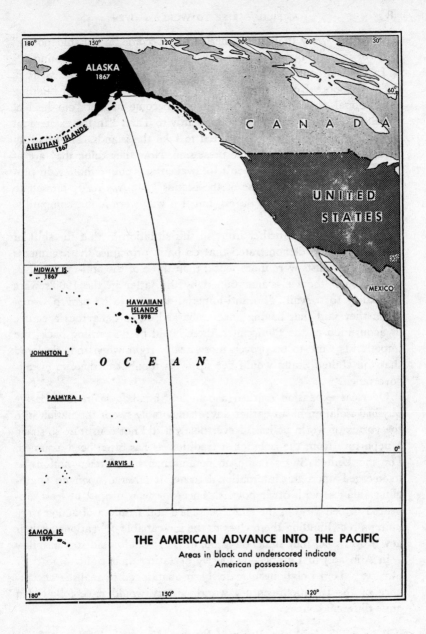

THE AMERICAN ADVANCE INTO THE PACIFIC

Areas in black and underscored indicate
American possessions

commented wryly that now America had become "a wurruld power" and cut into the big game, "be Hivens, we have no peace iv mind." [47]

In ironical contradiction of so much that he had said and written, even Theodore Roosevelt was soon to admit that, far from building up national power, the Philippines had become in fact "our heel of Achilles." In 1907 he wrote despondently to Taft: "In the excitement of the Spanish War, people wanted to take the islands. They had an idea they would be a valuable possession. Now they think they are of no value . . . it is very difficult to awaken any public interest in providing any adequate defense of the islands." He was ready himself to give them up—not under duress, but if a way were found compatible with national honor. [48]

There was a still further irony in this situation in that the shift of popular attitude demonstrated that on basic principles the arguments of the imperialists were more sound than those of the anti-imperialists, even though the views maintained by the latter in the 1900's were ultimately to prevail. The anti-imperialists were to be proven wrong when they said that having once embarked on so dangerous a course as acquisition of the Philippines, there could be no turning back; the imperialists were to be proven more nearly right when they declared that the United States would live up to its republican theories of self-government.

Overseas expansion marked a complete breakdown in the relative physical isolation of an earlier day; it inevitably swept the nation into the vortex of world politics. Nevertheless it did not constitute so sharp a departure from the isolationist tradition as has often been assumed. For the United States made no commitments to foreign nations as it emerged upon the international scene; it entered upon no entangling alliances with other powers. The American people, at least, appeared to believe that their independence and freedom of action were unimpaired. Blinding themselves to the inescapable obligations of their new world role, they somehow thought they could avoid responsibility —in Asia and in Europe—by merely declaring their right to go their own way. Had isolationism really been abandoned in realistic acceptance of the twentieth-century world, history would have followed a quite different course.

[47] Elmer Ellis (ed.), *Mr. Dooley at His Best* (New York, 1938), p. 135.
[48] Roosevelt to Taft, Aug. 21, 1907, in Morison, *The Letters of Theodore Roosevelt*, V, 762. See also Henry F. Pringle, *The Life and Times of William Howard Taft* (2 vols., New York, 1939), I, 302; Pringle, *Theodore Roosevelt*, p. 409.

CHAPTER 4

A New World Role

FOR ALL the excitement and drama of American entry upon the world stage as a consequence of military victory over Spain and overseas expansion, other international developments at the turn of the century were quite as important. The European powers were reaching out in dangerous competition to extend their influence and control in both Africa and Asia. The mounting strength of an aggressive Germany challenged the century-old world leadership of Great Britain. Czarist Russia was seeking to build a new dominion in pursuit of her own expansionist goals. In the clash of rivalries that now encircled the globe, the old balance of power was gravely threatened.

Entirely apart from her own colonial problems, America could in these circumstances no longer stand aside and calmly ignore what was taking place in this larger sphere of international politics. Her new position in the Caribbean and vital concern over an isthmian canal inevitably led to the positive assertion of broader interests in Latin America and an even more determined stand against possible European encroachments in the Western Hemisphere. The possession of the Philippines drew her ever deeper into the political rivalries of the Pacific and eastern Asia with what were to prove momentous consequences. And in the new interplay of power politics, she moved steadily toward a closer *rapprochement* with Great Britain as that nation whose interests most nearly coincided with her own.

This Anglo-American *rapprochement,* as already urged by so many public figures during the 1890's, had an increasing significance with the passing years. It did not mean the complete disappearance of old-time rivalries. Nevertheless the constant threat to both nations in the imperialistic ambitions of Germany continued to draw them together, creating a solidarity that when put to the test became a vital factor in the international alignments of the twentieth century.

Yet quite as significant as America's increased participation in world affairs was a continued refusal to make any commitments that infringed upon the nation's freedom of action. The United States took part in the international peace conferences that were held at The Hague in 1899 and 1907 and accepted the convention establishing the Permanent Court of International Arbitration. On both occasions, however, its signature to the agreements reached was qualified by the unequivocal reservation that nothing therein "shall be so construed as to require the United States to depart from the traditional policy of not intruding upon, interfering with, or entangling itself in the political questions or policy or internal administration of any foreign state." [1]

In the same spirit, active intervention in the affairs of eastern Asia was predicated on the maintenance of complete independence. Writing Theodore Roosevelt on August 2, 1903, Secretary of State John Hay stated that a good deal had been accomplished through American policy in the Far East, but "without the expense of a single commitment or promise." When the American delegation attended the Algeciras Conference, dealing with wholly European rivalries in North Africa, its role was subject to equally careful safeguards. The Senate affixed to ratification of the Moroccan convention a reservation reiterating that it had been signed "without purpose to depart from the traditional American foreign policy." [2]

The United States was in fact assuming far-flung responsibilities whose real significance the American people again sought to ignore by denying their existence. Although theory and practice could hardly be reconciled, they appeared to believe that their traditional foreign policy could be upheld by a reassertion of principles which these new commitments directly violated. Unwilling to go any further than the exercise of a moral influence in world affairs, they blinded themselves to the realities of the power politics in which the country was now so unavoidably enmeshed. A pattern of conduct was emerging that was to have increasingly dangerous consequences in the 1920's and 1930's.

[1] *Procès-Verbaux of the First Hague Peace Conference*, Part I, 69; *Foreign Relations, 1907*, Part 2 (Washington, 1910), 1144.

[2] Hay to Roosevelt, Aug. 2, 1903, quoted in Tyler Dennett, *John Hay* (New York, 1933), p. 406; *Statutes at Large of The United States*, XXXIV (Washington, 1907), Part 3, 2946.

Theodore Roosevelt recognized the implications of this ambivalent attitude and was obsessed with the difficulty of arousing his countrymen to the need for a more active and responsible foreign policy. In an interview in 1908 with André Tardieu, the future French statesman, he fully unburdened himself: "Here in the United States what is most lacking to us is to understand that we have interests in the whole world. I wish that all Americans would realize that American politics is world politics; that we are and that we shall be involved in all great questions . . . the whole American people must become accustomed to this idea. They must be made to feel and understand these international interests . . ." [3]

Other voices were raised to point out potential dangers to American security and the necessity for making adequate provision against them. The designs of Germany and Russia were interpreted as compelling the United States to accept definite commitments that would help to maintain a balance of global power in the interests of world peace. The earlier suggestions for an Anglo-American alliance were renewed in the belief that only through such a united front could Germany and Russia be held in check. The country was warned that policies suitable for the nineteenth century had no relevancy in the new world of the twentieth century.

Two interesting spokesmen of such views were Brooks Adams and Henry Adams.

The former was convinced that the economic center of the world was moving westward and that the great struggle of the future would be over Asia. In the face of Russian imperialism, it was consequently essential that the United States should take over the world leadership that Great Britain was perforce relinquishing. While Brooks Adams believed that in assuming this role America still needed the help of England, since the latter's geographic position made it the "fortified outpost of the Anglo-Saxon race," the United States had to face up to its own responsibilities: "The civilization which does not advance declines: the continent which, when Washington lived, gave a boundless field for the expansion of Americans, has been filled; and the risk of isolation promises to be more serious than the risk of alliance." [4]

[3] André Tardieu, "Three Visits to Mr. Roosevelt," *The Independent*, LXIV (Apr. 16, 1908), 862–863.

[4] Brooks Adams, *America's Economic Supremacy* (reprint, New York, 1947), pp. 174–175, 81–82. The chapter from which this quotation is taken first appeared under the title "The Spanish War and the Equilibrium of the World," *Forum*, XXV (Aug., 1898), 641–651.

Henry Adams also felt that the United States should adapt itself more realistically to changed circumstances. Germany rather than Russia was in his opinion the immediately disturbing element in the world. Linking her rise with England's decline, he saw no alternative to foreign commitments if America was to play an effective role in maintaining any sort of international equilibrium. At the time of the Algeciras Conference in 1906 he wrote: "We have got to support France against Germany and fortify the Atlantic System beyond attack; for if Germany breaks down England or France, she becomes the center of a military world, and we are lost. The course of concentration must be decided by force—whether military or industrial matters not much in the end." [5]

Some years later an even more prophetic note was sounded in an article attributed to Lewis Einstein, onetime officer of the State Department, which first appeared in the *National Review* and was then reprinted in February, 1913, in the *Living Age*. Einstein stressed the dangers to the United States in the existing Anglo-German rivalry, declared there was no basis for the illusion that an isolationist policy could preserve American interests, and argued that to sustain its own security the United States must be ready to uphold England, ultimately by the use of force. [6]

These warnings, however, hardly reached the general public. In spite of the realization that as a result of overseas expansion and a dwindling world the aloofness of an earlier day was no longer possible, there continued to be stubborn opposition to any foreign commitments. In no circumstances were the American people prepared to give up that freedom of action which had been the indestructible core of their foreign policy ever since colonial times.

The first important international move made by the United States after war with Spain—even before it had consolidated its position in the Philippines—was the announcement of the Open Door policy in China. The roots of this policy are clearly found in the efforts that

[5] Henry Adams, quoted in Forrest Davis, *The Atlantic System* (New York, 1941), p. 197. See also Henry Adams to Brooks Adams, June 11, 1897; Henry Adams to Sir Robert Cunliffe, May 19, 1898, quoted in Philip Rahv, *Discovery of Europe: The Story of American Experience in the Old World* (Boston, 1947), pp. 342, 345.

[6] [Lewis Einstein], "The United States and Anglo-German Rivalry," reprinted from the *National Review* in the *Living Age*, CCLXXVI (Feb. 8, 1913), 323–332.

had been made to protect American trade ever since the "most favored nation" principle had been written into the first treaty with China in 1844.[7] Secretary Hay's famous notes to the powers in 1899, however, were in themselves a reflection of the new position of the United States in eastern Asia resulting from its expansion in the Pacific. The commercial interests that had finally swung their support to retention of the Philippines as the key to Oriental trade now demanded a "vigorous policy" in China itself.[8]

The McKinley administration was not originally interested in any such program. In spite of the establishment of foreign spheres of influence in China and what appeared to be the threatened partition of the country, British suggestions in 1898 for cooperative action in supporting an "open door" to trade were rejected. In his message to Congress at the close of the year, the President denied that the European powers' encroachments in China in any way endangered American interests. Within a few months, however, such complacency appeared to be giving way to serious concern. The American Asiatic Association, spearhead of the drive for a more active policy, stated that the administration had been completely won over to the necessity of safeguarding trade expansion in the vitally important Far Eastern market. It was still uncertain of public support for further intervention in this distant part of the world, and consequently added to its report that the time had come for the concentrated "education of the people, the press, and the politicians." [9]

If the Open Door notes were basically a response to the pressure exerted by commercial interests, they nevertheless grew more directly out of the suggestions of William W. Rockhill, a State Department

[7] Foster Rhea Dulles, *China and America* (Princeton, 1946), pp. 24 ff.

[8] The *North American Review* had already run a special series of articles under such titles as "Our Future in the Pacific," "America's Interest in China," and "America's Opportunity in Asia." There were numerous other articles along such lines in other contemporary periodicals. For a full discussion of this topic, see Charles S. Campbell, Jr., *Special Business Interests and the Open Door Policy* (New Haven, 1951).

[9] James D. Richardson (ed.), *A Compilation of the Messages and Papers of the Presidents, 1789–1902* (10 vols., Washington, 1904), X, 102–103; *Journal of Commerce*, Mar. 18, 1899. The proposals for cooperation with Great Britain had won considerable press support. *The New York Times*, for example, strongly criticized the McKinley administration because American interests in China had "not been intelligently represented or adequately appreciated by the State Department." See Dulles, *China and America*, pp. 106–107, and also A. Whitney Griswold, *The Far Eastern Policy of the United States* (New York, 1938), pp. 23–24.

advisor on Far Eastern questions, and Alfred E. Hippisley, an Englishman and close friend of Rockhill's who had served with the Chinese Imperial Maritime Customs Service. These two men felt that the United States had to act promptly to protect its own position in the Far East, and they were also concerned over the future of China. Their suggestion for a series of notes urging the powers to accept the principle of trade equality in their respective spheres of influence appealed at once to Hay. He not only endorsed their plan, but accepted their text for the proposed notes, dispatched in September, 1899, without any significant alteration.[10] Rockhill would have liked to go further than the mere assertion of trade equality—"a pledge on our part to assist in maintaining the integrity of the empire"—but in existing circumstances this idea was recognized as impractical.[11]

There was something surprisingly casual about the initiation of a policy whose ultimate consequences were to be so far-reaching. It was not part of any general plan. Secretary Hay was actually on vacation when the Open Door notes were originally drawn up, and final approval by President McKinley appears to have been almost perfunctory. Nor was the public informed of what was under way. In November, the *Literary Digest* referred to a "widely credited report" of some move to ensure the Open Door and this was about all that was known at the time.[12]

The powers were reluctant to accept the restrictions that the Open Door policy implied, but Hay chose to ignore their equivocations. On March 20, 1900, he announced that their replies had been "final and definitive." [13] The nation promptly hailed his diplomacy as a brilliant achievement. The exchange of notes was said to constitute one of the most important negotiations of the age, a guarantee of America's impregnable position in eastern Asia, and a noble work of peace. The Springfield *Republican* was almost alone in viewing what had taken

[10] The Rockhill-Hippisley correspondence has been extensively quoted in Griswold, *Far Eastern Policy*, pp. 36–77, 475–500. However, his inference that Hippisley represented the British point of view, and that the Open Door policy was therefore British-inspired, does not appear to be borne out by the facts. Great Britain had swung away from support of the Open Door principle by the latter part of 1899 and never fully accepted it as set forth by Hay. See Paul Varg, *Open Door Diplomat—The Life of William W. Rockhill* (Urbana, 1952), pp. 26–36.

[11] Rockhill to Hippisley, Aug. 3, 1899, *ibid.*, p. 31.

[12] *Literary Digest*, XIX (Nov. 18, 1899), 607.

[13] The text of the notes and the replies of the powers are in *Foreign Relations, 1899* (Washington, 1901), pp. 128–143.

place in a coldly realistic light. Its editorial writer found something "rather funny" in believing that the powers' bland assurances really amounted to very much. He warned that the United States had gone

W. A. Rogers in *Harper's Weekly*, November 18, 1899

Uncle Sam: "I'm out for commerce, not conquest!"

far toward placing itself in a position where, if it was to be consistent, "it must guarantee by military force the political integrity of China, or share in a possible partition." [14]

[14] Quoted in Dulles, *China and America*, pp. 112–113.

Within a few months the outbreak of the Boxer Rebellion and foreign intervention to rescue the besieged legations in Peking appeared
to confront the United States with some such dilemma. But a middle
course was found. Hay announced that in taking part in the Allied
rescue expedition the United States would seek a solution of the situation that would preserve China's territorial and administrative entity,
protect all treaty rights, and safeguard for the world the principle of
equal and impartial trade.[15] How much effect this announcement had
may be questionable. The rivalries of the powers were undoubtedly a
more important factor in preserving Chinese independence. However,
the stand taken by the United States demonstrated a willingness to
intervene in the affairs of eastern Asia, even though no specific commitments were made, that drew dramatic attention to the nation's new
role as world power.

How deeply enmeshed in European as well as Far Eastern politics
the country had become through these moves was recognized by the
American envoy in Peking if not by the American public. Rockhill had
been sent out to negotiate a settlement of the Boxer controversy and
soon found himself "sick and tired of the whole business." It appeared
an impossible situation. As he wrote his friend Hippisley in July, 1901,
"England has her agreement with Germany, Russia has her alliance
with France, the Triple Alliance comes in here, and every other com-
bination you know of is working here just as it is in Europe. I trust it
may be a long time before the United States gets into another muddle
of this description."[16]

Hay soon reached somewhat similar conclusions. In undertaking
championship of the Open Door policy, he was getting beyond his
depth. The powers, and especially Russia, were unwilling to act upon
the principles it set forth; the United States was not prepared to support them in any decisive manner. The Secretary of State chafed at
the public reaction for which he was himself so largely responsible in
stating that the original American policy had been accepted. "The talk
of the papers about 'our pre-eminent moral position giving us the
authority to dictate to the world,'" he exclaimed, "is mere flapdoodle."[17] He had to face up to the realities of world politics. When
Japan asked about American policy in view of continued Russian

[15] *Foreign Relations, 1900*, p. 299.
[16] Rockhill to Hippisley, July 6, 1901, quoted in Griswold, *The Far Eastern
Policy of the United States*, p. 83.
[17] Quoted in Tyler Dennett, *John Hay* (New York, 1933), p. 326.

encroachments in Manchuria, he gave, on February 1, 1901, a blunt and unequivocal answer: the United States was not prepared "to attempt singly, or in concert with other Powers, to enforce these views in the east by any demonstration which could present a character of hostility to any other Power." [18]

Some seven months after Hay's note to Japan—that is, in September, 1901—Theodore Roosevelt became President of the United States. For the next eight years American foreign policy bore the sharp imprint of his dynamic personality. Roosevelt generally acted as his own Secretary of State. On occasion he even by-passed his Cabinet and members of the diplomatic service. Imparting to the conduct of foreign affairs his own restless energy and untiring vigor, he made policy as he himself thought it should be made.[19] There were at times signs of the belligerency that had characterized his attitude in earlier years. He paid scant respect to the rights of Latin American nations and delighted in the image of "the big stick." The moderation that Roosevelt displayed when confronted with a serious crisis was, however, far more significant. He had an understanding of power politics and a realistic conception of America's world role that were in sharp contrast with the much more limited views of his predecessor.

No one could have believed more thoroughly that the days of isolation were over, or have been more convinced that it was essential for the United States to build up the power commensurate with its new international responsibilities. The nation would surely go down before other more aggressive powers if it followed a course of "unwarlike and isolated ease," he said on one occasion. On another, he warned against huddling within national borders as "an assemblage of well-to-do hucksters who care nothing for what happens beyond." It was Roosevelt's lasting conviction that the guns of the Spanish-American War "left us echoes of glory, but they also left us a legacy of duty." [20]

He campaigned zealously for a larger Navy, insisting upon a program of two battleships a year, and in spite of all opposition succeeded

[18] Quoted in Alfred L. P. Dennis, *Adventures in American Diplomacy, 1896–1906* (New York, 1928), p. 242.

[19] In addition to Elting E. Morison (ed.), *The Letters of Theodore Roosevelt* (8 vols., Cambridge, Mass., 1951–1954), see John Morton Blum, *The Republican Roosevelt* (Cambridge, Mass., 1954), pp. 125–141.

[20] *The Works of Theodore Roosevelt* (20 vols., New York, 1926), XIII, 322, 324.

in obtaining the necessary appropriations. Ten battleships and four armored cruisers were added to the fleet by 1905. Roosevelt then stated only replacements would be necessary, but soon developing friction with Japan led him to demand additional construction. After a desperate struggle with Congress in 1907 he won renewed support for his program, and before leaving office was able to boast that during his two administrations the size of the fleet had been doubled.[21] Only through strength, Roosevelt constantly asserted, could America adequately safeguard her interests: "The American people must either build and maintain an adequate navy or else make up their minds definitely to accept a secondary position in international affairs, not merely in political, but in commercial, matters. It has been well said that there is no surer way of courting national disaster than to be 'opulent, aggressive, and unarmed.' "[22]

The power that he sought for America was to be exercised not only in her own defense, however, but in the broader interests of world peace. This was made clear in his first annual message to Congress. He spoke neither of imperialism nor of overseas expansion, but of the humanitarian program being applied in the colonies and the dedication of America to international accord. It was to seek peace not from weakness but in the name of justice, as he once wrote Andrew Carnegie, that the nation should be strong.[23]

At the same time Roosevelt would insist again and again that while peace was important, an even higher obligation was to seek what he vaguely called righteousness. He professed to judge a nation on the same moral basis as an individual. He believed that it should be the country's steady aim to raise the standard of national action "just as we strive to raise the standard of individual action." In spite of his intoxication with war, his scorn for pacifism, and his belief in power for its own sake, Roosevelt sincerely believed that he acted in the formulation of foreign policy under the restraints of moral law.

He himself had no difficulty in reconciling what other nations might

[21] Roosevelt to Sydney Brooks, Dec. 28, 1908, Morison, *Letters of Theodore Roosevelt*, VI, 1444. See also Gordon C. O'Gara, *Roosevelt and the Rise of the Modern Navy* (Princeton, 1945).

[22] *Messages of the Presidents*, X, 445. The final phrase in this quotation, "opulent, aggressive, and unarmed," was Brooks Adams', and frequently borrowed by Roosevelt. Roosevelt to Lodge, June 5, 1905, *Letters of Theodore Roosevelt*, IV, 1206. On occasion Roosevelt consulted Brooks Adams in regard to his messages, Roosevelt to Adams, Sept. 27, 1901, *ibid.*, III, 152–153.

[23] Roosevelt to Carnegie, Aug. 6, 1906, *ibid.*, V, 346.

have considered a contradiction between theory and practice. Justice and righteousness were determined by his own conception of justice and righteousness. The policy that he judged to be in the interests of the United States as a responsible member of the world community obviously conformed to moral law. He valiantly tried to uphold his ideal of the larger aims of foreign policy while President, and his address on receiving the Nobel Peace Prize in 1910 returned to what had been the favorite theme of so many presidential addresses: "Peace is generally good in itself, but it is never the highest good unless it comes as the handmaiden of righteousness." [24]

McKinley too had placed a strong emphasis upon ethical considerations. It has sometimes been said that the injection of moral concepts into American foreign policy, in supposed contrast with the more realistic views of Washington and Jefferson, Monroe and John Quincy Adams, was an unhappy innovation. This is to deny the idealism that has always affected American policy and was fully shared by the statesmen of the past—as much a fact as power politics is a fact. Furthermore, Theodore Roosevelt had no thought of relying solely on moral precepts in the hard interplay of power politics, or of sacrificing what he believed to be the national interest in seeking some vague international Utopia. He was completely realistic in his idealism. Nor did he want to leave the future to chance or cosmic tendency or providential will. The nation should be prepared to make its own destiny and to fulfill its historic mission through the conscious exercise of a commanding world influence.[25]

In line with these views Roosevelt was determined on assuming office to maintain the new overseas empire, uphold the Open Door policy, push forward the project for an isthmian canal, build up the Navy, and generally assert the world power of the United States. In his brief inaugural address as Vice-President only six months earlier, he had said: "We stand supreme in a continent, in a hemisphere. East and West we look across two great oceans toward the larger world life

[24] *The Works of Theodore Roosevelt,* XV, 384; XV, 255; XVI, 310; XVI, 306. See also chapter on "The Peace of Righteousness" in *Theodore Roosevelt—An Autobiography* (New York, 1927 edition), pp. 532–559.

[25] Charles A. Beard, George F. Kennan, Walter Lippmann, and Hans J. Morgenthau have made much of the injection of moral concepts into American foreign policy at the turn of the century. For example, Charles A. Beard and G. H. E. Smith, *The Idea of National Interest* (New York, 1934), 370 ff., but see also later discussion in Chapter 14.

in which, whether we will or not, we must take an ever-increasing share." [26]

There were to be unexpected difficulties in implementing his ambitious ideas. The Far East especially presented problems Roosevelt had hardly foreseen. He was not greatly concerned with the economic aspects of foreign policy, as he candidly stated in one letter written in July, 1901, but as the Russians pressed down into Manchuria in complete disregard of what had been accepted as their pledge to respect the Open Door, he became increasingly irritated with their "mendacity" and "treachery." His old belligerency asserted itself, and on one occasion he told Hay that he did not intend to give way, and if he were sure neither Germany nor France would join in, he "should not in the least mind going to 'extremes' with Russia." [27] But responsibility had a sobering influence. Roosevelt soon accepted the realities of the situation. The United States had neither the power nor the will to make its views prevail in eastern Asia if they were challenged by Czarist Russia, and the President gave up any idea, as had Hay, of seeking to uphold American policy by any suggestion of force.

Japan, however, could not disregard the threat to her national security in the Russian advance in Manchuria. She took up arms in 1904 and throughout the United States there was widespread sympathy for the little nation that dared war with the eastern colossus. In the public mind at that time, Japan stood for progress and civilization; she was fighting America's battle in defense of the Open Door in China. Russia symbolized tyranny, oppression, and barbaric reaction.[28] In evaluating a situation that was to have such close parallels a half century later, the *Arena,* a liberal journal, wrote: "The organization and control of the millions of China by Russia is far more dangerous to the world than would be their control by the Japanese." [29]

Roosevelt shared the popular sympathy for Japan and was even ready to come to her support should the European powers intervene in the war (at least he so wrote Cecil Spring-Rice), but he also realized that too sweeping a Japanese victory might well prejudice American interests. While certain that a victorious Russia would "organize

[26] *The Works of Theodore Roosevelt,* XV, 77.

[27] Roosevelt to Hay, July 29, 1903, *Letters of Theodore Roosevelt,* III, 532.

[28] E. Tupper and G. E. McReynolds, *Japan in American Public Opinion* (New York, 1937), pp. 4–9; Winston B. Thorstein, "American Public Opinion and the Portsmouth Peace Conference," *American Historical Review,* LIII (Apr., 1948), 439–464.

[29] Quoted in Dulles, *China and America,* p. 126.

northern China against us," he was also fearful that, if the Japanese won out, it "may possibly mean a struggle between them and us in the future." His analysis convinced him that it would be unfortunate if Japan drove Russia completely out of eastern Asia, and that it would be a great benefit for the United States if a balance of force could be maintained between the two rival nations "so that each may have a moderative action on the other." [30]

His mediation to bring the Russo-Japanese war to a close was thus motivated by a desire for the restoration of peace along lines that would secure the independence of China through the continued interplay of international rivalries. Such a settlement of the Far Eastern problem would best protect American interests, Roosevelt believed, in view of the impracticality of the United States intervening any more directly in support of the Open Door policy.

Following the conclusion of peace, Roosevelt was prepared to acknowledge Japan's right to annex Korea and develop her special interests in Manchuria in return for assurances that in every other respect the existing *status quo* of the Pacific area would be maintained. The so-called Root-Takahira agreement of 1908, which embodied these principles, was sometimes criticized as a political alliance, a dangerous entanglement. It was actually little more than a candid acceptance of the facts of life in eastern Asia.[31]

The danger of a clash of interests between Japan and the United States was heightened at this time by the national feeling aroused in both countries over the immigration issue. Roosevelt was all the more determined to provide a basis for friendly understanding. Yet he had no idea of letting such concessions as he was prepared to make be interpreted as weakness. When he sent the American fleet on its around-the-world voyage in 1908, he was in effect notifying Japan that the United States had the power to support its new role in international affairs. Roosevelt wanted peace, but a peace that did not in any way infringe upon legitimate national interest.[32]

[30] Roosevelt to Spring-Rice, June 13, 1904; to Whitelaw Reid, June 5, 1905; to Lodge, June 16, 1905, *Letters of Theodore Roosevelt,* IV, 831–832, 1206, 1230. See also Pauline Tompkins, *American-Russian Relations in the Far East* (New York, 1949), pp. 24–25; and, for a general account, Tyler Dennett, *Roosevelt and the Russo-Japanese War* (New York, 1925).

[31] Philip C. Jessup, *Elihu Root* (2 vols., New York, 1938), II, 34–43; Griswold, *The Far Eastern Policy of the United States,* 125 ff.; *Literary Digest,* XXXVII (Dec. 5, 1908), 832.

[32] Roosevelt to George Kennan, May 6, 1905, *Letters of Theodore Roose-*

His later views on Far Eastern policy were summarized in a well-known letter to his presidential successor in 1910. He told Taft that he considered the Open Door policy an excellent thing—so far as it could be maintained by diplomatic agreement. He then pointed out that the whole history of Manchuria demonstrated that the Open Door completely disappeared as soon as a powerful nation decided to disregard it, and was willing to run the risk of war rather than forego its intention. In keeping with his often-repeated statement that the United States should never take a position unless it could make good, and with his further conviction that a war over Manchuria was far outside America's real interest and beyond her military capacity, he advocated a policy of doing everything possible to adjust outstanding differences with Japan.[33]

The situation confronting Roosevelt in Latin America in no way paralleled that in eastern Asia. Here the United States had immediate and important interests at stake and it was logical that the President should pursue a more vigorous, if not aggressive, policy. While the United States had surprised the rest of the world by upholding its pledge to grant Cuba her independence, there had never been any intention of withdrawing from the Caribbean upon the conclusion of hostilities with Spain. Cuba was obliged to grant the United States a naval base and the right to intervene should Cuba's republican government be threatened from within or without, Puerto Rico remained a colonial possession, and steps were promptly taken to clear the way for construction of the long-proposed American-controlled isthmian canal. Roosevelt was determined not only to carry through the canal project, but to build up American power in an area which was now judged to have become vital to national security.

Secretary Hay succeeded, after a first less advantageous agreement had been rejected by the Senate, in concluding a treaty with Great Britain in which that country surrendered her interests in an isthmian canal as incorporated in the fifty-year-old Clayton-Bulwer Treaty. The United States was given a free hand not only to build the canal, but to control and fortify the canal zone. There was for a time violent controversy over proposed routes in Nicaragua and Panama, clouded

velt, IV, 1169; Autobiography, pp. 548–549; Literary Digest, XXXV (1907), 40, 313, 595, 946, 979.

[33] Roosevelt to Taft, Dec. 22, 1910, quoted in Griswold, Far Eastern Policy of the United States, pp. 131–132.

by the intrigues of a French canal company which had some years earlier secured the right to construct a canal across the isthmus, but Congress finally accepted Panama as the logical site. In January, 1903, Hay thereupon signed a treaty with Colombia, of which Panama was then a part, for the cession of the necessary canal zone in return for a payment of $10,000,000 and an annual rental of $250,000.

At this point Colombia balked, demanding greater compensation, and the Hay-Herrán Treaty was rejected by her congress. Roosevelt's impatience to get construction started had steadily mounted during the delays occasioned by American congressional indecision and diplomatic negotiations, and he was now incensed at what he considered the wholly obstructive tactics of Colombia. The tangled skein of subsequent events is not easy to unravel, but what happened was a revolt in Panama, the hasty establishment of a provisional government, and its proffer to the United States of the rights to a canal zone on the same terms that Colombia had refused. If Roosevelt did not actually encourage this revolt, certainly nothing was done to hamper the activities of the insurgent Panamanians. On the contrary, American naval forces, under the terms of an old treaty, refused to allow the transit of Colombian troops to suppress the revolt, and the United States recognized the new Republic of Panama with a promptitude that awoke uneasy suspicions of collusion. Nor was there any further delay in concluding the treaty with Panama that gave the United States a perpetual lease of the canal zone and provided an American guarantee of Panama's independence.[34]

The methods followed in securing the canal zone illustrate Roosevelt's impetuosity, his easy ability to convince himself of the righteousness of whatever policy he had himself decided upon, and a blithe disregard of the broader consequences of such precipitate action which contrasted sharply with his more cautious policy in Asia. His self-conscious reiteration that in the course of the negotiations he had conformed to "the highest, finest, and nicest standards of public and governmental ethics," was ultimately belied by his frank avowal: "I took the Canal Zone and let Congress debate; and while the debate goes on the Canal does also."[35]

[34] H. F. Pringle, *Theodore Roosevelt* (New York, 1931), pp. 301–338; H. C. Hill, *Roosevelt and the Caribbean* (Chicago, 1927); W. D. McCain, *The United States and the Republic of Panama* (Durham, N.C., 1937).

[35] Roosevelt's defense of his policy is most explicitly set forth in Theodore Roosevelt, "How the United States Acquired the Right to Dig the Panama

The wine of national power had in this instance gone to Roosevelt's head. There was no need for such haste. Here was Yankee imperialism overriding all opposing interests and the sorry spectacle awoke grave misgivings throughout Latin America as to where this new and powerful United States stood in relation to the rights of weaker nations.

Yet Roosevelt was not through. To forestall any possible threat to the newly asserted American interests in the Caribbean, he was ready to take whatever measures were necessary to block the extension of any foreign influence over the little republics in this general area. A first incident had arisen in 1902 when Great Britain and Germany (later followed by Italy) instituted a blockade of Venezuela to compel her recalcitrant government to meet certain debt payments. At this time, however, Roosevelt followed a hands-off policy, and when informed of the proposed blockade he raised no objections. "If any South American State misbehaves toward any European country," he had written the year before, "let the European country spank it." [36] But the continuation of the blockade after Venezuela agreed to arbitrate the dispute began to arouse distrust of at least Germany's intentions. As in the boundary dispute involving England and Venezuela seven years earlier, there was considerable concern over possible violation of the Monroe Doctrine and popular insistence that the United States take a firm stand. But no drastic measures were necessary. In tacit recognition of the new position of the United States, the European powers soon hastened to bring their intervention in Venezuelan affairs to an end and accepted arbitration of the entire controversy. [37]

With the canal project getting under way, Roosevelt sought to prevent the further recurrence of any such incident. When difficulties developed over debt payments on the part of the Dominican Republic, with warnings of possible intervention by France and Italy, he consequently took occasion to declare that in all such cases affecting the republics in the Western Hemisphere it was the prerogative of the United States to administer disciplinary action. Should there be any

Canal," *Outlook,* XCIX (Oct. 7, 1911), 314–318, and his *Autobiography,* pp. 521–29. The statement "I took the Canal Zone . . ." is reported in *The New York Times,* Mar. 25, 1911—just seven months before the *Outlook* article which justified his action as "right in every detail and at every point."

[36] Roosevelt to Speck von Sternberg, July 12, 1901, *Letters of Theodore Roosevelt,* III, 116.

[37] For discussion of the discredited story of Roosevelt's ultimatum to Germany, see Pringle, *Theodore Roosevelt,* pp. 285–289.

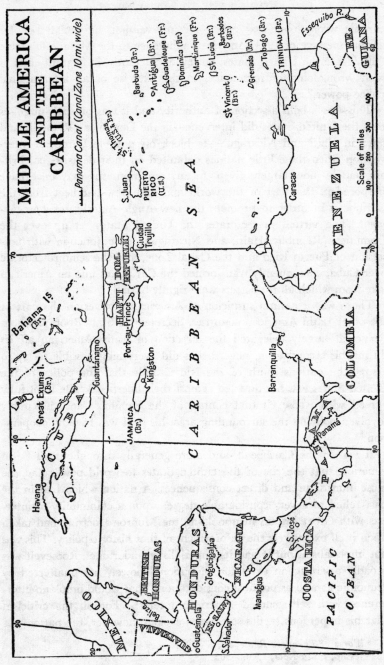

MIDDLE AMERICA
AND THE
CARIBBEAN

Panama Canal (Canal Zone 10 mi. wide)

MEXICO

BRITISH
HONDURAS

GUATEMALA
Belize
oGuatemala
EL SALVADOR
S.Salvador

HONDURAS
oTegucigalpa

NICARAGUA
Managua

COSTA RICA
S.José

PACIFIC
OCEAN

Havana

CUBA

Great Exuma I.
(Br.)

Bahama Is.
(Br.)

Guantánamo

JAMAICA
(Br.)
Kingston

HAITI
Port-au-Prince

DOM.
REPUBLIC
Ciudad
Trujillo

CARIBBEAN SEA

PANAMA
Panamá

Barranquilla

COLOMBIA

VENEZUELA

Caracas

PUERTO
RICO
(U.S.)
S.Juan

St.Thomas
(U.S.& Br.)

Barbuda (Br.)

Antigua (Br.)
Guadeloupe (Fr.)

Dominica (Br.)

Martinique (Fr.)

St.Lucia (Br.)

St.Vincent.
(Br.)

Barbados
(Br.)

Grenada (Br.)

Tobago (Br.)

TRINIDAD (Br.)

Essequibo R.

BR.
GUIANA

Scale of miles
0   100 200 300 400

© Council on Foreign Relations, Inc.

chronic wrongdoing that called for intervention, he declared in his annual message of 1904, American adherence to the Monroe Doctrine "may force the United States, however reluctantly, in flagrant cases of such wrongdoing or impotence, to the exercise of an international police power." [38]

This was a bold assertion of authority and it was on such premises that the United States did intervene—in the Dominican Republic and later in Haiti and Nicaragua—to block off possible European intervention when these little nations defaulted on their debts. Great Britain had by now largely given up any ambitions she may once have harbored in this part of the world and withdrew her fleet from the Caribbean in order to promote the new Anglo-American *rapprochement*. The virtual protectorates the United States set up over the Dominican Republic, Haiti, and Nicaragua, in conjunction with possession of Puerto Rico and the Canal Zone, and the semiprotectorate over Cuba, consequently transformed the Caribbean into an American lake from which all trespassers were rigidly barred.

There was a natural suspicion of American motives on the part of the other Latin American countries. Secretary of State Root, to whom Roosevelt largely delegated the direction of Latin American affairs during his second term, nevertheless did everything possible to try to assure the nations south of the Rio Grande that the policy of the United States was not directed against their liberties. While Root fully agreed with Roosevelt that control of the Panama Canal inevitably involved policing the surrounding area, his goal was friendly cooperation.[39]

It was in the Caribbean, and more generally throughout all Latin America, that the rise of the United States to world power had the most immediate and direct consequences. A nation which had in the past relied to a very considerable degree upon a community of interests with Great Britain in upholding the Monroe Doctrine had taken upon itself exclusively the enforcement of that historic policy. This was not imperialism, but it had its imperialistic undertones. Roosevelt was broadly asserting an extension of national power, not unaffected by economic as well as political considerations, that would brook no interference with self-assumed American interests. For all the criticism that his impetuous tactics sometimes evoked, however, the nation was

[38] *Works of Theodore Roosevelt*, XV, 257.
[39] Jessup, *Elihu Root*, I, 560–563.

prepared to support the Monroe Doctrine and defend the Caribbean on what appeared to be the indisputable grounds of national security.

Through its more active role in both eastern Asia and Latin America, the United States promptly found itself involved in the overseas projection of European politics. If the objective of American policy in Latin America was to reinforce the traditional separation of the Old World and the New, there could be no escaping European rivalries when the United States intervened in the Far East. Roosevelt had learned this the hard way in the course of his mediation in the Russo-Japanese War. He fully sensed the growing dangers to peace as an insurgent Germany continued to threaten the existing balance of power. He agreed with Henry Adams that if she succeeded in breaking down England or France, she would become the center of a new military world. He was resolved to exercise American influence, so far as it could be done without commitment to force, in maintaining world equilibrium.

This was the background for such a far departure from traditional policy as American participation in the Algeciras Conference, which met early in 1906 in an attempt to settle the dangerous clash between France and Germany in Morocco. A year earlier, Roosevelt had told Taft that the United States would not interfere in the burgeoning quarrel—"we have other fish to fry"—but his latent fears of European war soon led him, at the Kaiser's suggestion, to try to bring the disputants together in the hope that negotiations would create a more friendly relationship among Germany, France, and England. As he phrased it in a number of personal letters, the United States had a very real concern in "trying to keep matters on an even keel in Europe." [40]

The role enjoined upon the American delegation which he sent to the Algeciras Conference was one of official neutrality. His instructions to Henry White, however, clearly revealed his conviction that Germany's ambitions were the real threat to peace. American influence was consequently to be exercised, with diplomatic discretion, in support of the position of the Atlantic powers. [41]

[40] Roosevelt to Taft, Apr. 20, 1905; to Choate, Aug. 16, 1905; to Henry White, Aug. 23, 1905, *Letters of Theodore Roosevelt*, IV, 1162, 1302, 1313.

[41] Pringle, *Theodore Roosevelt*, p. 394; Allan Nevins, *Henry White* (New York, 1930), p. 268. See also Eugene N. Anderson, *The First Moroccan Crisis, 1904–1906* (Chicago, 1930).

The result of the conference was an uneasy reaffirmation of the existing balance of power. Roosevelt was content that without openly taking sides the United States had played what he exaggeratedly considered a very significant role in helping to maintain peace. "In this Algeciras matter," he later wrote Whitelaw Reid with happy abandon, ". . . I stood him [the Kaiser] on his head with great decision." [42] There was little realization at the time that the forces making for European war could not be reconciled by any such simple device as a reluctant agreement upon the status of Morocco, and that the ultimate showdown between the Triple Alliance and the Triple Entente had been merely postponed.

The question of whether participation in the conference was a dangerous departure from the traditional policy of not meddling in European affairs was raised in both Congress and the press. It did not excite a great deal of interest, but the introduction of what amounted to a resolution of censure in the Senate led to a lively discussion of both basic doctrine and the powers of the President. There was a familiar ring to the arguments of opposition speakers. They stressed the danger of getting mixed up in European politics, and attacked Roosevelt for seeking to demonstrate the world power of the United States beyond the limits of any reasonable conception of national interest. Among the President's supporters, Senator Lodge took the lead in denying that the President had in any way violated the traditional injunction against entangling alliances. He stated that it had always been the policy of the United States to exert all the moral influence at its command in behalf of world peace.[43]

In spite of declarations by Secretary Root and the Senate reservation that ratification of the convention did not mean any departure from traditional policy, the role played by the United States at Algeciras demonstrated, almost unconsciously, how closely American interests were becoming linked with those of Great Britain and France. Roosevelt was acting on his own in 1906—he had no popular mandate to intervene in European affairs—but his vision of America's world role made him realize that the United States could not remain on the

[42] Roosevelt to Whitelaw Reid, June 27, 1906, *Letters of Theodore Roosevelt*, V, 319.

[43] *Congressional Record*, XXXX, 59th Congress, 1st Session, pp. 792 ff., 1421 ff., 2139 ff.; *Literary Digest*, XXXII (Jan. 27, 1906), 112–113; and Henry Cabot Lodge, "The Monroe Doctrine and Morocco," *Harper's Weekly*, L (March 10, 1906), 332–333.

sidelines in conflicts that might have their origin in Europe, but necessarily had a global impact. In 1911 he was to state clearly that if England were unable to preserve the balance of power, the United States
would have to step in to do so: "in fact, we ourselves are becoming,
owing to our strength and geographic situation, more and more the
balance of power of the whole globe." [44]

William Howard Taft, succeeding to the Presidency in 1909, was
at once less aggressive, less perceptive, and less imaginative than
Roosevelt in his approach to world affairs. He did not set his sights so
high and was candidly prepared to conduct foreign policy along lines
that would most successfully promote trade and overseas investments.
Such factors had of course affected earlier American policy in both
the Caribbean and the Far East. The preservation of an open door for
trade in Morocco had even been advanced as justifying participation
in the Algeciras Conference. But while Roosevelt had never been
greatly interested in trade and investments, or importantly influenced
by those who approached foreign policy on such a basis, both Taft
and his Secretary of State, Philander C. Knox, tended to interpret the
national interest almost exclusively in terms of the interests of the
business community.

If there was nothing exceptional in such an attitude, it had perhaps
never been more frankly or persistently avowed. President Taft vigorously defended what he liked to call a substitution of dollars for bul-
lets. He was not afraid of the term "dollar diplomacy" and actively
encouraged investment bankers and commercial salesmen to build up
American influence overseas. Yet at the same time he had a deep interest in world peace. He insistently argued that there was no contradiction between this more expansive, altruistic goal and the promotion
of trade. His program, he declared in reaffirmation of the traditional
aims of American foreign policy, appealed alike "to idealistic humanitarian sentiments, to the dictates of every sound policy, and to legitimate commercial aims." [45]

An example of his efforts along idealistic, humanitarian lines was
the negotiation of a series of arbitration treaties as a means of bringing
about greater stability in international relations. Taft was ready to
submit to arbitration even questions of "vital interest" and those affect-

[44] Quoted in Dennett, *Roosevelt and the Russo-Japanese War*, p. 1.
[45] *Foreign Relations, 1912*, p. x.

ing "national honor."[46] He hoped to make the United States the leader in a movement that would finally eliminate war as a means of settling international disputes. No real progress was made, however. Even though the period was one notable for its peace societies, studies of the causes of war, and pervasive peace propaganda,[47] the restrictions upon the nation's freedom of action implicit in Taft's all-inclusive arbitration treaties could hardly hope to win effective support. The Senate, jealous of maintaining the nation's complete independence, would have none of them. Taft was far ahead of public opinion. The nation was still unwilling to go any further in active support of peace than to lend this ideal its moral support.

In other respects Taft's policies marked a shift in emphasis rather than any sharp break with those pursued by Roosevelt. If there was no meddling with European affairs comparable to taking part in the Algeciras Conference, foreign intervention was in some ways carried further than it ever had been before in both eastern Asia and Latin America. On the one hand, there was an attempt to reinvigorate the Open Door policy; and on the other, new moves to consolidate the protectorates over the little nations of the Caribbean. The technique was that of the new dollar diplomacy, but political as well as economic considerations were clearly involved.

Where Roosevelt had finally given over any hope of sustaining the Open Door, Secretary Knox elaborated a complicated scheme that would have meant the internationalization of Manchuria, and Taft himself sought to bring direct pressure to bear upon the Chinese government to admit American capital for economic development. Neither program was successful. Without Roosevelt's more realistic understanding of the international rivalries in eastern Asia, the new President and his Secretary of State blundered into complications that seriously impaired both American prestige and American influence. Dollar diplomacy in this part of the world succeeded in creating new frictions in American relations with both Russia and Japan, failed to justify itself from the point of view of a China going through the throes of an epochal revolution, and did not materially advance the interests of the United States.[48]

[46] Jessup, *Elihu Root*, II, 79–80; Henry F. Pringle, *The Life and Times of William Howard Taft* (2 vols., New York, 1939), II, 737.

[47] Merle Curti, *Peace or War—The American Struggle, 1636–1936* (New York, 1936), pp. 196–227.

[48] Griswold, *The Far Eastern Policy of the United States*, pp. 133–175.

Nor could it be said that this same dollar diplomacy succeeded any better in Latin America. Whether the State Department was pushing American investments to build up political power or exerting political power to safeguard the trade and investments it had originally encouraged, American policy was interpreted as economic imperialism. The United States maintained its military and naval dominance in the Caribbean and extended its sphere of economic control.[49] Failure to take Latin American susceptibilities into account, however, fortified the impression that in the pursuit of its own interests the United States was ready to ride roughshod over those of smaller nations.

In general it may perhaps be said that on the broader world stage Taft would have substituted a new alliance of diplomacy, commerce, and finance for the idea that diplomacy should be the servant of national power in making American influence felt on a global basis. In his last annual message to Congress, in 1912, he called upon his countrymen to recognize that the nation had emerged full grown as a peer in the great concourse of nations, was too mature to view foreign policy in terms of temporary expedients, and in adjusting itself to modern conditions could no longer confine itself to outworn dogmas as to its relationship with other powers: "We must not wait for events to overtake us unawares. With continuity of purpose we must deal with the problems of our external relations by a diplomacy modern, resourceful, magnanimous, and fittingly expressive of the high ideals of a great nation." [50]

Throughout these years in which Roosevelt and Taft sought to adjust American foreign policy, however different their methods, to the realities of the twentieth-century world, the American people continued to maintain that noncommittal attitude about which Roosevelt so often complained. They had hailed the Open Door policy as a triumph of diplomacy, applauded mediation in the Russo-Japanese war, and generally—although by no means universally—approved a Caribbean policy that secured American control of the Panama Canal and neighboring areas. Aside from their reaction to such specific developments,

[49] This sphere embraced Nicaragua, Honduras, Haiti, and the Dominican Republic. See the very critical Scott Nearing and Joseph Freeman, *Dollar Diplomacy* (New York, 1925), and C. L. Jones, *The Caribbean Since 1900* (New York, 1936).

[50] *Foreign Relations, 1912,* p. xxvii.

however, there appeared to be a mounting indifference to what was happening in other parts of the world.

The widespread interest in the cause of peace was a vague and idealistic, rather than practical, phenomenon. The point was never approached when public opinion would have been willing to approve commitments that would have definitely pledged the United States to cooperative internationalism. This was clearly demonstrated at the peace conference at The Hague in 1907, and in the Senate's refusal to accept effective arbitration treaties.

Where sentiment was most clearly revealed was in the annual debates on naval appropriations. While Roosevelt succeeded in building up the Navy into an effective fighting force, it was in the face of continual opposition. There was a substantial popular feeling that instead of emphasizing national power, the United States should take the lead in demonstrating that armaments could be reduced. Taft faced the same situation. He too favored building up the Navy, but every appropriation bill set off a battle. He was able to carry forward the program of two capital ships a year but only at the expense of other units in the fleet. The Navy definitely fell behind in its relative strength as compared with the fleets of the other powers.

It was senseless to build up the Navy, ran the general argument of the foes of such expansion, when the United States was at peace with all the world and nowhere was there any threat of war. One representative stated during the congressional debate on naval appropriations in 1910 that the federation of the world had become a reality as a consequence of the international meeting at The Hague, when the powers "in solemn council made laws for all the people of the earth." Another declared with equally shallow optimism that the prospect of the United States ever becoming involved in war was "as chimerical, and unlikely as a descent on our coast of an army from the moon." [51]

A minority report of the House Naval Committee three years later reflected a widespread view. "For the purpose of defending our country against attacks from any nation on earth," it stated, "we confidently believe that our navy is amply sufficient and fully adequate, and for any other purpose we need no navy at all." [52] Certainly the American people as a whole were not to be convinced, in spite of all

[51] *Congressional Record*, XLV, 61st Congress, 2nd Session, Part 4 (Mar. 25 and Mar. 26, 1910), pp. 3780, 3831; Appendix (Apr. 8, 1910), p. 119.

[52] Quoted in Harold and Margaret Spout, *The Rise of American Naval Power* (Princeton, 1939), p. 295.

the propaganda of big-Navy enthusiasts, that their own security could in any way be endangered by European power politics.

Even more important than such views, in accounting for a generally isolationist attitude, was a heightened absorption in domestic affairs. If Roosevelt for a time during his "imperial years" turned popular attention to foreign policy, the period between the Spanish-American War and the First World War was far more importantly marked by the impact upon domestic policies of the Progressive movement. The battle over the trusts, the campaign to regulate the railroads, conservation and pure food laws, the drive to curb the money power, and many other activities associated with Progressivism left the country little time to worry over those possible threats to the world balance of power that had first been discerned in the aggressive imperialism of Germany and Russia at the turn of the century.

The Progressives themselves, especially those from the Midwest, were largely uninterested in foreign affairs, and always ready to subordinate such issues to the demands of domestic reform. In spite of his early ambition to become "the forming and the shaping mind which is to mark out foreign policy," Senator Beveridge reflected this attitude. As chairman of the Senate Committee on Foreign Relations in the early 1900's, he was so remiss as to provoke open complaints on the part of his colleagues that he was neglecting his responsibilities. Equally revealing is the later comment of Walter Lippmann, who upon his graduation from Harvard in 1910 became at once absorbed in domestic political reform. Writing in 1943 he recalled: "I cannot remember taking any interest whatsoever in foreign affairs until after the outbreak of the First World War . . . I remained quite innocent of the revolutionary consequences of the Spanish-American War." In September, 1914, William Allen White, Kansas editor, wrote: "how sad it is that the war is taking the national attention away from justice." [53]

An exception to any such generalization was Herbert Croly, whose writings were an important expression of the "New Nationalism" proclaimed by Roosevelt. Croly had become convinced by 1910 of the need for a vigorous and vital foreign policy to promote the national interest in eastern Asia and Latin America. And while persuaded that there

[53] Claude G. Bowers, *Beveridge and the Progressive Era* (New York, 1932), p. 215; Walter Lippmann, *U. S. Foreign Policy* (Boston, 1943), p. xi; Walter Johnson, *William Allen White's America* (New York, 1947), p. 252.

should be scrupulous avoidance of any entanglement in European politics as such, he nonetheless felt that the United States could not escape its broader responsibilities, and should be prepared for the ultimate creation of a democratic alliance for the preservation of universal peace.[54]

While the more general Progressive attitude was explainable on the grounds of widespread indifference to foreign affairs, many liberals felt that whatever happened in Europe the United States had too much to do in putting its own house in order to venture abroad. The nation could not afford to dissipate its energy trying to play a larger international role. The Progressives believed that America was entirely safe in her relative geographic isolation, and that her all-important mission—both for herself and for the world—was to make democracy work at home. They were not to be beguiled out "of the high way of Heaven." In their concern with freedom and justice, they were determined to keep the "lamp burning brightly on this western shore as a light to all nations."

A few of them had been briefly converted to imperialism, persuaded perhaps, in Lyman Abbott's phrase, that it was "the new Monroe Doctrine, the new imperialism, the imperialism of liberty."[55] Others upheld Roosevelt's ambitious program in foreign policy because they were ready to accept his leadership on any issue. Senator George W. Norris of Nebraska, not yet perhaps a full-blown Progressive, later wrote that in the fight over Panama, "I followed him [Roosevelt] step by step"—and also confessed that, even at the time, "doubts assailed me."[56] The more general feeling in Progressive ranks, however, was that imperialism and Roosevelt's ambitious policies involved risks that were dangerous and unnecessary. In the assertion of American power, whether in the Far East or Latin America, they saw a denial of republican or democratic principles, and advantage only for those conservative business interests which they were so strenuously battling on the home front. Some few Progressives, chiefly Easterners like Croly, upheld dollar diplomacy, but not many. "What next?" Senator La

---

[54] Herbert Croly, *The Promise of American Life* (New York, 1910), pp. 293–313.

[55] *Outlook*, LIX (Aug. 27, 1898), 1006.

[56] Quoted in William E. Leuchtenberg, "Progressivism and Imperialism: The Progressive Movement and American Foreign Policy, 1898–1916," *Mississippi Valley Historical Review*, XXXIX (Dec., 1952), 488. This entire article, pp. 483–504, is most interesting, although it somewhat confuses changing attitudes toward the Spanish-American War, imperialism, and dollar diplomacy.

Follette of Wisconsin asked in 1911 in his *Weekly,* which usually ignored foreign affairs altogether. "Is there anything more; anything which Mr. Knox and President Taft will not give to foreign nations in exchange for 'business' desired by their friends in Wall St.?" [57]

William Jennings Bryan, representative of another school of Midwestern Progressivism, also strongly opposed an aggressive foreign policy. A consistent and unrelenting foe of imperialism (in spite of his later contradictory policy in the Caribbean as Secretary of State), he believed that the United States should seek to exercise only a moral influence in international affairs. His deep devotion to peace made him an eager advocate of arbitration treaties, and as early as 1905 he announced a peace plan of his own devising. Its underlying idea, subsequently incorporated in thirty "cooling off" treaties negotiated in 1913 and 1914, was the submission of all international disputes to The Hague Court, with the provision that until its report had been made there would be no resort to war. Throughout this period there was no one more anti-imperialist, anti-big-Navy and anti-foreign involvement than the silver-tongued orator who preached to a thousand Chautauqua audiences on "The Prince of Peace." [58]

When war finally broke out in Europe, and circumstances drew the United States closer and closer to intervention, the Progressive ranks would split. Many liberals would follow Wilson's lead in foreign as in domestic affairs. The Midwestern bloc that made up the original core of Progressivism, however, was to oppose American involvement in this foreign quarrel to the bitter end. La Follette expressed its point of view when he described Europe "as cursed with a contagious, a deadly plague." His major concern was in avoiding all contact with the decadent continent in order to protect the national health.[59]

Every attempt on the part of a Roosevelt or a Taft, or of any other public man with an international point of view, to awaken the nation to a realization of what being a great power really meant failed in these years before the First World War. The implications of the entanglements to which overseas expansion had led, the significance of the shifting balance of European power, and the meaning of the role

[57] *La Follette's Weekly Magazine,* III (Mar. 4, 1911), 1.

[58] See Merle E. Curti, "Bryan and World Peace," in *Smith College Studies in History,* XVI (Apr.-July, 1931).

[59] Ellen Torelle (ed.), *The Political Philosophy of Robert M. La Follette* (Madison, 1920), p. 209. See also Belle Case La Follette and Fola La Follette, *Robert M. La Follette* (2 vols., New York, 1953), I, 502-503.

that the United States was actually playing in world affairs were alike ignored by a people completely absorbed in their efforts to broaden political liberty and economic opportunity in their own land. The "spell of the Washington legend" was all-powerful. What Secretary Olney had once written, on the eve of war with Spain, remained just as true on the eve of a far greater war: "A rule of policy originating with Washington, pre-eminently wise for his epoch, ever since taught in schools, lauded on the platform, preached in the pulpit, and displayed in capitals and italics in innumerable political manuals and popular histories, almost becomes part of the mental constitution of the generations to which it descends. They accept it without knowing why and they act upon it without the least regard to their wholly new environment." [60]

No general warnings or advice, indeed, were ever to shake the conviction of the American people that "entangling alliances" were not for them. It took the unanswerable logic of decisive events to persuade them that only through collective security could the United States hope to maintain either its own safety or the principles for which it stood.

[60] Richard Olney, "International Isolation of the United States," *Atlantic Monthly*, LXXI (May, 1898), 583.

CHAPTER 5

The Impact of War

WHEN Woodrow Wilson became President in 1913, his primary interest was to carry through that broad program of domestic reform which he had outlined as the New Freedom.[1] International problems did not appear to have great urgency. In his first annual message to Congress, he voiced the buoyant faith of the American people "in a growing cordiality and sense of community interest among the nations, foreshadowing an age of settled peace and good will."[2] Yet in spite of his confidence that a rule of law was gradually replacing the rule of force in world relations, he still apparently felt a gnawing doubt whether he would be left free to concentrate as entirely as he hoped on his battle for tariff revision, currency and banking reform, more rigid control of the trusts. "It would be the irony of fate," he confided privately to a friend on the eve of his inauguration, "if my administration had to deal chiefly with foreign affairs."[3]

His attitude toward the nation's world role, so far as he had thought it out, reflected an intense conviction that America should always exercise her moral influence to promote liberty, justice, and a righteous peace. He had originally been opposed to overseas expansion but later swung over to support the "large policy" of 1898, brushing aside Washington's advice as meaning only "be good boys . . . until you are big enough to be abroad in the world." He had come to realize

[1] See Arthur S. Link, *Woodrow Wilson and the Progressive Era* (New York, 1954).

[2] R. S. Baker and W. E. Dodd, *The Public Papers of Woodrow Wilson* (6 vols., New York, 1925–1927), III, 70.

[3] Ray Stannard Baker, *Woodrow Wilson: Life and Letters* (8 vols., Garden City, N. Y., 1927–39), IV, 55.

that in a contracting world where "the whole had already become a simple vicinage; each part had become the neighbor to the rest," there was no avoiding the interdependence of nations.[4] However much the American people might like to stay at home, Wilson sternly believed they had an imperative duty to help other countries, and could not escape the obligations of their historic mission to do so.

He was far more deeply committed to such idealistic principles than his predecessors. Where Roosevelt had been primarily concerned with establishing the naval power that would make the United States a truly effective force for peace, and Taft had sought to promote both the national interest and world stability through economic expansion, Wilson thought almost exclusively in moral terms. He was equally opposed to militarism and dollar diplomacy. The strength of the nation lay in its idealism, and its leadership would be established through precept and example. "We have an object lesson to give to the rest of the world," he declared on one occasion; and on another stated even more succinctly, "The idea of America is to serve humanity." [5]

His first expression of such views as President was contained in a speech on Latin-American relations delivered at Mobile, Alabama, on October 27, 1913. Its primary purpose was to reassure the Latin American nations of the friendship of the United States, to impress upon them that this country would never seek to acquire further territory by conquest, and to place the relationship of the nations of the Western Hemisphere upon the high plane of mutual devotion to true constitutional liberty. The task of the United States, the President stated, was to demonstrate a friendship based upon honor and equality:

> We must show ourselves friends by comprehending their interest whether it squares with our own interest or not. It is a very perilous thing to determine the foreign policy of a nation in terms of material interest. It is not only unfair to those with whom you are dealing, but it is degrading as regards your own actions. . . . We dare not turn from the principle that morality and not expediency is the thing that must guide us and that we will never condone iniquity because it is most convenient to do so.[6]

The reality, however, often fell short of the ideal. Although both Wilson and his Secretary of State, William Jennings Bryan, had the

---

[4] Dec. 22, 1900; March, 1901. *Public Papers of Woodrow Wilson*, I, 367, 412.

[5] May 23, 1914; June 5, 1914. *Ibid.*, III. 118, 127.

[6] *Ibid.*, III, 67, 69.

highest motives, politics and economics persistently intruded in the determination of policy. When national interests in the Caribbean seemed to be jeopardized, the policy of the Wilson administration did not differ in practice very much from that of Taft or Theodore Roosevelt. Intervention in the affairs of the Central American republics might be based on principle, but this was slight consolation to these little republics or Latin America generally—particularly when the consequences were an extension of the economic or political power of the United States.[7]

The most severe test for Wilsonian policies in the early days of the administration was Mexico. The revolution which in 1911 broke the iron rule of the old dictator Porfirio Díaz left a heritage of plot and counterplot, seething political unrest, and bloody violence. American lives and property were constantly endangered. The situation further worsened when another rebellion led to the overthrow and cold-blooded assassination of Díaz' successor. Victoriano Huerta then set himself up as the new provisional president and in 1913 sought United States' recognition.

Wilson was prepared to follow a policy of patience and forbearance toward Mexico, one soon popularly known as "watchful waiting." But while he refused to be bullied into any active intervention to safeguard American interests, he was unwilling to condone the violence that had marked Huerta's rise to power. The influence of the United States was to be exercised in support of constitutionalism.

Since the days of Thomas Jefferson the *de facto* recognition of any established government, without inquiring too closely how it might have come into power, had been established American policy. It did not in any sense imply approval of the government concerned. It meant no more and no less than a willingness to enter into diplomatic relations once the new regime had demonstrated that it was in control of the administrative machinery of the state, popularly supported, and prepared to discharge international obligations. In his abhorrence of the violence that had marked Huerta's accession to power, however, President Wilson chose to ignore this tradition, which also conformed to the general practice of other nations, and he refused to recognize the new Mexican government.[8] He hoped that his policy would

[7] For a detailed discussion of Wilson's Latin American policy—which he aptly terms "missionary diplomacy"—see Link, *Woodrow Wilson and the Progressive Era*, pp. 81–106.

[8] Wilson's nonrecognition policy in Latin America was in theory reversed,

weaken the position of Huerta, give him an opportunity to mediate among the still warring factions in Mexico, and then enable him to promote new elections under orderly conditions that would bring about real peace and stability.

The opposition of the United States to Huerta was ultimately to force his withdrawal from the presidency and a new government headed by Venustiano Carranza was set up. Before Huerta's surrender, however, a further incident occurred that led to what seemed a direct repudiation of the noninterventionist policy that President Wilson proclaimed.

In April, 1914, the Mexican authorities arrested a boatload of American sailors that had gone ashore at Tampico, and when their commanding officer, Admiral Mayo, insisted on official apologies with a salute to the American flag, Huerta refused to comply with his demands. Wilson backed up Admiral Mayo and ordered a retaliatory blockade of the Mexican coast. When it was challenged in an attempt to smuggle arms into Vera Cruz from a German ship, American forces bombarded and then occupied this Mexican port.

In seeking authority from Congress for these drastic measures, the President tried to explain the contradiction to his declared principles. The honor of the United States was at stake, he stated, and only by maintaining national honor could America retain the respect of other nations. He was determined to sustain a point which he interpreted as having an importance over and beyond any immediate issue in relations with Mexico.[9]

This incident has been singled out from the highly complicated story of the relations between the United States and Mexico at this time because of the light it throws on Wilson's approach to foreign policy. The President did not fully understand the Mexican situation. His position was at once unrealistic and self-righteous. Yet underlying his blundering were principle and conviction. In asking Congress, on April 20, 1914, for authority to blockade the Mexican coast, Wilson

with a return to the Jefferson tradition, by Secretary Stimson in 1931. Ruhl J. Bartlett, *The Record of American Diplomacy* (New York, 1954), pp. 549–551. The issue remained open in the case of Soviet Russia (1917–33) and has continued in dispute in respect to Communist China.

[9] For relations with Mexico and the Vera Cruz incident, see J. F. Rippy, *The United States and Mexico* (New York, 1931), Chaps. XX and XXI; Harley Notter, *The Origins of the Foreign Policy of Woodrow Wilson* (Baltimore, 1937), pp. 221 ff.; and, more particularly, Link, *Woodrow Wilson and the Progressive Era*, pp. 107–144.

said: "There can in what we do be no thought of aggression or selfish aggrandizement. We seek to maintain the dignity and authority of the United States only because we wish always to keep our great influence unimpaired for the uses of liberty, both in the United States and wherever else it may be employed for the benefit of mankind." [10]

On further developments in relations between the United States and Mexico, which remained in a state of recurrent crisis until a stable Mexican government was finally formed, we cannot dwell. For in the meantime, national attention had been abruptly shifted in another direction. The problems of the Western Hemisphere, however troublesome, were thrust into the background by the drama of far more momentous events in Europe.

The assassination of an Austrian archduke at Sarajevo, a brief period of heightening international tension, the mobilization of impatient armies, a crisscross fire of ultimatums, precipitated in August, 1914, the First World War. The "age of settled peace and good will" tragically gave way to a new era of devastating world conflict, and little though the American people may have realized it—as they read the staggering headlines of the advance of Russian and German armies, of the invasion of Belgium, of the rallying of the French and the arrival on the continent of a British expeditionary force—a new era in their own history was opening. The United States was to find itself in a position where the policy it followed—whether of intervention or nonintervention—was to have a decisive effect in determining both the outcome of war and the kind of world in which twentieth-century man was to live.

At the beginning of hostilities the American people were largely persuaded they had no concern with the war. President Wilson declared that it was "a war with which we have nothing to do, whose causes cannot touch us"; or as he later phrased it, "it looked like a natural raking out of the pent-up jealousies and rivalries of the complicated politics of Europe." [11] The obvious conclusion seemed to be that the United States in the old phrase of the Swedish ambassador talking to John Adams in 1784, should be content to let the peoples of Europe "cut each other's throats with a philosophic tranquillity." Little disposition was shown to quarrel with the President's injunction

[10] *Public Papers of Woodrow Wilson*, III, 102.
[11] Dec. 8, 1914; July 4, 1919. *Ibid.*, III, 226; V, 527.

that the nation should observe neutrality in fact as well as in name; remain impartial in thought as well as in action.

An instinctive sympathy for the Allies was countered in 1914 by a good many doubts over their war aims, and the somewhat less than enthusiastic attitude of German-Americans and Irish-Americans toward everything British.[12] The one thing upon which the American people appeared to be generally agreed was the importance of maintaining neutrality and, as a corollary of this position, respect for the nation's rights as a neutral. Unfortunately, neutrality and neutral rights were not necessarily the same thing.

Wilson firmly believed in neutrality not merely to keep the United States out of war for its own sake, but because of the nation's obligations to the rest of the world. There was something more important for the country to do than fight. "We are the mediating nation," the President stated; it was the country's duty to remain at peace so that it could exercise the full force of America—"the force of moral principle." [13]

At the same time, Wilson was prepared to insist that the belligerents rigidly respect all neutral rights. As early as February, 1915, he took the unequivocal position that if Germany violated such rights through her submarine warfare, destroying American ships or American lives, the United States would hold her to "a strict accountability." He was to maintain that a nation could be "too proud to fight" and so certain of its course that "it does not need to convince others by force that it is right," yet make a tacit threat of the possible resort to force should Germany step over the lines he drew.[14]

In his own mind, Wilson apparently had little trouble in justifying a neutrality that in its commitment to the defense of self-determined neutral rights held the seeds of its own destruction. As in relations with Mexico, the dignity and authority of the United States were paramount in his thought. If the fundamental reason for neutrality was the opportunity to exert a moral influence for peace, that influence had to be kept inviolate. National honor was once again correlated with national responsibility.

His position became even more clear when the issue arose of forbidding travel by Americans on belligerent ships as a means of avoiding incidents that might create new friction with Germany and thereby

---

[12] See *Literary Digest*, XLIX (Aug. 8, 1914), 215, and (Nov. 14, 1914), 939.
[13] *Public Papers of Woodrow Wilson*, III, 304, 332.
[14] May 10, 1915. *Ibid.*, III, 321.

inflame public opinion. The President strongly—and successfully—opposed any such move:

I cannot consent to any abridgement of the rights of American citizens in any respect . . . Once accept a single abatement of right, and many other humiliations would certainly follow . . . What we are contending for in this matter is of the very essence of the things that have made America a sovereign nation. She cannot yield them without conceding her own impotency as a nation, and making virtual surrender of her independent position among the nations of the world.[15]

Again in 1916 he was to tell his countrymen that should a situation arise where he could not preserve both peace and honor, they should not expect of him "an impossible and contradictory thing."

The first important test of Wilson's neutrality policy was the sinking of the *Lusitania,* on May 7, 1915, with 128 Americans among the nearly twelve hundred persons drowned.[16] The United States promptly protested and demanded immediate disavowal of an act which it declared to be in clear violation of the established principles of warfare. When Germany refused to disavow or make reparation for the attack, on the ground that the *Lusitania* was carrying contraband cargo, a second note insisted even more vigorously on the American position. It appeared to be so strong that the President's pacifist-minded Secretary of State resigned in protest. William Jennings Bryan did not believe that Americans were justified in traveling on contraband-carrying ships in the war zone. Insistence on the right to do so, he was certain, would carry the nation into a war with which it should have nothing to do. The country as a whole sustained Wilson rather than Bryan; [17] indeed, the former was widely criticized for not taking an even more positive stand.

Further diplomatic exchanges got nowhere. But while refusing to abandon the right to sink contraband-carrying merchant vessels, the German government did seek to avoid another crisis in American relations by privately issuing orders to submarine commanders to spare large liners and to take every precaution for the safety of their pas-

[15] Wilson to Stone, Feb. 24, 1916, *Papers Relating to the Foreign Relations of the United States, 1916 Supplement* (Washington, 1929), pp. 177–178.
[16] For full discussion of the *Lusitania* incident, see Thomas A. Bailey, "The Sinking of the Lusitania," *American Historical Review,* XLI (1935), pp. 54–73.
[17] Bryan's position, however, would be endorsed by the neutrality acts of 1935–37.

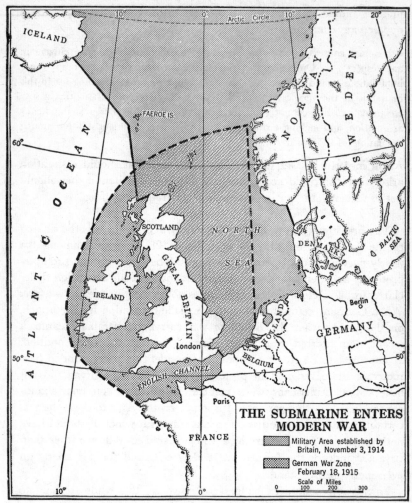

THE SUBMARINE ENTERS
MODERN WAR

Military Area established by
Britain, November 3, 1914

German War Zone
February 18, 1915

Scale of Miles
0   100   200   300

Reprinted from *A Short History of American Diplomacy*, L. Ethan Ellis

sengers. Nevertheless on August 19, 1915, another U-boat sank the
Arabic with a further loss of American lives. Robert Lansing, who
had replaced Bryan as Secretary of State, immediately summoned the
German ambassador and protested in the strongest terms. Greatly
alarmed, the latter gave an immediate pledge that passenger ships
would not again be attacked without warning. His government at least
partially backed him up in officially stating that the new orders to
submarine commanders were so stringent that the recurrence of any

such incident as the sinking of the *Arabic* was considered out of the question.

For some seven months there were no further critical incidents, but on March 24, 1916, a French vessel, the *Sussex,* was torpedoed in the English Channel with serious injury to several Americans. The United States protest—Lansing would have made it even stronger—was a virtual ultimatum. Unless Germany immediately abandoned its existing methods of submarine warfare against passenger and freight-carrying vessels, the United States would have no choice other than to sever diplomatic relations.

Germany now retreated—though not all the way. She definitely promised that there would be no further attacks on merchantmen without full warning and every effort being made to provide for the safety of passengers and crew, but at the same time reserved liberty of action if the United States did not induce the other belligerents to observe the "laws of humanity." It was clear that whenever Germany became convinced that she could successfully defend herself against any retaliatory measures which the United States might take, submarine warfare would be resumed.[18]

This final challenge was postponed until early 1917. In the meantime, other factors had come into play that were helping to prepare the country for war—or at least supporting a rigid insistence on neutral rights that made American entry into the conflict increasingly probable. For if submarine warfare was to prove the immediate cause for war, no such oversimplified explanation of what happened tells the whole story.

Real neutrality, in fact, had gone by the board long before Germany adopted unrestricted submarine warfare. While trade with the Central Powers had dwindled away to virtually nothing, the United States was extending vital economic aid to the Allies through an increasing flow of both munitions and food upon which they had become increasingly dependent. In statistical terms, the value of American exports to Allied countries rose between 1914 and 1916 from $824,860,000 to $3,214,000,000. If this trade were to be cut off, the Allies would have been shorn of their power to continue the war. The continued avail-

[18] The entire diplomatic correspondence is found in *Foreign Relations, Supplements, 1914–1917,* and valuable interpretations in Charles Seymour's *American Diplomacy During the World War* (Baltimore, 1934) and *American Neutrality, 1914–1917* (New Haven, 1935).

ability of such essential American supplies held out the only hope of Germany's eventual defeat.[19]

At the same time, this expanding commerce had become such an integral factor in the national economy of the United States that its interruption would have had almost disastrous domestic consequences. Much was made in congressional debates in 1916, and again twenty years later,[20] of the role played by the munitions makers and international bankers in blocking every move to place an embargo on munitions and thereby keeping the nation on the road to war. The fact was that the entire country was greatly concerned in a trade that embraced not only munitions but other manufactures and such basic farm products as wheat, cotton, and beef. Once it had been allowed to develop as it did, the people as a whole—farmers, industrial workers, businessmen—were unwilling to forego the commercial activity which largely accounted for their domestic prosperity.

While such considerations strengthened the opposition to any munitions embargo or other restriction on trade, the economic motive was by no means decisive in determining American policy. President Wilson accepted the practical arguments of business and financial groups in the matter of extending financial credits to the Allies, but there is no evidence that their influence persuaded him to keep on the course that sustained the historic principle of freedom of the seas and the privilege of trading wherever the nation chose. His insistence upon holding Germany to a strict observance of neutral rights, as already noted, was founded upon a conception of national honor and national prestige that in his opinion transcended any idea of economic gain.[21]

Apart from all else, moreover, a basic reason for both popular and administration concern with the continued shipment of supplies to England and France was the very fact that American economic aid had become of such importance to these nations. A mounting sympathy for their cause ran parallel with the demands of economic self-interest in encouraging this measure of Allied support, however loud Germany's outcries that American policy was no longer neutral. The

[19] The economic aspects of neutrality are fully discussed in the many wartime histories and especially elaborated in Charles C. Tansill, *America Goes to War* (Boston, 1938). See also Harold C. Syrett, "The Business Press and American Neutrality, 1914–17," *Mississippi Valley Historical Review*, XXXII (Sept., 1945), 215–230.

[20] See later discussion of the Nye Investigating Committee.

[21] Link, *Woodrow Wilson and the Progressive Era*, pp. 197 ff., and particularly pp. 278–281.

possibility that it might lead to war was considered less dangerous to the national interest than the weakening of the Allied position through any sort of embargo.

For as the European conflict wore on, the natural ties of blood, language, and common ideals that since 1900 have always drawn England and America together in spite of "family quarrels," as well as the bonds of a traditional friendship for France, increasingly eclipsed original doubts about Allied war aims. Propaganda had some part in swinging public opinion toward this more favorable attitude toward the Allies. The American people came largely to see the war through British eyes. Still, the influence of propaganda in 1914–17 is often overemphasized.[22] The impact of actual events was of far more importance than anything that was said about them. German violation of Belgium's neutrality, the sinking of the *Lusitania,* the deportation of Belgian civilians, and other instances of flagrant violation of accepted standards of international conduct were the determining factors in building up popular resentment against Germany's policy and therefore increasing sympathy for her foes.

The world was moving into an era when the rights of neutrals and civilians were to be given less and less consideration by any belligerent as groups of nation-states struggled for survival. But this could not affect contemporary judgments in 1914–17. Germany was the first to break the ancient rules. Because of her submarine attacks on passenger ships, a horrified American public held her responsible for a return to barbarism. She was running amok, threatening the very foundations of western civilization. The sinking of the *Lusitania* was itself enough to condemn Germany in the eyes of many people. "She has affronted the moral sense of the world," the *Nation* exclaimed, "and sacrificed her standing among the nations." [23]

Entirely apart from either economic or humanitarian considerations, some Americans favored support for the Allies, and eventually called for active entry into the war, on the ground that a victory for Germany would directly imperil American security. This point of view reflected the earlier idea that the United States would be gravely endangered by any continental power upsetting the Atlantic system. A Germany victorious over England and France would sooner or later,

[22] H. C. Peterson, *Propaganda for War* (Norman, Okla., 1939), and also Link, *Woodrow Wilson and the Progressive Era,* pp. 145–148.
[23] *The Nation,* C (May 13, 1915), 528, quoted in Thomas A. Bailey, *A Diplomatic History of the American People* (New York, 1940), p. 627.

according to such arguments, challenge this country's position in the Western Hemisphere. Walter Lippmann has written that the other factors making for war would never have carried the day "if a majority of the American people had not recognized intuitively, and if some Americans had not seen clearly, what the threatened German victory could mean to the United States." [24]

While such fears undoubtedly had some part in determining the popular attitude toward the war, there is little evidence that they carried the weight ascribed to them by Lippmann. The American people hardly understood the implications of an overturn in the existing European balance of power. They wanted the Allies to win because of their feeling that England and France stood for the things in which they themselves believed, rather than because of fear for their own safety. The Atlantic Ocean remained, in popular opinion, an effective barrier to any further German conquests.

A willingness to stand firmly in defense of the right to trade with the Allies—however strongly such a policy might be attacked as a departure from the real spirit of neutrality—and the ultimate decision to take up arms against Germany, were primarily due to a deepening popular conviction that the United States could not stand aside when the fundamental principles for which it stood were so precariously at stake and its national honor assailed by Germany's brazen disregard of American rights.

Although the tides of public opinion were already running strongly in favor of the Allies in 1916, there were very considerable elements among the American people who remained highly skeptical of their war aims, were not concerned over Germany's supposed assault upon American interests, and feared that the stand taken in defense of neutral rights would carry the nation into a war that they emphatically believed to be none of this country's concern. William Jennings Bryan was by no means alone in his conviction that the course the United States was following—selling munitions to the Allies, extending them

[24] Walter Lippmann, *U. S. Foreign Policy* (Boston, 1943), pp. 33–34. Lippmann cites an editorial, "The Defense of the Atlantic World," in the *New Republic*, X (Feb. 17, 1917), in support of this thesis. Later editorials in this journal (for example Apr. 7), strongly emphasize the identity of the Allied cause with American liberalism as justifying intervention. For extensive discussion, see Robert E. Osgood, *Ideals and Self-Interest in American Foreign Relations* (Chicago, 1953), pp. 114–134.

financial credits, denying German submarines the right to attack contraband-carrying vessels—could not be reconciled with real neutrality. His resignation at the time of the *Lusitania* incident had a strong impact on public opinion. Although a popular majority may have upheld Wilson's stand, there was considerable support for the view that national honor did not demand a position in respect to submarine operations that was untenable under the changed circumstances of modern war.[25]

The proponents of a more rigid neutrality were active in Congress. They repeatedly urged that steps should be taken to refuse credits to the belligerent nations, to embargo the shipment of munitions, to forbid the entry of armed merchantmen into American ports, and to bar American travel on belligerent ships. Those who favored these measures considered peace, rather than the protection of professed neutral rights or support for the Allies, as the all-important goal of foreign policy.[26]

And they soon found a further cause for concern in the preparedness movement that began to gain increasing headway after 1915. Sensing no danger to America whatever the outcome of events in Europe, they could find little justification for building up a powerful Navy and saw in this program a new force making for war.

Wilson had at first been completely uninterested in preparedness: if the force of America was moral principle, a Navy was irrelevant. He realized that the nation could not wholly disregard naval defense, but on one occasion, in December, 1914, he said that he turned away from the subject because "it is not new. There is no need to discuss it." Within the year, however, popular backing for preparedness persuaded him to take steps "to vindicate our right to independent and unmolested action by making the force that is in us ready for assertion." The administration therefore supported appropriation bills that were to lay the foundation for a Navy "second to none" as a practical and concrete expression of American power.[27]

[25] W. J. Bryan and M. B. Bryan, *The Memoirs of William Jennings Bryan* (Chicago, 1925), pp. 395–428.

[26] *Congressional Record*, LII, 63rd Congress, 3rd Session (Feb. 26, 1915), pp. 4705 ff.

[27] *Public Papers of Woodrow Wilson*, III, 227, 373–374, 387. For naval debates, see *Congressional Record*, LII, 63rd Congress, 3rd Session, pp. 4705 ff.; also Harold and Margaret Sprout, *Toward a New Order of Sea Power; American Naval Policy and the World Scene, 1918–1922* (Princeton, 1940), p. 36.

The critics of an uncontrolled munitions trade and of naval expansion remained certain that these were twin movements bound to lead the nation into unjustified hostilities. They were a varied group— characterized by an increasingly belligerent Theodore Roosevelt as a "flapdoodle pacifist and mollycoddle outfit"—and they were highly vocal. Sincere and liberal proponents of neutrality worked with pro-German elements, foes of British imperialism, and traditional isolationists. They were agreed only in their common conviction that America must be kept out of war. The cry of freedom of the seas and neutral rights meant nothing to them if such conceptions had to be defended by force of arms.

The issues arising from the fear of a gradual drift into war naturally enough entered into the presidential campaign of 1916. There was no sharp cleavage between the Democratic and Republican position, however. The Democrats coined the slogan "He kept us out of war" and urged Wilson's election as the way to peace; the Republicans, who had nominated Charles Evan Hughes, criticized administration policy as weak and vacillating, but, concerned over the German-American vote, failed to advocate more forceful measures. The President was re-elected primarily on domestic issues.[28] In spite of this relative subordination of foreign affairs during the campaign, however, the question of war or peace was drawing to a crisis by the close of 1916.

Although the threat of breaking off diplomatic relations after the torpedoing of the *Sussex* had forced Germany to countermand submarine attacks on merchant vessels, Wilson knew that the U-boat commanders would be unleashed whenever the German rulers felt it to be advisable. He realized that the United States would find itself in a position almost surely leading to war because of his own decision to hold Germany to a "strict accountability" for any attacks on American shipping. Convinced in these circumstances that the only way to avoid war was to make peace, he sought some effective way to mediate the conflict.

He had made several previous efforts along these lines. Early in 1915 and again a year later, he sent Colonel Edward M. House, his most intimate advisor, on special foreign missions to explore the possibilities of bringing about a peace conference. The astute Colonel, al-

[28] Kirk H. Porter, *National Party Platforms* (New York, 1924), pp. 395–396; *Literary Digest*, LII (June 17, 1916), 1828–29. For full discussion considering the interrelation between foreign and domestic policies, see Link, *Woodrow Wilson and the Progressive Era*, pp. 223–225.

ways strongly pro-Ally, had on the latter occasion gone so far as to assure the British Foreign Secretary, Sir Edward Grey, that if a peace conference were held and Germany proved recalcitrant, the United States would *probably* enter the war on the side of the Allies. But Great Britain was not willing to talk peace nor is it clear that Wilson was willing to make war, so the Colonel's maneuvers came to nothing. Now, however, the President was ready to try again and on December 18, 1916, he made a major appeal for an end to hostilities.

Acting upon the premise that "the objects which the statesmen of the belligerents on both sides have in mind are virtually the same"—a statement that badly shocked his pro-Ally advisors—Wilson called upon both the Allies and Central Powers to set forth their specific peace aims.[29] When they failed to give any satisfactory reply to this appeal, he then took the further step of outlining what he himself considered the sort of settlement they should seek. This was his famous "peace without victory" address. The new world order to which he called the warring nations to subscribe was not to be based upon a balance of military power or entangling alliances, but rather on a peace incorporating those principles of self-government, freedom of the seas, and limitation of armaments for which the United States had always stood—"a peace made secure by the organized major force of mankind."[30]

The European belligerents showed no interest in bringing the war to an end on any such terms. And this failure to promote the idea of a negotiated peace had elements of tragedy going far beyond its immediate effects on American prospects for staying out of war. It was a critical turning point in modern history. A peace between equals represented perhaps the only chance of a rational approach to settlement of the issues that had brought on Europe's conflict and the reestablishment of a stable world society. This was Wilson's prophetic warning. A peace imposed by the victors upon the vanquished, he declared, "would rest, not permanently, but only as upon quicksand."

The unsuccessful "peace without victory" address was almost immediately followed by Germany's declaration of unrestricted submarine warfare on January 31, 1917. The long-feared crisis was at hand. The alternatives before the country were forceful insistence on neutral rights or surrender to the German challenge.

[29] *Foreign Relations, 1916, Supplement,* pp. 97–99.
[30] Jan. 22, 1917. *Public Papers of Woodrow Wilson,* IV, 407–414.

There was an immediate popular demand for positive action. The swelling ranks of interventionists insisted that the time for temporizing was past and that the United States could no longer stand aside while its rights were so arrogantly assailed by threatened attack on American lives and American property.[31] When Wilson, his hand forced, announced that, in fulfillment of the stand taken at the time of the sinking of the *Sussex*, diplomatic relations would be broken with Germany, Congress and the country generally approved.[32] Typical of the position taken by a great majority of the nation's newspapers was the forthright statement of the Boston *Transcript:*

> From the quixotic adventure of imposing upon the Old World a "peace without victory," we are brought up with a sharp turn by the imperative necessity of defending American honor, American rights, American lives, American property—against a war without quarter with which Germany has threatened, not the New World only, but the whole world. . . .[33]

Yet for all the clamor of the interventionists—Senator Stone was to state on March 3 that "about all we have heard in Washington for months has been a prolonged shriek for war"[34]—there remained a very articulate opposition. Congressional spokesmen for the peace faction bitterly repeated that the United States had never been really neutral and was being maneuvered into an entirely false position. The real forces making for war, they maintained, were the bankers and munitions makers seeking to rescue their trade and investments. They hotly denied that any vital American rights or interests were endangered, or that the national honor was at stake.

Such opposition stemmed not only from antiwar feeling as such. It also reflected the old isolationist tradition. Intervention in the European conflict was seen as not only leading to a needless sacrifice of American lives, but to what would become a permanent involvement in European intrigue and rivalries. The debates in Congress brought out once again, in the recurrent pattern of the past, all the old arguments over the nation's world role.[35]

One school of thought advocated a "limited war." Its spokesmen

[31] Tansill, *America Goes to War*, pp. 650 ff.

[32] *Literary Digest*, LIV (Mar. 3, 1917).

[33] Quoted in Foster Rhea Dulles, *Twentieth Century America* (Boston, 1945), p. 208.

[34] *Congressional Record*, LIV, 64th Congress, 2nd Session (Mar. 3, 1917), p. 4886.

[35] *Ibid.*, pp. 4636 ff., 4864 ff., 4893 ff.

were ready to accept war as inescapable if Germany attacked American shipping, and yet remained strongly opposed to any entanglement in the strife of Europe. "We will vote to maintain by force, if need be, our liberties upon the sea," Congressman Lenroot of Wisconsin stated; "but that does not mean we will vote a general declaration of war against Germany." The Milwaukee *Sentinel* stated that if forced into hostilities "Uncle Sam 'would fight his own hand' and having gained his own end would cease fighting." [36]

Without going quite this far, Senator Borah vigorously stressed national aims. He agreed reluctantly upon the necessity of countering Germany's action with force, but was nonetheless stubbornly opposed to what he already considered Wilson's dangerous internationalism. Immediately after the declaration of war he would introduce a resolution, strongly supported by Henry Cabot Lodge, that reaffirmed the policies of Washington, Jefferson, and Monroe, and declared it to be the Senate's intention to conform "to these time-honored principles so long and so happily a part of our foreign policy." Borah's defense of his stand was emphatic: "I join no crusade; I seek or accept no alliance; I obligate this government to no other power. I make war alone for my countrymen and their rights, for my country and its honor." [37]

Among other Progressives and liberals who had earlier reflected isolationist views, there were now many who were ready to accept the call to defend liberty and justice in a wider sphere. Their progressivism took on international overtones. This was especially the case among such faithful followers of Theodore Roosevelt as Albert J. Beveridge and Harold Ickes. There were others. In grappling with the issues of the world, Walter Lippmann had long since written, the old isolationism in which everyone had been educated would have to be abandoned. The United States could not avoid the theaters of trouble; it should seek a coalition "with the powers whose policy is most nearly like our own." The editorials in the *New Republic* were soon to reveal a complete conversion to Wilsonian principles in declaring that "the liberal peoples of the world are united in a common cause." [38]

[36] *Literary Digest*, LIV (Mar. 3, 1917), 538.

[37] *Congressional Record*, LV, 65th Congress, 1st Session (Apr. 6, 1917), p. 440; Claudius O. Johnson, *Borah of Idaho* (New York, 1936), p. 203.

[38] Walter Lippmann, *The Stakes of Diplomacy* (New York, 1915), pp. 226–227; *New Republic*, X (Apr. 7, 1917), 280. See also David W. Noble, "The New Republic and the Idea of Progress, 1914–20," *Mississippi Valley Historical Review*, XXXVIII (Dec., 1951), 394–396.

It still remained true, however, that the bitter-end opponents of war continued to represent, perhaps more than any other single element in national life, the progressive forces of the West and Midwest. There could be no persuading men like Senators La Follette and Norris that the United States should join the Allies, involve itself in a bloody imperialistic struggle, and surrender its freedom of action. Their instinctive isolationism was only reinforced by the idea of taking up arms in defense of democracy. They were afraid it would only endanger a democracy still unfulfilled in America.[39]

Again and again La Follette declared that in taking part in this European quarrel, the United States was denying rather than vindicating everything for which it stood, inviting all those troubles against which the founders of the Republic had so farsightedly warned. "Are we," he asked, "seizing upon this war to consolidate and extend an imperial policy?"[40]

Senator Stone had only ridicule for the idea that any real danger confronted the United States. "This is so ludicrous," he stated, "that it is almost impossible to treat it seriously. . . . When did it come to pass that Uncle Sam must lay his head on the palpitating breast of Uncle Johnny Bull with a timid sense of dependence?"[41]

The antiwar faction, however, was a minority. Both Congress and the American people as a whole were fully persuaded by March, 1917, that the United States could not retreat in the face of the German challenge of unrestricted submarine warfare. They were prepared if necessary to take up arms in defense of national rights and national honor.

Further events now hurried the country along its fateful path. A first move to protect American interests—short of war—was the arming of American merchantmen, which was at first blocked by a senatorial filibuster but then authorized by executive action. While the public was still excitedly debating the implications of such a move, the State Department published an intercepted note from the German Foreign Minister to the German minister in Mexico—the so-called Zimmermann note—proposing a German-Mexican alliance, with the

[39] Eric F. Goldman, *Rendezvous with Destiny* (New York, 1952), pp. 241, 463.
[40] *Congressional Record*, LV, 65th Congress, Special Session (Apr. 4, 1917), pp. 225 ff.; see also Belle Case La Follette and Fola La Follette, *Robert M. La Follette* (2 vols., New York, 1953), I, 595–625.
[41] *Congressional Record*, LIV, 64th Congress, 2nd Session (Mar. 3, 1917), p. 4893.

possible adherence of Japan, should the United States enter the war. The bait was to be the recovery by Mexico of Texas, Arizona, and New Mexico. Some ten days later came the startling news of revolution in Russia, and its promise of a democratic regime to replace the arbitrary rule of czars. The only obstacle to believing that the European conflict was in truth a struggle between autocracy and freedom was removed. Then, on March 12, Germany made good her threat of unrestricted submarine warfare by sinking the unarmed American merchantman *Algonquin;* six days later three more ships were torpedoed.

Still, President Wilson struggled to avoid the consequences of this mounting crisis. In spite of the intensive pressure which he was under, both from the public and his advisors, he was reluctant to ask for war. He did not want to abdicate his leadership as had McKinley two decades earlier: "We are not governed by public opinion in our conclusion," he told his war-minded Cabinet on March 20. "I want to be right whether it is popular or not." [42] Yet there appeared to be no way he could lead his countrymen except into war. "What else can I do?" was his frantic question, and he must already have known in his own mind that he had no real choice. [43]

If war had to come, however, Wilson was determined that it should not be waged in a narrow self-interest, but in fulfillment of the historic destiny of the United States to promote liberty and justice. In no other way could he condone the failure of his policy to make a neutral United States the decisive influence in a negotiated peace. And the issues had to be drawn so clearly that the American people would be prepared to accept the sacrifices of war in fighting for an even greater cause than national rights or national security. The war had to become a struggle between Right and Wrong.

On April 2, 1917, Wilson appeared before Congress and asked for a formal declaration of war. Neutrality was no longer feasible or desirable, he now declared, where the peace of the world and the freedom of its people were at stake. The United States had no selfish interests to serve but was prepared to battle for those things that were

[42] *War Memoirs of Robert Lansing, Secretary of State* (Indianapolis, 1935), p. 237.

[43] The question was asked of both Colonel House and Frank Cobb of the New York *World. The Intimate Papers of Colonel House* (4 vols., Boston, 1926–28), II, 462–463; John Heaton, *Cobb of "The World"* (New York, 1924), p. 268.

even more precious than peace—for democracy, for the rights and liberties of small nations, and for

. . . a universal dominion of right by such a concert of free peoples as shall bring peace and safety to all nations and make the world itself at last free. To such a task we can dedicate our lives and our fortunes, everything that we are and everything that we have, with the pride of those who know that the day has come when America is privileged to spend her blood and her might for the principles that gave her birth and happiness and the peace that she has treasured. God helping her, she can do no other.[44]

However sober the attitude of the President himself, the response of the listening congressmen was excited, tumultous approval. On April 4 the Senate adopted the war resolution by a vote of 82 to 6, and two days later the House followed its lead with a vote of 373 to 50. The fateful die was cast.[45]

The United States had gone to war because the position in which the nation found itself, as a result of the policy that President Wilson had adopted toward submarine warfare, finally left no other choice compatible with what was considered national honor. Germany had taken the immense gamble of directly challenging America in the belief that unrestricted submarine warfare would bring the Allies to their knees before further aid from this country could become effective. The American people were not only ready to accept this challenge, but compelled a now reluctant President to carry his policy through to its logical and perhaps inescapable conclusion. It was too late to reverse an attitude which had been built up during the war years because of a growing economic dependence on trade with the Allies, a mounting sympathy for the cause which this trade was sustaining, and a deepening conviction that the defeat of Germany—at whatever cost —was in the national interest.

Once the decision was reached, the war then became sublimated in the minds of a majority of the American people into a great crusade. Following Wilson's inspired leadership, they believed that this was a vastly different war from the age-old struggles of the past. It was the war to end all wars. The great goal of enduring peace would

[44] *Public Papers of Woodrow Wilson*, V, 9–16.
[45] For general debate, *Congressional Record*, LV, 65th Congress, 1st Session, Appendix, pp. 1–150.

be finally achieved with the overthrow of German tyranny. The confidence in continuing social progress and the unlimited faith in a beneficent future that had characterized the Progressive era were given a global scope.[46]

President Wilson continued to sustain this lofty vision. In the face of all the natural disillusionments of war, he sought to keep the sights of the people fixed on their ultimate aims. If the idea of a peace without victory had given way to a determination to use force—"force to the utmost, force without stint or limit"—to bring Germany to her knees, the war was still to be one of "high disinterested purpose." As the nation's cause was just and holy, the President told his countrymen, so must the final settlements be just and holy; and "for this we can fight, but for nothing less noble or less worthy of our tradition." In his mind here was the summation, the final climax, of the world mission of America. "Once more we shall make good with our lives and fortunes the great faith to which we were born, and a new glory shall shine in the face of the people." [47]

This was the underlying spirit in which the nation went to war in April, 1917.

[46] "The fact is," Reinhold Niebuhr has written, "that every nation is caught in the moral paradox of refusing to go to war unless it can be proved that the National interest is imperiled, and in continuing in the war only by proving that something much more than the national interest is at stake." *The Irony of American History* (New York, 1952), p. 36.

[47] *Public Papers of Woodrow Wilson*, V, 53, 131, 138, 67.

CHAPTER 6

The Great Retreat

A LITTLE over a year and a half after his call to arms against Germany, on December 4, 1918, President Wilson sailed for the peace conference at Paris.

During the intervening months the reinforced Allies, after their long years of bloody struggle, had finally broken down the strength of the Central Powers. The mobilization of the massive industrial resources of the United States, the growing bulk of food and of war materials ferried across the Atlantic, the arrival of fresh American troops on the battle-scarred plains of northern France, had tipped the scales of war. There had been cruel fighting and heavy loss of lives, but at last the Allied forces were everywhere triumphant. On November 11, with revolution at home and a dethroned Kaiser fleeing ignominiously to Holland, the German authorities had signed the Armistice.

The President was now going overseas, not to conclude the negotiated settlement between equals that he had once declared held out the only hope of permanent peace in a war-torn world, but to take part in drawing up peace terms that would be imposed upon the vanquished by the victors.

There had already been some signs of a weakening of his leadership. The Republican victories at the mid-term elections in 1918 were a portent of the shifting political tides. Wilson was nonetheless confident that the American people shared his vision of a new world order and would not turn back from the course on which they had embarked. Perhaps he had forgotten Senator Borah's forceful statement: "I join no crusade; I seek or accept no alliance." Certainly he explained away the Democratic losses in Congress, criticism of his peace delegation and of his own trip to Europe, as irresponsible partisanship that could be easily overcome. The great war leader appeared to have no misgivings over his ability to play a comparable role as the great leader in establishing peace.

His ideas for the future had been set forth within the vague contours of the Fourteen Points (later supplemented by some ten additional "points") that he announced on January 8, 1918 as a statement of war aims. Apart from a number of specific territorial proposals, they embraced such general conceptions as the self-determination of peoples, freedom of the seas, removal of economic barriers, limitation of armaments, and an association of nations to guarantee the independence of great and small states alike. Through this program, Wilson said, ran one basic principle, the principle of justice; unless this principle was made the foundation of peace, peace could not stand.[1] Its practical application was the duty that now devolved upon the statesmen meeting in Paris.

The course of negotiations was not a smooth one. Hammering steadily at his main objective—the League of Nations—Wilson refused to be diverted or deterred. And he succeeded not only in winning approval for the covenant of the proposed League, but in integrating it so closely with the over-all peace settlements that it became inseparable from them. No matter what later befell the League, this was his victory and his triumph.

There were other issues which had to be decided, however, if there was to be any general peace, and therefore any League. Here the harassed President found himself combating the determined views of the European statesmen who were still playing the power politics he abhorred. "Mr. Wilson bores me with his Fourteen Points," growled the cynical Clemenceau, "why, God Almighty has only ten!" The French Premier, Prime Minister Lloyd George, and Premier Orlando considered themselves realists. Their willingness to accept the League was predicated upon peace terms that would assure the nations they represented the maximum of advantage. The fears and prejudices born of century-old rivalry and conflict, in some instances already reflected in secret treaties that would have divided the spoils of war regardless of Wilsonian principles, were not dissipated by the glittering promise of a brave new world.

[1] R. S. Baker and W. E. Dodd, *The Public Papers of Woodrow Wilson* (6 vols., New York, 1925–27), V, 155–162.

Peacemaking soon found the United States involved in problems that opened up all those "vials of perplexities and ills" against which its early statesmen had warned and from which the nation had heretofore so successfully held aloof. The President had to take a stand on

Ireland in Columbus *Dispatch*

"I wonder just where I stand with him, anyway!"

the boundaries of the new succession states in eastern Europe, the project for creating a Franco-German buffer in the Rhineland, Italy's claims to Fiume, the status of the Saar, the territorial limits of Poland, the future title to German colonies, Japanese rights in Shantung, and the determination of reparations. No one of these problems was of immediate or direct concern to the United States. Their equitable settlement was nevertheless essential if the organized major force of mankind was to guarantee the future peace.[2]

Wilson sought valiantly and doggedly to achieve a just peace. "Tell me what is right," he had said to the experts charged with the study of all these immensely complicated issues, "and I'll fight for it." [3] But right and wrong, even in the abstract, were not so easily determined. The principle of self-determination was oftentimes in conflict with the most fundamental demands of economic justice; the rights of one nation could not always be adjusted to the equally defensible rights of another. Moreover there was no withstanding certain practical con-siderations at war with abstract justice, and no diverting the powerful force of national interests that too insistently demanded protection. The settlements that were written into the Treaty of Versailles inevi-tably involved compromise and concession. They could not, in all too many instances, be easily reconciled with the ideals on which Wilson had declared they must be based.

The President realized this. In his own mind these concessions were justified, however, as measures necessary to secure general adherence to the League of Nations. For it was to be one of the functions of the League to review the decisions made at Paris. He did not envisage peace as something static, but as a dynamic force bulwarking world justice. What was above all essential was to create, through such an agency as the League, the machinery to adjust international disputes without recourse to war: "Settlements may be temporary, but the actions of the nations in the interests of peace and justice must be permanent. We can set up permanent processes. We may not be able to set up permanent decisions." [4] Yet there will always be controversy whether even an effective League—with American membership— could have successfully unraveled the dangerously tangled skein of the decisions reached at Paris. Compromises were of course essential, but in a number of instances they went so far as to undermine the basic principles Wilson had set forth as necessary for an enduring peace. In his determination to maintain support for the League, the President

[2] For negotiations, see *Foreign Relations, 1919: The Paris Peace Conference* (13 vols., Washington, 1924). They are fully discussed, among other books, in Thomas A. Bailey, *Woodrow Wilson and the Lost Peace* (New York, 1944).

[3] R. S. Baker, *Woodrow Wilson and World Settlement* (3 vols., New York, 1922), I, 10. These "experts" were representative of a group, largely college professors, assembled by Colonel House and named The Inquiry. Bailey, *Woodrow Wilson and the Lost Peace,* pp. 108–109.

[4] Jan. 25, 1919, Baker, *Woodrow Wilson and World Settlement,* I, 239.

sometimes gave ground too easily, hesitant to exercise American influence as forcefully as he might have in trying to modify the competing demands of national self-interest.

The more fundamental question may also be raised as to whether the settlements reached at Paris did not actually perpetuate the old order rather than provide a sound basis for the new. Deep-seated economic problems had played a major part in bringing on the war. For all his emphasis, in 1917 and 1918, on the political implications of the conflict, his insistence that it was basically one between autocracy and democracy, Wilson fully recognized and later frankly acknowledged the importance of the economic background. During his campaign to win American acceptance of the Versailles Treaty he asked of one audience in 1919:

Is there any man here or any woman, let me say is there any child here, who does not know that the seed of war in the modern world is industrial and commercial rivalry? The real reason that the war we have just finished took place was that Germany was afraid her commercial rivals were going to get the better of her, and the reason why some nations went into the war against Germany was that they thought Germany would get the commercial advantage of them. . . . This war in its inception was a commercial and industrial war. It was not a political war.[5]

This was an uncharacteristic oversimplification of the causes of war, but industrial and commercial factors were significant, and Wilson cannot be absolved of his share of responsibility in the failure of the conference to give them more serious consideration in drawing up the terms of peace. While the third of his Fourteen Points had called for "the removal, so far as possible, of all economic barriers and the establishment of an equality of trade conditions," he appeared to have completely forgotten it. Indeed, the President told one of his advisers on the eve of the peace conference that he was "not much interested in the economic subjects." [6] This was hardly realistic. His reluctance to give adequate attention to matters economic and financial, and to their effect upon the new world order, was to have far-reaching and unhappy consequences.[7]

[5] Aug. 5, 1919, *Public Papers of Woodrow Wilson,* V, 637, 638.
[6] Baker, *Woodrow Wilson and World Settlement,* II, 319.
[7] The economic aspects of the settlement were most pointedly brought out in the controversial study: J. M. Keynes, *The Economic Consequences of the Peace* (New York, 1920), and reviewed twenty years later in Étienne Mantoux, *The Carthaginian Peace* (New York, 1946). See also the discussion in Eric F.

It is true that Wilson tried to control the old forces of imperialistic rivalry through treaty provisions making the former German colonies mandates of the League of Nations instead of distributing them among the victorious powers. When his original idea that the mandatory nations should be such small neutral countries as Holland, Sweden, and Denmark was given up, however, the purposes of his plan were largely nullified.[8] Imperialistic rivalries had by no means been eliminated, and were with time to flare up once again with fresh virulence.

Wilson had to recognize the overwhelming obsession of France with security—and her general skepticism over the proposed League guarantees. In countering French demands for the creation of an independent Rhineland, he consequently went so far as to agree to a special Treaty of Guarantee with France, paralleling a similar Anglo-French pact. This was a curious incident in the negotiations at Paris. For such a security treaty—to an even greater degree than American membership in the League of Nations—was a flat repudiation of the policy of no entangling alliances. It contained a firm and definite commitment. Should France, pending the effective establishment of the League of Nations, become the victim of an "unprovoked movement of aggression" on the part of Germany, the United States would at once come to her assistance. Oddly enough, this treaty won the support of some isolationists who opposed League membership. Here was an entanglement, but it was considered a temporary one, and it did not involve—for example—possible intervention in the even more distant affairs of Yugoslavia, Poland, or Greece. The Franco-American Treaty, however, was to meet an even more ignominious fate than that of the Treaty of Versailles. Submission to the Senate was postponed and it was then permanently pigeonholed in the dark recesses of the files of the Committee on Foreign Relations.[9]

Goldman, *Rendezvous with Destiny* (New York, 1952), pp. 267–270, and the interesting correspondence between Wilson and George L. Record as quoted in Richard Hofstadter, *The American Political Tradition* (New York, 1948), pp. 272–273.

[8] For discussion of mandate system, Bailey, *Woodrow Wilson and the Lost Peace*, pp. 163–178; *Memoirs of Herbert C. Hoover: Years of Adventure* (New York, 1951), pp. 454, 455.

[9] *Congressional Record*, LVIII, 66th Congress, 1st Session (July 29, 1919), pp. 3311–12, for treaty text. Attitude of Lodge as quoted in Claude G. Bowers, *Beveridge and the Progressive Era* (Boston, 1932), p. 507; and Philip C. Jessup, *Elihu Root* (2 vols., New York, 1938), II, 401–403. See also *Harvey's Weekly*, II (Aug. 9, 1919), 1–2; *Literary Digest*, LXI (May 3, 1919), 20, and

The peace terms which Germany was finally compelled to accept were a compromise between the harshly punitive settlement that the victor might have imposed upon the vanquished and a freely negotiated peace based upon the mutual accommodation of conflicting interests. Wilson was to characterize the Treaty of Versailles as severe, but no more severe than the defeated enemy deserved. It completely disarmed Germany; deprived her of her colonies; compelled her to restore certain territories acquired by previous conquest, such as Alsace-Lorraine; and held her liable to indeterminate reparations, including payment for both civilian damages and military pensions. Yet it did not so limit or restrict Germany's recuperative powers as to prevent her recovery from the ravages of war and the ultimate reassertion of national power. The treaty settlement as a whole could be attacked—and was attacked—as both too harsh and too soft. It could be attacked—and was attacked—as both ignoring the realities of power politics and failing in many respects to embody the principles underlined in the Fourteen Points.[10]

From the American point of view, the League was always the treaty's most important feature, for membership constituted an implicit undertaking to uphold the general peace settlements. Going even further, the famous Article Ten of the Covenant pledged the signatory nations to respect and preserve against external aggression the territorial integrity and existing political independence of all League members. In signing the Versailles Treaty, President Wilson consequently not only accepted the terms of peace, but seemed to have committed the United States to their continued support.

America had taken up arms not alone in defense of national rights, but to promote certain broad and idealistic aims. On the assumption that these aims had either been incorporated in the peace settlements or could be realized through the League of Nations, the American people were now being asked to confirm what had been done in their name. Completely rejecting the traditional noninterventionist policy, the President called upon the nation to subscribe to a universal pact for safeguarding the peace and security of all the world. There was no

---

LXII (July 19, 1919), 12; and Bailey, *Woodrow Wilson and the Lost Peace*, pp. 231–237.

[10] Contemporary newspaper opinion is usefully summarized in the *Literary Digest*, LXI (May 17, 1919), 11. For later estimates, see Paul Birdsall, *Versailles Twenty Years After* (New York, 1941), and Mantoux, *The Carthaginian Peace*.

alternative, he stated in one speech on September 6, 1919, to this basic shift in American policy:

The isolation of the United States is at an end not because we chose to go into the politics of the world, but because by the sheer genius of this people and the growth of our power we have become a determining factor in the history of mankind and after you have become a determining factor you cannot remain isolated, whether you want to or not. Isolation ended by the processes of history, not by the processes of our independent choice, and the processes of history merely fulfilled the prediction of the men who founded our Republic.[11]

There is every evidence that the overwhelming majority of the American people were prepared, in the early spring of 1919, to approve the Treaty of Versailles and American membership in the League of Nations. Newspaper polls, resolutions adopted by thirty-two state legislatures, the declarations of labor unions, farm groups, women's organizations, and professional associations, all substantiate this interpretation of public opinion. Even the Midwest seemed to fall in line. From the *Ohio State Journal* came the anguished cry that if there were no League, "God pity us all, for there will be war from now to kingdom come." [12] It was the opinion of both Lodge and Borah, already desperately seeking ways to defeat Wilsonism, that if League membership were put to an immediate popular test, it would win a sweeping nationwide victory.[13]

The President's lofty confidence that the country would support his foreign policy would not appear entirely misplaced in view of such evidence. Had pro-League sentiment remained as powerful as it was during the spring of 1919, even a Republican dominated and strongly anti-Wilson Senate might have been compelled to give way before public pressure and accept the Treaty of Versailles without crippling reservations. But this was not what happened. Other factors came into play. And they brought about not only the rejection of the League, but what was even more important and more unfortunate, the nation's complete recoil from any collective action to meet the political and economic problems resulting from Germany's defeat.

Long before the President's return from Paris with the Treaty of

[11] *Public Papers of Woodrow Wilson*, VI, 18–19.

[12] *Literary Digest*, LX (Mar. 1, 1919), 11–13; *ibid.*, LX (Mar. 29, 1919), 32.

[13] Henry Cabot Lodge, *The Senate and the League of Nations* (New York, 1925), pp. 146, 147.

Versailles, the latent forces of anti-Wilsonism had assumed significant proportions. His Republican foes had become increasingly resentful of what they regarded as his highhanded and domineering tactics. Their opposition was then intensified by his challenge to the Senate, on his brief interim return to the United States during the peace conference, to dare to reject the pledges he had made for American membership in the League. On the eve of sailing again for Paris in March, 1919, Wilson had told a New York audience: "When that treaty comes back, gentlemen on this side will find the covenant not only in it, but so many threads of the treaty tied to the covenant that you cannot dissect the covenant from the treaty without destroying the whole vital structure." [14]

Wilson did not create the opposition to the peace that he offered the American people, but his attitude was not always calculated to provide an atmosphere that would have encouraged calm deliberation on the momentous issue that League membership represented. It is true that in response to criticism, and especially to the outspoken attack on his policy contained in a "Round Robin" expression of senatorial opposition signed by thirty-nine senators or senators-elect and presented by Lodge on March 3, he induced the peace conference to accept certain Republican proposals for changes in the Covenant as originally drawn up. Domestic issues were excluded from the League's province, the right of withdrawal from membership was stipulated, and—most important—"regional understandings like the Monroe Doctrine" were specifically safeguarded.[15] Nevertheless Wilson would not be persuaded that any further amendments or reservations should be considered. He did not believe they were being urged in good faith, and felt in any event that further revision of the League Covenant should be left to later consideration after American ratification of the peace treaty. Whatever the justification for his position, his insistence that it was the duty of the United States to accept in full everything that had been finally determined at Paris lost him support. Nor did he help his cause with his repeated dismissal of all opposition within the Senate as nothing more than factious partisanship.

For even as he returned to Paris for the final stage of the negotiations, the peace was being subjected to a cold scrutiny by elements within the country which were not motivated by partisan rancor.

[14] Mar. 4, 1919, *Public Papers of Woodrow Wilson*, V, 451.
[15] Denna Frank Fleming, *The United States and the League of Nations* (New York, 1932), pp. 153–159, 183–185.

Nationalistic groups with strong ties with the Old World—German-Americans, Italian-Americans, Polish-Americans, Irish-Americans—bitterly criticized the treaty for its failure to satisfy all the demands of their native lands. Many liberals who had heretofore generously supported both the domestic and foreign policies of the Wilson Administration, such as those associated with the *New Republic* school, strongly resented a settlement that seemed to them to perpetuate the basic evils of the old order rather than to provide any hope for realizing the war aims of democracy. From their point of view, the League was an agency designed to freeze the *status quo*. And most important of all, the old forces of isolationism threw off the enforced acquiescence of war days to rise in revolt against the reversal of traditional policy represented by membership in a League whose basic purpose was to sustain the territory and independence of all its members.[16]

The American people as a whole were not to take so strong a stand as the hyphenates, the liberals, or Wilson's partisan foes. Some time earlier an editorial in the New York *Sun* had predicted that when the war came to an end, "a lot of people will pick up their 1913–14 thoughts right where they laid them down." As the actual struggle over League membership was being fought out in the Senate, this popular reversion to the old isolationist habit of mind was just exactly what was taking place.

The process was hastened by domestic developments. The year 1919 was marked by skyrocketing inflation, violent and disturbing industrial disputes, the outbreak of bloody race riots in half a dozen cities, and a pervasive fear of the Bolshevik activity which was believed to underlie much of the social unrest of the period. These issues began to steal newspaper headlines and force foreign affairs further and further into the background. There was continued interest in the League and strong pressure from many quarters in favor of American membership, but the grave import of problems immediately at hand fostered an increasingly indifferent attitude on the part of the public as a whole.

[16] *Literary Digest*, LXI (Apr. 26, 1919), 9–11; editorials in the *Freeman, Nation,* and *New Republic; Congressional Record,* LVII, 65th Congress, 3rd Session, pp. 1383 ff., 1395 ff., 1810 ff., 1917 ff., 1983 ff., 1996 ff. An especially forthright statement of the liberal attitude may be found on the cover of the *New Republic,* May 24, 1919.

"THIS IS NOT PEACE—Americans would be fools if they permitted themselves to be embroiled in a system of European alliances. America promised to underwrite a stable peace. Mr. Wilson has failed. The peace cannot last. America should withdraw from all commitments which would impair her freedom of action."

Moreover the slump from wartime idealism intensified the growing skepticism over what good could ever come from American membership in the League. The returning soldiers had in many instances undergone shattering experiences that appeared to them to have little relation to the high goals for which they had believed themselves fighting. The mass destruction that had taken place on the bloody fields of northern France could not be easily reconciled with the concept of battling for freedom and democracy. In the disillusionment born of harsh experience, the only policy that justified itself in the minds of many veterans was one that barred any possible likelihood of the United States ever again becoming involved in foreign war.[17]

This negative and cynical attitude was to find enduring expression in much of the postwar literature—the writings of Dos Passos, Hemingway, Fitzgerald, Cummings, and others of the "lost generation." Perhaps nowhere has it been more faithfully reflected than in the words of Hemingway's hero in *A Farewell to Arms*: "I was always embarrassed by the words sacred, glorious, and sacrifice and the expression in vain. . . . I had seen nothing sacred, and the things that were glorious had no glory and the sacrifices were like the stockyards at Chicago if nothing was done with the meat except to bury it. . . ."[18]

When to such disillusionment were added the disappointments of the peace itself, it was not surprising that the war veterans helped to foster a growing conviction that the country should think twice before inviting further entanglement in European affairs.

The original popular reaction in favor of League membership, as this gradually changing attitude suggested, had been largely an emotional one—a carry-over of the crusading fervor that had marked American entry into the war. Under such circumstances a decision to join the League, without full realization of what membership implied in terms of traditional American policy, might have had as unhappy consequences as the refusal to become a member. There would have been no certainty that on sober second thought the American people might not have refused to carry out obligations they had not really understood.[19] But if the Republican leaders in the Senate, including

[17] Thomas A. Bailey, *Woodrow Wilson and The Great Betrayal* (New York, 1945), p. 36; Dixon Wecter, *When Johnny Comes Marching Home* (Cambridge, Mass., 1944), pp. 470–476.

[18] Ernest Hemingway, *A Farewell to Arms* (Modern Standard Authors edition, New York, 1949), p. 191.

[19] Root and Stimson favored strong reservations on the ground that the

Lodge, were justified in insisting that there should be full consideration of what approval of the Versailles Treaty really meant, their tactics most certainly did not encourage a rational approach to the problems involved. They delayed action for the sake of delay; they appealed to prejudice rather than principle.

In the light of the underlying conflict between a traditional freedom of action and membership in a League dedicated to collective security, the partisan maneuvering in the Senate, the endless disputes over the terminology of reservations, and all the political quarreling of the summer of 1919 seem largely irrelevant to the real issues at stake. The arguments of pro-League forces as well as those of opponents of the League, indeed, often served to confuse rather than to clarify the question which the American people were called upon to answer.[20]

The two opposing views that most definitely came to grips with the main issue were those of Wilson and Borah. The latter was supported by the so-called irreconcilables, and in varying degree by other Republicans who followed Lodge's leadership in the anti-League fight; the former had his Democratic followers, but as time went on became a more and more lonely figure. Both men—and they had a mutual respect for one another that rose above the pettiness of so much of the League struggle—stood firmly on principle. Their dispute was in the tradition of the great debate over intervention in world affairs that had come down through all American history.

Borah was utterly and completely convinced that the United States would not only best serve its own interests, but would most effectively promote world peace and the democratic cause, by rigidly maintaining a complete independence in all foreign relations. Having supported entry into war in 1917 solely on the grounds of defense of American rights, he now fought every move that would further entangle the United States in world affairs through pledge or commitment. Although he was later to play a leading role in bringing about the naval

---

American people might later refuse to carry out the commitments in Article 10 and that this would destroy the League. Henry L. Stimson and McGeorge Bundy, *On Active Service in Peace and War* (New York, 1948), pp. 102–103. Root to Adelbert Moot, July 11, 1919, quoted in Ruhl J. Bartlett, *The League to Enforce Peace* (Chapel Hill, N.C., 1944), p. 131. See also Fleming, *The United States and the League of Nations*, pp. 165–175.

[20] For this discussion in the Senate see Bartlett, *The League to Enforce Peace*, pp. 113–204; Bailey, *Woodrow Wilson and the Great Betrayal*, pp. 149–270; Fleming, *The United States and the League of Nations*, pp. 232–336, 359–450; W. Stull Holt, *Treaties Defeated by the Senate* (Baltimore, 1933), pp. 249–307.

disarmament conference of 1921–22, and in the movement for the outlawry of war that culminated in the Kellogg-Briand Anti-War Treaty,
he always believed that the exercise of a moral influence was the
farthest that the United States should go under any and all circumstances. Any deeper involvement in world affairs, in Borah's opinion,
would weaken rather than strengthen the helpful role that the country
might otherwise play in promoting peace and freedom.[21]

He feared above everything the contamination of democracy and
the undermining of American leadership should this country tie itself
to a Europe which persisted in its imperialistic policies and armament
races. There could be no health for the United States in a League that
he saw as little more than a reincarnation of the nineteenth century's
Holy Alliance. Borah believed that the mission of America was to
demonstrate the basic values of democracy, and that democracy was
something more than a form of government. "It is a moral entity, a
spiritual force as well," he declared. "And these are things which live
only and alone in the atmosphere of liberty." Reservations in regard
to such a matter as American membership in the League consequently
seemed to him immaterial. Such an important step was either fundamentally right or fundamentally wrong: the United States should
either accept the full responsibility of League membership or forthrightly reject such responsibility.[22] And Borah never wavered in his
certainty that rejection was the only sound policy for the United
States to follow. During the Senate debate in July, 1919, he said:

If I have had a conviction throughout my life with which it has been
possible for me to be consistent at all times, it has been the conviction that
we should stay out of European and Asiatic affairs. I do not think we can
have here a great, powerful, independent, self-governing Republic and do
anything else; I do not think it possible for us to continue to be the leading
intellectual and moral power in the world and do anything else. I do not
think we can achieve the task now confronting us, that of establishing here
an industrial democracy, as we have achieved a political democracy, and do
anything else.[23]

Wilson's position was just as uncompromising and just as much a

[21] There is no really adequate study of Borah, but see the rather uncritical
biography, C. O. Johnson, *Borah of Idaho* (New York, 1936), pp. 225 ff.
[22] *Congressional Record*, LVII, 65th Congress, 3rd Session (Jan. 14, 1919),
pp. 1384–87.
[23] *Ibid.*, LVIII (July 25, 1919), p. 3143.

matter of principle. He had become convinced that a League of Nations was the one hope for maintaining world peace, and that it was consequently the moral obligation of the United States to join the League and assume its leadership. He also was persuaded that every legitimate interest of the United States had been safeguarded through the changes already effected in the Covenant under Republican pressure, and that any further reservations would endanger the entire structure of the postwar settlements. The President insisted that Article Ten was all-important. And while he again and again affirmed it did not legally obligate the United States to use armed force, he was nonetheless determined there should be no reservations weakening its implications. It was "binding in conscience only," but to limit its effectiveness was to strike at the very heart of the Covenant.[24]

This confusion between a legal and a moral responsibility weakened Wilson's position. Through Article Ten the League members undertook "to respect and preserve as against external aggression" the territorial integrity and existing independence of all other members, but there was no automatic provision for carrying out this commitment. The Council was to advise upon the means by which aggression should be met, and as a member of the Council the United States would have been able to block action which it did not approve and thereby escape any obligation to impose sanctions on an aggressor nation. But in emphasizing that the United States assumed no legal responsibility because the pledge it would make in support of collective security was binding in conscience only, the President was making a distinction that could hardly be reconciled with his own repeated declarations of the moral duty of that country which he proudly called "the only idealistic nation in the world."

Membership in the League of Nations clearly meant the rejection of the traditional policy of complete freedom of action. Even entry into the war, in which the United States participated as an "associated" rather than "allied" power, had not so clearly broken the pattern of the past. The implications of Article Ten, as the backbone or heart of the Covenant, were much too definite. There was a great deal said about other aspects of the League in congressional and public debate. The fundamental issue remained the willingness or unwillingness of the United States to make the pledges—implied if not spelled

[24] See Wilson's testimony before the Senate Foreign Relations Committee, Aug. 19, 1919, *Senate Document 76*, 66th Congress, 1st Session, III, 6. Also *Public Papers of Woodrow Wilson*, V, 579.

out under Article Ten—for cooperative action in maintaining collective security.

As the issue sharpened, Wilson declared that the proponents of reservations—even the so-called mild reservationists—were demanding a sacrifice of principle that he could not make. What was at stake, he repeatedly stated, was "the nation's honor." Convinced in his own mind that approval of the treaty with the Lodge reservations was not ratification but nullification, he continued to believe that the American people would uphold him.[25] He could not imagine that having entered the war to attain certain objectives—a reign of law based on justice—his countrymen would suddenly withdraw from a job which they had really just started: "This nation went into this war to see it through to the end, and the end has not come yet. This is the beginning, not of the war but of the processes which are going to render a war like this impossible."[26]

What Wilson did not understand was that the American people had not undergone the great conversion to the cause of collective security that he himself had experienced. Their emotional response to his wartime leadership, and their support for the idealism of the Fourteen Points, did not necessarily mean that they were ready to follow him in time of peace in abandoning the traditional policy associated with the names of Washington and Jefferson. The President told them that a League was actually a great disentanglement, recognizing the validity of their fears of becoming too deeply involved in European affairs; but in the cold afterdawn of the great crusade, they wanted more convincing proof that the League would really mean peace and security rather than further foreign adventure.

In his speeches and addresses throughout 1919, Wilson continually stressed the great obligations of world leadership. He spoke of the "supreme sacrifice of throwing in our fortunes with the fortunes of men everywhere." Reminding his audiences that the United States had entered the war as the disinterested champion of right, he declared that the nation could interest itself in the terms of peace in no other capacity.[27] He tried to sustain an idealistic tone among a people tired of idealism. Though his eloquence could still touch their emo-

[25] *Ibid.*, V, 557; VI, 483; Edith Bolling Wilson, *My Memoir* (Indianapolis, 1913), p. 297; letter of Nov. 18, 1919, in *Congressional Record*, LVIII, 66th Congress, 1st Session, p. 8768.
[26] Sept. 5, 1919, *Public Papers of Woodrow Wilson*, V, 644.
[27] *Ibid.*, V, 452, 538.

tions, it could not in times of peace arouse the enthusiasm of the days of war.

Again and again the President predicted that without an effective League, in which the United States played its full part, the world was doomed once more to experience all the horrors of the war. Yet in his own mind the compelling reason for joining the League remained not so much American security as the creation of a new world order. This was the measure of his idealism and it was impossible for him—however unfortunate this was for his cause—to stress the more realistic arguments that might possibly have gained more converts. There had to be some nobler motive for national action than even an enlightened self-interest. The choice that the American people were called upon to make—and the most solemn in all their history, he declared—was this:

Shall America redeem her pledges to the world? . . . She has said to mankind at her birth: "We have come to redeem the world by giving it liberty and justice." Now we are called upon before the tribunal of mankind to redeem that immortal pledge. . . .[28]

And again upon another occasion:

The stage is set, the destiny disclosed. It has come about by no plan of our conceiving, but by the hand of God who led us into this way. We cannot turn back. We can only go forward, with lifted eyes and freshened spirit, to follow the vision. It was of this that we dreamed at our birth. America shall in truth show the way. The light streams upon the path ahead, and nowhere else.[29]

Here was the eloquence of old, the idealism of the New Freedom and the Great Crusade, but it did not answer the shrewd, practical—and more narrowly selfish—arguments of his isolationist opponents. He did not meet his foes on their own ground because his vision reached so far beyond them. There was no clear demonstration in terms the common people could understand why the United States should surrender its freedom of action to bulwark his noble conception of world peace and security. Whether anything Wilson might have said would have inspired such popular enthusiasm as to force a change in senatorial attitudes may be highly doubtful. His speeches, however, were too lofty in the circumstances of the time—a time of disillusionment and mounting nationalism.

A western tour undertaken in September broke the President's health.

[28] Sept. 5, 1919, *ibid.*, V, 645.
[29] July 10, 1919, *ibid.*, V, 551–552.

The cause for which he fought lost its one great leader. There was no letup, however, in the attacks made either against Wilson or against the Wilson League. "He has had his say," Colonel Harvey wrote bluntly after the stricken President's return. "He has shot his bolt. He has done his worst. He is no more to be considered. Now let the Senate act." [30]

Within little more than a month it had. The treaty was defeated both with and without reservations—by the decisive votes of 39 to 55 and 38 to 53. The United States had renounced the great effort, for which it had itself provided the leadership in the person of Woodrow Wilson, to substitute for the rivalries and military alliances of the past a new system of collective security. In spite of its world war experience, it was prepared to fall back upon isolationism.

This was not quite the end—although it was clearly forecast. The treaty's friends were determined to keep up the struggle for ratification. And they were able to marshal sufficient support to induce the Senate to make one more effort to find a reasonable compromise on reservations on which both moderate Republicans and moderate Democrats could agree.

It was again to prove impossible. Other factors of course entered the situation, but perhaps more than anything else the coldly hostile attitude of Lodge, more concerned with political advantage than national interest, and Wilson's reaffirmed refusal to make any further compromise, were now the decisive barriers to any accommodation of conflicting senatorial views. There had been at all times a majority apparently willing to approve the treaty with moderate reservations— for only the Borah-led irreconcilables had taken a stand against League membership under any circumstances—but no way was found to agree on such reservations and then change this simple majority into the necessary two thirds majority. [31]

At the end Wilson stood almost by himself, a lonely, ill, and deserted figure. He would not give in. On March 8, 1920, he wrote his Democratic followers in the Senate: "Either we should enter the League fearlessly, accepting the responsibility and not fearing the role

---

[30] *Harvey's Weekly,* II (Oct. 4, 1919), 1–3.

[31] Whether acceptance of the Lodge reservations would merely have inspired additional reservations, whether their author would in any circumstances have accepted the League, are unanswerable questions. For a strong defense of Lodge's position, see comments by his grandson, Henry Cabot Lodge, in John A. Garraty, *Henry Cabot Lodge* (New York, 1953), p. 358, n.

of leadership which we now enjoy, contributing our efforts toward establishing a just and permanent peace, or we should retire as gracefully as possible from the great concert of powers by which the world was saved." [32] In these circumstances the final vote on the Treaty of Versailles—49 yeas to 35 nays—fell just seven votes short of the required number.

The proponents of League membership still refused to accept final defeat or to believe that their cause was permanently lost. They clung to the hope that in the forthcoming presidential election, whose long shadow had stretched out over the entire debate, the American people might declare themselves so clearly in favor of the rejected League that the question could be revived. Wilson had already called for a great popular referendum; he insisted that League membership be made the paramount issue of the campaign.

Any hope of such a referendum, however, was illusory. In no election in American history has foreign policy been sufficiently disentangled from domestic problems to afford a clear-cut mandate for any proposed course of action. That of 1920 was no more an exception to this generalization than the 1900 campaign had been. Indeed, the foreign policy issue was hopelessly confused, in addition to being pushed into the background. While the Democrats called for ratification of the Versailles Treaty without reservations which would impair its essential integrity, and their candidate, James M. Cox, stood foursquare on the League, the Republicans successfully played things both ways to the complete bafflement of many voters.

As the Republican presidential nominee, Warren Gamaliel Harding took a strong enough stand against the League to retain the support of the irreconcilables; at the same time, by vaguely promising some other approach to international cooperation, he kept in line those Republicans who felt the United States should not sacrifice its world leadership. He stated that he was not interested in clarifying our international responsibilities—"It is not interpretation but rejection that I am seeking"—and at the same time he called for the establishment of an "association of nations" based on justice rather than force.[33] While Borah supported the Republican nominee as an isolationist, an influential group including Hughes, Hoover, Root, and Stimson declared

---

[32] *Congressional Record,* LIX, 66th Congress, 2nd Session (Mar. 8, 1920), p. 4052.

[33] *The New York Times,* July 23, Oct. 8, Oct. 9, Oct. 25, 1920, quoted in Bartlett, *The League to Enforce Peace,* pp. 181, 182.

Harding's election would be the best way to advance international cooperation. The partisanship that had so directly affected the Senate debates engulfed foreign policy even more completely, and left the League issue to be decided by default rather than through any positive expression of well-considered opinion.

Whatever the actual views of Republican voters on foreign policy, the triumphant Harding, swept into office by a popular vote of 16,152,000 to 9,147,000, promptly interpreted his victory as a popular mandate for rejecting membership in either the existing League or any other international association. His own personal convictions, so far as they were discoverable through the hazy fog of earlier statements, had always leaned toward isolationism. Now there was no need for further equivocation: the votes were all counted.

The United States was ready at all times to associate with other nations for conference and counsel, Harding declared in his Inaugural Address. It would continue to seek world disarmament and to promote the processes of arbitration and mediation. In pursuing such ends, however, every commitment had to be made in the exercise of national sovereignty, rather than through a world supergovernment which was "contrary to everything we cherish and can have no sanction by our Republic." He recognized the new position the United States held in the world, but denied that it called for any such change in foreign policy as one whereby "internationality was to supersede nationality." The nation had spoken: "We turned to a referendum, to the American people. There was ample discussion, and there is a public mandate in manifest understanding." [34]

The continued acceptance of isolationist doctrine would appear to go far toward justifying Harding's interpretation of the election. The advocates of League membership dwindled away in the 1920's; nothing more was heard of any new association of nations. Little opposition was voiced when the United States withdrew still further from European affairs. There was general endorsement—if never completely universal approval—of the reaffirmed principle that the United States should studiously refrain from any international agreement that could possibly be construed as an alliance. The experience of the war was unhappily forgotten. Eventually, even participation in the Allied

[34] *Supplement to Messages of the Presidents, 1921–1925* (Washington, 1925), p. 8942.

struggle against Germany would be considered by many Americans to have been a grave mistake.[35]

The battle which League membership symbolized had been won by adherents of the old tradition forever associated with the names of Washington and Jefferson and Monroe. The further concentration of world power in America, so greatly accelerated by the war, was not to be accompanied by any commensurate assumption of the new obligations that such power entailed. The United States was as always ready to exercise its moral influence in promoting peace, but it refused to make any commitment for more active support of collective security. The nation was still following the path that had been marked out when it was weak and struggling, without realizing that in its maturity such a course was no longer defensible.

For Wilson, who had envisaged a new international order in which America would play her full part in defending the principles of freedom and justice, who believed so sincerely that making the spiritual power of democracy prevail was "surely the manifest destiny of the United States," [36] this was final defeat.

From the depths of his disillusionment he sadly commented that America had repudiated a "fruitful leadership for a barren independence. The people will have to learn now by bitter experience just what they have lost. . . . We had a chance to gain the leadership of the world. We have lost it, and soon we shall be witnessing the tragedy of it all." [37]

[35] See later discussion of popular attitudes in the 1930's.

[36] Annual Message, 1920. *Public Papers of Woodrow Wilson*, VI, 514.

[37] Joseph P. Tumulty, *Woodrow Wilson as I Knew Him* (New York, 1921), pp. 501–502.

CHAPTER 7

Giant of the Western World

ALTHOUGH the nation may have sought to withdraw after the election of 1920 into a new isolationism, this shuffling off of international responsibility did not mean a parallel loss of influence. America's rise to pre-eminent world power had been graphically demonstrated by its decisive intervention in the war and its dominant role at the peace conference. As in every instance in which it has engaged in war, the nation had emerged from the conflict of 1917–18 far stronger than it had been when it entered. The implications of its new power could not be brushed aside by President Harding's strictures against "internationality."

Woodrow Wilson may have thought primarily in terms of moral influence for the realization of his idealistic peace aims, but he had by no means been insensible of material factors. He had been confident, at Paris, that the powerful position the United States had attained would persuade the stricken and devastated countries of Europe to follow wherever he led. And in urging American membership in the League of Nations, he had spoken of this country's role as that of a senior partner: "The financial leadership will be ours. The industrial primacy will be ours. The commercial advantage will be ours. The other countries of the world are looking to us for leadership and direction." [1] What Theodore Roosevelt had envisaged some years earlier— the United States playing the dominant role in the balance of world power—was more than ever an indisputable fact.

[1] Aug. 5, 1919, R. S. Baker and W. E. Dodd, *The Public Papers of Woodrow Wilson* (6 vols., New York, 1925–27), V, 640.

The sinews of American strength remained natural resources, the technique of industrial technology, and the dynamic drive of an enterprising and vigorous people. This was not all, however. Wartime demand had immensely speeded up the processes of invention and production; the world-wide interruption of trade had enabled American business to develop new foreign markets, and the financial capital of the world had shifted from London to New York. Rarely if ever in all history has a country risen so rapidly to economic pre-eminence as did the United States in the period from 1914 to 1919.[2] Moreover, it was the one nation that faced the postwar world with the certain promise of still further economic advance.

Its basic resources could be approximately measured. In 1920, the United States produced nearly 40 per cent of the world's coal, or more than twice that of its nearest rival, Great Britain; a somewhat larger proportion of the world's production of pig iron; and nearly 70 per cent of all crude petroleum. Its wealth in other raw materials, including lumber and agricultural crops, was immense. While it lacked certain products—rubber; some strategic metals, such as manganese, chromite, and tungsten; and the tropical or semitropical crops of coffee, tea, and sugar—it was nevertheless more nearly self-sufficient than any other country.

As the decade advanced, its position as the leading commercial and financial nation would be consolidated. The United States accounted for nearly 16 per cent of world exports, and with approximately 12 per cent of total imports was second only to Great Britain in this branch of trade. Its industrial production was even more impressive. In the latter part of the 1920's, the value of American manufactures was nearly half that of the world total—an estimated 46 per cent— and far exceeded that of any possible rival. In terms of national income, further statistics equated the total for the United States, in 1929, with the aggregate total for twenty-three other leading nations, including the United Kingdom, Germany, France, Canada, and Japan.[3]

Even more striking was the financial position of the United States.

[2] Raymond F. Mikesell, *United States Economic Policy and International Relations* (New York, 1952), p. 7.

[3] United States Department of Commerce, Bureau of Foreign and Domestic Commerce, *Commerce Yearbook*, 1930 (2 vols., Washington, 1930), II, 648, 650, 677; *The United States in the World Economy*, Economic Series No. 23 (Washington, 1943), pp. 28, 29.

Here wartime developments had not so much accentuated an earlier trend as in the case of foreign trade, production, and national income, but had rather brought about a complete reversal in the country's prewar position. A debtor nation with outstanding obligations, amounting to $3.7 billion on net balance in 1914, had become five years later a creditor nation which was owed $12.5 billion. Some $10 billion of this figure represented war debts but the account of nongovernmental items on the international balance sheet showed that such assets had approximately doubled while liabilities were nearly cut in half. By the close of the 1920's, additional foreign loans and direct investments had built up net assets on private account to over $8 billion.[4]

These developments meant that the United States was, almost in spite of itself, playing the decisive world-wide role in economic and financial matters. It was in large measure financing the rehabilitation of Europe through gifts and loans. Huge sums were spent in relief and reconstruction by both public and private agencies; extensive advances were made to enable Germany, France, and Italy to stabilize their currencies. Other loans were extended to local governmental units, public utilities, and private corporations. The United States was aiding in the construction of railroads in Poland, harbors in Yugoslavia, and housing developments in Austria. There was comparable activity—foreshadowing the still more extensive operations of the 1940's and 1950's—in other parts of the world. Funds were made available for digging new oil wells in the Middle East, planting rubber in Malaya and the Dutch East Indies, establishing sugar plantations in Cuba, and developing public utilities in Tokyo and Shanghai.

So far as direct investments were concerned, the overseas branches of American manufacturing companies and commercial establishments ringed the globe. Automobile assembly plants on the Continent, five-and-ten-cent stores in England, refineries in the Caribbean, trading firms in China, were but a few examples of industrial America abroad. The roster of companies engaged in such activity was a roll call of big business: Standard Oil, General Motors, the Ford Company, International Business Machines, Singer Sewing Machine, International Harvester.

There was even considerable economic exchange with Soviet Russia. Although the United States withheld diplomatic recognition until

[4] Cleona Lewis, *America's Stake in International Investments* (Washington, 1938), pp. 447, 450; George Soule, *Prosperity Decade*, Vol. 8 in *The Economic History of the United States* (New York, 1947), pp. 252–255.

1933, business was not dissuaded from seeking new markets. General Electric sold millions of dollars of electrical equipment to the Bolsheviks, Standard Oil and Vacuum Oil had Russian contracts, the Ford Company aided in establishing a Soviet automobile industry, American technical assistance helped build the great Dneprostroi Dam, and the American Locomotive Company did business with Stalin.[5]

The shift from a debtor to a creditor nation with such expansive overseas interests and holdings had a significance not always appreciated at the time. In the money markets of the world, as in those of trade and commerce, the policies followed by the United States called the tune. Other capitals necessarily looked to New York and Washington as they tried to work out their own financial and economic problems. Nevertheless the United States made little effort to develop a broad-scale program that took such considerations into account. The retreat from international cooperation was quite as emphatic in this sphere as in that of political relations. In defiance of the realities of international exchange and the demonstrable advantages of a more cooperative policy, the United States continued throughout the 1920's to insist on payment of the war debts and to maintain a high tariff policy. The economic nationalism of this era was to have fully as grave consequences as political isolationism.

The total of loans extended to the Allies, during the war and after the armistice, was in round numbers $10,350 billion. Through settlements primarily based on ability to pay, the period for discharge of all such indebtedness was extended over some sixty-two years, with an average interest rate scaled down to 2.1 per cent. These were generous terms. However, the United States persistently refused to recognize any connection between Germany's reparation payments and Allied payments to the United States. The inability of the Allies to collect from Germany consequently led to the ultimate breakdown of the entire program. President Hoover was compelled, in 1931, to declare a moratorium on all intergovernmental payments, and it was to prove impossible thereafter ever to renew them on either the reparations or war debts accounts.[6]

The American tariff policy was even more inimical to world eco-

[5] Foster Rhea Dulles, *The Road to Teheran: The Story of Russia and America, 1781–1943* (Princeton, 1944), pp. 184–186.

[6] For general discussion, see H. G. Moulton and Leo Pasvolsky, *War Debts and World Prosperity* (Washington, 1932); Benjamin H. Williams, *Economic Foreign Policy of the United States* (New York, 1929), pp. 217–242.

nomic stability than the policy on war debts. Import duties were promptly raised following the war and the Fordney-McCumber tariff of 1922 imposed the highest average rates in the country's history. Eight years later they were again stepped up. The average incorporated in the Hawley-Smoot tariff of 1930 was no less than 40 per cent. Some thirty-four foreign countries strongly protested this action, and after passage of the law many of them were driven to retaliatory action to safeguard their own economies. The Hawley-Smoot tariff was in no small measure responsible for an almost world-wide increase in tariff rates, import quotas, exchange restrictions, and other impediments to the international flow of goods and services.[7]

A committee of one thousand economic experts—and one thousand economic experts are rarely in agreement on anything—strongly protested against the dangerous implications of this raising of the American tariff wall.[8] They pointed out that the European nations could not obtain the exchange for meeting war debt payments and for buying in the American market unless they were able to sell to the United States, and emphasized the shortsightedness of trying to solve this dilemma by a policy of making further loans to Europe which would only increase a burden that the debtor nations could not sustain. Nevertheless President Hoover brushed aside the experts' report, and the United States continued on its way.

The consequent curtailment of world trade coincided with other economic dislocations that were unsettling the delicate balance of international payments. American foreign loans and investments—apart from the war debts—thereupon largely collapsed under the devastating impact of what was becoming a global depression. Economic insecurity was added to political insecurity in paving the way for another war.

The dire effects of this economic nationalism can hardly be exaggerated. The United States controlled so much of the world's material wealth and industrial production, so great a proportion of international trade, and such a large share of world capital resources that American policy could not fail to have decisive consequences in every part of the globe—whether the money markets of Europe, the trading centers of the Middle East, the commerce of Asia. In the final analysis,

[7] Percy Wells Bidwell, *Tariff Policy of the United States: A Study of Recent Experience* (New York, 1933).
[8] *The New York Times*, May 5, 1930.

the basis for this pervasive influence was found in the cold, hard, indisputable facts of economic and financial dominance.

There was not only a continental America. The United States was still an empire, and its outlying possessions and spheres of political influence, as well as its own domain, importantly affected its world position. It is true that the Philippines had no more than been taken under the American wing than there began what was in effect a long, slow, steady retreat from the imperialism of 1900. Still, the United States retained possessions directly extending its influence southward into Latin America and westward to the shores of Asia. It was supreme on a continent, and dominant over the broad reaches of the Pacific.

As one of the first overseas colonies, Puerto Rico had gradually acquired an increasing measure of self-government since its acquisition from Spain. The powers of the legislative assembly had been steadily broadened and, through a new organic act in 1917, an elective upper house replaced an appointed council. Puerto Rican citizens were also made citizens of the United States and given their own Bill of Rights. In time the appointment of the governor gave way to his popular election, and finally, in 1950, the way was cleared for a new Puerto Rican constitution which would make the island completely self-governing. Two years later its status became that of a free, associated commonwealth.[9]

Of even greater strategic importance in the Caribbean area—and indeed of significance only on this account—were the Virgin Islands and the Panama Canal Zone. The former was the one new overseas possession secured since the opening of the century. The islands were finally purchased from Denmark, after a long history of unsuccessful negotiations, in 1916.[10] At first under the Navy Department, they were in 1931 transferred to the Department of the Interior. The Canal Zone had of course been under American control since 1903, and was administered directly by the President through the War Department.

The control over the Caribbean established by these outright possessions was strengthened by other elements of power. The United States had an important naval base in Cuba and still maintained the right of intervention in that country; the Republic of Panama, Nica-

[9] Julius W. Pratt, *America's Colonial Experiment* (New York, 1950), pp. 188–190, 281–283; *United States Statutes at Large,* LXIV, Part I, pp. 319–320.
[10] Charles Callan Tansill, *The Purchase of the Danish West Indies* (Baltimore, 1932), pp. 454–516, Appendices, pp. 517–537.

ragua, Haiti, and the Dominican Republic were virtual protectorates. By the close of the 1920's, the United States was preparing to give up most of these special privileges and the treaty right to intervene in Cuba was abrogated in 1934. The American position in the Caribbean was not materially weakened by such concessions, however. The little republics in this area remained within the American sphere of influence, and the power of the United States in the Western Hemisphere could hardly be disputed.[11]

In the Pacific, the defense perimeter of the United States was a line that ran from the tip of the Aleutian Islands through Hawaii to the Panama Canal Zone. The value of Alaska and the Aleutians—Seward had called the latter "this drawbridge between America and Asia, these stepping stones across the Pacific Ocean"—had increased immensely with the passage of time. Brigadier General William Mitchell was to express the view, in 1935, that air power would ultimately make Alaska the most strategic place in all the globe—"I think whoever holds Alaska will hold the world." [12] If the developments of the Second World War did not entirely substantiate this prediction, they were greatly to emphasize Alaska's importance.

Among the nation's island possessions in the Pacific, Hawaii was most closely and intimately bound to the mainland. Neither its strategic nor economic importance had been questioned since it had been taken over during the Spanish-American War. Hawaii's status, like that of Alaska, was that of an "incorporated territory" and the islands were clearly destined for eventual statehood.[13] Guam and American Samoa, the latter acquired through treaty in 1899, were distant outposts administered by the Navy, and almost completely forgotten by the American people.[14]

Far and away the most significant and troublesome of all overseas possessions were the Philippine Islands. The high promise held out for their role in giving the United States both naval and commercial supremacy in the Pacific had not been fulfilled. The feeling had grown with successive years that they could not be defended in case of attack; experience had shown that they were of no significant value in the

[11] American policy in the Caribbean is usefully summarized in J. Fred Rippy, *The Caribbean Danger Zone* (New York, 1940).

[12] Quoted in Dulles, *The Road to Teheran*, pp. 76–77.

[13] Pratt, *America's Colonial Experiment*, pp. 178–239.

[14] See Earl S. Pomeroy, *Pacific Outpost, American Strategy in Guam and Micronesia* (Stanford, 1931).

development of trade with eastern Asia. The tremendous cost, in both lives and money, of subduing the Filipino revolt against American rule at the turn of the century had been an important factor leading to the popular revulsion against imperialism.[15]

From the outset it had been the declared intention of the United States to give the Filipinos the largest possible measure of self-government and to prepare them for ultimate independence. They had been granted an elective legislature in the organic act of 1902, and in the ensuing years steady progress was made along the road to self-government. It was greatly accelerated during the Wilson administration. The Jones Act of 1916 specifically stated that independence would be granted as soon as a stable government could be established. This trend was for a time interrupted with the return of the Republicans to office in 1921, but the persistent demand of the Filipinos for freedom was now matched by a rising sentiment in Congress that it should no longer be postponed.

A measure providing independence after a ten-year transition period was finally passed in 1932. However, it was vetoed by President Hoover, and, when re-enacted over his opposition, rejected by the Filipinos themselves. They maintained that the proposed retention of American naval and military bases in the islands would infringe upon their sovereignty. This proved to be only a temporary setback. In 1934, another independence bill—the Tydings-McDuffie Act—only slightly modifying the provisions of the previous measure, was passed by Congress, signed by President Roosevelt, and accepted by the Filipinos. During the next year, a constitution was drawn up and a new government organized. The islands were to be a semiautonomous commonwealth until July 4, 1946, and then become the Philippine Republic. In spite of occupation by Japan during the Second World War, this program was carried out. After liberation by American forces, the Philippines became fully independent on the date originally set.[16]

The movement for Filipino freedom did not derive its real strength from an idealistic determination on the part of the American people to fulfill their pledges. It was the end result of the powerful pressure exerted upon Congress in the early 1930's by certain farm and labor

[15] See Garel A. Grunder and William E. Livezey, *The Philippines and the United States* (Norman, Oklahoma, 1951).

[16] *Ibid.*, pp. 195 ff. For the text of the Tydings-McDuffie Act, see most conveniently Henry Steele Commager, *Documents in American History* (New York, 1950), pp. 467–471.

groups which wanted to see the Philippines free so that they could set up more complete barriers against competing Filipino products and cheap Filipino labor. It was the American Farm Bureau Federation, the National Dairy Union, the National Grange, and the American Federation of Labor that, for their own economic benefit, provided the impetus to carry out a promise that had originally been based on democratic and humanitarian ideals.

The Hoover administration had opposed independence on the double ground that the Filipinos were not yet fully prepared for complete self-government, and that their immediate freedom would have a dangerously unsettling effect on international relations in the Pacific. Congressional advocates of independence hardly bothered to discuss such aspects of the situation. The old contest between imperialists and anti-imperialists, centering on freedom and democracy, was almost completely forgotten as Congress debated about tariff-free sugar, coconut oil, tobacco, cordage, and immigrant labor. There were a number of men in both the Senate and the House who were acting upon conviction in their belief that the United States should fulfill its independence pledges to the Filipinos. The militant farm and labor groups, concerned only with the promotion of the economic interests they represented, nevertheless dominated the situation.[17]

American policy toward the Philippines had been curiously paradoxical. Their people had been encouraged to seek independence through careful tutelage in self-government, and at the same time economic policy had tied the islands so closely to the continental United States as to fasten upon them a new dependence. This was a very real problem, but the public was largely oblivious of it. There was very little interest in the Philippines, and no popular desire whatsoever to keep them under American control or to continue any longer as a colonial power. It could be argued that while the old political imperialism was dead, it had been replaced by a new economic imperialism. Even this was dubious. The new policy, in any event, was a far cry from the ambitious visions of the Roosevelts, Lodges, Mahans, and Beveridges of 1900.[18]

[17] Grunder and Livezey, *The Philippines and the United States,* pp. 196–200, 209–210; Pratt, *America's Colonial Experiment,* 301–304.

[18] An interesting illustration of changed attitudes was the proposal of Henry Cabot Lodge, grandson of the most vigorous exponent of acquisition of the Philippines, that the islands might be turned over to Germany. "Our Failure in the Philippines," *Harper's Magazine,* CLX (January, 1930), 209–218. See also Julius W. Pratt, "Collapse of American Imperialism," *American Mercury,* XXXI (March, 1934), 269–278.

A further development in building up world power which had paralleled the overseas expansion of the turn of the century was the growth of the American Navy. The implications of that control of the seas which Mahan had emphasized so strongly continued to have great significance in a world of international rivalry. The rise of the United States to a position where it could challenge England's naval supremacy was of the utmost importance. If economic strength was the fundamental basis for the influence wielded by this country, its most concrete expression in strategic terms was the American Navy.

Thanks largely to Theodore Roosevelt's strenuous efforts, the fleet had grown steadily in the early 1900's. But while a strong continental base, and the naval stations in Cuba and Hawaii, enabled the United States wholly to control the Caribbean and the eastern Pacific, it could not hope with its existing Navy to exert any such leverage in world politics as that at the command of Great Britain. The war had been responsible, however, for a tremendous upsurge of navalism. When the Naval Appropriation Act of 1916 specifically set forth the goal of "a navy second to none," England's historic command of the seas was doomed.[19]

The actual fleet-in-being, for all the construction of the war years, had still not caught up with the British Navy when hostilities came to an end in November, 1918. It included sixteen battleships aggregating four hundred thousand tons, but England had thirty-three battleships and nine battle cruisers with a displacement of nearly a million tons. This, however, was only part of the story. When vessels authorized or under construction were taken into consideration, the United States forged ahead. While England had only four new battleships under way, this country had thirteen, including ten "superdreadnoughts," and an additional six battle cruisers. If the new program were continued, the United States within a few years, probably by 1925, would have a battle line superior to that of Great Britain in almost every respect. Moreover the future plans of the Navy Department went even beyond this. As presented to Congress in December, 1918, they called for a Navy whose over-all combat strength would eventually add up to thirty-nine battleships and twelve battle cruisers—far beyond anything planned or conceived by British naval authorities.[20]

[19] H. and M. Sprout, *Toward a New Order of Sea Power; American Naval Policy and the World Scene, 1918–1922* (Princeton, 1940), pp. 21–22, 36.

[20] Statistics from War and Navy Departments, *Joint Army and Navy Action in Coast Defense* (1920), and report of Navy General Board (Feb. 2, 1921) in

President Wilson, in spite of his earlier lack of interest in the Navy, supported these ambitious plans. The United States had started on a building program and it would clearly be unwise, he told Congress, to attempt to adjust it "to a future world policy as yet undetermined." [21] He was thinking of the League of Nations. Perhaps his compelling reason for backing naval expansion was to have some bargaining power in trying to win British acceptance for a League of Nations that would acknowledge the Monroe Doctrine.

His advisors were more concerned with American naval power in its own right. Should the peace conference fail, one policy statement said, the United States should bend its energies, its money, all its will, to creating "incomparably the greatest navy in the world." Secretary Daniels related this goal to the nation's world mission. If the United States were to fulfill its "destiny as a leader of democratic impulse," he stated, it should be "incomparably strong in defense against aggressors and in offense against evil-doers." [22]

Even if a league should undertake to safeguard international security, the big-Navy advocates believed that the program of expansion should be continued. Their new theory appeared to be, as advanced in a memorandum forwarded to President Wilson by Admiral Benson, that while the American Navy could always be counted upon to uphold collective sanctions against an aggressor nation, there could be no certainty that Great Britain would follow such a course. Consequently, the United States should have a Navy at least equal to that of Great Britain to enforce sanctions in the interests of world peace.[23]

When agreement had been reached with England on League issues, Wilson was himself willing to consider naval limitation. Administration support was withdrawn from the pending appropriation bill, and future plans were put on a short-term basis in the revised naval estimates for 1919–20. Wilson's tactic now was to combat the anti-League forces with the threat that far greater appropriations would be necessary unless the United States joined the new League of Nations and supported collective security.[24]

House Naval Committee, 66th Congress, 3rd Session, *Hearings on Sundry Legislation, 1920–21*, pp. 952 ff., as summarized in Sprout, pp. 49–53.

[21] Dec. 2, 1918, *Public Papers of Woodrow Wilson*, V, 318.

[22] *The New York Times*, Dec. 31, 1918, quoted in Sprout, *Toward a New Order of Sea Power*, p. 56.

[23] Letter from Admiral Benson, Apr. 7, 1919, in Ray Stannard Baker, *Woodrow Wilson and World Settlement* (3 vols., New York, 1922), III, 214–216.

[24] *Ibid.*, III, 379–392; Josephus Daniels, *The Wilson Era: Years of War and*

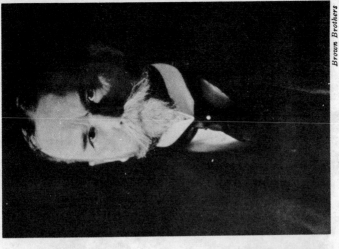

3. JOHN HAY

2. HENRY CABOT LODGE

1. ALFRED THAYER MAHAN

THREE IMPERIALISTS OF THE TURN OF THE CENTURY

4. PRESIDENT McKINLEY and the then VICE PRESIDENT THEODORE ROOSEVELT

Brown Brothers *Brown Brothers*

5. ELIHU ROOT 6. PHILANDER C. KNOX

FOUR SECRETARIES OF STATE

7. WILLIAM JENNINGS BRYAN 8. ROBERT LANSING

Brown Brothers *Brown Brothers*

9. The "Big Four" at the Paris Peace Conference. Left to right, Lloyd George, Italy's Orlando, Clemenceau of France and President Wilson

10. Premier Clemenceau inviting the Germans to sign the Treaty of Versailles

11. SECRETARY OF STATE
CHARLES EVANS HUGHES

Brown Brothers

12. SECRETARY KELLOGG signing the Kellogg-Briand Anti-War Treaty

Brown Brothers

Underwood & Underwood

13. PRESIDENT HOOVER with his outgoing and incoming Secretaries of State, FRANK B. KELLOGG (left) and HENRY L. STIMSON

14. The isolationists confer: SEN-
ATORS HIRAM JOHNSON, ARTHUR
VANDENBERG and WILLIAM E.
BORAH

15. PRESIDENT ROOSEVELT and
SECRETARY HULL on former's return to Washington to meet European crisis, August 24, 1939

16. PRESIDENT ROOSEVELT signing declaration of war on Japan, December 8, 1941

17. Signing the Four Power Pact in Moscow, November 11, 1943. Seated, left to right, China's AMBASSADOR FU PIN-SHEUNG, SECRETARY OF STATE CORDELL HULL, FOREIGN MINISTER MOLOTOV and FOREIGN SECRETARY ANTHONY EDEN

18. PRESIDENT ROOSEVELT and PRIME MINISTER CHURCHILL at Casablanca, January 29, 1943

19. PREMIER STALIN, PRESIDENT ROOSEVELT and PRIME MINISTER CHURCH-
ILL at Teheran, November, 1943

20. GENERALISSIMO CHIANG KAI-SHEK, PRESIDENT ROOSEVELT, PRIME MIN-
ISTER CHURCHILL and MADAM CHIANG KAI-SHEK at Cairo, November, 1943

Brown Brothers

21. PRIME MINISTER CHURCHILL, PRESIDENT ROOSEVELT and PREMIER STALIN at Yalta, February, 1945

22. PRIME MINISTER ATTLEE, PRESIDENT TRUMAN and PREMIER STALIN at Potsdam, July, 1945

Brown Brothers

23. SECRETARY OF STATE JAMES F. BYRNES

24. SECRETARY OF STATE GEORGE C. MARSHALL

25. PRESIDENT TRUMAN, SECRETARY OF STATE STETTINIUS and FIELD MARSHAL SMUTS at the San Francisco Conference, 1945

26. PRESIDENT TRUMAN with his new SECRETARY OF STATE DEAN ACHESON, January, 1949

27. PREMIER YOSHIDA signs Japanese-American Security Pact; JOHN FOSTER DULLES and SECRETARY OF STATE DEAN ACHESON look on, September 8, 1951

28. The "Big Three" meet German CHANCELLOR KONRAD ADENAUER in Bonn, May 24, 1952, preparatory to signing the Allied-Germany Peace Contract. Left to right, British FOREIGN MINISTER ANTHONY EDEN, CHANCELLOR ADENAUER, SECRETARY OF STATE DEAN ACHESON and French FOREIGN MINISTER ROBERT SCHUMAN

29. SECRETARY OF STATE JOHN FOSTER DULLES and MUTUAL SECURITY ADMINISTRATOR HAROLD E. STASSEN report to PRESIDENT EISENHOWER following their fact-finding trip to Europe

30. Two members of the Indian Repatriation Commission lead a group of Korean prisoners of war to a processing center

31. Red Chinese PREMIER CHOU EN-LAI (left) at the Geneva Conference, April 26, 1954. Behind the Chinese delegation can be seen ANDREI GROMYKO and Soviet FOREIGN MINISTER MOLOTOV

32. PRESIDENT EISENHOWER bids SIR WINSTON CHURCHILL good-by at the end of the latter's visit to Washington in June, 1954

The American people were not persuaded that the choice was either a tremendous Navy or the League. With the destruction of the German fleet, they did not really fear for national security, even though the rising power of Japan in the Pacific meant that America could not afford to lower her guard too much. At least the public did not believe a Navy superior to that of Great Britain was essential. The attitude of both Congress and the press reflected in some measure partisan disapproval of any program recommended by a Democratic administration; it was also influenced by a revived opposition to militarism in a world supposedly made safe for democracy. Most importantly, it registered the emphatic national desire to reduce government expenditures and government taxation.

This attitude blocked the naval expansion originally planned, and finally induced the Harding administration, at first very Navy-minded, to summon the Washington Conference for the Limitation of Armaments. Such developments did not entirely invalidate, however, the premise which had been accepted in 1916. The United States might not feel it necessary to outbuild Great Britain, but it was still to have "a navy second to none."

Now that America had become so much stronger in so many ways— and perhaps just because of such strength—there seemed to be a compelling urge to maintain at least naval parity. It was derived in part from a conception of power for its own sake. Even though an economy-minded nation was inclined strictly to limit appropriations, the feeling was almost universal that the United States should have a Navy commensurate with its new standing in the world community.

The Washington Conference, as we shall see, importantly affected the whole question of naval policy. In spite of self-imposed restrictions on further expansion, however, the big-Navy issue continued to be debated throughout the 1920's. Strong pressures were exercised by the economic interests that stood to profit from naval construction and by zealous patriotic societies, especially the Navy League, to win support for an American Navy that would outrank all others. Nevertheless the United States failed to maintain even that fleet which was permissible under existing treaties. Its over-all strength fell below that of the British Navy and in the western Pacific the United States was definitely weaker than Japan.[25] Congress could not be spurred to make the

After, 1917–23 (Chapel Hill, N. C., 1946), p. 368; Sprout, *Toward a New Order of Sea Power*, pp. 47–84.

[25] Donald W. Mitchell, *History of the Modern American Navy* (New York, 1946), pp. 276–297.

necessary appropriations. Not until after the complete breakdown of the principle of limitation in the 1930's was construction renewed on any considerable scale.

Less tangible in any evaluation of the position of the United States in the 1920's than any of these concrete expressions of power was the influence exercised abroad through American exports—exports of goods, dollars, personnel, and ideas. In Europe and in a different but no less significant sense in many parts of Asia, the social institutions and cultural values of the United States had a direct impact on the way of life and civilization of other countries. Scores of books and hundreds of magazine articles labored the thesis of America's "invasion of Europe," with foreign contributors to this symposium almost invariably viewing the prospect with considerable alarm.[26]

An expanding foreign trade, promoted with increasing vigor as the decade wore on, spread over the face of the globe the manifold products of American manufacture. Automobiles, bicycles, sewing machines, office equipment, typewriters, and household articles with the stamp "made in the U.S.A." could be found almost everywhere: throughout Europe and the Middle East, in Japan and China, in the Latin American republics, and sometimes deep within the interior of Asia and Africa. They could hardly fail in many instances to bring about far-reaching changes in native mores.

The competition of such imports with European manufactures also had the effect of compelling foreign firms to adopt the mass production and assembly line techniques so successful in the United States. The "rationalization" of production became foreign industry's goal. Japan was especially influenced by the American example; Soviet Russia studied a technological system which was succinctly labeled "Fordismus," and Europe borrowed what it could as its manufacturers looked enviously across the Atlantic.

Many critics assailed our influence along such lines. The battle between what were considered the materialistic ideals of American culture and the spiritual ideals of Europe raged relentlessly. The lines were drawn, as Charles Beard wrote rather sardonically, with "prose against poetry; dollars against sacrifice; calculation against artistic

[26] On this vast subject two pioneer studies (although they do not deal specifically with the 1920's) may be cited: Richard Heathcote Heindel, *The American Impact on Great Britain, 1898–1914* (Philadelphia, 1940), and Halvdan Koht, *The American Spirit in Europe* (Philadelphia, 1949).

abandon." [27] While Beard was very skeptical of the validity of these distinctions, he nevertheless heavily stressed the importance of the export of American products, customs, and ideas in remolding the contemporary world.

From this point of view, overseas investments were in some ways even more significant than foreign trade. In making loans to foreign states and municipalities, public utilities and private firms, American bankers often retained rights of control or supervision. In the case of direct investments in the form of branch factories, assembly plants, or distributing firms owned by American corporations, there was even greater evidence of the authority with which the United States spoke in the world of international business.

This conspicuous display of wealth and power did not make for the most harmonious relations. Europeans were naturally resentful of a nation so rich and powerful that it could greatly influence—almost wilfully it seemed at times—their own economy and their own way of life. The aid that was given toward reconstruction in the immediate postwar period had not endeared the United States to the recipients of its charity, and the concessions made in meeting war debt payments had little meaning in countries where it was firmly believed that those debts, contracted in the common cause of defeating Germany, should have been canceled altogether. The economic power of the world's richest nation was often considered, in the phrase used in the title of one foreign study of American civilization, as a dangerous "menace" to the institutions and way of life of other countries.[28]

Joining the march of American goods and American money by the latter half of the 1920's was a tremendous army of American tourists. They penetrated to every part of Europe, some half a million strong every year, and in lesser numbers went on round-the-world voyages which took them to the countries of the East. The persuasive attraction of their money compelled the host countries to cater to their needs. Businessmen, students, vacationists, alike became salesmen of American culture, introducing ideas and customs which further strengthened the impact of the United States abroad.[29]

[27] Charles A. Beard, "The American Invasion of Europe," *Harper's Magazine*, CLVIII (Mar., 1929), 475.

[28] Georges Duhamel, *America: The Menace* (Boston, 1931).

[29] Hiram Motherwell, "The American Tourist Makes History," *Harper's Magazine*, CLX (Dec., 1929), 70–76; F. P. Miller and H. D. Hill, "Europe as a Playground," *Atlantic Monthly*, CXLVI (Aug., 1930), 226–231; André

"Can Paris Be Retaken by the Parisians?" asked the correspondent of one New York paper in a story sent home during the mid-1920's: "The French claim they cannot walk on the Boulevard St. Germain and hear a word of their native tongue. They claim that the high prices following in the wake of the American visitor are driving them from the best restaurants in Paris. They mourn the days of yesterday and scorn the Americanized Latin Quarter of today." [30]

A great vogue for American movies supplemented other cultural influences. Hollywood was as supreme in western Europe as it was in its homeland, and millions of foreigners made up their minds as to what American civilization was really like by what they saw on the screen. To a degree which could never be accurately measured, but was sufficiently important to be taken very seriously, films made in the United States affected the fashions and customs of aspiring middle-class Europeans in Paris and Rome, Oslo and Berlin, London and Madrid.

Neither administrative facilities for the conduct of foreign policy nor popular concern over foreign issues could be compared with the attributes of national power in the 1920's. As Secretary of Commerce, Herbert Hoover made strenuous efforts to promote trade. He would later write that the experts stationed at his department's fifty-seven foreign offices were "hounds for American sales." The State Department was reorganized. Its diplomatic and consular services were merged, new opportunities and higher rewards provided for career men, and staffs at foreign consulates, ministries, and embassies were considerably expanded. Nevertheless, it could hardly be said that the agencies charged with the direction of American policy, whatever that policy might be, were entirely adequate in terms of the position that the United States actually held. The State Department budget was some $2 million annually; its home personnel about 600 men and women.[31]

The same lag occurred in popular understanding of the needs of a foreign policy. Granted the increased interest in international affairs

---

Siegfried, "Will Europe be Americanized?" *The Yale Review*, XIX (Mar., 1930), 433–446.

[30] New York *Herald Tribune*, Jan. 24, 1926.

[31] *Memoirs of Herbert C. Hoover: Cabinet and Presidency* (New York, 1952), pp. 79–80; Graham H. Stuart, *The Department of State* (New York, 1949), pp. 275, 276, 307.

made evident in newspaper handling of foreign news, magazine articles dealing with such issues, and the many associations that sprang up to educate the public, the American people still did not have a very realistic conception of the kind of world in which they lived, or of the role the United States was playing in that world. The rejection of the League of Nations had first shown their willingness to see the nation withdraw from active participation in international policies. A comparable urge for independent action was demonstrated by popular endorsement of highly nationalistic economic policies. Still further evidence of this same general attitude was revealed in the immigration laws of the 1920's, bringing to a virtual end the role of the United States as the haven for the oppressed of other lands. Political aloofness, high tariffs, and immigration quotas were facets of the same national impulses in rejecting Europe.

By failing to direct the tremendous material power that was theirs toward a constructive internationalism, and by limiting the conscious influence of the United States on world affairs to moral suasion, the American people ignored the inescapable effects of their technology, their money, their prosperity. Nevertheless, these phenomena continued to have direct and important consequences for the rest of the globe.

The United States had become "the real empire of modern civilization," wrote Reinhold Niebuhr, theologian and philosopher, in May, 1930, but it was not by force of arms that it was extending its sway—"our legions are dollars." He thought, however, that the American people were "awkward imperialists," naïvely believing that "it is our virtue rather than our power which the other nations envy." In such circumstances he wondered whether the country could successfully meet the issues raised by expansion overseas. Niebuhr concluded with the perennial question: Would America be able to "develop a political genius equal to the responsibilities thrust upon us by our imperial power?" [32]

[32] Reinhold Niebuhr, "Awkward Imperialists," *Atlantic Monthly*, CXLV (May, 1930), 670–675.

CHAPTER 8

The Ideal and the Real

AMERICAN foreign policy during the 1920's represented a retreat to traditional isolationism, again not in the sense of complete withdrawal from world affairs but of consistent refusal to make any political commitments infringing upon the nation's freedom of action. The internationalism preached by Woodrow Wilson was rejected; participation in any program of collective security carefully avoided. But the American people were prepared to throw the full weight of their moral influence in support of world peace, and energetically promote their own economic interests throughout the globe. The same decade that witnessed continued rejection of membership in either the League of Nations or the World Court saw the United States take the lead in urging disarmament, assume the initiative in the movement for the outlawry of war, and also seek in every possible way to win control over the world's strategic oil reserves, increase foreign investments, and expand trade and commerce.

There was nothing either new or paradoxical in such seeming contradictions. Ever since the turn of the century the United States had perforce played an important role on the international stage, yet even during the war had never agreed to any limitations upon its complete independence. It could only be said, in comparison with the past, that American policy during the 1920's reflected a heightened emphasis on moral and ethical concepts which more than ever ignored the practical political responsibilities inherent in the nation's global position.

As a leading spokesman for this approach to foreign affairs, Senator Borah invariably stated that the United States was always ready to fulfill its obligations to mankind. But the point he constantly stressed was that the nation should always act independently—neither at the bidding nor through the permission of other countries. Arthur H. Vandenberg, at this time editor of the Grand Rapids *Herald* and destined to take over Borah's position as isolationist leader in the Senate, had very much the same ideas. He also believed that the American people should take their full part in world affairs, but in strict observance of the historic tradition that insisted upon "the preservation of our absolute and untrammeled right of self-decision." [1]

This was the isolationism of the 1920's. Its underlying spirit often served to create a distrust of any dealings whatsoever with foreign nations. It affected tariff policies, immigration legislation, the insistence upon war debt payments. It encouraged other strongly nationalistic activities. Within the broad reaches of foreign policy itself, however, isolationism meant no more and no less than the inability of the American people to realize that moral platitudes about peace were no substitute for acceptance of the responsibilities of collective security. [2]

This isolationist attitude, as in earlier periods, derived its strength from various sources. It cannot be attributed to any one factor in the life of the nation, whether political partisanship, Midwest provincialism, conservative or liberal pressure, ethnic considerations, or the influence of any single group of national leaders. Isolationism was a way of thinking that most Americans, to a greater or less degree, continued to accept without bothering very much about what it involved. After the war, wrote the journalist and foreign policy expert, Frank H.

---

[1] William E. Borah, "American Foreign Policy in a Nationalistic World," *Foreign Affairs*, XII (Jan., 1934), Supplement; Arthur H. Vandenberg, *The Trail of a Tradition* (New York, 1926), p. 314.

[2] The debate over "isolationism" in the years between the two world wars largely turns—as it always has—on the interpretation of this confusing label. In such a study, for example, as William Appleman Williams, "The Legend of Isolationism in the 1920's," *Science and Society*, XVIII (Winter, 1954), 1–20, the writer bases his entire thesis on the theory that the foreign relations of the United States in this period "were marked by express and extended involvement with—and intervention in the affairs of—other nations of the world." This was of course true. But if isolationism is interpreted as it was by the isolationists themselves—freedom from any binding political commitments— then American policy during these years remained basically isolationist. A far more active participation in world affairs than in prewar days does not invalidate the fundamental point that the United States expressly rejected the collective security advocated by internationalists. The extensive literature on this subject—contemporary comment and historical monographs—is discussed in the Bibliography.

Simonds, the people "returned to their accustomed practices and to their familiar conceptions . . . That return was due to instinct rather than intellect . . ." [3]

The situation in 1919 had given isolationism an unusual partisan aspect, as the bitter struggle over the League of Nations had so clearly shown, and this political division over foreign policy was in some measure to continue throughout the 1920's. Although the ranks of both parties were actually divided, the Republicans' opposition to internationalism remained a potent force. Their earlier tradition was expansive and interventionist. Support for imperialism, Theodore Roosevelt's conception of world power, and the backing of party leaders, including Lodge, for the original League to Enforce Peace all served to suggest that, politically, the Republicans should have urged a more responsible approach to foreign affairs. But this was not generally the case.

Toward the Far East a rather different attitude prevailed and much has been made of the seemingly paradoxical policy of the United States, largely under such Republican influence, in following one course in Europe and quite another in Asia. "The dichotomy of our active, 'interventionist' policy in the Far East and our passive, 'isolationist' policy toward Europe," Edward Mead Earle has written, "is an enigma and a paradox." [4] Yet so far as the Republicans are concerned, and perhaps public opinion as a whole, this may perhaps be explained by the political heritage of 1900. The early interests of the Republicans in trade expansion throughout the Pacific area, and also in missionary enterprise among the peoples of China and Japan, provided the basis for a continuing concern over the American position in Asia. And among Midwest Republicans, traditionally suspicious of Great Britain, an attitude typified in its most extreme form by the fulminations of the Chicago *Tribune,* there was a further reason to look favorably on an active Far Eastern policy. So far as it countered British pretensions to predominant influence in Asia, it could command support that the isolationists would never extend to any interventionist European program that involved Anglo-American cooperation.

In spite of such apparent contradictions or divisions within the ranks,

[3] Frank H. Simonds, *American Foreign Policy in the Post-War Years* (Baltimore, 1935), p. 152.

[4] Edward Mead Earle, "A Half Century of American Foreign Policy," *Political Science Quarterly,* LXIV (June, 1949), 172.

however, the Republican party remained basically isolationist in its general approach to foreign affairs. While its interest in the exercise of American influence in the Pacific continued to stand out in sharp contrast with the policy of withdrawal from Europe, even in this part of the world there was a firm determination to avoid any binding obligations. The Republicans actually had no more idea of limiting the nation's freedom of action in eastern Asia than of doing so in Europe.

Isolationism was undoubtedly strengthened by Midwest provincialism. The French traveler André Siegfried noted an entirely different point of view in the Mississippi Valley as compared with that in either the East or on the Pacific coast.[5] There had been some half dozen senators from eastern states among the little band of "irreconcilables" in 1919, but Midwest congressmen were almost a unit in their opposition to the League. This attitude continued to be reflected in their votes on analogous issues, and as a group they showed little enthusiasm for an active foreign policy.

Yet the fact remains that the attitude toward foreign policy of senators and representatives from the Mississippi Valley paralleled the majority view of those from the nation as a whole. In both cases there was emphatic opposition to participation in any program of collective security. At no time did Midwestern opinion run counter to national opinion; it was at the most just a little more cautious about international cooperation than opinion in other parts of the country.[6]

Any attempt to correlate isolationism with either conservative or liberal political alignments shows no more than that the lines were constantly crossed. There were internationalists in both camps, and also isolationists. If many of the old Progressives were relentless in their continuing fight against foreign commitments, there were conservatives no less adamantly opposed to them. Such representatives of the business community as Andrew Mellon and Henry Frick had fought

[5] André Siegfried, *America Comes of Age* (New York, 1927), p. 307.

[6] Among recent articles on this issue are William G. Carleton, "Isolationism and the Middle West," *Mississippi Valley Historical Review*, XXXIII (Dec., 1946), 377–390; Ray A. Billington, "The Origins of Middle Western Isolationism," *Political Science Quarterly*, LX (Mar., 1945), 44–64; Richard W. Leopold, "The Mississippi Valley and American Foreign Policy, 1890–1941," *Mississippi Valley Historical Review*, XXXVIII (Mar., 1951), 625–642. In still further discussion the political analyst, Samuel Lubell has written: "The hard core of isolationism in the United States has been ethnic and emotional, not geographical. By far the strongest characteristic of the isolationist-voting counties is the residence there of ethnic groups with a pro-German or an anti-British bias." *The Future of American Politics* (New York, 1952), p. 132.

League membership just as vigorously as Robert La Follette and George Norris. From quite different points of view, liberals and conservatives could be equally fearful of the consequences of entangling alliances. The *Nation's Business* and the *New Republic* believed that the causes for which they spoke—the conservative *status quo* on the one hand and liberal reform on the other—would be best promoted by a rigid insistence upon this country's complete freedom in international affairs.[7]

In the presidential campaign of 1924, there was no backing from any political group for League membership. It was a closed issue for the Republicans, shunted aside by the Democrats with an impractical suggestion for a national referendum on foreign policy, and ignored by the Progressives backing La Follette.[8]

The latter's stand, however, was especially interesting. La Follette had been one of the most unrelenting foes of the League, and the elements that promoted his presidential candidacy—progressive farm groups, labor, the socialists—were considered significant strongholds of isolationism. As the spokesman of the combined labor-farmer forces of the nation, La Follette nevertheless called for a vigorous foreign policy aimed at revision of the Versailles Treaty, disarmament, and the outlawry of war. His primary interest remained domestic reform, and he did not believe national attention should be diverted from fundamental problems at home, but he never ignored world issues. Progressive philosophy in respect to the underlying aspects of foreign policy was noninterventionist only so far as intervention might restrict freedom of action. It differed only in degree from the philosophy of the Harding and Coolidge administrations. There was the same wish to exercise a moral influence in carrying out the American mission, and the same determination to avoid all foreign commitments.

Many other factors that had entered into the isolationism of an earlier day were still present in the 1920's. There was the old feeling

[7] For the conservatives' attitude toward the League, Denna F. Fleming, *The United States and the League of Nations* (New York, 1932), pp. 209, 210, and Ruhl J. Bartlett, *The League to Enforce Peace* (Chapel Hill, N.C., 1944), p. 213. On the progressives see Eric F. Goldman, *Rendezvous with Destiny* (New York, 1952), pp. 233–283, and Kenneth C. MacKay, *The Progressive Movement of 1924* (New York, 1947), p. 146.

[8] Kirk H. Porter, *National Party Platforms* (New York, 1924), pp. 503, 491, 522; statements on party positions in Norman H. Davis, Theodore E. Burton, and Robert Morss Lovett, "American Foreign Policy," *Foreign Affairs,* III (Sept., 1924), 22–60.

of self-sufficiency, and a continuing sense of superiority over the nations of Europe. It was still believed to be of utmost importance to stay at home in order to develop most effectively a democratic way of life. If the mission of America in the regeneration of the world was to provide an example of the good and the true, the nation could not afford to be contaminated by too close an association with any foreign country.

There was of course diversity of opinion—as there always had been. In broad terms, however, Republicans and Democrats, conservatives and liberals, the people as a whole, appeared to be determined to maintain the traditions of the past. In the popular mind nothing in the country's experience—neither overseas expansion, world war, nor a League of Nations—seemed to have demonstrated that an isolationist policy was any less sound than when it was first initiated.

The first important move in postwar foreign policy after the conclusion of peace with Germany was the summons officially issued by President Harding, in 1921, for an international conference at Washington to deal with both the political questions of eastern Asia and the problem of disarmament. Looking out across the western ocean, the new Republican administration conjured up dangers that appeared to justify some measure of collective action in the Pacific at the very time that it was so abruptly refusing further cooperation in the Old World.

The original impetus behind the call for the Washington Conference was the popular demand for arms limitation inspired by the tremendous cost of naval competition. Although the United States could better afford an extended building program than either Great Britain or Japan, even the completion of new vessels already authorized would have constituted an extremely heavy burden at a time when every effort was being made to reduce all government expenditures. Senator Borah initiated the movement for disarmament with the introduction in the Senate of a resolution urging an immediate naval parley with Great Britain and Japan. His proposal fell upon fertile ground through its immediate appeal to an economy-minded Congress, and with its hand forced the Harding Administration prepared to act. It so happened, moreover, that just at this time Great Britain, which was concerned over renewal of the old Anglo-Japanese alliance, was about to suggest a meeting that would take up both Far Eastern issues and naval limitation. There was actually something of a race with England in calling a conference now broadened, beyond Borah's original idea, to include all nations with interests in the Pacific and to place political questions as well as disarmament on its agenda.

The Washington Conference met on November 12, 1921, under the chairmanship of Secretary of State Hughes. An internationalist at heart, Hughes had originally favored American membership in the League of Nations with clear-cut reservations, clung during the 1920 campaign to the idea that some new world association might still be established, and then realistically accepted the popular verdict that under existing circumstances this was impossible. When reproached for apparently abandoning his own principles, set forth as one of the leading Republicans urging Harding's election as the best means to promote international cooperation, he refused to resurrect the old controversy. "Nothing good will come of it," he wrote one correspondent, "and very likely it will stand in the way of much that might otherwise be accomplished." [9] Acting on this theory, he was ready to do everything he could to secure concrete results from this new move to strengthen international security in the Pacific.

The circumstances were dramatic as Hughes opened the conference proceedings. Largely dispensing with the usual formalities, he at once introduced a far-reaching proposal for the limitation of capital ships, which constituted a formidable challenge to the other naval powers. As the negotiations proceeded on these proposals, the conference also took up the political issues affecting the general security of the Pacific area and the status of China. Seldom has any international conference grappled so resolutely with important questions, and much of its success in meeting these problems, especially that of naval limitation, was due to the brilliant leadership of the Secretary of State.

The major achievements of the Washington Conference were reflected in the adoption of three closely interrelated treaties. The United States, Great Britain, France, and Japan agreed in a Four Power Treaty to respect one another's rights in their insular possessions in the Pacific and to consult together should such rights be threatened. With the addition of Italy, these same nations concluded a Five Power Treaty limiting their strength in capital ships and barring the fortification of their naval bases in the Pacific. In specific terms, the United States and Great Britain were to maintain a ratio of 525,000 tons each in battleships; Japan was allotted 315,000 tons; France and Italy

[9] Merlo J. Pusey, *Charles Evans Hughes* (2 vols., New York, 1951), II, 431–436.

accepted 172,000 each for their capital vessels. And finally, all those countries with interests in the Pacific (with the exception of Soviet Russia, which had not been invited to the conference) joined in a Nine Power Treaty in which they undertook to respect the sovereignty and independence of China and to uphold the principles of the Open Door.[10]

From one point of view, American leadership in the negotiation of these treaties appeared to constitute intervention on a broad scale in Far Eastern politics. At the same time, it could also be interpreted as marking a partial withdrawal from Asia in that the United States sought international support for a program that it had heretofore tried to uphold virtually alone. In any event, the all-important consequence of the Washington Conference was the establishment of an embryonic security system in the Pacific whereby it was profoundly hoped that peace and order would be substituted for the rising threat of possible war. Taken as a whole—and the Harding administration was to insist they should be taken as a whole—the new treaties incorporated mutual pledges of nonaggression, delimited the three principal naval powers' areas of strategic control, and checked further armament expansion in battleships.[11]

For all such advance, however, there was still no departure so far as American policy was concerned from the basic traditions of isolationism. The United States had agreed not to fortify its Pacific outposts, to restrict battleship construction, and to respect both the integrity of China and the existing status of the other powers' insular possessions. But it had made no commitments whatsoever as to its future action should any of the treaties be violated.

This was made abundantly clear in the treaties themselves, in repeated statements by those responsible for their negotiation, and, in the case of the Four Power Treaty, through the double reinsurance of Senate amendment. There was nothing here comparable to the League's controversial Article Ten.

[10] *Conference on the Limitation of Armaments, Senate Document 125,* 67th Congress, 2nd Session (Washington, 1922). Major treaty texts also in Ruhl J. Bartlett, *The Record of American Diplomacy* (New York, 1954), pp. 486–491.

[11] See A. W. Griswold, *The Far Eastern Policy of the United States* (New York, 1938), pp. 305–332; Pusey, *Charles Evans Hughes,* II, 453–522; Foster Rhea Dulles, *China and America* (Princeton, 1946), pp. 150–162; Harold and Margaret Sprout, *Toward a New Order of Sea Power* (Princeton, 1943), pp. 149 ff., and especially 282–296. For excerpts of newspaper opinion, *Literary Digest,* LXXII (Feb. 18, 1922), 7–10.

President Harding stressed this point of view in submitting the treaties for ratification. He was enthusiastic over the results of the conference—"it is all so fine, so gratifying"—and he was confident of the permanence of the treaties' contribution to peace.[12] At the same time, he told the Senate that he could bring it every assurance that nothing in any of the several pacts "commits the United States, or any other Power, to any kind of an alliance, entanglement or involvement. It does not require us or any Power to surrender a worthwhile tradition. . . . The Senate's concern for freedom from entanglements, for preserved traditions, for maintained independence, was never once forgotten by the American delegates." [13] In answering the charge of some critics that if the treaties had no provision for their own enforcement, express or implied, they became virtually meaningless, the President simply refused to consider this negative point of view: "Let us accept no such doctrine of despair as that." [14]

Senator Lodge, to whom was somewhat ironically given the task of guiding the Four Power Treaty through the Senate, met directly the criticism of a skeptical Borah, a fearful La Follette, and a denunciatory Reed. He denied that the treaty represented any sort of a link with the imperialist powers or involved any obligation other than that of consultation. It had been concluded "without alliances or penalties or the sanction of force lurking in the background." Should ratification be withheld, Lodge warned, the United States would "sink back into sullen solitude . . . a hermit nation armed to the teeth and looking forward always to wars as inseparable from the existence of mankind upon the earth." [15]

The treaties were approved after considerable debate and in their apparent settlement of political rivalries in the Pacific and Eastern Asia they seemed to hold out a new hope for continuing peace in that part of the world. Ultimately this hope was shattered by the aggressive expansion of an imperialistic Japan, but neither the events of 1931 nor those of 1941 could be foreseen. It has been said, with all the wisdom of hindsight, that in view of Japan's expansionist ambitions,

---

[12] *Supplement to Messages of the Presidents, 1921–1925* (Washington: 1925), pp. 9068–9069.

[13] *Ibid.*, p. 9075.

[14] *Ibid.*, p. 9072.

[15] Quoted in J. Chal Vinson, "The Parchment Peace: The Senate Defense of the Four-Power Treaty of the Washington Conference," *Mississippi Valley Historical Review*, XXXIX (Sept., 1952), 305, 306. See also D. F. Fleming, *United States and World Organization* (New York, 1938), pp. 89–105.

the United States blundered in surrendering its lead in battleship construction and in agreeing not to fortify its Pacific bases. Walter Lippmann wrote, in 1943, of "the exorbitant folly" of the Washington Conference and reproached himself for at the time celebrating "the disaster as a triumph." [16]

In 1922, however, the United States was not giving up as much as the naval treaty suggested. The temper of Congress was such that there was little likelihood of its appropriating the funds to maintain naval supremacy or to fortify Pacific naval bases.[17] More important, the concessions represented by limitation of United States strength in the western Pacific were largely responsible for the adherence of the other powers, most notably Japan, to the political agreements that constituted international recognition of the sovereignty and independence of China. The subsequent breakdown of the accords does not nullify their importance as marking at the time a substantial victory for American policy in eastern Asia.

A more valid criticism of the Washington Conference was its failure to provide in any way for the enforcement of the treaties concluded or for joint action should the sovereignty of China be imperiled. The great mistake was not in going too far, but in not going far enough. The limitation of armaments was primarily based on a new conception of Pacific security. Had that security been practically safeguarded, there would have been far less likelihood of the later breakdown of the Washington accords. Even a military-dominated Japan would have been reluctant to challenge the treaty system of the Pacific if she had known that aggression would have been met by the concerted resistance of the treaty signatories. In refusing to consider any program that might involve the use of sanctions, and emphasizing so heavily its freedom from any entanglement, the United States fatally weakened the structure of the peace for which its own leadership at the Washington Conference was so largely responsible.

Another part of the world in which Secretary Hughes showed an active interest was Latin America. If his policies were not always completely successful, they helped to prepare the way, subject to later

---

[16] Walter Lippmann, *U. S. Foreign Policy* (New York, 1943), pp. xii–xiii.

[17] "In last analysis, therefore," Donald W. Mitchell has written, "the sacrifices of the United States at the Washington Conference were of warships and naval bases that would quite probably not have been built." *History of the Modern American Navy* (New York, 1946), p. 274.

temporary reverses under President Coolidge, for a progressively more friendly attitude toward the countries south of the Rio Grande. His approach led to the good-will measures that were initiated during the Hoover administration, and ultimately to the Good Neighbor policy of Franklin D. Roosevelt.

American influence—economic and political—had continued to expand throughout Latin America and there was no part of the world where the United States had assumed broader responsibilities. The basic assumptions of the Monroe Doctrine, even though they were not yet embodied in treaty form, had been strengthened with the passing years and commanded full popular support. Under no circumstances would the United States tolerate any interference on the part of European nations in the political life of the New World.

This was particularly true in the Caribbean. The region's importance as an area vital to the strategic defense of the United States had been recognized in the Roosevelt Corollary to the Monroe Doctrine, Taft's dollar diplomacy, and the interventionist policies of Woodrow Wilson. Whatever the American people might think of involvement in either European or Asiatic affairs, they fully recognized the need for a strong, positive policy in the Caribbean and Latin America generally, and they accepted the possibility that it might have to be upheld by force.[18]

Hughes had no idea of limiting the nation's commitments in Latin America. He acknowledged the importance of maintaining paramount influence in the Caribbean. What he tried to do, however, was to convince the countries in that part of the world—along the lines initiated by Secretary Root—that the United States had no ulterior motives in respect to their freedom and independence, and no intention of employing superior power to their disadvantage. He told their representatives in an important address in December, 1922: "The Government of the United States has no ambition to gratify at your expense, no policy which runs counter to your national aspirations, and no purpose save to promote the interests of peace and to assist you, in such manner as you may welcome, to solve your problems to your own proper advantage. The interest of the United States is found in the peace of this Hemisphere and in the conservation of your interests." [19]

Hughes constantly emphasized the principle that the Monroe Doctrine was a policy of self-defense rather than aggression. He was not

[18] See J. Fred Rippy, *The Caribbean Danger Zone* (New York, 1940).
[19] Quoted in Pusey, *Charles Evans Hughes*, II, 532.

prepared to go so far as to suggest that its enforcement should be made a matter of common action, and insisted on reserving to the United States full freedom in its application. Nevertheless, he recognized the equality and complete independence of all the American republics.

Hughes resigned as Secretary of State in 1925 to become Chief Justice of the Supreme Court, and for a time under his successor, Frank B. Kellogg, there appeared to be a retreat from the more beneficent Latin American policy that Hughes had tried to implement. The insistence of President Coolidge on the right of the United States to protect the person and property of its citizens, wherever they might be, as part of the general domain of the nation [20] opened the way to renewed intervention in the internal affairs of a number of Latin American countries.

The most important instance of such interference—apart from the continued control directly or indirectly exercised over the fiscal affairs of a number of other Caribbean republics—occurred in Nicaragua, where the United States landed some five thousand troops in 1927 to maintain order and protect American interests. It was a complicated situation that found the United States supporting a government which it had too hastily recognized while Mexico continued to uphold the rival regime. President Coolidge, widely criticized for waging a "private war," finally sent Henry L. Stimson as his personal representative to try to work out some agreement between Nicaragua's opposing factions. This Stimson succeeded in doing. New elections held in 1928 under American supervision brought at least relative stability to Nicaragua and also improved United States relations.[21]

A quarrel with Mexico, growing out of the nationalization policy of President Calles, also for a time threatened trouble. Business interests insistently called for intervention to safeguard American property rights, but the Coolidge administration had no thought of any such dangerous move. It was determined to avoid possible hostilities. The issues in dispute were finally resolved through the skillful diplomacy of Ambassador Dwight Morrow, and before Coolidge left office substantial progress had been made in placing relations with Mexico on a better footing than they had been for many years.[22]

[20] *The New York Times,* Apr. 27, 1927, quoted in Julius W. Pratt, *America's Colonial Experiment* (New York, 1950), p. 317.

[21] George H. Stuart, *Latin America and the United States* (New York, 1943), pp. 366 ff., and Henry L. Stimson, *American Policy in Nicaragua* (New York, 1927).

[22] J. M. Callahan, *American Foreign Policy in Mexican Relations* (New York, 1932), Chap. XV.

Soon after his election in 1928, Herbert Hoover embarked upon a good-will tour of Latin America. Both in the course of this trip and upon subsequent occasions, he repeatedly emphasized the desire of the United States for the most cordial ties with its southern neighbors. He declared it to be American policy never to interfere in any other country's internal affairs, repudiated the idea of using force to sustain financial contracts, and stated that "we must clothe faith and idealism with action." [23] A further assertion of these principles was contained in a memorandum on the Monroe Doctrine, drawn up by Under Secretary of State J. Reuben Clark in 1930, which finally freed this policy of the incubus of the Roosevelt Corollary and did much to relieve Latin America's fears of further interference by the United States. "So far as Latin America is concerned," the Clark Memorandum stated, "the Doctrine is now, and always has been, not an instrument of violence and oppression, but an unbought, freely bestowed, and wholly effective guarantee of their freedom, independence, and territorial integrity against the imperialistic designs of Europe." [24]

In complete acceptance of this memorandum, Stimson, now Secretary of State, practically applied its principles. The United States withdrew in 1932 the American marines that had been stationed in Haiti ever since the intervention of Wilsonian days, and early the next year recalled the last troops from Nicaragua. The State Department also steadfastly resisted all pressure for intervention in the revolutionary situation that about this time developed in Cuba. The United States had not allowed the preponderance of its material and military power, Stimson declared in reviewing these developments, to prescribe a different rule of conduct in the Western Hemisphere than it was prepared to follow in other parts of the world. It had sought to make its policy "so clear in its implications of justice and good will, in its avoidance of anything which could be even misconstrued into a policy for forceful intervention . . . as to reassure the most timid and suspicious . . ." [25]

This could never be wholly achieved. The United States was too

[23] R. L. Wilbur and A. M. Hyde, *The Hoover Policies* (New York, 1937), pp. 588, 589; William Starr Myers, *The Foreign Policies of Herbert Hoover* (New York, 1940), pp. 43, 55.

[24] Bartlett, *The Record of American Diplomacy*, pp. 546–549.

[25] From contemporary article in *Foreign Affairs*, Apr., 1933, quoted in Henry L. Stimson and McGeorge Bundy, *On Active Service in Peace and War* (New York, 1948), pp. 186–187.

THE IDEAL AND THE REAL

strong, its power too overshadowing, its economic interests too pervasive, for the republics of Latin America ever to feel completely safe from possible exploitation or interference. There was always the shadow of imperialism. The important forward strides taken before the Republicans went out of office succeeded, however, in greatly improving relations. In this part of the world, America recognized and accepted her responsibilities.

In their general attitude toward possible commitments in either Europe or eastern Asia, both the Coolidge and Hoover administrations conformed to the pattern set by the Harding administration. The views of Coolidge himself, however, were more limited than those of Harding and particularly those of his predecessor's Secretary of State. His accession to the Presidency, indeed, brought to that post whose incumbent is charged with the final responsibility in determining foreign policy a man whose provincialism could hardly be exaggerated.

Europe and Asia could not have been more beyond his field of interest. Although Coolidge often spoke of the position of great power and responsibility which the United States had attained, his succinct conclusion was "our first duty is to ourselves." He was convinced that the role of the United States should be one of complete detachment, and firmly believed that its influence for peace would be effective just in proportion as its disinterestedness was clearly recognized by other countries. In his Inaugural Address in 1925 Coolidge said: "We have been and propose to be, more and more American. We believe that we can best serve our own country and most successfully discharge our obligations to humanity by continuing to be openly and candidly, intensely and scrupulously, American. If we have any heritage, it has been that. If we have any destiny, we have found it in that direction." [26]

Apart from Latin America, he actually had little influence on foreign policy. The most interesting development during his term of office was one with which he had nothing to do. This was the conclusion, in 1928, of the Kellogg-Briand Anti-War Treaty, to which virtually all the nations of the world—including Japan, Germany, and Italy—ultimately became signatories and pledged themselves to renounce war as an instrument of national policy.[27]

[26] *Supplement to Messages of the Presidents, 1921–1925,* pp. 9401, 9741, 9482.

[27] A number of studies deal with the Kellogg-Briand Anti-War Treaty, in-

This treaty may be interpreted as a sincere expression of the hopes and aspirations of a people hungry for some assurance of enduring peace. Its failure to provide any means whatsoever to give practical validity to its antiwar pledge was also the measure of the continuing

Rollin Kirby in New York *World*, December 5, 1923

"I sympathize deeply with you, Madame, but I cannot associate with you."

isolationism which belied the pact's illusory promise. The Kellogg-Briand Treaty did not pretend to deal with the causes of war, and did

cluding J. T. Shotwell, *War as an Instrument of National Policy* (New York, 1929), and D. H. Miller, *The Peace Pact of Paris* (New York, 1928), but the most recent and authoritative is Robert H. Ferrell, *Peace in Their Time* (New Haven, 1952).

not suggest any machinery for settling international disputes by peaceful means. It simply outlawed war, and placed an entire reliance upon moral compulsion for the observance of its provisions. It was the product of complete idealistic confusion. The American people felt an inner compulsion to do something about world peace, unable perhaps to escape some feeling of guilt for their rejection of the League, and yet they were still determined to avoid any commitment for collective security.

The negotiations leading to conclusion of the antiwar treaty followed an unusual course. As early as 1923, Senator Borah introduced in the Senate a resolution for the outlawry of war, and the idea had also been incorporated in the Progressive platform a year later.[28] The actual initiative for the treaty came, however, from a quite different quarter. At least in part upon the suggestion of Professor James T. Shotwell of Columbia University, Premier Briand of France proposed a pact renouncing war between the United States and France. His purpose was not to encourage the general action American proponents of the outlawry of war had in mind, however, but rather to win this country over to what was, in effect, a negative alliance assuring France that the United States would never engage in war against her. This proposal was studiously ignored by the State Department until public opinion, aroused by outlawry-of-war advocates, forced a response to Briand's overtures. Secretary Kellogg thereupon suggested broadening the proposed treaty to include all peace-loving nations. While this had been far from the French statesman's idea, he felt compelled to go along with the new plan. A diplomatic maneuver to avoid any guarantee of French security thus led to official acceptance of the principle of outlawing war by international agreement.

The diary of Assistant Secretary of State Castle reveals the stages in this development and his own surprise when his chief, as noted on March 6, 1928, began to take the outlawry of war seriously: "For weeks the press has chorused approval of F. B. K.'s exchange of notes with Briand on outlawing war . . . actually it is futile . . . I think it is about time for the correspondence to stop. The political trick has been turned and now we should take a well deserved rest. The funny thing is that Olds [Under Secretary of State] and the Secretary seem to take it all with profound seriousness." [29]

[28] Claudius O. Johnson, *Borah of Idaho* (New York, 1936), pp. 392–394; Porter, *National Party Platforms*, p. 522.
[29] Quoted in Ferrell, *Peace in Their Time*, 165.

In spite of this cynical attitude in the lower echelons of the State Department, the treaty was concluded and immediately applauded in official pronouncements and many newspaper editorials as a brilliant achievement. President Coolidge and Secretary Kellogg agreed that it promised more for world peace than any other pact ever negotiated; Senator Borah rejoiced that it incorporated the basic principle of organizing peace through moral suasion rather than force. An acquiescent Senate voted its approval—although in a highly doubtful and sometimes derisive mood—with only a single dissenting vote.[30]

Among the skeptics in the country as a whole were a number of public figures whose impressions had interesting implications for the future. In a contemporary article in *Foreign Affairs*, Franklin D. Roosevelt, destined to be the principal architect of the United Nations, declared that words without deeds were not enough, and that the outlawry of war led to a false belief that something important had been accomplished. "It does not contribute in any way," he wrote, "to settling matters of international controversy." [31] In very much the same vein, the young Henry Cabot Lodge, who would be the American delegate to the United Nations just a quarter of a century later, stated in *Harper's Magazine* that the idea of renouncing war by fiat was inherently absurd, and that nothing could be achieved without paying a price for it. The antiwar pact created "a sense of false security," Lodge concluded, ". . . and official sanction is thereby given to a most portentous misconception." [32]

In later years the views set forth by Roosevelt and Lodge were generally accepted. It was almost universally agreed that the Kellogg-Briand Treaty had exercised a harmful rather than a helpful influence on the cause of world peace. The outlawry of war served to satisfy the conscience of the American people without requiring of them any positive action, and also created an illusion of safety which seemed to obviate the need for any more direct participation in world affairs.[33]

---

[30] *Supplement to Messages of the Presidents, 1925–1929* (Washington, 1929), p. 9802; David Bryn-Jones, *Frank B. Kellogg* (New York, 1937), pp. 248–251; *Congressional Record*, LXX, 70th Congress, 2nd Session, p. 1065. See also *Literary Digest*, XCVIII (Sept. 8, 1928), 5–7.

[31] Franklin D. Roosevelt, "Our Foreign Policy—A Democratic View," *Foreign Affairs*, VI (July, 1928), 582, 585.

[32] Henry Cabot Lodge, "The Meaning of the Kellogg Treaty," *Harper's Magazine*, CLVIII (Dec., 1928), 41.

[33] Sumner Welles has characterized the Kellogg-Briand Pact as "a happy and decorous means of evading rather than accepting responsibility . . . a high

In looking back upon the support he had given the treaty, Henry L. Stimson later marveled at his willingness to fall in line with public opinion, and expressed the fear that he had given "aid and comfort to the very irresponsibility he hated." [34]

Whatever its consequences, the treaty remains a classic example of the naïveté of much popular thinking on America's world role. Rarely if ever have moral and ethical factors been played up in such sharp contradiction of reality. The outlawry of war was accepted as the final realization of a historic dream even as the nation refused any sacrifice that might have given that dream substance. There could have been no more telling illustration of a natural desire on the part of the American people to have their cake and eat it too—to assure world peace and yet avoid any responsibility should such assurance fail.

When Herbert Hoover came to the White House in 1929, the unreality of American foreign policy was not yet apparent. The Washington Conference accords still held out high hopes for continuing peace in the Pacific, relations with Latin America showed considerable improvement over prewar days, and the popular expectations aroused by the Kellogg-Briand Treaty were still undiminished. With partisan undertones, the Republicans proudly declared that, while effectively steering clear of any foreign entanglements, they had so directed foreign affairs as to make the moral influence of the United States a decisive instrument in safeguarding peace. The specter of war, if not entirely banished, did indeed seem to be retreating into the background.[35]

Although the new President was more international-minded than Harding or Coolidge, his views were nevertheless basically isolationist in the traditional meaning of the term. His experiences at the Paris peace conference, and in dealing with postwar European governments on relief measures, had convinced Hoover, in 1919, that the attitudes of the Old World and the New World were so diametrically opposed that close collaboration was impossible. If the American people were

---

point in isolationist thinking . . . a fitting climax to a foreign policy which even in its least harmful aspects was totally negative." *The Time for Decision* (New York, 1944), p. 48.

[34] Stimson and Bundy, *On Active Service*, p. 260.

[35] For example, the statement of so authoritative a writer as Hamilton Fish Armstrong that war seemed "on the whole less likely to come than at any time since the last one ended." "After Ten Years: Europe and America," *Foreign Affairs*, VII (Oct., 1928), 18.

to participate in foreign power politics, he had written, "we must become something other than a free people as we conceive it." An intense desire to promote peace led him for a time to favor membership in the League, but only on the basis of very specific reservations safeguarding the nation's freedom of action. The United States constituted the world's "one great moral reserve," he stated on one occasion, and added that the independence of action through which this reserve could be maintained would be impossible if the nation let itself be dragged into European entanglements.[36]

The developments of the early 1920's had not moderated Hoover's cautious approach to international affairs. His Inaugural Address made this clear. He fully accepted what he stated to be the American people's decision not to commit themselves in advance to becoming involved in the settlement of foreign disputes. Reaffirming his deep concern with peace, he declared his further conviction that the nation's freedom from such obligations had increased its availability for service in all fields of human progress.[37]

The all-important foreign issue that arose during the Hoover administration—overshadowing war debts, tariff policy, relations with Europe or Latin America—was crisis in eastern Asia. In 1931 Japan opened an attack on Manchuria. This was a direct challenge to China but also an indirect one to the United States through its flagrant violation of the two major political treaties to which the Japanese and the Americans were a party. There could be no reconciling Tokyo's military action with its undertaking, in the terms of the Nine Power Treaty, to respect China's territorial integrity, or with its pledge, embodied in the Kellogg-Briand Treaty, never to resort to war as an instrument of national policy.

The United States was under no obligation, as the careful phraseology and supplementary reservations of both treaties made clear, to take any action. Here was the pay-off of the policy so carefully maintained since 1919. There was no commitment to take part in collective sanctions to restrain an aggressor nation. Yet Japan's defiance of the Far Eastern treaty system gravely threatened American interests. Whatever the theoretical implications of an isolationist policy, it was impossible to ignore these ominous developments.

[36] *The Memoirs of Herbert Hoover, The Cabinet and the Presidency* (New York, 1952), pp. 377–378; *Years of Adventure* (New York, 1951), pp. 473, 476, 457; Myers, *The Foreign Policies of Herbert Hoover*, p. 17.

[37] *Supplement to Messages of the Presidents, 1925–1929*, p. 9848.

The course followed by the United States wavered between aloofness and intervention. Every effort was made to exert a maximum
moral influence in behalf of peace. Secretary Stimson repeatedly protested Japan's infraction of her treaty obligations, summoned her before the bar of world opinion for her international wrongdoing, and
even allowed the American consul in Geneva to be present as an observer at League discussions in regard to possible collective measures
to moderate the crisis. So far—and no further. There would be no
American commitments, no promise of action.[38]

As time went on, Stimson would himself have liked to follow a
bolder course. He came to favor a greater degree of cooperation with
the League and the consideration of economic sanctions. President
Hoover, however, was adamantly opposed to the latter step. Developments in eastern Asia, he told his Cabinet, did not imperil the freedom
of the American people, or their economic or moral future. Since the
League had taken up the issue, the United States should cooperate
with it in any proposals for negotiation or conciliation. "But," he concluded, "that is the limit. We will not go along on war or any of the
sanctions either economic or military, for those are the roads to
war." [39] Hoover could not believe in "the magic wand of force by
which all peace could be summoned from the vasty deep." The
strength of the Nine Power Treaty and the Kellogg-Briand Treaty lay
in the fact, he stated, that they were not military alliances but enforce-
able solely by "the moral reprobation of the world." [40]

The conflict between the views of Hoover and Stimson was com-
promised—so far as two really irreconcilable positions could be com-
promised—by the President's suggestion that the United States should
explicitly state its refusal to recognize any territorial changes in eastern
Asia violating existing treaty engagements or brought about by force
of arms.[41] This nonrecognition policy—to which Stimson's name was

[38] Henry L. Stimson, *The Far Eastern Crisis* (New York, 1936), pp. 31–69;
Hoover, *The Cabinet and the Presidency*, pp. 365–379; Stimson and Bundy,
On Active Service, pp. 220–263. For general discussion of entire episode, Sara
R. Smith, *The Manchurian Crisis, 1931–32* (New York, 1948), and also two
special articles: Paul H. Clyde, "The Diplomacy of 'Playing No Favorites':
Secretary Stimson and Manchuria," *Mississippi Valley Historical Review*, XXXV
(Sept., 1948), 187–202, and Richard N. Current, "The Stimson Doctrine and
the Hoover Doctrine," *American Historical Review*, LIX (Apr., 1954), 513–542.

[39] Hoover, *The Cabinet and the Presidency*, pp. 368–370.

[40] *Ibid.*, pp. 377–378; see also Wilbur and Hyde, *The Hoover Policies*, p.
600; Myers, *The Foreign Policies of Herbert Hoover*, pp. 158–159.

[41] Stimson and Bundy, *On Active Service*, p. 234; Myers, *The Foreign Policies of Herbert Hoover*, pp. 164–168.

given—was a final effort to exert some influence on Japan. It was completely ignored. Yet even Stimson at this time stated his belief that in the long run the only effective force making for peace was world opinion, and he sought by every possible means to mobilize such opinion behind nonrecognition. He was perhaps making the most of his inability to apply direct sanctions. In later years, he came to feel that the policy of moral condemnation failed as completely as it did because America lacked the courage to back up her position by force when such a move held out any possible risk of war.[42]

The policy of the United States during the Manchurian crisis was in keeping with tradition. There could be little question, in 1931–32, that Hoover rather than Stimson reflected the prevailing climate of opinion. The American people had no wish to make commitments that might involve them in war against Japan; they had no enthusiasm for either economic or military sanctions.[43] They had accepted increasing participation in world affairs—the Washington Conference treaties, the Kellogg-Briand pact, even consultation with the League Council—but there had been no shift in their basic determination to insist on full freedom of action and to avoid anything that smacked of an entangling alliance.

Nothing could have been more ironical, however, than this further demonstration of the belief that by avoiding formal engagements the United States actually retained complete freedom of action. The stand taken during the Manchurian crisis, even if the nonrecognition doctrine again did not involve any definite or binding future commitment, was another step along the road that led directly to Pearl Harbor. Although intervention in eastern Asia might always stop short of anything in the nature of an entangling alliance, the ultimate responsibilities devolving upon the United States for a policy that embraced the Open Door in China, the Washington Conference treaties, and nonrecognition of any territorial changes brought about by force could hardly be avoided. The Stimson doctrine mired the nation ever more deeply in Asiatic affairs and made any escape from the crisis of 1941 impossible except through the repudiation of all previous policy and a conscienceless abandonment of China.

[42] Stimson and Bundy, *On Active Service,* pp. 260–262.
[43] Eleanor Tupper and G. E. McReynolds, *Japan in American Public Opinion* (New York, 1937), Chap. IX.

The policies and attitudes brought out by Japan's attack in Manchuria found expression in relation to another problem facing the Republican administrations of the 1920's. This was disarmament. The United States was again ready to exercise its moral influence in promoting a cause so dear to the collective heart of the American people; and again it flatly refused to assume any obligations in helping to safeguard the international security on which disarmament was so completely dependent.

While the Washington Conference agreements limiting battleship construction were extended to certain other categories of naval vessels at a further conference in London in 1930, a far more difficult aspect of disarmament was involved in the status of land forces. The League of Nations sought to come to grips with this problem with plans for a world parley in 1932, and the United States promptly agreed to take part in both the preliminary discussions and the conference itself. President Hoover, in fact, took the lead in advancing a program to ban all offensive weapons—had not the nations of the world agreed to give up war as an instrument of national policy?—and to reduce by one third all other military components. The powerful peace forces of this country enthusiastically supported this plan. For a time there were hopes that something beyond naval limitation might actually be accomplished. Every attempt to reduce the armies of the world, however, foundered on the rocks of political distrust.[44]

America had her full share of responsibility for this failure. Although her own actual military strength was not important, the potential power of her immense economic and industrial resources was obviously too vital a factor in any balance of world power to be ignored. What the European nations—and especially France—repeatedly sought was some assurance that in the event of any threat to peace American influence would be realistically exerted in support of collective security. Again and again proposals were made at Geneva that would have put the United States on record as at least agreeing to consult with the other powers should aggressive action from any quarter endanger European stability.

This the United States would not do. It was so strongly wedded to its no-commitment policy that even a consultation agreement was rejected. Premier Laval of France urgently pressed such a suggestion in

<hr />

[44] Myers, *The Foreign Policies of Herbert Hoover,* pp. 134–152; Stimson and Bundy, *On Active Service,* pp. 264–281.

1931, following similar and unsuccessful overtures at the London Naval Conference a year earlier, as "a great gesture" in the cause of disarmament. Hoover's immediate reaction was that it was a political impossibility.[45] The chance that an agreement to consult might be construed as an agreement to act could not be accepted by a statesman so obdurately opposed to any foreign commitment and to the use of coercion against other nations.

The American people did not consider disarmament a major issue. They were deep in the throes of a depression that largely eclipsed interest in everything else. So far as they thought of arms limitation at all, they continued to believe that it would be somehow obtainable without having to do very much about it. They appeared to be unable to realize that in the always close relationship between arms competition and war, the growth of armaments was a consequence of fear and insecurity—the symptom of the disease rather than its real cause. Although their desire for peace could not be called into question, they remained unwilling to take the risks that effective support for peace demanded.

The failure of disarmament was the triumph of timidity. Here perhaps was the final and conclusive example of the unhappy alliance between idealism and irresponsibility that was the most significant aspect of American policy during a period in world history when forces still hardly perceived had begun their inexorable march toward another war.

[45] Hoover, *The Cabinet and the Presidency*, p. 348; Stimson and Bundy, *On Active Service*, p. 275. See also Russell M. Cooper, *American Consultation in World Affairs* (New York, 1934), pp. 45 ff., and Denna F. Fleming, *The United States and World Organization, 1920–1933* (New York, 1938), p. 367.

CHAPTER 9

The Mirage of Neutrality

"THE REST of the world—Ah! there is the rub."[1] This phrase from President Franklin D. Roosevelt's Annual Message to Congress in 1936 underscores the basic dilemma of the mid-1930's. The United States was deeply committed to a moral approach to the problems of peace and war, and yet the entire program symbolized by the Kellogg-Briand Treaty was bankrupt. The principle of peaceful adjustment for all international disputes was completely undermined when other powerful nations "impatiently reverted to their old belief in the law of the sword." The question then was, Should America undertake to restrain these aggressive powers in alliance with other peace-loving countries, or abandon all idea of international cooperation and seek its own peace and security through a strict neutrality in other nations' quarrels?

A further problem intensified the dilemma. In the 1920's the world had still seemed reasonably safe for democracy. Fascism had not yet become a serious threat, and communism lacked the militant force that it would later acquire as the weapon of an imperialistic Soviet Russia. President Coolidge had been able to say that American foreign policy could "best be described by one word—peace." This conception was the basis for the proposals for the outlawry of war, and for the determination of so many Americans that their country would under no circumstances ever again take up arms. The refusal to consider

[1] Samuel I. Rosenman (ed.), *The Public Papers and Addresses of Franklin D. Roosevelt* (13 vols., New York, 1938–50), V, 9; and, more conveniently, *Roosevelt's Foreign Policy, 1933–41—Franklin D. Roosevelt's Unedited Speeches and Messages* (New York, 1942), p. 90.

alliances or any commitment to sanctions, Hoover later wrote, "was not isolationism. It was a belief that somewhere, somehow, there must be an abiding place for law and a sanctuary for civilization." [2]

As the 1930's wore on, however, the victories of fascism and growth of dictatorial controls in other lands changed prevailing ideas of what actually constituted national security and recalled the broader aims of American policy. The peace for which the United States had traditionally stood meant something more than mere absence of war. Theodore Roosevelt had always insisted upon a righteous peace; Woodrow Wilson continually emphasized a moral international order. The growing realization that the world was now faced with the menace of totalitarianism as well as the danger of war—"the twin spirits of autocracy and aggression"—revived the belief that peace of itself was not necessarily enough. Even if it could conceivably be preserved for the United States, could the nation avoid taking a stand in defense of freedom; indeed, could peace and freedom ever be disassociated?

When Roosevelt first came into office all such issues were subordinated to the more immediate demands of domestic policy. In his first Inaugural Address the new President made no reference to foreign policy other than the brief statement that he would dedicate the nation to "the policy of the good neighbor." The nation was convulsed by a country-wide banking crisis; millions of unemployed were vainly seeking work from coast to coast; the national economy seemed to be paralyzed. Throughout his first term, Roosevelt concentrated on these vital domestic issues, leaving his Secretary of State, Cordell Hull, as the latter has testified, almost in full charge of foreign policy.[3] Moreover the President's ideas on the role that the United States should play in world affairs appeared to have undergone a definite shift since his foursquare support for collective security as a loyal Wilsonian in 1920. He was generally content to have America stay at home. It was not until almost the eve of European war, and his realization that everything that might have been accomplished by the New Deal on the domestic front and the very security of the nation were threatened by events abroad, that Roosevelt returned to his original internationalism.

A first sign of his isolationist phase is found in an article written for

[2] *The Memoirs of Herbert Hoover: The Cabinet and the Presidency* (New York, 1952), pp. 377–378.

[3] *The Memoirs of Cordell Hull* (2 vols., New York, 1948), I, 194.

Foreign Affairs in 1928. Roosevelt then flatly stated, in behalf of himself and his fellow Democrats: "We are opposed to any official participation in purely European affairs or to committing ourselves to act in unknown contingencies." While he was quick to add that there should be continued cooperation with the League of Nations in all matters "which bear on the general good of mankind," and that it was neither possible nor desirable to maintain "an isolated national existence," his position clearly fell within the familiar postwar isolationist pattern.[4]

This was further emphasized in the campaign of 1932. Roosevelt repeatedly stressed a nationalistic approach to the problems arising from the depression and specifically repudiated political cooperation with other countries. The League of Nations was no longer the organization conceived by its founders, he stated on one occasion, and added emphatically: "I do not favor American participation." [5]

Roosevelt—like Wilson—had hoped to avoid having to deal with foreign issues in order to concentrate on domestic ones. He fell heir, however, to two unavoidable international problems: the disarmament conference at Geneva and a world economic conference at London. Both conferences were complete failures, and in part at least because of the attitude adopted by the United States.

An isolationist policy was modified at Geneva to the extent of expressing a willingness, should a general disarmament program be adopted, to consult with other nations in the event of any threat to peace, and to do nothing that would interfere with any collective effort to meet the emergency. But the United States would make no commitment to positive action.[6] At London, expected support for proposed moves to stabilize world currencies was dramatically withdrawn in order to leave the government free to take whatever measures were desired on the home front.[7] The Roosevelt administration, that is, was

[4] Franklin D. Roosevelt, "Our Foreign Policy—A Democratic View," *Foreign Affairs*, VI (July, 1928), 580–582. See also Frank Freidel, *Franklin D. Roosevelt: The Ordeal* (Boston, 1954), pp. 238–241.

[5] *Public Papers of Franklin D. Roosevelt, Forty-eighth Governor of the State of New York, Second Term, 1932*, pp. 551 ff., as quoted in Charles A. Beard, *American Foreign Policy in the Making* (New York, 1946), pp. 75–77.

[6] Department of State, *Peace and War, United States Foreign Policy, 1931–41* (Washington, 1943), pp. 10–12, 186–191. Innocuous as this statement seemed in many ways, it was nevertheless characterized by John Bassett Moore as "the gravest danger to which the country has ever been exposed, a danger involving our very independence." "An Appeal to Reason," *Foreign Affairs*, XI (July, 1933), 571.

[7] Roosevelt's abrupt message withdrawing support from any move to stabilize

no more willing at this point than its predecessors to assume any specific obligations in world affairs, and its foreign policy strongly accentuated the economic nationalism that had been initiated immediately after the war. Under the impact of the depression, there was actually a retreat from the more internationalist outlook toward which the country had appeared to be moving.

This is not to say that Roosevelt was blind to what was happening abroad. Before the close of his first year in office, he stated that with 10 per cent of the world's population threatening the peace of the remaining 90 per cent, concerted measures should be taken to strengthen international security. Discounting "the old policies, alliances, combinations and balances of power," he urged new agreements for the elimination of aggression and the abolition of weapons of offensive warfare.[8] He did not, however, press this program and it aroused little popular interest among a people still struggling back from depression depths and deeply absorbed in the trials and tribulations of the NRA and the AAA.

This generally uninterested attitude toward foreign affairs began to change early in 1935. The New Deal had by then succeeded in bringing about some measure of economic recovery and was about to launch its further program of social reform. International relations, on the other hand, had deteriorated so badly that they could no longer be shunted aside. The threatening attitudes of both Mussolini and Hitler gave a new immediacy to the fears first awakened by the collapse of collective security when Japan attacked in Manchuria. Roosevelt declared there was no ground for apprehension so far as the foreign relations of the United States itself were concerned, but warned that as new strivings for armaments and power "rear their ugly heads," the nation had to recognize that the maintenance of international peace was a matter in which "we are deeply and unselfishly concerned."[9]

A first move to give practical expression to this new concern merely demonstrated the continuing isolationist temper of the country. Dur-

world currencies, stemming from his growing interest in devaluation and a managed currency for the United States, has given rise to a great deal of controversy. For his own admission that his message fell upon the conference "like a bombshell," see *Public Papers and Addresses*, II, 265. For the reactions of the two principals at the conference, Raymond Moley, *After Seven Years* (New York, 1939), pp. 255–269, and *Memoirs of Cordell Hull*, I, 256–269.

[8] *Roosevelt's Foreign Policy*, p. 47.

[9] *Ibid.*, pp. 70–71.

ing the past fifteen years internationalists had made repeated efforts
to have the United States join the World Court. In order—as he
stated—that this country might throw its weight into the scales in
favor of peace, Roosevelt now urged approval of the protocol governing our prospective membership which had been carefully worked out
by Elihu Root in 1929. Still the Senate balked. First, it insisted on
additional reservations, one of them repeating the no-entangling-
alliances safeguard affixed to the convention setting up the old Hague
Tribunal; then it turned around and rejected the World Court protocol altogether.[10]

The opponents of American membership based their objections on
the familiar argument that whatever reservations might be adopted,
the United States would be making a commitment that prejudiced its
complete freedom of action. "We are different over here," one senator
perhaps unconsciously paraphrased George Washington; "Why go
abroad?" [11] Such original foes of the League of Nations as Borah,
Johnson, and Norris spearheaded the attack on the Court, and they
were vehemently supported by the Hearst press and the Detroit radio
priest, Father Coughlin. The latter's last-minute appeal ("keep America safe for Americans . . . and not the hunting ground for international plutocrats") was responsible for a deluge of anti-Court letters
and telegrams which swamped the offices of wavering senators.[12]

It is sometimes maintained that this final propaganda barrage played
a decisive role in defeating World Court membership. The evidence is
far from conclusive. The failure of Roosevelt to exercise any important influence in support of his proposal, and the decidedly lukewarm
attitude of what had unjustifiably been assumed to be a predominantly
favorable Senate majority, appear to have been more telling factors.
Certainly, the World Court awoke no great popular enthusiasm. The
Senate vote, falling seven short of the necessary two thirds' majority
with 52 yeas and 36 nays, was interpreted as substantially reflecting
"the public mind as it has stood for many years." [13] Moreover if the
United States had assumed membership in 1935 with the amendments

[10] *Peace and War*, pp. 21, 245–246; Denna F. Fleming, *The United States
and the World Court* (New York, 1945), pp. 118–133.

[11] Quoted *ibid.*, p. 123.

[12] *The New York Times*, Jan. 28, 1935.

[13] *New Republic*, LXXXII (Feb. 13, 1935), 2; *Christian Century*, LII (Feb.
13, 1935), 198–199; statement by Senator Robinson on vote, *The New York
Times*, Feb. 3, 1935.

and reservations proposed by the Senate, it would have meant very little in the balance between peace and war. The episode was most significant in that it clearly revealed how fearful the United States continued to be of any foreign commitments whatsoever.

This isolationist attitude was soon to receive even more decided confirmation in the neutrality program which was the American response to the growing threat of war in Europe. The naked aggression of the fascist powers provided the incentive for an unprecedented congressional intrusion into the realm of foreign policy whose hopeful purpose was to keep the United States out of harm's way in the event of any general European conflict.

A first ominous development on the European scene was the brutal attack that Mussolini launched against Ethiopia in October, 1935. Foreign protests against such unprovoked aggression were unavailing; the half-hearted efforts of the League to impose sanctions upon Italy were completely ineffectual. As the world watched with growing anguish, Mussolini's legions succeeded in wholly subjecting the hapless little country and Ethiopia was incorporated in the Italian Empire.

Emboldened by his fellow dictator's success, Hitler thereupon underscored his shrill demands for a complete revision of the Versailles Treaty by sending his troops into the demilitarized Rhineland in March, 1936. And then, during this same fateful spring, a civil war broke out in Spain that still further intensified the growing crisis. For Italy and Germany directly supported the antidemocratic forces under General Franco, the rebel leader, in their attack upon the loyalist defenders of the existing Republican regime. The fascist nations, soon to be even more intimately linked through formation of the Rome-Berlin Axis, were on the march.

The western democracies were no more willing to pick up the challenge of fascist intervention in the Spanish civil war than they had been to call Mussolini to account for the attack upon Ethiopia. Fearful that any positive move would plunge all Europe into war, England and France followed a cautious policy which aimed at localizing the conflict in Spain in spite of the assistance given the rebels by Germany and Italy. The result was a further victory for fascism and the setting of the stage for World War II.[14]

The American Congress reacted to the mounting crisis in Europe

[14] See Claude G. Bowers, *My Mission to Spain* (New York, 1954).

by insisting upon a program of strict neutrality. On August 31, 1935, it enacted a first and temporary measure providing that whenever the President proclaimed the existence of a state of war, it would be unlawful to sell or export arms or munitions to any belligerent nation, or for American vessels to transport such materials of war to the ports of any belligerent, and further authorizing the President to forbid travel by American citizens on the ships of a belligerent except at their own risk. These bans were put into effect against both nations when Italy and Ethiopia became engaged in hostilities.

Six months later, Congress further tightened the existing law by decreeing that no loans should be extended to any belligerent power. Following the outbreak of the Spanish war and the realization that existing legislation did not apply to civil strife, it adopted upon Roosevelt's urging, in January, 1937, a joint resolution forbidding the export of arms and ammunition to Spain.[15]

These measures were then replaced in May, 1937, by a so-called "permanent" law. This legislation re-enacted the earlier provisions against the shipment of arms and munitions and the extension of loans to any belligerent, made mandatory the ban on travel by Americans on belligerent ships, and introduced a new provision, to be in force for two years only, whereby wartime trade in certain nonmilitary commodities, as designated by the President, would be lawful only when the belligerent nations paid for such commodities purchased in this country and transported them on their own vessels. This was the famous cash-and-carry stipulation that constituted a compromise between cutting of all wartime trade—a complete embargo—and permitting the sale of raw materials under conditions that were designed to avoid the difficulties that had developed during the First World War. In response to overwhelming isolationist and pacifist pressure, America was prepared to surrender that freedom of the seas for which she had stood so resolutely in 1812 and again in 1917.[16]

Everything conspired in the mid-1930's to strengthen the isolationist demand for neutrality legislation. The early disillusionment over the consequences of participation in the First World War had hardly

[15] Rosenman, *Public Papers and Addresses of Franklin D. Roosevelt,* V, 626, 634.

[16] *Peace and War,* pp. 266–272, 419–420, 468–474. See also Allen W. Dulles and Hamilton Fish Armstrong, *Can America Stay Neutral?* (New York, 1939), pp. 60, 72; Edwin M. Borchard and William Potter Lage, *Neutrality for the United States* (New Haven, 1937), pp. 337–343.

been mitigated by the rise of fascism in Italy and nazism in Germany. The old distrust of Europe was intensified by default on the war debts after what was generally considered by Americans as a generous scaling down of interest charges. The renewed armaments race heavily underscored the risks of general hostilities and the consequent danger to the United States of any sort of entanglement in European affairs.

And finally, a report on the past and present traffic in arms issued by a Senate committee headed by Gerald P. Nye of North Dakota had a tremendous popular impact. Its disclosures of the value of the munitions trade during the First World War, widely publicized and further amplified in many contemporary books and articles, with constant emphasis upon the tremendous profits of bankers and munitions makers, fortified the isolationists' belief that the United States should not have gone to war in 1917. The Nye report appeared to prove that the country had been needlessly dragged into that conflict to safeguard special economic interests.[17]

If this facile and basically false interpretation of the events of 1914–17 was accepted, the way to keep out of future wars seemed self-evident. All that was necessary was to cut off all trade in munitions and ban loans to belligerent nations. The United States would then not have any economic interests to safeguard. The neutrality legislation of the 1930's actually incorporated the proposals of the noninterventionists of Wilson's day. Instead of meeting realistically the existing emergency, they appeared to many observers designed to keep the United States out of a war that had been fought twenty years earlier.

Seldom has the popular reading—or misreading—of history had a more important effect on the making of foreign policy; and the inaccuracy of the lesson drawn from the experience of 1917 was paralleled by the want of logic in its application. The reasons for American participation in the First World War were obviously far more com-

---

[17] *Senate Report 944,* 74th Congress, 2nd Session, V. Among contemporary writings the most sensational was Helmoth C. Engelbrecht, *Merchants of Death* (New York, 1935).

One of the earliest "revisionist" accounts of American entry into the war, heavily stressing economic factors, was C. H. Grattan, *Why We Fought* (New York, 1929).

In *The Road to War* (New York, 1935), Walter Millis also reflected this viewpoint, which he later modified in an article in *Life,* "1939 is Not 1914" VII (Nov. 6, 1939), 75 ff. In answer to such interpretations of the events of 1917 were two important articles in *Foreign Affairs:* Charles Seymour, "American Neutrality: The Experience of 1914–17," XIV (Oct., 1935), 26–36; and Newton D. Baker, "Why We Went to War," XV (Oct., 1936), 1–86.

plex than the Nye Committee's attribution of all responsibility to
Allied propagandists, wicked bankers, and greedy munitions makers.
It has been seen that mounting sympathy for the Allied cause, and the
belief that only the defeat of Germany could assure a peace founded
upon principles of justice and freedom, were far more important factors in persuading the American people to take up arms than any
consideration of trade and profits. Whatever might have happened
twenty years earlier, moreover, no such simple expedient as an arms
embargo could hope to assure peace for the United States in a world
successively challenged by fascism and communism.

Roosevelt was not happy over the neutrality laws. He had strongly
favored legislation that would at once have sought to maintain neutrality, and yet have enabled the President to exercise some influence
in support of peace by giving him a discretionary power in imposing
an arms embargo only against the aggressor nation. Congress had not
been interested. It was unwilling to make any distinction in its legislation between the aggressor and his victim, or to give the President
any real leeway in the application of the law. While both Hull and
Roosevelt remained fearful that the inflexibility of the congressional
program might draw the nation into war instead of keeping it out,
they felt that there was no way in which the executive branch of the
government "could withstand the isolationist cyclone." [18] The Secretary of State advised the President to approve the neutrality bills, and
Roosevelt—although he was later to state that he believed their adoption to have been a mistake—duly signed them.[19]

Whether a stronger stand might have influenced Congress is doubtful. In any event, it was not taken. The President in effect abdicated
his leadership in foreign affairs. He made no real or sustained effort
in the mid-1930's to win the approval of Congress for any more realistic program than that inspired by the revelations of the Nye Committee. He was content to remain on the sidelines while national policy
was largely shaped by the impact of events abroad on a strongly
isolationist-minded congressional majority.

In a Chautauqua address in August, 1936, moreover, Roosevelt expressed a rather middle-of-the-road position on the issues involved,
and appeared quite ready to accept the basic principles of the neutrality program. Declaring that the United States shunned all political

[18] *Memoirs of Cordell Hull*, I, 400.
[19] *Ibid.*, I, 410 ff., 415, 509; *Roosevelt's Foreign Policy*, pp. 76–77, 194.

commitments that might entangle the country in foreign wars, he warned also against the nation letting itself get into a position where it might be drawn into hostilities to safeguard economic interests. If the choice should ever be presented between profits and war, he stated emphatically, and with obvious reference to the disclosures of the Nye Committee, the nation "will answer—must answer—'we choose peace.' " [20]

Nor did Secretary Hull offer any forthright support for collective security. He was later to write that during this period the administration was fighting "week in and week out" to prove that the isolationism expressed in the neutrality program was a dangerous policy,[21] but there is little evidence of such sustained activity. The Secretary of State was highly cautious, and very much aware of the strength of the isolationist tide. His public statements did not seem to carry him much further than even Borah was willing to go. As late as September, 1937, Hull was abjuring internationalism in favor of what he called a policy of "enlightened nationalism." [22]

Whatever the actual views of either Roosevelt or Hull at this time, however, the failure to make a more decided fight against isolationism was largely due to domestic political considerations. The President was deeply concerned over what he was trying to accomplish at home. Enactment of the neutrality legislation coincided with consideration of the most important measures of the "Second New Deal"—labor legislation, social security, control of public utilities, and the attempted reform of the Supreme Court. Circumstances consequently placed a premium on maintaining a closely cooperative relationship between the executive and legislative branches of the government, and such cooperation would have been gravely prejudiced by a fight over neutrality.

It is of great significance that the foremost isolationists in Congress, largely representative, as in the past, of the progressive bloc within the Republican party, consistently backed the New Deal program and helped to make up the New Deal majority.[23] Roosevelt may well have

[20] *Ibid.*, pp. 102, 104.
[21] *Memoirs of Cordell Hull,* I, 666.
[22] *The New York Times,* Sept. 21, 1937.
[23] At one in support of Roosevelt's domestic program and in opposition to his proposed foreign policy were such Republican progressives as Senators Borah, Capper, Frazier, Johnson, La Follette, McNary, Nye, Norris, and Shipstead (Farmer-Laborite). Except in one or two instances, they all voted for the Social Security Act, the Public Utility Holding Act, the Wagner Act, the "Soak the Rich" tax bill—and the neutrality acts.

thought that he could not risk alienating their support for his reform projects by attacking their concepts of foreign policy. He was perhaps able to quiet his doubts on the wisdom of neutrality legislation when he set it alongside his assured conviction of the importance of liberal labor legislation and social security.

The administration therefore continued to move slowly and carefully in foreign affairs. The promotion of trade reciprocity, which was gradually modifying the old economic nationalism, and a series of conferences seeking greater understanding with Latin America were its most substantial achievements during Roosevelt's first term. A highly significant departure from the policies of the Republican administrations of the 1920's was the diplomatic recognition of Soviet Russia in 1933, but the hopes of more friendly relations between the United States and the U.S.S.R. did not materialize. There was continued friction over Communist interference in domestic affairs, no settlement of debts, and very slight gains in Soviet-American trade. Policy in eastern Asia at this same time was directed toward a possible *rapprochement* with Japan, within the framework of the nonrecognition doctrine proclaimed by Secretary Stimson. Here again not very much could be accomplished so long as Japan insisted on her paramount rights in Manchuria and steadily encroached on north China.

While Congress had nationwide backing for the general provisions of the neutrality legislation, there were vigorous attacks upon its application to the civil war in Spain. Critics of this phase of national policy maintained that the United States was actually penalizing the recognized government of a friendly nation by shutting it off from the American munitions market, and at least indirectly giving aid and comfort to rebels who were receiving substantial support from the fascist regimes of Germany and Italy. The soundness of the view that the United States was thereby itself serving the cause of fascism could hardly be disputed, but the isolationist ranks held firm in insisting upon what they declared to be the only safe course for the United States to follow.

The refusal to heed the pleas that the President should be given some discretionary power in the application of the neutrality laws in international war reflected in some measure the strong anti-Roosevelt feeling at a time when the President was repeatedly being charged with seeking dictatorial powers. The insistence with which anti-New Dealers—both Republican and Democratic—demanded absolutely rigid legislation was clearly affected by partisan bias. Yet this was not the whole story. The Neutrality Act of 1937 passed the House by a vote of 376 to 13, and the Senate by a vote of 63 to 6. The support for this measure was much broader than any political, sectional, or factional alignment.[24]

Newspaper and periodical opinion provided further confirmation of the heightened isolationist trend. This was if anything even more true in the case of liberal journals and farm and labor organs than in that of business reviews. Public opinion surveys also reported popular support for the neutrality program with sufficient decisiveness to have for once some real meaning. Only a very small minority of those interviewed in the polls taken in 1935–37 were willing to consider any sort of collaboration with the League of Nations, or the adoption of any form of sanctions in seeking to bring pressure upon an aggressor nation.[25]

In time the passion for peace would be countered by a mounting sympathy for the forces of democracy arrayed against the evil designs of fascism. The American people would be recalled to their commitment to liberty as well as their commitment to peace; the inner contradictions of their attitude would become more apparent.[26] In the mid-1930's, however, it was still almost universally agreed that come what might the United States could best defend its own interests—and therefore should do so—by carefully avoiding any direct intervention in the troubled world beyond its shores.

As if events in Europe were not sufficiently disturbing for the future of world peace, Japan chose this summer of 1937 to renew her attack upon China. The Japanese militarists, who had been jockeying for a stronger position ever since 1931, were now firmly in the saddle, and determined to establish national hegemony over the entire Far East. The growing international anarchy embraced Asia as well as Europe.

[24] *Congressional Record*, LXXXI, 75th Congress, 1st Session (March 3, 1937), p. 1807; (March 18, 1937), p. 2410.

[25] Any comparison of editorials in such periodicals as the *New Republic, Nation,* and *Christian Century* with those in the *Commercial and Financial Chronicle, Business Week,* and *The Nation's Business* brings this out clearly. Polls as reported by Hadley Cantril (ed.), *Public Opinion, 1935–46* (Princeton, 1951), pp. 966, 967. See also Francis S. Wickware, "What We Think About Foreign Affairs," *Harper's Magazine,* CLXXIX (Sept., 1939), 397–406.

[26] For the confusion in the position of "isolationists" and "internationalists," see particularly Basil Rauch, *Roosevelt: From Munich to Pearl Harbor* (New York, 1950), pp. 1–12.

This new development aroused President Roosevelt from the somewhat indifferent attitude with which he had appeared to regard foreign affairs. Realizing anew the danger to the United States should a general war break out, he tried to discover some positive way to align the United States with the forces working for peace. It was to be charged that his changed attitude represented no more than an attempt to divert public attention from the inadequacies of the New Deal and from the political defeat he had suffered this same June in the struggle over the Supreme Court. The mounting world crisis was of itself more than enough, however, to recall him to the advocacy of that collective security that he had once believed held out the only promise of peace for the United States.

In any event, the President decided to explore public reactions to a possible program calling the aggressor nations to account. The position of the United States seemed to be more and more becoming one of condoning aggression through advance notice that its victims would be unable to obtain arms or ammunition in the American market. While the failure of either China or Japan to declare war in 1937 made it unnecessary in this instance to invoke the ban on arms shipments, as it had been invoked in the Italian-Ethiopian conflict and Spain's civil war, this did not change the over-all situation.

Roosevelt's test of public opinion was his famous "quarantine speech," delivered in Chicago on October 5, 1937, in which he dramatically appealed to the country to face the realities of a world drifting toward war. If the existing "reign of terror and lawlessness" were to be overcome, the President stated, there had to be concerted action on the part of all peace-loving nations to uphold the standards of international morality. No escape from the consequences of the breakdown of world order was possible "through mere isolation or neutrality." Repeating his earlier statement that the freedom and security of 90 per cent of the world population were being jeopardized by the remaining 10 per cent, Roosevelt declared there must surely be some way whereby those who wanted to live in peace could make their will prevail.

So far these were rather general statements. At this point he departed from his speech as originally outlined by his State Department advisors and came more directly to grips with the basic issue:

It seems to be unfortunately true that the epidemic of world lawlessness is spreading.

When an epidemic of physical disease starts to spread, the community approves and joins in a quarantine of the patients in order to protect the health of the community against the spread of the disease.[27]

The reaction to the "quarantine speech," for that phrase was immediately singled out by the press, was varied. There were those who applauded an assertion of presidential leadership in foreign affairs that had long been wanting. "An eloquent voice," declared *The New York Times,* "has expressed the deep moral indignation which is felt in this country toward policies of ruthlessness and conquest." [28] More generally, however, newspaper editorials reflected either a very questioning attitude or an uneasy alarm. The suggestion that the speech was no more than an attempt to make political capital by a sensational, warmongering appeal to national emotions was occasionally advanced in the anti-New Deal press. Other newspapers emphasized the irresponsibility of urging departure from a policy that had been overwhelmingly approved by Congress. *Business Week* and the *New Republic* were agreed that the President appeared to be willing to run the risks of war in rejecting the neutrality program. He had made a "dangerous and tragic choice." [29]

Representing the pacifist elements that most vigorously rejected any idea of sanctions or force in upholding peace, the *Christian Century* also expressed an uneasy concern over what Roosevelt had in mind:

. . . his attitude toward the neutrality law, his use of the "quarantine" metaphor, his inveterate navalism, his need of distracting attention from certain unhappy features of his domestic policy and of rallying Congress to his support, his possible ambition to outdo the other Roosevelt with the latter's Treaty of Portsmouth, and the contingency of a possible third term ambition—these considerations work together in the public mind to cause and in considerable degree to justify much of the apprehension which exists.[30]

Roosevelt felt, as he later phrased it, that the speech upon which he counted so much had fallen "upon deaf ears—even hostile and resentful ears." Once again he was perhaps unduly impressed by the vociferousness of the isolationist outcry and failed to realize that further

[27] *Roosevelt's Foreign Policy,* pp. 129–132.

[28] *The New York Times,* Oct. 6, 1937.

[29] Summaries of newspaper opinion are to be found in Charles Callan Tansill, *Back Door to War—Roosevelt Foreign Policy, 1933–41* (Chicago, 1952), pp. 344–347; Samuel L. Rosenman, *Working With Roosevelt* (New York, 1952), pp. 166–168. For the next day's press conference see *Public Papers and Addresses of Franklin D. Roosevelt,* VI, 422–425.

[30] *Christian Century,* LIV (Oct. 20, 1937), 1287.

hammering at the points he had made in the quarantine speech might well have won increasing support for a more positive foreign policy. Secretary Hull was even more cautious in interpreting the popular reaction. He was convinced that the President had gone too far in suggesting a quarantine, and used all his influence in urging greater moderation in further policy statements. A good many years later Hull was to write that this speech set back the cause of educating the American public to internationalism by at least six months.[31] There is no more evidence to support this conclusion than the directly opposite verdict of some commentators that the speech significantly changed popular attitudes.

What further measures Roosevelt may have had in mind had he been certain of popular backing for a stronger policy are not entirely clear. There was the possibility of sanctions and also the project, first suggested by Under Secretary of State Sumner Welles, for a world conference to seek agreement on certain fundamental principles in support of peace.[32] Roosevelt for a time seriously considered the latter idea, planning a dramatic Armistice Day meeting of all foreign envoys to announce his plan. However, according to Welles, it was "almost hysterically opposed" by certain of the President's closest advisors and he reluctantly abandoned it.[33]

The caution imposed by the apparent lack of support for collective action against aggressors was even more conspicuous at the Brussels Conference, of November, 1937, on international policy toward Japan's renewed attack on China. The instructions given to the American delegate, Norman Davis, limited the scope of American participation to discussion of a possible settlement of the Chinese-Japanese controversy through peaceful negotiation, stressed the fact that the first objective of this country's foreign policy was its own national security, and carefully warned Davis to "observe closely the trend of public opinion in the United States and take full account thereof." [34]

In such circumstances there was no chance whatsoever that the conferees at Brussels would decide upon any active measures to restrain

[31] *Memoirs of Cordell Hull*, I, 545.

[32] Sumner Welles, *The Time for Decision* (New York, 1944), pp. 64–69; *Memoirs of Cordell Hull*, I, 546–549; Joseph Alsop and Robert Kintner, *American White Paper* (New York, 1940), p. 91; and particularly William L. Langer and S. Everett Gleason, *The Challenge to Isolation, 1937–1940* (New York, 1952), pp. 19–32.

[33] Welles, *The Time for Decision*, p. 66.

[34] *Peace and War*, pp. 50–52, 389–390. *Memoirs of Cordell Hull*, I, 552.

Japan. The idea of possible sanctions, which had at least been entertained in 1932 even if rejected, was not even considered. The failure of the Brussels Conference was complete. It emphasized anew the com-

Herbert Johnson in *Saturday Evening Post*, January 8, 1938

"Samuel! You're not going to another lodge meeting!"

plete collapse of collective security, and also the further retreat of the United States into uncompromising political isolation.

Still, Roosevelt made one more effort to stem the tide. Although he said nothing more about quarantining aggressors, he did revive the idea of a world conference in a somewhat different form, and early in 1938 sounded out the British Government as to its practicality. Prime Minister Chamberlain rejected the President's proposal. What Winston Churchill was later to call "the last frail chance to save the world from tyranny otherwise than by war" thus came to nothing.[35] Whether it could have commanded effective support either at home or abroad is doubtful, and the President was in any event finally convinced there was nothing more he could do. Apart from his measures to win greater Latin American cooperation in hemisphere defense, and the extension of the Monroe Doctrine to include Canada, he let things drift.[36]

Secretary Hull might reiterate, as he did in March, 1938, that isolationism could never become a means to security, but remained "a fruitful source of insecurity." [37] The public seemed indifferent. This period was the low point in popular disregard of the responsibilities and obligations, and also the dangers, that were the inescapable consequence of the position of world power that the United States had attained. This continued isolationist-pacifist attitude of the country had perhaps been most graphically revealed at the opening of the year in the agitation for a constitutional amendment requiring a popular referendum on any declaration of war. Although this proposal was defeated in the House, the narrow margin of votes—209 to 188—afforded striking evidence of the unrealistic nature of popular thinking on world affairs.

In the meantime, events in Europe were hurrying toward still graver crises. Strengthened in his resolve to create a greater Germany, if need be by force of arms, Hitler occupied Austria in March, 1938, and six months later began to press upon Czechoslovakia his demand for the surrender of the German-populated Sudetenland. While England and France passively acquiesced in Austria's incorporation into the Third Reich, they felt driven to action in support of Czechoslovakia, and Europe suddenly found itself confronted with possible war. The diplomatic wires linking Berlin, Prague, Paris, Rome, and London (Soviet Russia was largely ignored) ominously hummed as frantic efforts were made to avert the crisis. After a series of hectic preliminary discussions, Hitler finally agreed to a conference with the heads of state of Great Britain, France, and Italy.

[35] Winston S. Churchill, *The Gathering Storm* (Boston, 1948), pp. 254–255.
[36] *Roosevelt's Foreign Policy*, pp. 139–140, 143–144.
[37] *Peace and War*, pp. 57, 418; *Vital Speeches*, IV (Apr. 1, 1938), 368–372.

This meeting was held at Munich on September 29 in an atmosphere tense with a dread expectancy. The result was a new international accord—"peace in our time," as Prime Minister Chamberlain hopefully termed it—but what was to prove no more than a brief and fateful truce had been won only by appeasement. The western democracies deserted Czechoslovakia. And while Hitler agreed to occupy no more of that unfortunate country than the Sudetenland, even this cynical pledge was soon flouted. In March, 1939, the Nazi leader openly defied England and France by forcibly taking over all Czechoslovakia. Encouraged by his Axis partner's success, Mussolini thereupon seized little Albania. The whole structure of European peace was crashing into ruins.[38]

During these critical days of the autumn of 1938, Roosevelt sent abroad message after message expressing the hope of the United States that a way could be found to maintain peace. He appealed to Mussolini to exercise his good offices; he urged moderation on Hitler. While recognizing "our responsibilities as part of a world of neighbors," the President nevertheless always made it clear that the United States accepted no political involvements in Europe and would assume no obligations in the conduct of its negotiations.[39] There is little reason to believe that his messages at the time of the Munich crisis, or at any time during 1939, had any effect whatsoever on the course of events. In view of the neutrality legislation, if for no other reason, the President could hardly have expected that they would.

His Annual Message to Congress in January, 1939, was largely devoted to foreign affairs. Munich had all too obviously postponed rather than averted a final crisis. "All about us rage undeclared wars—military and economic," Roosevelt told the country. "All about us grow more deadly armaments—military and economic. All about us are threats of new aggression—military and economic." The peace-loving nations could not indefinitely stand aside without effective protest, he continued, and even though the United States was not prepared to intervene in this situation by force of arms, it could not continue to act as if there were no aggression. "There are many methods short of war, but stronger and more effective than mere words, of bringing home to aggressor governments the aggregate sentiments of our own people." Whatever the President had in mind, it was not the contin-

[38] For discussion of these events as affecting American policy, Langer and Gleason, *The Challenge to Isolation,* p. 32–51.
[39] *Roosevelt's Foreign Policy,* p. 152.

uation of the neutrality policy as written into existing law: "We have learned that when we deliberately try to legislate neutrality, our neutrality laws may operate unevenly and unfairly—may actually give aid to the aggressor and deny it to the victim. The instinct of self-preservation should warn us that we ought not to let that happen any more." [40]

Roosevelt tried to implement such ideas by calling for repeal of the arms embargo. But his political position was weak and he was afraid to stir up too much opposition on the part of the isolationists. Once again he was confronted by congressional fear that any tampering with the existing legislation would lead to a situation such as that which had drawn the United States into war in 1917. Even the expiration of the cash-and-carry provisions of the "permanent" neutrality law did not persuade Congress that anything should be done. It remained stubbornly opposed to any move whereby the United States could serve notice on potential aggressors that its policy would distinguish between them and the victims of their aggression.

Yet Congress no longer reflected public opinion on this issue as it had in 1937. Newspaper editorials and the polls suggest a pronounced shift in popular attitudes by mid-1939 in favor of a modification of the neutrality laws whereby arms and munitions, as well as other goods, could be purchased on a cash-and-carry basis.[41] This would have directly favored Great Britain and France, as opposed to Germany, through their control of the seas, and the desire to change the law clearly revealed a mounting sympathy for the western democracies. The isolationists, however, were still strongly entrenched in Congress, and the partisanship that had always affected the neutrality issue was perhaps fiercer than ever. The position of the foes of revision was most succinctly expressed by Representative Vorys of Ohio: "The President's policy is to use the threat of our power to preserve a balance of power in Europe. Opposed to this is the traditional American belief that the way to peace is for us to be neutral . . ." [42]

[40] *Ibid.*, pp. 155–156; Rosenman, *Working With Roosevelt*, pp. 183–187.
[41] Cantril, *Public Opinion*, pp. 967–968; William O. Scroggs and Whitney H. Shephardson, *The United States in World Affairs, 1939* (New York, 1940), p. 80.
[42] *Congressional Record*, LXXIV, 76th Congress, 1st Session (June 28, 1939), p. 8151. For further quotations from the debate in the House, Charles A. Beard, *American Foreign Policy in the Making, 1932–40* (New Haven, 1946), pp. 227–232; and for other evidence of public opinion, Langer and Gleason, *The Challenge to Isolation*, pp. 136–147; Rosenman, *Working With Roosevelt*,

The Republicans as a whole insisted vigorously upon retention of the mandatory embargo on arms and ammunition. The result was that the administration proposals for changing the law were amended out of all reason in the House, and their consideration was postponed in the Senate by a 12-to-11 vote of the Foreign Relations Committee. When Roosevelt made a further last-minute appeal to the Senate leaders, at a famous conference on July 18 at which Borah casually stated that his own sources indicated there was no immediate danger of European war, Vice-President Garner brought the discussion to a close. "Well, Captain," he is reported to have said, "we may as well face the facts. You haven't got the votes and that's all there is to it." [43] The policy of the United States remained as it had been: in the event of war the sale of munitions would be forbidden to all belligerents.

This was the final triumph of the isolationists. Never again would they hold the strategically dominant position which was theirs in midsummer 1939. Their influence remained formidable. It would be consistently thrown against every proposed move to enable the United States to play a more positive role in world affairs. With the outbreak of the European war, however, they were gradually forced back in a slow, strategic retreat. It was not complete surrender—as postwar developments would show—but the American people as a whole finally began to realize as never before that the United States could not stand alone in a world where aggression anywhere threatened every peace-loving nation.

---

pp. 184–187; Rauch, *Roosevelt: Munich to Pearl Harbor*, pp. 102–127. See also F. O. Wilcox, "The Neutrality Fight in Congress," *American Political Science Review* (Oct., 1939), 811 ff., and Kenneth Colegrove, *The American Senate and World Peace* (New York, 1944), pp. 58–59.

[43] It was claimed by Hiram Johnson that he could muster up to forty votes opposed to any change whatsoever in the existing legislation. *The New York Times*, July 9, 1939. Roosevelt himself stated that the committee decision was "about a cross section of the opinion of the Senate." *The New York Times*, July 12, 1939. The Garner statement is from Alsop and Kintner, *American White Paper*, p. 46.

CHAPTER 10

Challenge and Response

THE IMMEDIATE reaction in the United States to the challenge flung at the world when on September 1, 1939, Hitler sent his armed columns crashing into Poland was one of bewildered frustration. The American people hoped desperately that the United States could continue to remain at home and mind its own affairs, whatever happened in Europe. President Roosevelt's promise that so long as it lay within his power there would be "no black-out of peace in the United States" [1] reflected the devout wish of the country as a whole.

In spite of this general attitude, there was from the very outbreak of hostilities—in sharp contrast to 1914—almost universal sympathy for the Allied cause. This was at once revealed in a movement for revision of the existing neutrality legislation in the interests of England and France. The cash-and-carry provisions of the 1937 act had expired; the munitions embargo was still in effect. President Roosevelt called Congress into special session on September 21, to urge repeal of the embargo and substitution of a provision that would allow the belligerents to purchase munitions as well as raw materials on a strictly cash-and-carry basis.[2]

In seeking repeal of the arms embargo, administration spokesmen officially took a very careful position. They did not speak of the help such action would afford Great Britain and France; they emphasized the supposed strengthening of American neutrality. There was never any question, however, of the real intent of the proposed changes in the law. As a result of its own manufactures and the seizure of the

[1] *Roosevelt's Foreign Policy* (New York, 1942), p. 184.
[2] *Ibid.*, pp. 192–198.

great munitions works in Czechoslovakia while the world was nominally at peace, Germany had on hand military supplies that the Allies
could not match unless they somehow had access to the American
munitions market. Roosevelt actually sought neutrality revision because of a mounting conviction that the United States could not possibly follow a policy that penalized the nations fighting Hitlerism.

Still, public opinion was divided on the wisdom of the repeal of the
arms embargo. While something like four fifths of the nation's newspapers favored it, and business sentiment as reflected in trade and
financial journals approved, labor and farm organizations were generally fearful of such a move. Liberal opinion was much confused. The
New Republic, for example, continued to call for a strict neutrality,
but conceded the need for some modification in the existing law. While
the war aims of the Allies were still somewhat obscure, it declared
editorially, there appeared to be sufficient warrant to grant them the
"light additional aid" that repeal of the embargo would mean. Public
opinion polls, theoretically representing a cross-section of all these divergent elements, reported in October a favorable majority of 57 per
cent for revision.[3]

There was little more than sporadic popular interest in the actual
debates on the floor of Congress—everything had been said too many
times—and political partisanship often seemed to be the determining
factor in accounting for the alignment on the administration's proposals. However, the old isolationist bloc opposed strongly any modification whatsoever in the neutrality laws as they then stood. Revision
was interpreted not only as first step toward eventual participation in
the war, but as a repudiation of the basic premises on which it was
believed American foreign policy should be founded.

Such senators as Robert La Follette, Jr., Gerald Nye, and Hiram
Johnson led the attack, and there was to be no surrender on the part
of the aging but still intransigent Borah. In his last speeches to Congress and over the radio, he insisted that come what might America
should continue to steer clear of any European entanglement. So
fundamental a departure from neutrality as repeal of the arms embargo, he declared, would be disastrous, for it would constitute a moral
commitment for intervention should all not go well with the Allies—
"you will send munitions without pay and you will send your boys back

    [3] William O. Scroggs and Whitney H. Shephardson, *The United States in
World Affairs, 1939* (New York, 1940), pp. 167–179; the *New Republic,* C
(Oct. 18, 1939), 285; Hadley Cantril (ed.), *Public Opinion, 1935–46* (Prince-
ton, 1951), p. 967.

to the slaughter pens of Europe." [4] In spite of the isolationist campaign, however, Congress approved trade in arms and munitions on a cash-and-carry basis by a vote of 55 to 24 in the Senate and 243 to 172 in the House.

For six months—the period of the so-called phony war—no further action was taken; hope that the war would not spread persisted. Early in 1940, believing that the United States should somehow exercise its influence for peace, the President sent Under Secretary of State Welles abroad to discover whether there were any bases for possible mediation. It was a forlorn and hopeless mission. The only thing that could have given Hitler pause, Welles later wrote, would have been to impress upon him that if he carried a war of devastation to western Europe, the United States would ultimately intervene; [5] and, in the light of public opinion, any such pronouncement of policy was never even contemplated by the administration. Robert Sherwood has written that these six months were the one time in Roosevelt's career when he was at a loss what to do—"a period of terrible, stultifying vacuum." [6]

In his Annual Message in January, 1940, the President sought to arouse the nation to the dangers with which it was confronted and the impossibility of continuing on an isolationist course. There were those, he said, "who wishfully insist, in innocence or ignorance, or both, that the United States of America as a self-contained unit can live happily and prosperously, its future secure, inside a high wall of isolation, while outside the rest of civilization and the commerce and culture of mankind are shattered . . .

"I hope that we shall have fewer American ostriches in our midst. It is not good for the ultimate health of ostriches to bury their heads in the sand." [7]

Other than to emphasize "the leadership which this nation can take when the time comes for a renewal of world peace," the President proposed no definite action. Secretary Hull, also envisaging the possible role of the United States as the great neutral peacemaker, in his turn went no further than to try through several public addresses to prepare the public for the assumption of new responsibilities at the close of hostilities. [8]

[4] *Vital Speeches*, V (Oct. 1, 1939), 741–743; VI (Oct. 15, 1939), 21–23.
[5] Sumner Welles, *The Time for Decision* (New York, 1944), p. 119.
[6] Robert E. Sherwood, *Roosevelt and Hopkins* (New York, 1948), p. 123.
[7] *Roosevelt's Foreign Policy*, pp. 213–214, 215.
[8] *The Memoirs of Cordell Hull* (2 vols., New York, 1948), I, 732.

The sudden shock of Hitler's swift invasion of Norway and Denmark in April, 1940, the conquest of the Low Countries in May, the terrifying collapse of France in mid-June, and the mounting threat to a be-

Reprinted from *A Short History of American Diplomacy*, L. Ethan Ellis

leaguered Great Britain finally awoke the American people from their complacent attitude toward the war. The shattering impact of German conquests in western Europe overnight aroused them to the demands of national defense and to the urgency of aiding nations which alone stood between them and a possible future attack on American shores.[9] There was still no idea on the part of the administration of any commitment to active intervention in the war, in spite of the frantic pleas from both England and France. But Roosevelt felt it imperative to redefine American policy in the belief that "military and naval victory for the gods of force and hate would endanger the institutions of democracy in the western world."

At the very height of the crisis in France, as Italy attacked from the south and the German armies stood almost at the gates of Paris, he spoke to the country and to the world in a notable address at Charlottesville, Virginia. After castigating the Italian Government for its treacherous action—"On this 10th day of June, 1940, the hand that held the dagger has struck it into the back of its neighbor"—he declared:

In our unity, in our American unity, we will pursue two obvious and simultaneous courses; we will extend to the opponents of force the material resources of this nation and, at the same time, we will harness and speed up the use of those resources in order that we ourselves in the Americas may have equipment and training equal to the task of any emergency and every defense.

All roads leading to the accomplishment of these objectives must be kept clear of obstructions. We will not slow down or detour. Signs and signals call for speed—full speed ahead.[10]

There was always strong backing for hemisphere defense. In his calls for military and naval appropriations that before the end of 1940 reached the staggering total of $17 billion, for the creation of a two-ocean Navy, and for the adoption of peacetime conscription, Roosevelt faced no effective opposition. Universally approved, too, were the agreements reached at the Havana Conference in July, 1940, whereby the American republics undertook to prevent any change in the status of the European colonies in the Western Hemisphere and to consider any act of aggression in the New World as directed against them all,[11] and the plans shortly afterward adopted at Ogdensburg for the joint

[9] For full discussion, see William L. Langer and S. Everett Gleason, The Challenge to Isolation, 1937–1940 (New York, 1952), pp. 436–544.

[10] Roosevelt's Foreign Policy, pp. 252–253.

[11] Department of State, Peace and War: United States Foreign Policy, 1931–1941 (Washington, 1943), pp. 82, 562–563. Many of these wartime agreements, as well as other diplomatic documents, may be most conveniently found (though sometimes abridged) in Ruhl J. Bartlett, The Record of American Diplomacy (New York, 1954), in this instance, pp. 557–558.

defense of Canada and the United States.[12] Aid to the European nations still arrayed against Hitler, however, was a different matter. About this vital issue whirled for eighteen months the dark clouds of embittered controversy.

There could be no question that America had a tremendous stake in Allied victory, or—to put it another way—that she would be gravely imperiled by Hitler's conquest of all Europe. The question endlessly debated, however, was whether this stake—or this peril—called for a program that might lead to direct intervention in the war, or whether the United States could continue to rely upon its own resources for national safety even if the Axis powers were triumphant. Hovering somewhere between the extreme points of view represented by those who favored entry into the war and those who would have placed complete reliance upon continental defense were the great majority of the American people. Convinced that Germany's defeat was imperative if western democracy were to be safe, they at the same time believed that it was vital to keep this country at peace. As it became apparent that the United States held the balance of global power, and that the course followed might well prove decisive in determining the war's outcome, they felt themselves caught in a fateful dilemma. Moreover the issue at stake involved not only neutrality, but the basic and unresolved problem of just what should be America's role in world affairs generally.

The succession of important steps implementing the foreign policy of 1940–41—the destroyer–naval-base deal, the lend-lease program, the economic boycott of Japan, the acceptance of a shooting war in the Atlantic, and the firm stand taken in the Pacific—were primarily the consequence of the momentous events occurring abroad. As Hitler overran the greater part of western Europe, occupying the Low Countries and imposing his rule upon a truncated France, and then steadily intensified the air war against Great Britain with the constant threat of invasion, the situation confronting the United States grew ever more menacing. The logic of trying to help hard-pressed friends fight potential foes became increasingly unanswerable. Whatever the risks of involvement, to stand wholly aside meant that the United States might some day find itself a solitary fortress of democracy in a fascist-ruled world.

[12] *Roosevelt's Foreign Policy*, p. 272.

The destroyer–naval-base deal, inspired by the urgent need to aid Britain during her hour of greatest peril in the summer of 1940, was the first concrete measure of American assistance. The United States undertook to furnish England with fifty over-age destroyers, together with certain other military material. For its part, the British Government pledged itself never to surrender its fleet to Germany; transferred to the United States, as an outright gift, air and naval bases in Newfoundland and Bermuda; and further granted ninety-nine-year leases for additional bases in the Bahamas, Jamaica, St. Lucia, Trinidad, British Guiana, and Antigua. The agreement reached only after prolonged negotiations, was incorporated in an exchange of letters on September 2, 1940, between Secretary Hull and the British Ambassador, Lord Lothian.[13]

Here was a sharp departure from the strict neutrality originally envisaged for American policy, and it proved to be only a first step along such lines. Before the close of 1940, Roosevelt was considering a plan to make further aid available to Great Britain and the other nations fighting Hitlerism by lending or leasing essential war materials. The virtual exhaustion of available British funds for the purchase of munitions in this country, the general opposition to loans that might create a postwar debt situation comparable to the unhappy heritage of the First World War, and an importunate letter from Prime Minister Churchill emphasizing Great Britain's imperative needs provided the background for the lend-lease program. It was largely Roosevelt's own inspiration, and he took the occasion of both a news conference and a fireside chat to awaken public opinion to the need for prompt action.[14]

Early in January, 1941, the Treasury Department drafted a bill to implement Roosevelt's program and it was introduced in Congress with the symbolic title of House Resolution 1776. It authorized the President to sell, transfer, exchange, lease, lend, under such terms as he thought suitable, supplies of munitions, food, weapons, and other defense articles to any nation whose defense he deemed vital to the defense of the United States.[15] The provision of such assistance, Secre-

[13] *Peace and War*, pp. 83–84, 564–568.

[14] Sherwood, *Roosevelt and Hopkins*, pp. 221 ff.; Samuel I. Rosenman, *Working with Roosevelt* (New York, 1952), pp. 256 ff.

[15] *Peace and War*, pp. 100–102, 627–630; Edward R. Stettinius, Jr., *Lend-Lease—Weapon for Victory* (New York, 1944), for general discussion and terms of act, pp. 335–339. Also William L. Langer and S. Everett Gleason, *The Undeclared War, 1940–1941* (New York, 1952), pp. 213–289.

tary Hull explained in supporting the bill, was imperative in order that control of the high seas should remain in the hands of law-abiding nations. This was "the key to the security of the Western Hemisphere," for should control of the seas fall into the hands of the Axis powers, the danger to the United States "would be multiplied manyfold." [16]

Two months were consumed in impassioned debate. The President rallied to his support those who agreed with him that the defeat of the Axis was vital to American security and were willing to follow his leadership in whatever steps seemed advisable to aid the Allies. He was opposed by two groups. The first was made up of those isolationists who were convinced that this further abrogation of neutrality would ultimately draw the United States into war, and that in the meantime resources would be dissipated that might better be held for the defense of the nation itself. The second group comprised congressmen who tended to favor aid for Great Britain, but were reluctant to grant the President such sweeping powers or to authorize him to extend support to any nation—possibly including Soviet Russia—whose defense, on his own sole authority, he deemed vital in the American interest. Only after several amendments seeking to limit the presidential powers had been beaten down did Congress finally fall in line. The final votes—260 to 165 in the House and 60 to 31 in the Senate—were nevertheless decisive, and on March 11, 1941, the Lend-Lease Act became law with the President's signature. Shortly afterward a first appropriation of $7 billion got this important program underway.[17]

Unknown to the public, still another development at this time reflected the growing *rapproachement* between the United States and Great Britain. Secret discussions in Washington during February and March between representatives of the American and British Chiefs of Staff led to acceptance of a joint report—the ABC-1 Staff agreement—outlining a common strategy that would make lend-lease aid most effective, and also provide for future contingencies should the United States actively enter the war. To make clear that no commitments were involved, the President did not formally approve this report, but it was nonetheless highly revealing of the progress of Anglo-American cooperation.[18]

[16] *Peace and War,* p. 100.

[17] For summary of legislation as found in the President's first report on lend-lease, see *Roosevelt's Foreign Policy,* pp. 412–420.

[18] Langer and Gleason, *The Undeclared War,* pp. 285–289.

In implementing the destroyer–naval-base deal and the lend-lease program, Roosevelt never wavered from the decision reached during the crisis of the spring of 1940. His ideas were expressed most simply in the homely analogy he had employed in calling for support of lend-lease: "Suppose my neighbor's home catches fire, and I have a length of garden hose . . . If he can take my garden hose and connect it up with his hydrant, I may help him to put out his fire." [19]

The President was firmly convinced that there should be no quibbling about how the hose was to be paid for, when all that really mattered was to prevent the conflagration from spreading further. The only guarantee of American security, that is, was the defeat of Hitler and everything for which he stood.

After the adoption of the lend-lease program, Roosevelt projected, on March 15, 1941, the arsenal of democracy concept of America's role:

The British people and their Grecian allies need ships. From America, they will get ships. They need planes. From America, they will get planes. They need food. From America, they will get food. They need tanks and guns and ammunition and supplies of all kinds. From America, they will get tanks and guns and ammunition and supplies of all kinds. . . .

Our country is going to be what our people have proclaimed it must be— the arsenal of democracy.[20]

The Roosevelt administration was not seeking war when it adopted this policy of all-out aid to the Allies, any more than it was seeking war on the other side of the world when in the summer of 1941 it would cut off the flow of all supplies to Japan. In the conviction that the triumph of fascism would be intolerable, its purpose was to try to assure victory for the nations combating this evil force without the commitment of American military power. The President repeatedly expressed his belief that if the United States did everything possible to support the Allies, there was far less chance of being drawn into hostilities than if it stood aside and did nothing. There is no evidence that he pursued the course he did in order to bring about intervention. On the contrary, there is every good reason to believe that he did not want war. Yet he accepted the risks inherent in his program because he remained convinced that there could be no safety for America in a

[19] *Public Papers and Addresses of Franklin D. Roosevelt* (13 vols., New York, 1938–50), IX, 607.
[20] *Roosevelt's Foreign Policy*, pp. 346–347.

world dominated by Hitler. And he knew that isolation was not security.[21]

When this policy led to war—as the isolationists all along vociferously insisted that it would—it was not demonstrated that the United States could have avoided ultimate conflict with the Axis powers by any other course. It was instead shown that in spite of all hopes only active American participation in the world struggle could encompass the overthrow of fascism and remove its continued threat to the peace of all nations. The immense difficulties encountered in the final defeat of Germany and Japan, when the full might of America's military, naval, and air forces were thrown into combat, made clear that the menacing expansion of the Axis powers could not otherwise have been halted. That the victory over the Axis did not at once lead to universal peace, but was followed by the new threat of Soviet imperialism, has no bearing upon the urgencies of the situation created by German and Japanese aggression in 1941.

In the eighteen months between the fall of France in June, 1940, and Pearl Harbor in December, 1941, the maintenance of any effective foreign policy, whether of war or peace, was continually hampered by the sharply conflicting views of the American people. Yet wholehearted support for the Roosevelt program was essential in order that national production could be geared to meet the needs of both national defense and lend-lease aid. If the United States were to act effectively, the American people had to be convinced of the necessity for undergoing the sacrifices national policy entailed, as well as the need to accept its inherent risks. Seldom has a President faced a greater challenge of national leadership.

Roosevelt felt himself to be under a vast restraint because of the strength of isolationist sentiment. Uncertain of full support, his reaction was to move with great caution at every stage of the development of his program—a caution that exasperated some of his advisers and Cabinet members. Both Secretary of War Stimson and Secretary

[21] On this highly controversial point of Roosevelt's attitude, the most objective treatment is found, as on so many of the issues of this period, in the studies of William L. Langer and S. Everett Gleason. In quoting Hopkins' belief that the President was "loath to get into this war," and the further Stimson comment of Roosevelt's fear of any assumption that "we must invade Germany and crush Germany," they nevertheless state that the fragmentary evidence available makes it impossible to speak with certainty of Roosevelt's views and intentions. *The Undeclared War*, pp. 456, 735.

of the Navy Knox, as well as Attorney General Jackson and Secretary of the Interior Ickes, were disturbed at his failure to follow up his victory in the Lend-Lease Act. Stimson tells the story of a Cabinet meeting at which the President spoke of a program for patrolling the western Atlantic: " 'Well, it's a step forward.' I at once replied to him," Stimson wrote in his diary for April 25, 1941, " 'Well, I hope you will keep on walking, Mr. President. Keep on walking.' The whole cabinet burst into a roar of laughter which was joined in by the President." [22]

Caution often gave Roosevelt's policy, in spite of its underlying consistency, a highly equivocal character. In seeking to emphasize the dangers of an Axis victory, and at the same time assure the American people that there was no great risk of their being drawn into the war, he left the door open to charges of irresponsibility or insincerity that cannot always be easily answered. This was particularly true during the presidential campaign of 1940, which took place between the destroyer–naval-base deal and passage of the Lend-Lease Act.

His Republican opponent, Wendell Willkie, though highly critical of many aspects of administration policy, was yet prepared to support aid to the Allies—short of war—as essential to American security. Far more internationalist than the Republican party as a whole, he nevertheless carried his party with him at this critical juncture. Roosevelt felt obliged, however, to defend himself against the charge that he was dragging the country into war by constantly reiterating that there was no danger of direct involvement. On one occasion he said emphatically: "I have said this before, but I shall say it again and again and again: Your boys are not going to be sent into any foreign wars." [23]

This statement could hardly be reconciled, whatever reservations Roosevelt may have had in respect to "foreign wars," with the increasing probability, which he himself had to recognize, that intervention might become necessary if Hitler were to be defeated. Nevertheless the President could not at this time bring himself, for fear of further isolationist attacks, to be more straightforward in publicly assessing the actual risks of American policy. Under these circumstances, the leadership that he might have exerted in preparing the nation for the role that it was destined to play often appeared weak and vacillating. His

[22] Henry L. Stimson and McGeorge Bundy, *On Active Service in Peace and War* (New York, 1948), pp. 370–371. See also Sherwood, *Roosevelt and Hopkins*, p. 188.

[23] Quoted, *ibid.*, p. 191; see also Sherwood's comment, p. 201.

reluctance to be more decisive can only be explained by the compulsion that he felt himself under to avoid at all costs the "irrevocable act" that might fail of popular support and thereby endanger everything he was trying to do.[24]

As a matter of fact, the isolationists did not in any important instance defeat any move on which the administration was decided. Their attacks upon the destroyer–naval-base deal ("Dictator Roosevelt Commits an Act of War") were unavailing. Criticism of the President's failure to consult Congress was in many quarters thought to be justified, but it was impossible to deny the advantages of the deal itself in securing air and naval bases for the defense of the Americas. If lend-lease set off a prolonged and vehement debate on the ground that it was irreconcilable with any reasonable concept of neutrality, once again all attacks were beaten off.[25]

The isolationists were fighting a losing battle in 1940–41—not only on the immediate question of aid for the Allies, but on the underlying issue of America's future relationship with the rest of the world. In its broad and comprehensive scope, the lend-lease program was itself a commitment for which there was no parallel in national history. Senator Vandenberg wrote in his diary that he felt he was witnessing the suicide of the Republic: "This is what I believe is the result. We have torn up 150 years of traditional foreign policy. We have tossed Washington's Farewell Address into the discard. We have thrown ourselves squarely into the power politics and power wars of Europe, Asia and Africa. We have taken the first step upon a course from which we can never hereafter retreat." [26]

The advocates of a rigid neutrality showed no such concern over policy in the Pacific during this period as they did over that affecting Europe. Once again the isolationists conformed to tradition in being much more favorably disposed to measures that actually constituted intervention in the conflict between China and Japan than to any such move in the war against Hitler. Roosevelt was far more free to help Chiang Kai-shek, and then to tighten the economic noose about Japan, than to extend aid to Great Britain. Some of the most outspoken critics of his policy toward Europe, Senator Wheeler of Montana, for ex-

[24] *Ibid.*, p. 132.

[25] Langer and Gleason, *The Challenge to Isolation*, pp. 770–776, and *The Undeclared War*, pp. 252–289; Charles C. Tansill, *Back Door to War* (Chicago, 1952), pp. 584–615.

[26] Arthur H. Vandenberg, Jr., and J. A. Morris (eds.), *The Private Papers of Senator Vandenberg* (Boston, 1952), p. 10.

ample, strongly backed the interventionist moves in eastern Asia. The country generally favored abrogation of the commercial treaty with Japan in 1939, upheld a program of assistance for China, and was to have little criticism for the ultimate ban on all exports to Japan as adopted in midsummer, 1941.[27] This situation had its ironical aspects in view of the final consequences of the economic boycott of Hitler's Far Eastern partner. The dangers of entanglement in Europe loomed so large that the risk of being drawn into war through hostilities in the Pacific was often overlooked.

The truth of the matter was that the general isolationist position, reinforced by Republican distrust of Roosevelt, had changed very little under the impact of events. "If we go to war to save democracy in Europe," declared Philip La Follette in almost hackneyed phrases, "we shall wind up by losing democracy at home." [28] Again and again the old warning was repeated that once involved in the complicated maze of European power politics, there could be no telling in what future foreign quarrels the nation might needlessly become involved. After the entry of Soviet Russia into the war in the summer of 1941, this latter argument seemed to be strengthened. All the changes were rung on the irony of associating ourselves with the forces of communism in defense of democracy. This was a favorite theme of the isolationists as developed by such critics as Senator Charles W. Tobey of New Hampshire: "Today we would ally ourselves with Russia in her war with Germany, but it is possible that ten years from now we might ally ourselves with Germany to halt the menace of Communism sweeping Europe. . . . Why spend the lives of our richest blood on the battlefields of Europe on such uncertain and impermanent ventures?" [29]

The major attack upon the policies that the isolationists saw carrying the United States along the road that a quarter of a century earlier had led to war was spearheaded by the America First Committee. Presided over by Robert E. Wood, chairman of the board of Sears Roebuck and Company, its active leadership included such diverse figures as Colonel Charles A. Lindbergh and Senator Wheeler, the railway magnate Robert Young and William L. Hutchinson, vice-president of the American Federation of Labor. The character of the isolationist front was indeed shifting. Although Midwestern progres-

[27] In addition to studies already noted, see Herbert Feis, *The Road to Pearl Harbor* (Princeton, 1950).

[28] *Vital Speeches,* VII (Feb. 15, 1941), 265.

[29] *Ibid.,* VII (Oct. 1, 1941), 750.

sives were represented, they were by no means the dominant element in the America First Committee. Its principal backers were businessmen, it obtained its funds largely from banking and industrial sources, and it was most vehemently supported by the Chicago *Tribune,* the nation's most reactionary newspaper. In spite of the sprinkling of liberals within its ranks, the hard core of this noninterventionist movement was solidly conservative.

The America First program had the support of many political extremists, but the committee's national leaders tried to disassociate themselves from these irresponsible allies. Even so, there were strange bedfellows indeed in the ranks of America Firsters. Among its membership, or persons closely affiliated with it, were sincere noninterventionists who remained persuaded, on what they believed to be sound and even idealistic grounds, that in peace or war America should remain at home; there were also the Anglophobes, anti-Semites, the Roosevelt-haters, Coughlinites, and the fascist-minded. Never accepted by the America First Committee but hysterically anti-interventionist—until June, 1941 when Germany invaded Soviet Russia—were the Communists.[30]

In the forefront of the forces that supported all possible assistance for the victims of Nazi aggression, stood the Committee to Defend America by Aiding the Allies. Its membership crossed conservative-liberal as well as political lines, and reflected highly varying points of view. The committee campaigned vigorously and effectively in behalf of the destroyer–naval-base deal, lend-lease, and repeal of the neutrality laws. Its program was all aid short of war, but as time went on this did not seem enough to many members. The growing belief that only more positive action could forestall a fascist victory swelled the ranks of avowed interventionists within this active and influential organization.[31]

The original chairman of the committee was William Allen White, long-time editor of the Emporia (Kansas) *Gazette,* and the dilemma in which he found himself, as the scroll of history unwound in 1940–41, may perhaps be taken as a reflection of the uncertainties that plagued the great bulk of the American people who were neither rigid isolationists nor active interventionists. For White in turn urged with utmost vigor all possible assistance for those nations fighting fascism,

[30] See Wayne S. Cole, *America First: The Battle Against Intervention, 1940–1941* (Madison, Wis., 1953).

[31] See Walter Johnson, *The Battle Against Isolation* (Chicago, 1944).

drew back abruptly when he felt other members of the Committee were going too far along the interventionist road, subscribed to a public statement calling upon the President to do everything "that may be necessary to ensure defeat of the Axis powers," and then, in January, 1941, resigned his chairmanship of the committee.[32] Like so many of his countrymen he wanted both an Allied victory and American peace. When these two objectives seemed increasingly irreconcilable, he did not know where to turn. Following White's resignation, the Committee to Defend America campaigned ever more militantly under new leadership to strengthen Roosevelt's hand in aiding the Allies in every possible way.

In the meantime, the administration had taken a succession of gradual steps that were aligning the United States more and more definitely with the Allies, and at the same time providing for its own security against possible German encroachments in the western Atlantic. On April 10, 1941, the State Department announced that Greenland would be occupied to block the possible extension of German control over that Danish possession, and some three months later the President stated that an understanding had been reached with Iceland to station American troops there as a means of assuring its defense against possible attack.[33] "The United States," Roosevelt told Congress, "cannot permit the occupation by Germany of strategic outposts in the Atlantic to be used as air or naval bases for eventual attack against the Western hemisphere." [34]

A more sensational development was a mid-August secret meeting, off the coast of Newfoundland, of President Roosevelt and Prime Minister Churchill. The German armies had overrun Yugoslavia and Greece; they were advancing deep within Soviet Russia in apparently victorious consummation of the campaign launched in June. On the other side of the world, Japan had occupied southern Indo-China (by agreement with Vichy France) and was progressively expanding its area of control in the southwest Pacific. The leaders of the two great western democracies could not have held their conversations under more urgent or dramatic circumstances.

Their primary concern was the means whereby the assistance being given Great Britain by a still nominally neutral United States could be

[32] *Ibid.*, pp. 179–201.
[33] *Peace and War*, 103–104, 640–648; 111, 686–691.
[34] *Roosevelt's Foreign Policy*, p. 428.

made most effective. The meeting further led, however, to the announcement of "certain common principles in the national policies of their respective countries on which they base their hopes for a better future for the world." Henceforth known as the Atlantic Charter, this statement paralleled the Fourteen Points proclaimed by President Wilson nearly a quarter of a century earlier. Their countries, Roosevelt and Churchill declared, sought no aggrandizement or territorial changes that were not in accord with the wishes of the people concerned; would endeavor to bring about access to trade and raw materials on equal terms for all states; and hoped to see established, after the final destruction of Nazi tyranny, a peace that would enable all men in all lands to live out their lives in freedom from want and fear. Finally, the two men stated their belief that pending the establishment of a permanent system of general security, the disarmament of all aggressor nations was essential.[35]

The legal nature of the agreement was rather vague; its terms gave rise to a great deal of controversy. Within the United States, the Atlantic Charter intensified the fears of isolationists and encouraged the hopes of internationalists. Its significance at the time was not so much what the document contained, however, as the fact that the American President and the British Prime Minister agreed upon such a joint statement closely aligning their two countries in a common cause. The principles set forth in the Atlantic Charter were unhappily to have little chance of realization in a postwar world that saw no real peace.

Soon after this famous meeting of Roosevelt and Churchill, Germany stepped up her submarine warfare in the Atlantic, and the need to provide protection for the supplies being sent to Great Britain under the lend-lease program became increasingly urgent. A patrol system covering American ships was already in effect, and about September 1 Roosevelt decided to provide naval escorts for other vessels in the North Atlantic. He hesitated for a time to announce his plan, but on the fourth of the month an attack upon the destroyer *Greer*, carrying mail to Iceland, brought an end to further delay. Terming the attacks upon American vessels—for that on the *Greer* followed earlier instances of the torpedoing of merchant ships—"acts of international lawlessness" that revealed the design of the Nazis to abolish freedom of the seas, the President stated in a radio address on September 11

[35] *Peace and War*, pp. 111–113, 717–720. See also Langer and Gleason, *The Undeclared War*, pp. 663–692.

that henceforth protection would be given all merchantmen in "the waters which we deem necessary for our defense." American naval vessels and American planes, he stated, "will no longer wait until Axis submarines lurking under the water, or Axis raiders on the surface of the sea strike their deadly blow—first.[36]

So far had the United States departed from its neutrality under the mounting menace to its own security; so far had it gone in allying itself with the nations combating aggression. There remained only one further move—short of war itself—to make the United States an active participant in the struggle against Germany. This step was taken when, in response to appeals from the President, Congress finally revised the neutrality law to permit the arming of American merchant vessels and to allow them to carry cargoes to belligerent ports.[37]

Once again there was prolonged and vehement debate, for the isolationists were more than ever fearful that the consequences of Roosevelt's policy would be war, but the logical necessity of making sure that the goods being sent to England would be delivered eventually carried the day. The final vote on neutrality revision—50 to 37 in the Senate and 212 to 194 in the House—was a measure of the acute differences of opinion still prevailing in Congress and in the country, but the important thing was that the bill was passed. On November 17th it became law with the President's signature.[38]

While the debate in Congress was still under way, the President had again emphasized the national emergency and stressed the need for what he termed "total national defense":

Ours has been a story of vigorous challenges which have been accepted and overcome—challenges of uncharted seas, of wild forests and desert plains, of raging floods and withering drought, of foreign tyrants and domestic strife, of staggering problems—social, economic and physical; and we have come out of them the most powerful nation—and the freest—in all of history.

Today in the face of this newest and greatest challenge of them all we Americans have cleared our decks and taken our battle stations. We stand ready in the defense of our nation and the faith of our fathers to do what God has given us the power to see as our full duty.[39]

[36] *Roosevelt's Foreign Policy,* p. 474. In reporting the *Greer* incident, Roosevelt did not divulge the fact that the destroyer was reporting the submarine's presence to a British patrol.

[37] *Peace and War,* pp. 115–117, 787–788.

[38] The division of votes found the Republicans in opposition: 21 to 6 in the Senate, 137 to 22 in the House. Easterners were divided; the Midwest generally hostile.

[39] October 27, 1941. *Roosevelt's Foreign Policy,* p. 516.

There were the inevitable attacks upon this bold pronouncement of American policy. Those who continued to think in terms of a complete abstention from world affairs fought frantically this final abandonment of any real neutrality and what they instinctively realized was a basic change in the fundamental tenets of American foreign policy. Congressional opposition to arming American ships was again greatly augmented by partisan distrust of Roosevelt. In the country as a whole, public opinion was far more convinced than the vote on this move suggests that neutrality and isolation no longer had any validity in the modern world. Popular polls asking whether it was felt to be more important to maintain peace than to bring about the downfall of the Axis powers revealed a persistent decline in the number of persons who put peace first—from 64 per cent of those interviewed in May, 1940, to 32 per cent of those whose opinions were sought early in December, 1941.[40] This basic shift in popular attitudes, with all its implications for the future world role of the United States, was well under way before the Japanese bombers roared out of the Pacific skies to attack Pearl Harbor.

For it was through events in the Pacific theater of war, rather than developments in the Atlantic, that peace and neutrality were finally— and irretrievably—shattered. During that long summer which saw the United States drawing closer and closer to acknowledged hostilities with Germany, Secretary Hull had been patiently conducting the fruitless negotiations with the Japanese envoys in Washington that were finally to lead to a complete impasse.[41]

Japan's continued aggression in China, her alignment with the Axis powers in the autumn of 1940, her occupation of northern Indo-China, held out the constant menace of the spread of war to eastern Asia. American policy was designed to do what it could to check Japan by diplomatic and economic pressure and to provide such aid as possible, including lend-lease supplies, for Nationalist China. After abrogation of the Japanese-American commercial treaty in the summer of 1939, there had been a gradual tightening of export controls over goods shipped to Japan—most notably iron and steel scrap. The key material in bringing to bear decisive economic pressure, however, was oil. In spite of popular demand for more stringent sanctions, President Roosevelt was for long reluctant to embargo shipments of this commodity

[40] William A. Lydgate, *What Our People Think* (New York, 1944), p. 35.
[41] For complete account, Feis, *The Road to Pearl Harbor*.

for fear that it might drive Japan to the hostilities which he was anxious to avert.

In the summer of 1941, Japanese occupation of all Indo-China, and the consequent threat to British communications in the Far East, to the Netherlands East Indies, and to the Philippines, created a situation demanding more positive action to safeguard the interests of both the Allies and the United States. The rejection by Japan of all proposals for the withdrawal of her troops from either China or Indo-China thereupon led, on July 25, 1941, to the decision to impose what was in effect a complete embargo on Japanese-American trade—including shipments of oil—through the freezing of all Japanese assets in the United States.[42]

This step was taken with a full realization of the risks involved. Still, negotiations were continued in the attempt to discover some way in which the danger of war could be minimized or the threatened hostilities at least postponed. Both Secretary Hull and the Japanese envoys were actually sparring for time, however, and no progress was made at their frequent conferences in Washington. At the close of August, the Japanese suggested a meeting at sea of President Roosevelt and Prince Konoye, the Japanese Premier. While this idea was for a time discussed, Secretary Hull strongly advised against it without a previous agreement—which proved to be impossible—on the basic principles underlying any prospective accord. The question will always remain whether this proposed Roosevelt-Konoye meeting might possibly have been productive.[43] When it failed to materialize, the Konoye Cabinet resigned and on October 16 General Tojo, the former War Minister, became Premier under circumstances that still further intensified the mounting crisis.

A final exchange of notes between the two governments in November served only to emphasize anew the unbridgeable gulf between their respective positions. While Japan might have been willing to evacuate Indo-China, she was prepared to do so only on condition of being granted a completely free hand in China, with the United States agreeing to cease all aid to the Nationalist Government. For its part, the United States insisted on the withdrawal of Japanese troops from both

---

[42] *Peace and War*, pp. 126–127, 704–705; *Roosevelt's Foreign Policy*, p. 442.

[43] *Peace and War*, pp. 130–133, 733–735. Ambassador Grew believed—and has continued to believe—that such a meeting might have been productive. Joseph C. Grew, *Turbulent Era* (2 vols., Boston, 1952), II, 1353–54. See also his entire Chap. XXXIV, "Pearl Harbor: From the Perspective of Ten Years."

Indo-China and China, together with Japan's acceptance of the Chiang Kai-shek Government, as the only possible basis for the establishment of friendly Japanese-American relations and the restoration of normal trade.

Hostilities could have been averted—at least temporarily—if the United States had been at any time willing to surrender its basic position and allow Japan her free hand in China. For a time, indeed, some sort of *modus vivendi* was considered, but the idea was soon abandoned. The obligations long since assumed in upholding Chinese sovereignty, the danger to the Allies in the further military expansion of Hitler's Far Eastern partner, and America's own security all dictated a refusal to appease Japan even though this meant war.

With the exchange of these notes in late November, the end had in fact come. Japan's decisive answer was not her diplomatic reply to Secretary Hull's final *démarche*. On December 7, 1941, her planes rained down the bombs on Pearl Harbor that plunged the United States and Japan into war. The conflict raging in Europe became a global struggle that was to reach out to the farthest corners of the entire world.

The American people were shocked and horrified by the sudden attack on Pearl Harbor. There was no general realization that the crisis was so near at hand. Top officials in Washington were better informed. Throughout the final stages of the negotiations, they had known, as a result of the breaking of the Japanese code, that Japan had definitely reached the decision to break off negotiations and resort to arms. It was understood that war had become only a matter of Japan's choosing the time and place. From President Roosevelt on down, however, it was felt certain that the attack would take place in southeastern Asia. And on these grounds no special precautions were taken to safeguard the American fleet at Pearl Harbor. A conviction that the attack would come elsewhere may not justify this laxity, but all the evidence demonstrates that it was an error of judgment rather than any betrayal of the national interest.[44]

[44] The best accounts of these developments are again found in Feis, *The Road to Pearl Harbor,* pp. 291–341, and Langer and Gleason, *The Undeclared War,* pp. 464–493, 625–662, 693–731, 836–941. The so-called revisionist historians—see bibliographical notes—have intimated or directly charged a "Roosevelt conspiracy" inviting an attack upon Pearl Harbor. For example, Tansill, *Back Door to War,* p. 651, and—even more extravagantly—Rear Admiral Robert A. Theobold, *The Final Secret of Pearl Harbor* (New York, 1954). There is no evidence whatsoever to support such charges. For the de-

On December 8, Congress declared a state of war as a result of what the President termed "the unprovoked and dastardly attack by Japan." [45] Three days later it accepted war with Germany and Italy after those two nations had taken the initiative in declaring hostilities against the United States.

Roosevelt no longer had any need to temporize. In a radio address to the nation, he spiritedly called upon the American people to meet a crisis which could only be resolved by victory—final and complete— over the enemy:

We are now in the midst of a war, not for conquest, not for vengeance, but for a world in which this nation, and all that this nation represents, will be safe for our children. We expect to eliminate the danger from Japan, but it would serve us ill if we accomplished that and found that the rest of the world was dominated by Hitler and Mussolini.

We are going to win the war and we are going to win the peace that follows.

And in the difficult hours of this day—and through dark days that may be yet to come—we will know that the vast majority of the members of the human race are on our side. Many of them are fighting with us. All of them are praying for us. For, in representing our cause, we represent theirs as well—our hope and their hope for liberty under God. [46]

The assault on Pearl Harbor drove home, with compelling force, the lesson being so laboriously learned from the rising conflict with Germany in the Atlantic. Its tremendous emotional impact united the country almost overnight in a final realization that the United States, part of a world community with which its own destiny was inextricably interwoven, could not escape direct participation in the war because of its geographical position.

"In my own mind," wrote in later years Senator Vandenberg, upon whom had fallen the mantle of isolationist leadership after the death of Borah, "my convictions regarding international cooperation and collective security for peace took firm hold on the afternoon of the Pearl Harbor attack. That day ended isolationism for any realist." [47]

---

tailed testimony of what actually happened, see *Pearl Harbor Attack, Hearings Before the Joint Committee on the Investigation of the Pearl Harbor Attack,* 79th Congress, 2nd Session (39 parts, Washington, 1946), and *Investigation of the Pearl Harbor Attack, Report of the Joint Committee* (Washington, 1946).

[45] *Roosevelt's Foreign Policy,* p. 553.

[46] *Ibid.,* p. 565.

[47] *The Private Papers of Senator Vandenberg,* p. 1.

CHAPTER 11

The Search for Peace

THE WAR with which the American people were now confronted was in its general scope, in the world-wide deployment of American forces, in the effort and sacrifice involved, and in loss of lives to dwarf completely the experience of 1917–18. Neither the mobilization of national resources nor battles and campaigns, however, can form a part of this account of foreign policy. The strategic decisions reached at the series of wartime conferences among the war leaders are relevant only so far as they helped to mold the pattern of the postwar world. Still, the war itself remains the background—the vital, dynamic inspiration—for the efforts being made during these momentous years to prevent any future conflict that would again disappoint world hopes for enduring peace.

While the nation was going through the travail of those immense efforts that were finally to encompass the defeat of the Axis powers, its leaders never lost sight of the ultimate goals for which the United States was fighting. This time a way had to be found to make peace secure. The American people had to be prepared to play a full part in postwar world organization. And though a growing number of them had already accepted the fact that isolationism was no longer a viable national policy, it was far from easy for the nation to discard a tradition and a practice that had the authority of over a century and a half of history behind it.

A first move indicative of the new bases on which American policy was henceforth to be founded was seen in the Declaration of the United Nations, a joint statement of the war aims of the Allied powers

issued on January 1, 1942. The United States was not to be an associated power, as it had been when it joined the Allies in 1917. It was
to be a full-fledged partner in a Grand Alliance whose objective was
not only defeat of the common enemy, but the creation of a new world
order. For embodied in this Declaration of the United Nations were
the principles that President Roosevelt and Prime Minister Churchill
had written into the Atlantic Charter. However generalized, they set
forth the need, upon conclusion of the war and the disarmament of
aggressor nations, for establishing "some wider and permanent system
of general security." [1]

American diplomacy's primary task all during the war was of course
to uphold the Allied coalition. Everything else was subordinated to this
paramount need, and American leadership was most conspicuously
displayed in the wartime conferences that developed the common
strategy which was to lead to ultimate victory. Yet from Pearl Harbor
on, there were also continued discussion and planning within the State
Department, on the part of various private organizations, and among
the public at large of the means whereby the future world order envisaged in the Atlantic Charter could be guaranteed.

Throughout all this discussion one basic consideration stood forth:
the United States could not again slough off the international responsibilities inherent in its position as a world power. The policy makers
acted on this premise, and they were further decided, as Secretary Hull
made clear, that some international agency would have to be created
which could—by force if necessary—maintain the future peace. [2] The
achievement of this latter goal was not to wait upon conclusion of hostilities, and in another respect as well Roosevelt was determined to follow a different course than that Wilson had followed twenty-five years
earlier. The postwar program was to be developed on a bipartisan
basis, with congressional participation at every step, and along lines
that would command popular support. If the United States was to
take part in any world movement for the organization of peace, and
assume in good faith the obligations this involved, the experience of
the past clearly demonstrated that it could go only so far as the American people were willing to go.

[1] Senate Document 123, 81st Congress, 1st Session, A Decade of American
Foreign Policy, Basic Documents, 1941–45 (Washington, 1950), pp. 2–3.
[2] The Memoirs of Cordell Hull (2 vols., New York, 1948), II, 1638. See
also Department of State, Postwar Foreign Policy and Preparation 1939–45
(Washington, 1950).

Roosevelt predicted that with the collapse of the Axis there would be those who would say that the United States should in the future let the world "stew in its own juice" and never again become involved in pulling "the other fellow's chestnuts from the fire." But he emphatically stressed the folly of any return to such isolationist thinking. ". . . It is useless to win battles," he said, "if the cause for which we fight these battles is lost. It is useless to win a war unless it stays won." And in his State of the Union message in January, 1943, he declared that the United Nations "can and must remain united for the maintenance of peace . . ." [3]

A first concrete sign of waning isolationism, so far as its traditional political undertones were concerned, was the attitude shown by responsible Republican leaders. As candidate of his party in the election of 1940, Wendell Willkie had already performed yeoman service for the cause of internationalism. He now reaffirmed his support for the creation of some new League of Nations, and his book *One World* exerted an enormous influence in awakening the public to an understanding of the conception expressed in its symbolic title. Governor Dewey of New York was also to swing over—though more slowly—to the internationalist camp and help to take the issue of American membership in a world organization out of partisan politics. Even more significant, for eastern Republicans had generally been international-minded, was the new position of Senator Vandenberg. Convinced of the need for world cooperation, this onetime spokesman of Midwestern isolationism played an important role in reconciling divergent views on the postwar role of the United States. [4]

While this whole issue was being debated in Congress, where proposals had been introduced that would have definitely committed the United States to set up procedures for the peaceful settlement of international disputes, the Republicans formally moved, in August, 1943, to clarify their position. A conference of the party's advisory council adopted a resolution, known as the Mackinac Charter, which set forth what Vandenberg called a middle position "between those extremists at one end of the line who would cheerfully give America away and those extremists at the other end of the line who would attempt a total

---

[3] Samuel I. Rosenman, *Working with Roosevelt* (New York, 1952), pp. 363, 368.

[4] *Vital Speeches*, X (Nov. 1, 1943), 48; X (May 15, 1944), 451; Arthur H. Vandenberg, Jr., and J. A. Morris (eds.), *The Private Papers of Senator Vandenberg* (Boston, 1952), p. 37.

isolation which has come to be an impossibility." It put the party firmly on record as favoring "responsible participation by the United States in postwar cooperative organization among sovereign nations to prevent military aggression and to attain permanent peace with organized justice in a free world." [5]

However vaguely worded—and Roosevelt was to state that he was not paying much attention to "the language of debate" [6]—the Mackinac Charter helped to assure Republican support for administration foreign policy, the support which Wilson had so signally lacked when he brought home the covenant of the League of Nations. Overwhelming majorities now approved pending congressional resolutions expressing support for postwar cooperation. The Fulbright resolution in the House, and the Connally resolution in the Senate, both of which affirmed the need for world organization, were milestones on the road away from the isolationism of the 1930's.[7] And Secretary Hull was greatly strengthened in the negotiations already under way for the actual establishment of a new world league.

It was, indeed, while the Connally resolution was still under discussion that the foreign secretaries of the United States, Great Britain, China, and Soviet Russia met at Moscow, in October, 1943, and took the first step toward the formation of what was to become the peacetime United Nations. For in the Moscow Declaration issued at the close of the meeting, they officially recognized the necessity for establishing at the earliest practicable date a general international organization for the maintenance of international peace and security.[8] Hull returned triumphantly to express his conviction—over-optimistic and perhaps naïve—that with this understanding among the major powers, "there would no longer be need for spheres of influence, for alliances, for balance of power." [9]

Shortly after the Moscow meeting, Roosevelt met with Churchill and Chiang Kai-shek at Cairo, and then with Churchill and Stalin at Teheran. He reaffirmed this approach to postwar policy, and added that it was agreed among the four powers "that if force is necessary to keep international peace, international force will be applied—for as

[5] *Ibid.*, pp. 55, 58.

[6] Elliott Roosevelt (ed.), *F.D.R.—His Personal Letters* (2 vols., New York, 1950), II, 1460.

[7] *A Decade of American Foreign Policy*, pp. 9, 14.

[8] *Ibid.*, p. 12.

[9] *Memoirs of Cordell Hull*, II, 1648; *Vital Speeches*, X (Dec. 1, 1943), 102.

long as it may be necessary." [10] There was to be no repetition, so long as it lay within his power, of the tragic mistakes in foreign policy of the years after the First World War. And the fact was that the United States now stood committed, with the general endorsement of Congress, to a program of forthright collective security.

These developments of the closing months of 1943, both at home and abroad, were generally hailed as laying "the foundations of the world which we shall live in." [11] They met with almost universal popular approval. There were of course dissenting voices, but, in sharp contrast with the position they had maintained in the days before Pearl Harbor, even the isolationists rushed to point out the compelling need for America to assume her proper role in organizing peace. Thus Governor John Bricker of Ohio decried the past failure of the United States to acknowledge the implications of its commanding place in world affairs. "Instead of accepting, with intelligent self-interest, a degree of responsibility for world events commensurate with our rank," he declared, "we have allowed events to control us." No less emphatic on the need for a new approach to foreign policy was Senator Robert A. Taft. "We can only assure permanent peace and liberty in this country," he stated, "by the formation of some kind of association of nations to maintain the peace of the world." [12]

Public opinion followed the lead of national spokesmen. In the winter of 1943–44, there was every evidence that a large majority of the people believed that the United States should actively participate in a world organization for peace. Moreover there appeared to be little difference in attitudes among the various sections of the country.[13]

The war itself naturally held popular attention rather than discussions about peace, however important they might be for the future. And the immediate concern of the conferences both at Teheran and Cairo was much more with military planning than postwar organization. The meeting at Teheran consolidated the wartime alliance among the United States, Great Britain, and Soviet Russia; that at Cairo sought to strengthen China's will to fight by pledging the return

[10] Rosenman, *Working with Roosevelt*, p. 413.

[11] *Vital Speeches*, X (Dec. 15, 1943), 138.

[12] *Ibid.*, X (May 1, 1944), 422; X (June 1, 1944), 492.

[13] The polls reported a 73 per cent majority in the country as a whole, 72 per cent in the Midwest. William A. Lydgate, *What Our People Think* (New York, 1944), p. 47.

of territories seized by Japan and promising her the future status of a great power. Everything that was being done was first considered from the point of view of ultimate military victory.

The desperate holding operations in the Pacific before the United States was in a position to launch a counterattack against Japan, the build-up of national strength to make possible active participation in the war against Hitler, the campaigns in North Africa and the Mediterranean, the mounting air raids against Germany, and the preparations for the second front that was finally to take form with cross-Channel invasion—these were the great events of 1942 and 1943. All that was being planned in regard to postwar organization would have been rendered wholly futile if the forces arrayed against the Axis powers had not been victorious in their great trial at arms.

Then with 1944 and 1945 came the great advance across the Pacific, the westward sweep of the Russian armies, the Allied landings on the Normandy coast, the spectacular liberation of France, the final assault upon Germany, the steady march up the island ladder toward Japan. All this gave substance to the bright dreams of a new world order.

Against the background of such great events, the State Department, with the aid of a bipartisan committee of eight senators, went steadily ahead blueprinting the actual charter of a world organization.[14] On a more immediately practical basis, it also sponsored a series of international meetings marking a fresh new approach to world affairs. Between May, 1943, and July, 1944, the United States took part in the various conferences that set up the Food and Agricultural Organization, the United Nations Relief and Rehabilitation Administration, the International Monetary Fund and International Bank for Reconstruction and Development, and a revived International Labor Organization. Here were concrete steps that clearly revealed acceptance of the fact that the United States and the other nations of the world were—as Churchill had said of Britain and America at the time of the destroyer–naval-base deal—"somewhat mixed up together in some of their affairs." Moreover they emphasized the importance of economic as well as political collaboration in a postwar world that would face even more gigantic problems of reconstruction and recovery than had the world of 1919.

Finally, there was the conference at Dumbarton Oaks, in August,

[14] *Memoirs of Cordell Hull*, II, 1639; *The Private Papers of Senator Vandenberg*, pp. 90 ff.

1944, where a specific plan for a United Nations charter was drawn up by representatives of the United States, Great Britain, Soviet Russia, and China. This plan evolved from long study and debate. Different viewpoints centering upon the concept long held by Roosevelt of "the Four Policemen," [15] as opposed to broader recognition of the rights of small nations, had to be reconciled. Special care had to be taken to preserve the principle of national sovereignty as contrasted with the idea of a superstate. Compromises not entirely satisfactory to all elements in this country, to say nothing of the problem of reconciling the divergent views of other nations, were inevitable. Nevertheless the outlines of the proposed charter were approved at Dumbarton Oaks. Subject to the further negotiations among the Big Three at the Crimean Conference in early 1945, the basis was laid for the new world organization that with both American and Russian participation would replace the defunct League of Nations.[16]

The issues involved naturally affected the presidential election of 1944. In striking contrast to 1920, however, general approval of what was being done made it possible to remove the basic question of American membership in a world organization from campaign politics. After both parties had endorsed international cooperation in their platforms, an understanding was reached between Secretary Hull, on behalf of President Roosevelt, and John Foster Dulles, acting for Governor Dewey, that placed foreign policy on a nonpartisan basis at least so far as this major issue was concerned.[17]

It was too much to expect that any general agreement could silence all controversy over America's postwar role. As the campaign progressed, Dewey was to chide Roosevelt for the isolationist position the latter held in the 1930's, and Roosevelt charged insincerity in the Republican conversion to internationalism. "Can anyone really suppose," he asked after naming such men as Hamilton Fish, Gerald Nye, and Hiram Johnson, "that these isolationists have changed their minds about world affairs?" In answer to the important question of the powers to be given to the American representative on the proposed Security Council of the United Nations, Dewey tried to hedge. Roosevelt took advantage of the situation to make a forthright declaration: ". . . to my simple mind it is clear that, if the world organization is to

---

[15] *Memoirs of Cordell Hull*, II, 1642–43.

[16] Department of State, *Dumbarton Oaks, Documents on International Organization* (Washington, 1945).

[17] *Memoirs of Cordell Hull*, II, 1690 ff.

have any reality at all, our American representative must be endowed in advance by the people themselves, by constitutional means through their representatives in the Congress, with authority to act. . . ." [18]

Whatever the politics of attack and counterattack, however, the significance of the campaign for the nation was the added emphasis placed upon the importance of the new course on which the United States had embarked. It was still too much to say that isolationism was dead. As the ensuing years were to demonstrate, there could be a considerable lag between accepting internationalism in theory and putting it in practice. Nevertheless, the country appeared to be moving steadily ahead in what constituted a sharp reversal of the basic policy it had so long followed.

After Roosevelt's victory, a dramatic illustration of changing opinion was once again provided by Senator Vandenberg. In a notable speech in the Senate on January 10, 1945, he not only reaffirmed his support for world organization, but made the startling proposal that the major Allies should at once conclude "a hard-and-fast treaty" to guarantee the permanent disarmament of the Axis powers. Coming from the source it did, this was a revolutionary suggestion. Even more significant was Vandenberg's general expression of the new internationalism:

> I have always been frankly one of those who has believed in our own self-reliance . . . But I do not believe that any nation hereafter can immunize itself by its own exclusive action . . . Our oceans have ceased to be moats which automatically protect our ramparts . . .
>
> I want maximum American cooperation, consistent with legitimate American self-interest, with constitutional process and with collateral events which warrant it, to make the basic idea of Dumbarton Oaks succeed. I want a new dignity and a new authority for international law.[19]

Vandenberg created something of a sensation. The most important thing about his proposal, James B. Reston wrote in *The New York Times*, "was not that Vandenberg made it but that the American people responded to it with such enthusiasm." Walter Lippmann accorded it even greater significance as actually affecting the course of events: ". . . This speech can, if it is understood and appreciated, break the vicious circle in which American foreign policy has been revolving so ineffectually . . . The immense importance of Senator

[18] *Vital Speeches*, XI (Nov. 1, 1944), 40–41; Rosenman, *Working With Roosevelt*, pp. 484, 485.
[19] *The Private Papers of Senator Vandenberg*, p. 135.

Vandenberg's proposal is that it would end the policy of postponement and thus restore American influence in the settlement of Europe." [20]

The time of this speech was the eve of Roosevelt's departure for a meeting with Churchill and Stalin at the Crimean resort of Yalta. Early in February, the three statesmen and their large staffs foregathered for this most famous of all wartime conferences to complete plans for the final assaults upon the Axis powers, draw up a program for the occupation of Germany and for government of the liberated states of eastern Europe, and resolve the remaining problems in establishing a postwar world organization. What were considered at the time mutually satisfactory settlements of most of these issues were reached. Roosevelt, Churchill, and Stalin agreed upon the occupation zones (including one under French control) to be established in Germany, a basis for setting up a new provisional government in Poland, free elections in the other liberated countries, representation for their respective governments in the projected world organization, and a compromise formula for the use of the veto power in the Security Council.

At the same time, Roosevelt and Stalin reached a secret understanding, with the concurrence of Churchill, that provided for the entry of Soviet Russia into the war against Japan within two or three months after the defeat of Germany. In return Stalin was assured of recognition of the autonomy of Mongolia, transfer to the Soviet Union of the Kurile Islands and the southern half of Sakhalin, and the recovery of all those privileges and special rights that Russia had held in Manchuria prior to the Russo-Japanese War. Moreover, Roosevelt undertook to secure the compliance of Generalissimo Chiang Kai-shek, uninformed of the results of the negotiations among the Big Three, with these territorial cessions to the Soviet Union. [21]

The Yalta agreements represented as a whole a pragmatic approach to issues whose settlement was intimately linked with the further prosecution of the war as well as with conditions underlying a future peace. Neither Germany nor Japan had yet surrendered; the practicality of the atomic bomb was not demonstrated. In the light of given circumstances, both Roosevelt and Churchill, as well as their principal advisors, were convinced that these agreements held out great promise for future collaboration among the wartime Allies.

[20] Quoted, *ibid.*, pp. 138, 141.
[21] *A Decade of American Foreign Policy*, 27–34; Edward R. Stettinius, Jr., *Roosevelt and the Russians* (New York, 1949), pp. 295–307; William D. Leahy, *I Was There* (New York, 1950), pp. 291–323.

There has perhaps been no other international meeting in modern times that has aroused such continuing controversy and embittered debate as the Yalta Conference. It has become at once a myth and a symbol—often far removed from any factual background—in the American mind. The understandings reached with Soviet Russia, both in respect to the status of the countries of eastern Europe and more particularly in regard to settlements in eastern Asia, have been made the basis for condemnation of Roosevelt's entire policy. The critics of Yalta—their attitude often intensified by bitter partisanship—have insisted that Roosevelt betrayed the democratic cause by unjustified concessions to Russia that built up and immensely strengthened her postwar position.

It is always possible that had Roosevelt taken a stronger stand on certain points—as may also be said of Wilson's policy at Paris in 1919 —solutions more favorable to the western democracies might in some instances have been reached. Yet the fact remains that Stalin made substantial concessions to the American viewpoint—on occupation policies in Germany, the status of the governments in eastern Europe, procedures in the world organization—and he forthrightly reaffirmed Allied solidarity in both Europe and Asia. If the agreements reached at Yalta had been faithfully carried out, including continued Russian acceptance of the Nationalist Government in China, there would have been a sound basis for postwar Soviet-American cooperation. Moreover, in the light of existing military dispositions at the time of the conference—the position of the Russian armies in eastern Europe and on the borders of Manchuria—Roosevelt did not give anything away that the United States really had or controlled. He was hardly in a position—and no more was Churchill—to bring decisive pressure on Russia for any broader concessions than those that were actually made.

Over and beyond all such considerations, a further vital factor came into play at Yalta. Roosevelt—and Churchill as well—was not only very hopeful that mutual concessions had greatly strengthened the bonds between the United States, Great Britain, and Soviet Russia; he believed that it was imperative to operate on the premise that this was the case and to accept the Russian pledges of cooperation in good faith. On this the two western statesmen were in full accord. In later years Churchill justified his attitude. "Our hopeful assumptions were to be falsified," he wrote in *Triumph and Tragedy*. "Still, they were the only ones possible at the time." [22] The tragedy of Yalta did not lie in the agreements reached, but in the failure of Soviet Russia to honor her commitments.

Roosevelt, especially, believed that he was morally bound to do everything he could to promote understanding if America were to retain the confidence of other nations in her postwar leadership. The United States would have to take the responsibility for world collaboration, he declared, or bear the responsibility for another world conflict. And Roosevelt did succeed—the parallel with Wilson is again apparent—in attaining agreement on the creation of a world organization for peace. The compromises agreed upon at Yalta over exercise of the veto power in such an organization, votes in the assembly, the admission of member states—whatever difficulties arose in the future over their interpretation—were what made it possible to call the meeting at San Francisco for final action on the plans elaborated at Dumbarton Oaks.

"The conference in the Crimea," Roosevelt stated confidently, and his optimism was generally echoed by his American associates, and especially by Harry Hopkins, who played such an important role as Roosevelt's special emissary on many visits to Moscow, "was a turning point—I hope in our history and therefore in the history of the world." [23]

It was the President's fate not to live to see final establishment of the world organization for which he had worked so hard and for which he had such high expectations. Nevertheless it was the tribute of Winston Churchill that his leadership had been decisive in bringing the United Nations into being. Roosevelt, the Prime Minister of Great Britain declared, had "altered decisively and permanently, the social axis, the moral axis, of mankind by involving the New World inexorably and irrevocably in the fortunes of the old." [24]

A first and highly important act of the President's successor, Harry S. Truman, was to state that there would be no postponement of existing plans for the San Francisco Conference because of Roosevelt's death. Moreover Truman refused to give way before the obstructive tactics that Soviet Russia soon began to adopt in respect to a number of still unresolved questions relating to conference procedures. "Our

[22] Winston S. Churchill, *Triumph and Tragedy* (Boston, 1953), p. 402.
[23] Rosenman, *Working With Roosevelt*, p. 529; Robert E. Sherwood, *Roosevelt and Hopkins* (New York, 1948), p. 870.
[24] Quoted, *ibid.*, pp. 933–934.

agreements . . . so far," he was quoted as saying at a White House meeting, "had been a one-way street . . . it was now or never." [25] Truman was no less international-minded than Roosevelt. He was no less determined to do everything he could to fulfill the nation's hopes and aspirations for the creation of an enduring structure of world peace. The San Francisco conference met in April, 1945 and in due course carried through the program that led to formation of the United Nations.[26]

There was no real danger of either popular or congressional opposition. This time the way had been prepared; the preliminary work was well done. No partisan or sectional alignment opposed American membership in the United Nations. The newspapers, the radio commentators, and other molders of public opinion were almost unanimous in favor of the United States playing its full part in this new movement for collective security. The polls all showed decisive popular majorities following their lead. The Senate quickly fell in line. "Well—the battle is over," Vandenberg wrote happily to his wife after the votes were counted, ". . . 89 to 2!" [27]

In accepting the United Nations, the American people as a whole acted in a spirit of easy optimism created by impending victory over the Axis powers. The entire movement for world organization was predicated upon the assumption that the Grand Alliance of the war would be maintained, and that the major powers—especially the United States and Soviet Russia—would be able to work in continued harmony in restraining aggression. There was little popular realization of the stresses and strains to which collective security might be subject, and the sacrifices that it might entail. A will for peace on the part of every great power was taken for granted, once the aggressor nations were shorn of their strength. In such a cordial atmosphere, the American commitment to international cooperation did not conjure up the dangers that had formerly seemed inherent in any political connection with the rest of the world.

Yet there were already signs that the Soviet Union might not be as willing to cooperate in peace as in war. Further controversy had arisen over boundaries in eastern Europe, the status of Poland, and other issues that were not too promising for the future. Experienced observers were certain that power politics could not be brushed aside in

---

[25] Walter Millis (ed.), *The Forrestal Diaries* (New York, 1941), p. 50.
[26] *A Decade of American Foreign Policy*, pp. 117–140.
[27] *The Private Papers of Senator Vandenberg*, p. 218.

romantic enthusiasm over a new system of collective security. They feared that the stage was being set for new clashes of interest that might well precipitate another world crisis.

The reports of Averill Harriman, ambassador to Moscow, strongly advised that the outward thrust of communism was not dead. His warning in April, 1945, that the United States might well find itself facing ideological warfare "as vigorous and dangerous as Fascism or Nazism" made a deep impression in informed circles. Secretary of the Navy Forrestal was among those who were convinced that the United States could not afford to place any reliance upon Russia's peaceful intentions. In urging that the United States maintain its armed forces, he declared that "the means to wage war must be in the hands of those who hate war." [28] One of the most prescient statements of this attitude was in a memorandum set down, in May, 1945, by Joseph C. Grew, at this time Acting Secretary of State:

This war, so far as the interests of the United States are concerned, will have achieved one purpose and one purpose only, namely protection from the military expansion of Germany and Japan. For that purpose we had to fight, for had we not fought, our nation itself would have been in direct peril. It was and is, so far as our own interests are concerned, purely a war of self-defense, forced upon us.

But as "a war to end wars," the war will have been futile, for the result will be merely the transfer of totalitarian dictatorship and power from Germany and Japan to Soviet Russia which will constitute in [the] future as grave a danger to us as did the Axis.[29]

The public was neither as well informed nor as realistic in its thinking. That the overthrow of Germany and Japan would create power vacuums leading almost inevitably to fierce competition between the Communist and free worlds was scarcely understood. The American people still placed their faith in the new order that they believed was in the making. As its acknowledged leader, the United States would be in a position to carry out its great mission of promoting the universal cause of liberty and justice. It was in this hopeful spirit that they were at long last prepared to reject isolationism and accept the obligations and responsibilities of collective security.

[28] *The Forrestal Diaries*, pp. 47, 97.
[29] Joseph C. Grew, *Turbulent Era* (2 vols., Boston, 1952), II, 1445.

CHAPTER 12

Cold War

THE POSITION of the United States at the close of the war, as in 1898 and again in 1918, was one of greater influence in every way than had been the case at the opening of hostilities. Moreover a startling new development characterized the world situation of 1945. While five nations had nominal status as great powers through their membership in the Security Council of the United Nations, only one rivaled the immense resources and prestige of the United States. After more than a century, the prophecy of Alexis de Tocqueville in the mid-1830's appeared to be realized:

There are at present two great nations in the world, which started from different points, but seem to tend towards the same end. I allude to the Russians and the Americans . . . The principal interest of the [latter] is freedom; of the [former], servitude. Their starting point is different and their courses are not the same; yet each of them seems marked by the will of Heaven to sway the destinies of half the globe.[1]

War had served to strengthen rather than weaken America, in sharp contrast to what had befallen almost every power, and the prosperity of the postwar years was to confound those observers who had been certain of depression as a consequence of the shift from a wartime to a peacetime economy. The Marxian theory of capitalist collapse seemed to have no validity—to the confusion of Soviet planners—as the United States continued to expand its productive capacity, increase employment, and enjoy further phenomenal gains in national income.

[1] Alexis de Tocqueville, *Democracy in America* (new edition, 2 vols., 1945), I, 434.

Its fundamental economic structure appeared to be more stable than ever before.

At the same time, the nation's military strength had been built up immeasurably. A Navy superior to the combined fleets of the rest of the world dominated the seven seas; the Air Force commanded greater striking power than that of any other country; and American overseas bases in the general areas of the Atlantic, the Mediterranean, and the Pacific rimmed the Eurasian continent which lay under the shadow of the vast land forces of Soviet Russia. It is true that the great armies which had fought their way across western Europe and up the island ladder to the shores of Japan were within two years to be precipitately reduced from twelve million to only a million and a half men.[2] This weakening of the military forces, however, appeared to be compensated by the incalculable addition to the American armory of the atomic bomb. Possession of this terrible engine of destruction gave the United States a decisive advantage in the scales of global power in war's immediate aftermath, and continuing responsibilities that were without parallel in history.

All this raised at once the question of how such power would be used, and how it would affect the attitude of a country that had so recently abandoned its traditional isolationism and still lacked the political experience and maturity of the older nations. Would the United States be swerved from what had always been considered its great mission of promoting peace and freedom? Would its ideals be subverted by the temptation to exercise its power in self-aggrandizement?

The potentialities of commanding moral as well as political leadership were implicit in America's position. In common with its Allies, the nation had taken up arms in defense of its security and had fought with no other goal than the defeat of fascism and the restoration of a peaceful world. It had no thought of territorial gains. In spite of occasional rhapsodizing about the coming "American Century," there was no recrudescence of the imperialism that had briefly exercised such a beguiling influence after war with Spain. On the contrary, there was a vital interest in the world-wide promotion of freedom and democracy in the belief that only in a free world was American freedom secure. Wartime policies, indeed, had built up a tremendous "reservoir of

[2] John C. Campbell, *The United States in World Affairs, 1945–47* (New York, 1948), pp. 33–36, 457–458. See also Walter Millis (ed.), *The Forrestal Diaries* (New York, 1951), pp. 89, 102, 128–129.

good will" upon which wise statesmanship could draw in helping to establish the new world order.

The ordinary difficulties that might have been expected in developing an effective course of action and working out postwar problems, however, were completely overshadowed as Russian intransigency appeared to shatter all hopes for orderly progression toward a peaceful world. The American people were hardly prepared for what was in store for them. Their tradition and history had inculcated the idea— or the illusion—that America could always have her way in foreign policy, and that if any program the United States sponsored fell short of complete success, failure was entirely due to lack of foresight, or even disloyalty, on the part of those charged with determining policy. They did not realize the weight of imponderables in world politics, or the necessary dependence on other nations in international cooperation. They failed to appreciate the bitter fact that there were no easy solutions to the world problems with which they were faced.[3]

In these circumstances, there was a harsh awakening to the realities of postwar power politics, to the dangers born of the deepening chasm between democratic and Communist ideology, and to the irony of finding that the promotion of liberty and the pursuit of peace could not always be easily reconciled. To bear the immense weight of their new international responsibilities was a far sterner task than had been envisaged as the bright dream of "One World" gave way to the reality of a world even more sharply divided than that of the 1930's and 1940's.

The hope that wartime cooperation with Russia would carry over into the making of peace had not yet died at the time of the Potsdam Conference among the Big Three and the first meetings of the United Nations in 1945. It was believed to be entirely feasible to handle whatever issues arose in the projected four-power control of an occupied Germany by mutual accommodation, and to settle other postwar problems through the normal processes of diplomatic negotiation. The United States was ready to meet the Soviet Union more than halfway.

A highly significant sign of this attitude was the proposal made toward the close of 1945, with the concurrence of Great Britain and Canada, to set up some form of international control over the development of atomic energy whereby the uses of this source of power could

[3] For a stimulating discussion along these lines, see Charles B. Marshall, *The Limits of Foreign Policy* (New York, 1954).

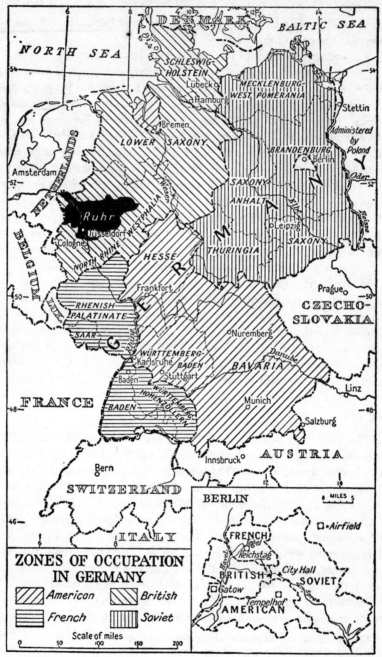

ZONES OF OCCUPATION
IN GERMANY

American   British
French   Soviet

Scale of miles
0   50   100   150   200

BERLIN

FRENCH
Tegel
Reichstag
BRITISH   City Hall
Gatow   SOVIET
Tempelhof
AMERICAN

MILES
Airfield

© Council on Foreign Relations, Inc.

be limited to constructive rather than destructive purposes and the world freed from the terrifying menace of atomic warfare. The United States was willing to exchange basic atomic energy information, recognizing that in any event it could not long keep the secret of the bomb, if adequate measures of international inspection and control could give assurance that there would be no production of atomic weapons. The United Nations would then take over the responsibility of guaranteeing that the further development of this new source of power would always be for peaceful ends.

The specific proposal presented to the United Nations by the American representative on its Atomic Energy Commission, Bernard Baruch, provided not only for rigid international inspection, but for the elimination of the veto in cases involving the illegal manufacture of atomic bombs. To implement this program, the plan contemplated an International Atomic Authority with over-all controls in the entire field of atomic energy. The United States expressed its willingness both to stop the further manufacture of bombs and to destroy existing stockpiles if this program were accepted.[4]

Although Soviet Russia, having agreed to the establishment of the Atomic Energy Commission, appeared for a time to be willing to accept the principles of control advanced by the United States, her unrelenting opposition to any means for their effective enforcement or for abolition of the veto in atomic matters soon rendered any hope of action illusory. This all-important, vital issue, upon whose settlement also depended any prospect of limiting conventional armaments or creating an international police force, was hopelessly deadlocked. Soviet Russia's membership in the United Nations, it became all too clear, did not mean that cooperation in building a peaceful world too easily assumed at San Francisco.

On other issues the Communists were also following increasingly obstructive policies. Disregarding the promises made at Yalta for free and democratic elections in the liberated countries of eastern Europe, the Soviet Union gave decisive support to the Communist parties in Poland and Hungary, Bulgaria and Rumania; ignoring the agreements

[4] See State Department, *A Report on the International Control of Atomic Energy* (The Acheson-Lilienthal Report), Publication 2498 (Washington, 1946), and *International Control of Atomic Energy*, Publication 2702 (Washington, 1946). Also James F. Byrnes, *Speaking Frankly* (New York, 1947), pp. 265–276; Arthur H. Vandenberg, Jr., and J. A. Morris (eds.), *The Private Papers of Senator Vandenberg* (Boston, 1952), pp. 220–236.

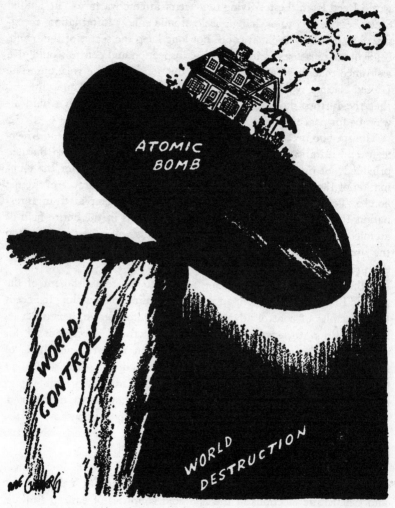

Rube Goldberg's Pulitzer prize cartoon in New York *Sun*, July 22, 1947

"Peace Today"

made at Potsdam, it insisted on its own program for reparations and effectively blocked plans for treating Germany as an economic unit. It refused to withdraw Russian troops from Iran, whose independence had been guaranteed at Teheran, and encouraged the infiltration of forces from Yugoslavia, Bulgaria, and Albania in support of the Communist guerillas at war against the recognized government in Greece. Through action taken by the United Nations, the Russians ultimately were constrained to abandon further intervention in the affairs of both Iran and Greece, and there were other instances of a reluctant accommodation to the views of the western democracies. Nevertheless the Soviet Union seemed determined to place every possible roadblock on the path to peace, both in the United Nations and in the Council of Foreign Ministers.[5]

The very fact of predominant American power, as well as certain aspects of American postwar policy, may have accounted in part for what often seemed to be Soviet intransigence. For the United States not only had the atomic bomb, the world's greatest Navy, and a global ring of strategic air bases; in addition, its position in occupied Germany and occupied Japan carried its influence close to Russia's frontiers. Moreover such actions as the abrupt termination of lend-lease aid, and the casual ignoring of the Kremlin's request for a postwar reconstruction loan, were not in Soviet eyes convincing evidence of American good will.[6] As a nation where fear and suspicion are endemic, it was not surprising that Russia should feel the need for loyal, friendly nations on her borders, and be determined to keep such nations under her influence if not direct control. As time went on, however, what might originally have been a defensive position inspired by fear seemed to the western world increasingly characterized by imperialist ambition.

The American public was not yet—in 1945–46—very much aroused over these developments. Its immediate worries were naturally enough demobilization, the reconversion of industry to peacetime production, and continuing economic progress. Inflation, the housing shortage, and industrial warfare appeared to be much more serious problems than the status of Iran, Communist influences in Greece, or even the lower-

[5] For a vivid account of postwar developments in Europe, see Theodore White, *Fire in the Ashes* (New York, 1954).

[6] Edward R. Stettinius, Jr., *Roosevelt and the Russians* (New York, 1949), pp. 318–319; Campbell, *The United States in World Affairs, 1945–47*, pp. 32–46, 344–350, 369–374.

ing of the Iron Curtain in eastern Europe. There was always grave concern over the control of atomic energy, but even here the public seemed optimistically convinced that the problem could be solved. While the reaction upon the end of the war was nowhere nearly so severe as that symbolized a quarter of a century earlier by Harding's desire for a return to normalcy, domestic issues tended to absorb popular attention.

As greater stability was attained at home, however, increasing attention was paid to the disputes that were being aired at the United Nations' "town meeting of the world." The American people could not escape the unhappy realization that Soviet-American relations had become the most serious problem of the postwar era. "What is Russia up to now?" Vandenberg asked as early as February, 1946, in an important speech in the Senate: "We ask it in Manchuria. We ask it in Eastern Europe and the Dardanelles. We ask it in Italy . . . We ask it in Iran. We ask it in Tripolitania. We ask it in the Baltic and the Balkans. We ask it in Poland. We ask it in Canada. We ask it in Japan. We ask it sometimes even in connection with events in our own United States. "What is Russia up to now?"

He did not despair of ultimate accord, but insisted on a vigorous defense of American interests at all times, and the assumption of "a moral leadership which we have too frequently allowed to lapse." [7]

In other quarters where the hopes of cooperation had not yet been dimmed by the realities of increasing friction, there was a feeling that American policy was too rigid. In particular, the followers of Henry A. Wallace, who was to break with the Truman administration and run as a presidential candidate of the Progressive party in 1948, urged a more conciliatory attitude in dealing with the Soviets. This was already a minority view, however. Popular pressure was mounting for a "get-tough-with-Russia" policy as the only means of safeguarding the interests of the free world. [8]

Secretary of State Byrnes reflected such influences in the increasingly firmer tone which he adopted at the periodic meetings of the Council of Foreign Ministers: "If we are to be a great power we must act as a great power." He had revived Senator Vandenberg's earlier suggestion of a four-power treaty to guarantee continued German disarmament in an attempt to calm Russian fears that the attitude of the United

[7] *The Private Papers of Senator Vandenberg*, 247, 248.
[8] Campbell, *The United States in World Affairs, 1945–47*, pp. 446–448.

States toward Germany was so lenient as to raise the specter of Germany winning back her old power.[9] When the Soviets would have none of this treaty, Byrnes made a forthright statement on the situation in Germany that marked a significant turning point in postwar American policy.

This was the speech summarizing American policy toward Germany delivered at Stuttgart on September 6, 1946: the German level of industry should not be so lowered as to prevent the recovery of reasonable living standards, the purposes of occupation were not a prolonged alien dictatorship but the building up of political democracy, and the eastern boundaries were to be determined by a peace conference rather than by unilateral action on the part of Russia or Poland. The United States did not want to see Germany become the pawn in an East-West struggle, Byrnes declared, but it was prepared to fulfill its responsibilities as an occupying power for as long as necessary. He assured Europe that this was not the 1920's: "We are staying here and will furnish our proportionate share of security forces." [10]

A month later, in a talk before the American Club in Paris, Secretary Byrnes gave a simple and homely explanation of just what America was trying to do—an explanation that was to have continuing validity: "The people of the United States did their best to stay out of European wars on the theory that they should mind their own business and that they had no business in Europe. It did not work . . . They have concluded that if they must help finish every European war, it would be better for them to do their part to prevent the starting of an European war." [11]

As both Soviet and American policy continued to stiffen, the implications of what was becoming the "cold war" could no longer be ignored. Peace treaties were finally concluded with Italy and the Russian satellites in eastern Europe, but the Council of Foreign Ministers made no headway on those with either Austria or Germany. The hoped-for cordiality in Soviet-American relations, as the key to international cooperation, had given way to a grim contest that was at first centered on German policy, and then spread gradually to other parts

---

[9] Byrnes, *Speaking Frankly,* pp. 171–174; *Private Papers of Senator Vandenberg,* pp. 263–264.

[10] *Senate Document 123,* 81st Congress, 1st Session, *A Decade of American Foreign Policy: Basic Documents, 1941–49* (Washington, 1950), pp. 522–527; Byrnes, *Speaking Frankly,* pp. 188–191.

[11] Byrnes, *Speaking Frankly,* p. 193.

of the world. The United States took the lead in seeking to mobilize and unite the free democracies of western Europe against the constant threat of Soviet-inspired Communist expansion. This was both a

Fitzpatrick in St. Louis *Post-Dispatch,* March 16, 1947
Burdens of Empire

struggle for political power and a struggle between opposing ideologies. At stake was not only national security, but, in a broader sense, maintenance of that sort of world in which liberty and democratic principles could survive.

The American people had not reckoned upon anything like this when they gave up isolationism and pledged their support to collective security. Here was a much more perilous involvement than they had contemplated. Yet they had to recognize—and did recognize—that there could be no withdrawal or retreat.

It was on March 12, 1947, that President Truman sent to Congress that significant message which finally and unequivocally accepted the challenge of Soviet expansion and laid the bases for a counterpolicy of containment. The Communist satellites were intervening more and more directly in the internal affairs of Greece, and her liberty and independence were gravely jeopardized. The Soviet Union itself was exercising direct pressures upon Turkey that seriously threatened that country's freedom of action. At stake was the security of the entire area of the eastern Mediterranean, where Great Britain had once wielded a decisive influence but no longer had the strength to do so. In these circumstances, President Truman specifically asked for authorization to extend to Greece and Turkey immediate economic and military aid to a total of $400 million. He went beyond this specific request, however, in outlining what became popularly known as the Truman Doctrine:

One of the primary objectives of the foreign policy of the United States is the creation of conditions in which we and other nations will be able to work out a way of life free from coercion.

I believe that it must be the policy of the United States to support free peoples who are resisting attempted subjugation by armed minorities or by outside pressures. . . .

The world is not static and the status quo is not sacred. But we cannot allow changes in the status quo in violation of the Charter of the United Nations by such methods as coercion, or by such subterfuges as political infiltration.[12]

Here was a broad and challenging conception of America's new world role, and one which necessarily involved intervention and entanglement on a heretofore unimagined scale. Well over a century earlier, pleas for aid to Greece when her struggle for independence was threatened by the intervention of the Holy Alliance had inspired John Quincy Adams to warn his countrymen not to go abroad "in search of monsters to destroy." There could have been no more telling illustra-

[12] *A Decade of American Foreign Policy,* pp. 1253–57.

tion of a changed world than Truman's message. The American people were called upon to back up their declared conviction that a threat to freedom anywhere was in a very real sense a threat to their own freedom. The nation was to embark upon a course which was designed, as George F. Kennan wrote in an inspired article giving the philosophic basis for the containment policy, to confront the Russians "with unalterable counter-force at every point where they show signs of encroaching upon the interests of a peaceful and stable world." [13]

The Truman Doctrine was accepted—and the President's specific requests for aid to Greece and Turkey approved—only after long debate. The new policy was criticized in the first instance for ignoring the United Nations. Before the appropriations were granted, Senator Vandenberg introduced an amendment making the contemplated assistance to Greece and Turkey subject to the United Nations' review and termination.[14] Other objections were raised on the ground of the impracticality of venturing so far afield, and the risks of becoming involved in what might develop into direct conflict with Russia in the Near East. However reluctant the approval finally given the new program, it was nevertheless decisive. The vote of 287 to 107 in the House and 67 to 23 in the Senate constituted a first victory for bipartisan support of foreign policy in a Congress that since the mid-term elections of 1946 was controlled by the Republicans.[15]

The Truman Doctrine was an important milestone in the development of postwar policy. It was also the harbinger of a project for even broader and more extensive foreign aid, in this instance limited to economic assistance, that was soon broached as a means of helping to restore the economy of a still prostrate Europe. First suggested by Under Secretary of State Acheson on May 8, 1947, and then set forth in more explicit terms by Secretary Marshall just a month later, the European Recovery Program—or Marshall Plan as it became generally known—had a scope and breadth that were something new in history.

[13] The Kennan article, "The Sources of Soviet Conduct," originally appeared anonymously in *Foreign Affairs*, XXV (July, 1947), 566–582. It is reprinted in George F. Kennan, *American Diplomacy, 1900–1950* (Chicago, 1951), pp. 107–124. See also Walter Lippmann, *The Cold War: A Study in U. S. Foreign Policy* (New York, 1947).

[14] *Private Papers of Senator Vandenberg*, pp. 345–346.

[15] Public opinion polls reported some 65 per cent of those interviewed, and knowing about the program, as in favor of aid for Greece, 49 per cent ready to extend assistance to Turkey, and 68 per cent favoring help to other countries in a similar situation. *Public Opinion Quarterly*, XI (Summer, 1947), 285–286.

From one point of view it was a generous and expansive undertaking to help other people that appealed at once to American idealism. It was also good business. So far as the Marshall Plan helped to restore the economy of Europe, it broadened the market for American goods and would work to the benefit of the economy of the United States.

Crocodile (Moscow), 1947

American Motor of the Latest Type

Still more important, anything that served to raise the standard of living among the peoples of Europe would operate to block the spread of communism and thereby strengthen national security. All in all, the Marshall Plan stood out most conspicuously as an unprecedented expression of enlightened self-interest.

The United States had already made substantial and generous contributions to European relief and recovery. In the form of loans and grants, gifts through private relief organizations, and the shipment of goods and supplies through the United Nations Relief and Rehabilitation Administration, it had extended to Europe between V-E Day and the spring of 1947 assistance totaling more than $11 billion. This aid had not proved sufficient, however, to overcome the existing economic stagnation. It was becoming increasingly apparent that only a broad program of reconstruction for the European nations as a whole could ward off the disintegrating forces that were providing such fertile ground for the further growth of communism in Italy, France, and other countries.

Pointing out that human beings, nations, and democratic institutions exist within narrow economic margins, Acheson had declared that it should be the policy of the United States to do everything it could to widen these margins. He believed that in the world as it existed this was an American responsibility, not only from humanitarian considerations, but as a guarantee of national peace.[16] Taking up this theme, Secretary Marshall was more specific. He urged European aid, not as relief that would be no more than a temporary palliative, but as a basic contribution to enable Europe to help herself. Let the nations of Europe draw up a joint program of economic recovery, submit their plans and their needs to the United States, he advised, and American assistance would be possible on a practical and realistic basis:

It is logical that the United States should do whatever it is able to do to assist in the return of normal economic health in the world . . . Our policy is directed not against any country or doctrine but against hunger, poverty, desperation, and chaos. Its purpose should be the revival of a working economy in the world so as to permit the emergence of political and social conditions in which free institutions can exist.[17]

The invitation to submit a common program of economic recovery did not exclude the Soviet Union, and for a time it was believed that Russia would feel obliged to participate. The clear intent of the Marshall Plan to strengthen the forces of the free world against communism, however, almost inevitably caused the Soviets to refuse to have anything to do with it and to exercise a decisive pressure on the satellite nations of eastern Europe to follow their lead. Even Czechoslovakia

[16] McGeorge Bundy (ed.), *The Pattern of Responsibility—From the Record of Secretary of State Dean Acheson* (Boston, 1952), pp. 49–50.
[17] Department of State *Bulletin,* XVI (June 15, 1947), 1160.

was forced to withdraw her original acceptance of the invitation. The countries of western Europe, on the contrary, eagerly embraced the opportunity offered them. After long months of protracted negotiations, a sixteen-nation group drew up plans for a recovery program that, as finally modified by the United States, called for the extension of American aid to the over-all total of approximately $17 billion, spread over a four-year period.[18]

These proposals were submitted to Congress in December, 1947, with an urgent appeal by President Truman for their adoption. They were designed to restore Europe's economy, he stated, and a stable Europe was vital to the United States because "it is essential to the maintenance of the civilization in which the American way of life is rooted." [19] This concept was a far departure from the idea, as once expressed by John Dos Passos, that "repudiation of Europe is, after all, America's main excuse for being." The threat of communism was driving home a new realization that, whatever their differences, western Europe and America had very much the same basic ideals and principles.

In the light of political circumstance, with the Democrats in a minority in Congress, the attitude of the Republican leaders was quite as important as that of the Truman administration. Reporting unanimous approval of the European aid bill by the Senate Foreign Relations Committee, Vandenberg took the lead in urging favorable action:

The greatest nation on earth either justifies or surrenders its leadership. We must choose. There are no blueprints to guarantee results. We are entirely surrounded by calculated risks. I profoundly believe that the pending program is the best of these risks. I have no quarrel with those who disagree, because we are dealing with imponderables. But I am bound to say to those who disagree that they have not escaped to safety by rejecting or subverting this plan. They have simply fled to other risks, and I fear greater ones. For myself, I can only say that I prefer my choice of responsibilities.[20]

No more severe test could have been presented of the American people's willingness to accept their new international obligations. The issue was hotly debated. The opponents of the bill attacked aid on

[18] *A Decade of American Foreign Policy*, pp. 1284–98. The original Marshall Plan countries were Austria, Belgium, Denmark, France, Greece, Iceland, Ireland, Italy, Luxembourg, the Netherlands, Norway, Portugal, Sweden, Switzerland, Turkey, and the United Kingdom.

[19] *Ibid.*, p. 1285.

[20] *Private Papers of Senator Vandenberg*, p. 390.

such a scale as an intolerable economic burden, characterized it as un-justified intervention in European domestic affairs, and declared it was an invitation to new risks and dangers. There was still a fighting mi-nority that favored American withdrawal from commitments already made, rather than the assumption of new ones. Far more general, espe-cially in the Midwest, was an attitude of cautious skepticism as to this particular program's feasibility. Nevertheless the Marshall Plan at-tracted growing popular support. Editorial opinion approved it by a wide margin; all the major farm organizations, and both the A.F. of L. and the C.I.O. went on record as favoring it; and the National Association of Manufacturers (with a rather ambiguous provision against extending aid to any country which adopted a program of socialization) gave it strong endorsement. Such other evidence of public opinion as was available reinforced these indications of the will-ingness of the American people to accept the sacrifices that the pro-gram would mean.[21]

While the issue was still being debated, Soviet Russia provided the final incentive for both popular and congressional approval. Early in March, 1948, came the dramatic news of a startling *coup d'état* estab-lishing Communist control over Czechoslovakia. The reduction of this eastern outpost of democracy to Soviet domination was compelling evidence of the danger of still further extension of Russian influence unless heroic measures were taken to stem the Red tide. Before the month was over, the Marshall Plan, as embodied in the Economic Cooperation Act of 1948 with an initial appropriation of $5.3 billion, was accepted by overwhelming votes in both houses of Congress.[22]

While the Truman Doctrine and the Marshall Plan were the most important developments in the realm of foreign policy in 1947–48, the United States found itself engaged on many other fronts. It was con-cerned with the removal of national barriers to world trade, sought to draw the countries of the Western Hemisphere into closer accord, was caught up in the complex of Middle East problems centering about Palestine, and became involved more deeply than ever in the affairs of

[21] Leonard S. Cottrell, Jr., and Sylvia Eberhart, *American Opinion on World Affairs* (Princeton, 1948), pp. 38–52; John C. Campbell, *United States in World Affairs, 1947–48* (New York, 1949), pp. 487–488.

[22] For the Economic Cooperation Act, see *A Decade of American Foreign Policy*, pp. 1299–1321.

eastern Asia. There could be no separating the world into small segments; global responsibility meant exactly what the phrase stated.

In some ways the most difficult of these problems involved economic readjustment, and the opposition of the Republicans to reductions in tariff led to an increasing gap between promise and performance in the position taken by the Truman administration. Congress again approved the reciprocal trade program, initiated by Roosevelt back in 1934, but adopted amendments to the existing legislation which seriously limited its effectiveness. American representatives played an important part in the economic conferences at Geneva and Havana that led to creation of the International Trade Organization, but the Senate refused to sanction American membership. While the United States, that is, accepted in principle a program of world cooperation in reducing tariffs and promoting commerce, it was not prepared to go very far in implementing this program. Yet there was no question, as President Truman stated, that this country was "the giant of the economic world" and that its choice of policy could "lead the nations to economic peace . . . or plunge them into economic war." [23]

Policy in Latin America followed the lines which had led at the close of the war to agreement in the Act of Chapultepec that an attack upon any one of the American states would be considered an attack upon them all. The developing friction in the relations between the United States and the Argentine had for a time blocked further action to give this policy permanent form. In the summer of 1947, however, twenty-one nations meeting at Rio de Janeiro signed a treaty that not only reaffirmed the position they had taken in the Act of Chapultepec, but definitely pledged themselves in the event of any attack to active cooperation in defense of their common safety.[24]

This treaty gave a final multilateral sanction to the principles originally set forth in the Monroe Doctrine, and also provided protection against aggression originating in the Western Hemisphere itself. It in effect incorporated guarantees, although limited to this part of the

[23] Seymour E. Harris (ed.), *Foreign Economic Policy for the United States* (Cambridge, Mass., 1948), pp. 254–270; Campbell, *The United States in World Affairs, 1947–48*, pp. 245–275.

[24] The texts of these and other postwar treaties may be found in the State Department series *Treaties and Other International Acts*, the annual Raymond Dennett and Katherine D. Durand (eds) *Documents on American Foreign Relations*, and (usually abridged) Ruhl J. Bartlett, *The Record of American Diplomacy* (New York, 1954). In this instance, see Bartlett, pp. 559–560 and 730–733.

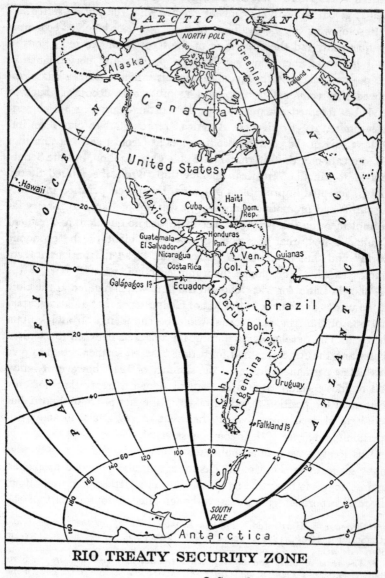

RIO TREATY SECURITY ZONE

© *Council on Foreign Relations, Inc.*

world, that clearly violated the old doctrine of abstention from permanent foreign commitments. The defense of Latin American nations from foreign attack, however, had always been implicit in the Monroe Doctrine, and not even the most extreme isolationists were opposed to this further undertaking to uphold the peace of the Americas. Still, it was a striking indication of changed attitudes that the more general implications of earlier policy should now be so specifically set forth in a hard-and-fast treaty which the Senate approved with only one dissenting vote. A year later, to carry out the purposes of the treaty, there was formally set up the Organization of American States.

As for affairs in eastern Asia, the war against Japan had brought about a tremendous extension of American power and American influence in the entire Pacific area. While independence was granted the Philippines as promised a decade earlier, close ties were continued with the island republic, and a ninety-nine-year agreement provided for the maintenance of United States military and naval bases.[25] Moreover, to other American outposts in Hawaii, Guam, and Samoa were added the former Japanese-mandated islands in the western Pacific, while the United States retained exclusive control over the Ryukyus and the Bonin Islands. The mandated islands were officially designated as a strategic area trusteeship under the jurisdiction of the United Nations, and legally Japan held a "residual sovereignty" over the Ryukyus.[26] Nevertheless the authority of the United States was absolute in its capacity as guardian of the security of the Pacific. What Secretary Acheson would call "our defensive perimeter" now stretched from the Aleutians to Japan, then turned southward pivoting on the bastion of Okinawa, and reached down to the shores of the Philippines.[27]

Far Eastern developments were soon to prove as threatening to American interests as those in Europe. This danger was not fully apparent, however, in the first postwar years. Because the United States had a virtually free hand in carrying out its reconstruction program, the occupation of Japan did not give rise to any such difficulties as the occupation of Germany. If the situation in Korea, where separate

[25] Garel A. Grunder and William E. Livezey, *The Philippines and the United States* (Norman, Okla., 1951), 270–275.

[26] Bartlett, *The Record of American Diplomacy*, pp. 759–760, 764–765. For trusteeship agreements, see also *The Forrestal Diaries*, pp. 130–131, 213–216, 233–234, and later discussion in Ralph J. D. Braibanti, "The Outlook for the Ryukyus," *Far Eastern Survey*, XXII (June, 1953), 73–78.

[27] Statement of January 12, 1950, Bartlett, *The Record of American Diplomacy*, p. 762.

zones of Russian and American occupation were divided by the 38th parallel, did not promise too well for the creation of a united and independent country, military conflict here was certainly not anticipated in the first postwar years. Although the perennial problem of China was intensified by incipient civil war, and mounting indications that control of that vast country might fall into Communist hands, the fateful consequences of Nationalist weakness were still not fully exposed.

It will be necessary to return to developments in eastern Asia. In the meantime, Europe continued to hold the major attention of both the American Government and the American people.

The extension of aid to western Europe through the Economic Cooperation Administration got off to an immediately successful start. This program had a tremendous psychological impact, over and above the material relief it afforded, in arousing new hopes for European recovery. It was largely responsible for preventing Italy—perhaps France—from being swept into the Communist camp in the 1948 elections in those two countries. Yet at the same time, and in part because of the very success of the Marshall Plan, the conflict between Soviet Russia and the western democracies grew increasingly tense.

Its focus remained Germany. The collapse of all efforts to bring about economic or political union between the eastern and western occupation areas had finally led the United States, Great Britain, and France, in February, 1948, to merge their zones and set up a joint administration in West Germany. The Soviets retaliated by tightening their hold on East Germany and attempting to drive the western Allies out of Berlin. When the Russians established a blockade of that city in June, however, the western powers responded with a dramatic counterstroke. Acting upon the advice of the American military commander, General Lucius Clay, who declared that retreat would be disastrous, they provided an "air lift" to sustain their position. Throwing hundreds of planes into the operation, they maintained during the winter of 1948–49 a highly successful transport service that provided Berliners—for a time at the rate of 4,000 tons daily—with the food, coal, and other essentials that enabled them to withstand all the rigors of their enforced isolation.[28]

The situation was for a time highly critical. American military leaders in Washington repeatedly and gravely discussed the possibility

[28] See Lucius Clay, *Decision in Germany* (New York, 1950).

of war and the question of using the atomic bomb should hostilities break out. Withdrawal from Berlin, however, was never really considered. At one top-level conference where the suggestion was made, it is recorded in *The Forrestal Diaries*, President Truman interrupted and emphatically stated that "there was no discussion on that point, we are going to stay, period." [29] He was determined to demonstrate beyond misunderstanding that the United States was not to be intimidated, and that there would be no retreat from its established policy to combat Soviet aggression anywhere. In the face of this indisputable evidence of the American intention to stand firm, and the almost incredible feats performed by the air lift, Russia capitulated. In April, 1949, the blockade of Berlin was raised. A bold and decisive policy had achieved a vitally important success.

The belief was nevertheless growing during this same period that the economic aid rendered through the Marshall Plan could not guarantee the ability of western Europe to protect itself from aggression. The Economic Recovery Program had brought about substantial improvement. Expenditures of some $6 billion by the United States and $4.3 billion by the participating countries resulted before the close of 1949 in an increase of approximately 25 per cent in western Europe's total production of goods and services, and of some 57 per cent in its production of bread grains. Still, something had to be done to strengthen military as well as economic defenses. The times seemed to call for more concrete evidence of American interest in building up continental security. In such circumstances there gradually took shape a project that was to lead the United States into the most entangling of alliances.

Early in 1948, American public opinion was already swinging toward the idea of a possible military pact between the United States and the Marshall Plan countries. About the same time, the National Security Council began to discuss some form of association with the Western Union that had just been organized, at Brussels, by the European nations themselves.[30] Then in June, Senator Vandenberg introduced and the Senate adopted a resolution advocating the negotiation within the framework of the United Nations charter of further regional agree-

[29] *The Forrestal Diaries*, p. 454.
[30] *Public Opinion Quarterly*, XII (Summer, 1948), 549, 760; *The Forrestal Diaries*, p. 423.

ments for collective self-defense along the lines of the Treaty of Rio de Janeiro.[31]

Only ten years earlier Franklin D. Roosevelt had felt obliged to repudiate his alleged statement that America's frontier was along the Rhine. His countrymen were beginning to realize that it might lie along the Elbe. Buoyed up by such indications of both public and congressional support, the Secretary of State opened the negotiations that led to the North Atlantic Treaty.

The presidential election of 1948 intervened between the beginning and the conclusion of these negotiations. However, the bipartisan approach to foreign policy in Europe succeeded in keeping the treaty issue generally out of politics. Thomas E. Dewey, the Republican candidate, refrained from attacking at least this phase of Democratic policy.[32] When Truman was so surprisingly re-elected, he felt that his hand had been greatly strengthened. He was prepared to drive ahead with the further extension of European aid, proposed "a bold new program" to make the benefits of American scientific progress available for the improvement of the undeveloped parts of the world, and again called for close cooperation with the United Nations. In his Inaugural Address in January, 1949, however, he stressed most heavily among the major objectives of American foreign policy, the association of the free nations of the North Atlantic area in a "collective defense agreement." [33]

Dean Acheson, the new Secretary of State, now proceeded to complete the pact negotiations with the European countries, in constant consultation with the Senate Committee on Foreign Relations, and the new treaty was submitted to the Senate on April 12, 1949. It closely paralleled the Rio de Janeiro Treaty. In accepting the thesis that an attack on any one of them was an attack against them all, each of the twelve signatories pledged such action as it might deem necessary, *including the use of armed force,* to restore and maintain the security of the North Atlantic area.[34]

[31] *A Decade of American Foreign Policy,* p. 197; *Private Papers of Senator Vandenberg,* pp. 404–420.

[32] John C. Campbell, *The United States in World Affairs, 1948–49* (New York, 1950), pp. 500–501.

[33] *Senate Document 5,* 81st Congress, 1st Session, *Inaugural Address of President Harry S. Truman,* p. 3.

[34] *A Decade of American Foreign Policy,* pp. 1328–31, 1356–64. The original signatories were Belgium, Canada, Denmark, France, Iceland, Italy, Luxemburg, the Netherlands, Norway, Portugal, the United Kingdom and the United States.

Here nearly half a century later was the concrete embodiment of that proposal to "fortify the Atlantic system beyond attack" which Theodore Roosevelt had viewed sympathetically as a means to prevent any aggressor nation from winning domination of Europe. Here was the incorporation of the ideas that Woodrow Wilson had sought to implement after the First World War when he concluded his abortive

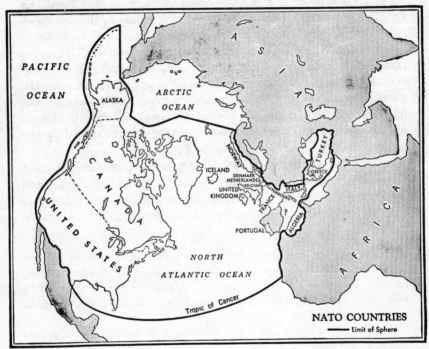

Reprinted from *Encyclopedia of American History,* Ed. Richard B. Morris

security pact with France. What had proved impossible in earlier years because the American people had such deep-seated prejudices and fears, because they were so stubbornly opposed to any entangling alliance, the menace of Communist aggression had finally brought within the realm of practicality. The experience of two world wars and the devastating potential of atomic warfare appeared to have persuaded the nation of two things: the only hope of restraining aggression was to have the aggressor unmistakably know in advance where the United States stood; and should war still come, the greatest promise of national safety lay in having allies among the free and democratic nations of Europe.

This further and most decisive departure from traditional isolationism was to cause wider discussion and debate than membership in the United Nations, the Truman Doctrine, or the Marshall Plan. Senator Vandenberg joined President Truman and Secretary Acheson in urging the treaty's prompt ratification.[35] The opposition in Congress centered in a small group of senators, of whom the most conspicuous was Taft. Their attitude was not isolationist in the sense that Borah, La Follette, and Hiram Johnson had been isolationists in their stubborn refusal to accept any commitment whatsoever for American action in world affairs. "Only an idiot would be an isolationist today," Taft once exclaimed indignantly.[36] In attacking the North Atlantic Treaty, however, this group reflected the old obsession against all alliances. Its members remained fearful that the United States would carry its commitments too far and let itself become too deeply involved in protecting other countries. They were most strongly opposed to making any pledges for sending American troops to Europe.

In his defense of the treaty, Secretary Acheson emphasized the grave danger of relying upon independent action to uphold world peace, and the vital importance of forestalling any such situation as that which had led to American involvement in the First and Second World Wars:

That experience has taught us that the control of Europe by a single aggressive unfriendly power would constitute an intolerable threat to the national security of the United States . . . It is a simple fact, proved by experience, that an outside attack on one member of this community is an attack on all members.

We have also learned that if the free nations do not stand together they will fall one by one.[37]

The Senate finally approved the North Atlantic Treaty on July 21, 1949, by a vote of 82 to 13. But notwithstanding the sweeping majority in its favor, discussion went on over the fundamental issues the treaty raised. Especially was there continuing and often vehement controversy over the military assistance the United States was called upon to provide its North Atlantic partners. Opposition to the administration's requests for funds represented in some instances a conservative but

[35] *Ibid.*, pp. 1332–56; *Private Papers of Senator Vandenberg*, pp. 474–501.
[36] Quoted in Richard P. Stebbins, *The United States in World Affairs, 1950* (New York, 1951), p. 412.
[37] Acheson, *Pattern of Responsibility*, p. 62.

sincere apprehension over the effect on the national economy of the continued drain on American resources. On occasion, it was little more than partisanship and political irresponsibility. Always it was strengthened by that persisting fear of entanglement that periodically flared up from the traditions of the past. For all such debate and discussion, however, ratification of the North Atlantic Treaty was a decisive commitment to collective security that the nation as a whole emphatically endorsed. The action taken by the Senate was justifiably hailed by President Truman as not the decision of the few, but a result of "the collective judgment of the people." [38]

[38] Quoted in Richard P. Stebbins, *The United States in World Affairs, 1949* (New York, 1950), p. 28.

CHAPTER 13

Broadening Tension

POPULAR acceptance of the North Atlantic Treaty reflected a general feeling that the threat of Communist imperialism represented one of the gravest dangers ever to confront the United States. Whether this was indeed the ultimate crisis that it sometimes appeared to be, only the perspective of time could tell. But as the cold war became steadily intensified in Europe and eastern Asia, and then suddenly erupted into open and bloody conflict in Korea and Indo-China, the alliance of the free world seemed to falter. The United States doubted its Allies; its Allies doubted the United States.

The American people had definitely accepted through membership in the United Nations and the North Atlantic Treaty Organization the proposition that in an atomic age there was no alternative to binding political ties with other countries. Yet they still hoped that this would not mean entangling too deeply their peace and prosperity "in the toils of European ambition, rivalship, interest, humor, or caprice." They had been led to think in terms of an effective world organization that would do away with power politics and spheres of influence. Even when these expectations were disappointed, they envisaged alliance with a united western Europe and the subsiding of continental rivalries under the necessity of preserving a common front against a common enemy.

It was soon found, however, that cooperation even in western Europe was not so easily achieved. Age-old fears and rivalries were not quickly forgotten. Historic ambitions could still hamper the consolidation of the forces of freedom. The United States was to become involved in spite of itself in the perennial conflict between France and Germany, the issues in dispute between Italy and Yugoslavia, the role of Spain, the independence movements in North Africa and the Middle East, and the interplay of conflicting nationalist and colonial rivalries in Indo-China and other parts of southeastern Asia.

Trying to hold the alliance of the western world together under these circumstances, the United States felt obliged to make concessions to the viewpoints of the European powers that sometimes could not be reconciled with the old American tradition of sympathy and encouragement for subject peoples struggling for self-government. It temporized with colonialism. Expediency rather than firm adherence to principle too often appeared to govern the policy of the "great exemplar of liberty." Granted that there was no easy way to reconcile the immediate, pragmatic needs of world security and the broader, more idealistic goals of universal freedom, the question remained whether a peace which sacrificed or endangered the basic values of liberty and justice was worth while; indeed, whether even as peace it was not illusory.[1]

A consequence of the compromises this situation imposed on American policy was a gradual shrinkage—especially in Asia—of that "reservoir of good will" that had been built up during the war. The moral basis of American leadership was disputed in many parts of the world that still had no sympathy with communism. Moreover, European recipients of American aid inevitably rebelled against the dependence that their need for this assistance imposed, strongly resenting such pressures as were brought to bear on either their domestic or foreign policies. The dominance that the United States exercised as a result of its tremendous economic and military power was not always conducive to complete confidence in America's ultimate aims.

At the beginning of 1950, Europe was still a major preoccupation. The need for further appropriations for the economic recovery program and for military aid brought Secretary Acheson constantly before congressional committees to justify and defend every step in the development of this phase of foreign policy. This was a new postwar development. For if the direction of policy remained a prerogative of the executive branch of government, with treaties subject to senatorial approval, the expenditure of the huge sums involved in foreign assist-

[1] For general discussion, see Charles B. Marshall, *The Limits of Foreign Policy* (New York, 1954).

ance called for legislation on the part of both houses of Congress. And this in turn demanded popular support all along the way to assure favorable action.

Congress, the newspapers, and public commentators continually debated the effectiveness of American policy. The immense burden of the economic and military aid programs, with high taxes still providing insufficient revenue to balance a tremendously expanded budget, built up a powerful opposition to what was considered by many people to be an unwarranted overextension of overseas commitments. Yet there was no abatement of the constant pressure being exercised by Soviet Russia. In spite of the fears of those who felt the United States was taking on too much of a task, the more international-minded proposed still more extensive foreign assistance.

They urged that, beyond aid to Europe, greater attention should be paid to "Point Four" of the Truman Inaugural Address, the bold new program advocating the expansion of technical assistance and capital investment in the undeveloped regions of the world. In support of a bill to implement this program, Secretary of State Acheson declared that it was in essence a vital security measure. Economic well-being throughout the world was the best possible safeguard against the further spread of communism. Anything that helped to bolster the economy of Latin America, the Middle East, Africa, and southeastern Asia —as well as Europe—was of direct benefit to the United States.[2]

The European Recovery Program, now moving into its final phase, certainly seemed to demonstrate the potentialities of economic assistance. The "dollar gap" between the European nations and the United States was narrowing in 1950, and industrial production on the Continent was continuing to gain substantial headway. The movement for closer economic integration was also being steadily advanced through the European Payments Union, the Schuman Plan for the pooling of western Europe's iron and coal resources, and the Organization for European Economic Cooperation.[3] At the same time, military coordination was being promoted through the North Atlantic Treaty Organization, and plans were under way for an integrated defensive force to

[2] State Department, *Strengthening the Forces of Freedom: Selected Speeches and Statements of Secretary of State Acheson* (Washington, 1950), pp. 68–72. On this general program, see State Department, *Point Four: Cooperative Program of Aid for the Development of Economically Undeveloped Areas*, Economic Cooperation Series, 24 (Washington, 1950).

[3] Richard P. Stebbins, *The United States in World Affairs, 1950* (New York, 1951), pp. 133–148; also Theodore White, *Fire in the Ashes* (New York, 1954).

be made up of separate divisions from its member nations. Western Europe was moving into a progressively stronger position to resist Communist infiltration or Communist attack.

The objective of the "total diplomacy" of the United States, Acheson stated in reviewing these progressive developments, was the continued building up of such "situations of strength"—military and economic—as would serve to give pause to Soviet imperialism. He insisted that it was "in the carrying out of such a policy . . . however long it takes and whatever it requires of us, that the frustration of the Kremlin's design for world dominion lies." [4]

Acheson's appeals for the necessary appropriations to carry through this program inevitably met stiff resistance. The bipartisanship that had supported the original acceptance of overseas commitments appeared to be breaking down in 1950; political factors sometimes played a greater part in congressional debate than national interest. Nevertheless the over-all policy was maintained. While the original requests of the administration for military and economic aid were almost invariably pared, Congress gave approval to substantially what the President and his Secretary of State proposed.

The country as a whole endorsed what was being done and accepted the premise that western Europe had to be supported as the first line of American defense. It went along with the necessary appropriations and taxes. Popular approval of this foreign policy, in fact, appeared to be so widespread that a Senate committee reported, in September, 1950, that the State Department might have "underestimated the willingness of the American people to accept the burdens that go with the position of leadership in the free world." [5]

Europe, however, was not the only region where the United States found itself dangerously involved in combating the menace of Communist aggression. Events in eastern Asia led to a series of crises that in mid-century underscored even more urgently than developments in Europe the perils of the global conflict in which the free world was engaged. The dramatic rise to power of the Chinese Communists, who swept their Nationalist foes from the mainland and then intervened in

[4] McGeorge Bundy (ed.), *The Pattern of Responsibility—From the Record of Secretary of State Dean Acheson* (Boston, 1952), pp. 24, 30; State Department, *Strengthening the Forces of Freedom*, p. 77.

[5] *Senate Report 2501*, 81st Congress, 2nd Session (Washington, 1950), pp. 4, 51.

the tense situations that developed in Korea and Indo-China, tended to counterbalance, if not more than counterbalance, the gains that the forces arrayed against communism were scoring in Europe and other parts of the world.

At the close of the war, American Far Eastern policy—apart from the occupation of Japan and southern Korea—was primarily directed toward ensuring the creation of a free, unified, democratic China which could take her place, as had been planned at the Cairo Conference of 1943, among the great powers devoted to maintaining world peace. The danger that the long-smoldering conflict between Chinese Communists and Nationalists might break out into open war was recognized. But President Truman hoped that American influence could somehow be exerted to avert such strife and bring about an accord that would make possible the formation of a reconstituted government in which all Chinese political factions would be represented. Should such a government be formed and enact the agrarian and other reforms demanded by the Chinese people, the American policy makers believed that the age-old problem of the status of China would finally be resolved.

To carry out such a program, President Truman appointed a special mission to China at the close of 1945 under the leadership of General George C. Marshall, wartime Chief of Staff and subsequent Secretary of State. The mission was instructed to try to bring about a truce between the Communists and the Nationalists and to urge the creation of a coalition government that would include, as well as Nationalists and Communists, representatives of the liberal, democratic elements in China. A temporary truce was effected, but soon broke down. For the Marshall mission never had any real chance of success. Neither the Nationalists nor the Communists were prepared to make the concessions that might have averted civil war; the democratic elements that might conceivably have served as a balance wheel in any coalition were unorganized and helpless. When fighting again broke out in March, 1946, the Marshall mission could do nothing, and after several months of fruitless activity gave up its task. The civil war that the United States had hoped to prevent was resumed with fresh fury.[6]

In these new circumstances, the Truman administration felt it had no alternative other than to stand aside and "let the dust settle." It

[6] The background for developments in China has been ably examined in Herbert Feis, *The China Tangle: The American Effort in China from Pearl Harbor to the Marshall Mission* (Princeton, 1953).

continued to recognize the Nationalist regime of Chiang Kai-shek, even extending financial aid that by 1950 totaled some $2 billion, but nevertheless abstained from any more direct intervention in the civil strife. Counsels were very much divided within administration circles on the wisdom of this policy. The predominant opinion among the Far Eastern experts in the State Department, however, was that any other program would be disastrous for American interests.

The advocates of nonintervention took the stand that the United States could not afford to support the Nationalists. Their attitude was based on the belief that the failure of Chiang Kai-shek to reform his government along democratic lines or to carry out other promised reforms had largely alienated the Chinese people, and that under such circumstances the Communists, with a program broadly appealing to the masses, were the only political force capable of uniting the country. Some proponents of these views were further convinced that the Communist movement in China was largely indigenous and consequently unlikely to fall under Soviet domination.

Critics of the policies of the Truman administration have violently attacked this interpretation of the relations between the Chinese Communists and the Russian Communists. They have charged that it was not only wholly false, but inspired by Communist sympathizers within the State Department.[7] Nevertheless the fact that in subsequent years Moscow and Peiping have drawn closer and closer together does not prove that in 1945–46 there were such incontrovertibly binding ties.

In any case, there is no evidence that the opinion of Far Eastern experts on the futility and danger of intervening more actively in China's civil war was based upon any other consideration than loyal support of what they believed to be the best interests of the United States. It was all too easy in later years, with the advantages of hindsight, to condemn the China policy of this period, yet even after the event there was no clear indication of how the situation could have been saved, if indeed it could have been, by anything short of all-out American intervention at the risk of precipitating another world conflict.

As the civil war went on, the Nationalists were unable to withstand the steady advance of the Communists. Desertions from their own ranks greatly weakened their power to offer any effective resistance. Soon the forces under Chiang Kai-shek were everywhere in full re-

[7] Stebbins, *The United States in World Affairs, 1950,* pp. 51–52.

treat, and by the close of 1949 were driven from the mainland to take refuge in Formosa, where the Generalissimo set up the seat of the Nationalist Government. By this time, it was abundantly clear that Soviet Russia was actively supporting Communist China, in spite of her 1945 treaty of friendship with the Nationalists, and the close ties that had now developed between the governments in Peiping and Moscow took on an increasingly unhappy significance. Communist imperialism was on the march in Asia. The defection of China from the free world, for this was what had happened whatever might be said about the undemocratic character of the government of Chiang Kai-shek, almost overnight upset the postwar balance of Far Eastern power.

The Truman administration, in which Dean Acheson had now replaced General Marshall as Secretary of State, continued to insist upon a noninterventionist policy. In mid-March, 1949, the State Department blocked a move sponsored by fifty senators for extending an additional $1.5 billion aid to the Chinese Nationalists on the ground that any such program would "embark this Government on an undertaking the eventual cost of which would almost surely be catastrophic." [8] But the policy makers had no other plan to cope with the rapidly deteriorating situation. In a White Paper issued in August, the State Department justifiably denied that anything could have been done to prevent the Communist victory—"the ominous result of the civil war in China was beyond the control of the government of the United States"—and acknowledged a complete impasse in trying to cope with this dangerous setback for the free world. [9]

The administration point of view was candidly expressed in testimony given in 1949 by General Bradley, chairman of the Joint Chiefs of Staff, on military assistance to Europe:

If the whole continent of Asia came under the influence of the Soviets we think it would be a great loss, of course. We are dependent on that area for considerable amounts of materials. However, we believe that Europe is more important from an industrial capacity standpoint than Asia. Furthermore there is, we believe, an effective way that you can render assistance to Europe, but no immediately apparent effective way that you can render assistance to Asia. [10]

[8] Quoted in John C. Campbell, *The United States in World Affairs, 1948–1949* (New York, 1950), p. 285.

[9] Department of State, *United States Relations with China With Special Reference to the Period 1944–49*, Far Eastern Series, 30 (Washington, 1949).

[10] *Military Assistance Program: Joint Hearings* (Washington, 1949), cited

Criticism of this realistic—but to the Asia Firsters seemingly defeatist attitude—mounted, with outraged attacks on Truman and Acheson. The whole issue became inextricably entangled in partisan controversy, and there was once again apparent that curious dichotomy in the Republican attitude between isolationism in respect to Europe and interventionism in Asia. Many of the most severe critics of the Marshall Plan and the North Atlantic Treaty became the most enthusiastic advocates of economic and even military aid for the Chinese Nationalists. There had never been any really consistent effort to develop a bipartisan policy in China,[11] and many Republicans consequently felt free to place the entire blame for the debacle in eastern Asia on the Democrats. They declared the Communist victory in that part of the world to be wholly due to the Truman administration's shortsightedness, vacillation, and ineptitude.

Such political leaders as Senators William F. Knowland of California, Henry Styles Bridges of New Hampshire, Patrick A. McCarran of Nevada, and Representative Walter H. Judd of Minnesota often went to unconscionable extremes in their attacks upon the China policy. Insinuating if not directly saying that Secretary Acheson was following a "soft policy" toward communism in Asia, they reiterated the charge that leftist influences in the State Department were responsible for his letting Chiang Kai-shek down and opening the way to the Chinese Communists' victory. Even Senator Taft followed this line and vigorously attacked the "pro-Communist policy of the Far Eastern Division of the State Department." The American "betrayal" of the Nationalists, he wrote in 1951, was owing to the influence of this group and to Secretary Acheson's strong prejudice against doing anything to help Chiang Kai-shek.[12]

Into this bitter fray there rushed Senator Joseph R. McCarthy of Wisconsin, with easily apparent political motivation, and the country was soon shocked and alarmed by his sensational charges. He declared that the State Department was "thoroughly infested" with Communists; spoke of "the unusual affinity for Communist causes" of the department's chief trouble shooter, Ambassador Philip C. Jessup; and characterized Owen Lattimore, one-time department consultant, as

in Richard P. Stebbins, *The United States in World Affairs, 1949* (New York, 1950), p. 105.

[11] Arthur H. Vandenberg, Jr., and J. A. Morris (eds.), *The Private Papers of Senator Vandenberg* (Boston, 1952), pp. 519, 527.

[12] Stebbins, *The United States in World Affairs, 1949*, p. 56; Robert A. Taft, *A Foreign Policy for Americans* (New York, 1951), p. 108.

being both the chief architect of Far Eastern policy and a top Soviet espionage agent.[13]

The earlier conviction of Alger Hiss, a high official in the State Department, on charges of perjury connected with alleged Communist activity and espionage, and other highly publicized disclosures of occasional Communist infiltration in government agencies made by the House Un-American Activities Committee, helped to create an atmosphere of suspicion and distrust on which Senator McCarthy throve. He took the lead in a violent anti-Communist campaign based on the thesis that the overwhelming danger confronting the United States was not so much communism abroad as communism, disloyalty, and treason at home.

The McCarthy technique was to gain headlines and publicity through sweeping accusations with which the denials could never quite catch up, to imply subversive activity through innuendo and indirect smears, to dwell upon guilt by association, and to make other blanket and unsubstantiated charges. The impact of what became known as "McCarthyism" heightened the fears, suspicions, and distrust from which it drew its strength. It endangered the basic freedoms that were the foundation of democracy and seriously undermined morale in all government agencies. When McCarthy moved on to active interference with State Department policies, attacking the Voice of America and insisting on the removal of certain suspect books from the libraries maintained abroad as part of the United States Information Program, the consequences were highly demoralizing both at home and overseas. His activities sowed dissension among the American people, and between the United States and its allies.

The phenomenon of McCarthyism was far more significant than Senator McCarthy himself in spite of his headline-catching skill and incessant drive for political power. For the support that his anti-Communist campaign attracted, in spite of its cynical disregard of civil liberties and of truth, would not have been possible except in an atmosphere of fear. Faced with the very real menace of Communist imperialism, the public seemed swept along by a wave of hysteria, conjuring up greatly magnified dangers within the country that denied the common sense and the basic loyalties of the American people. In embracing McCarthyism, too many Americans appeared to have

[13] Stebbins, *The United States in World Affairs, 1950,* pp. 56–57.

forgotten that a major citadel of their defense was the maintenance of their own liberties.[14]

The full consequences of McCarthyism in undermining morale were not yet apparent in 1950. Nevertheless the charges of Communist infiltration in the State Department could not be ignored. Secretary Acheson emphatically denied any subversion or disloyalty among his associates, but he was placed on the defensive. And when he continued to oppose any definite commitment for American defense of Formosa, should the Chinese Communists attack this last stronghold of the Nationalists, the attacks on him were redoubled. His leadership in the over-all anti-Communist policies of the Truman administration was forgotten as Formosa became an all-important political issue, symbolizing for the Asia Firsters a test of State Department loyalties.

Soon Acheson's critics became even more aroused over the stand he might take toward recognition of Communist China and its admission to the United Nations. Great Britain had already recognized the government set up at Peiping by Mao Tse-tung, the Communist leader. Soviet Russia was insisting on its right to the seat held by the Nationalists in the Security Council and other nations also viewed this proposal sympathetically. But the Asia Firsters, and Republicans generally, expressed the most vehement opposition to any dealings whatsoever with the Chinese Communists—either their recognition by the United States or their admission to the UN.[15]

These attacks and charges, which had considerable popular backing, importantly affected the further determination of policy. Whatever may have been its projected plans, the Truman administration now withheld recognition from the Chinese Communists, and took a strong stand against the Soviet Union's efforts to secure their entry into the United Nations. Secretary Acheson was unwilling to go so far as to state that the United States would exercise its veto power in the Security Council, should this become necessary to block the Soviet maneuvers. He seemed to hope that the issue could somehow be settled without reaching this point. His rather ambiguous attitude did not satisfy his Republican foes, and at the same time created considerable

[14] The literature bearing on McCarthyism and the "crisis of nerves" is immense. Among the many articles and books dealing with the issue and the defense of freedom, there may be singled out especially Henry Steele Commager, *Freedom, Loyalty, Dissent* (New York, 1954), and Elmer Davis, *But We Were Born Free* (Indianapolis, 1954).

[15] Stebbins, *The United States in World Affairs, 1950,* pp. 51–60.

resentment on the part of those members of the United Nations who favored the Chinese Communists' admission.[16]

In the midst of such controversy and confusion, while the State Department was almost frantically trying to work out some new approach to these seemingly insoluble problems, the situation in eastern Asia took a new and dramatic turn that overnight transformed the cold war into war in reality. On June 25, 1950, hostilities broke out in Korea.

The joint occupation of Korea by Soviet and American forces after the Japanese surrender in 1945 had been a temporary and almost fortuitous expedient. The powers had agreed, in conformity with the pledge made at the Cairo Conference, to establish an independent and unified Korea. Soviet Russia had blocked the efforts of the United Nations to hold elections for a general assembly in 1947, however, and the two sections of the country remained divided along the 38th parallel. In the south, the Republic of Korea was set up under the presidency of Syngman Rhee and recognized by the United Nations; in the north, a Democratic People's Republic was established under the aegis of the Soviets. Both Russian and American military forces were withdrawn from the Korean peninsula by 1949 and an uneasy truce had since then prevailed along the disputed boundary.[17]

Hostilities were precipitated when the North Koreans suddenly drove across the 38th parallel. Behind them, it was all too clear, were their masters in the Kremlin. The conflict between the free world and the Communist world had entered upon a new phase of active hostilities in a region where the forces pledged under American leadership to stem the further advance of Soviet imperialism were least united and most inadequately prepared to take effective action.

The North Korean onslaught confronted the United States with the necessity for a decision that had far greater significance than anything that had yet happened in the postwar world. President Truman acted unhesitatingly. The American deputy representative in the United Nations at once brought the crossing of the 38th parallel before an emergency session of the Security Council. The temporary absence of Soviet Russia, which was boycotting the Council because of its refusal to admit the Chinese Communists to UN membership, cleared the

[16] *Private Papers of Senator Vandenberg,* pp. 533, 540–541.
[17] Stebbins, *The United States in World Affairs, 1949,* pp. 458–460; *The United States in World Affairs, 1950,* pp. 185–189.

way, on June 25, for prompt passage of a resolution terming the action of the North Koreans a breach of peace. Taking this resolution as justifying the immediate extension of aid to the victims of aggression, Truman ordered American air and naval forces to give support to the South Koreans.

Two days later, on June 27, the Security Council adopted a further resolution specifically calling upon all members of the United Nations "to furnish such assistance as may be necessary to repel the armed attack." The President now sent American ground troops into action and also, on his own responsibility, without authorization from either the United Nations or Congress, ordered the American Seventh Fleet to enforce the neutrality of Formosa.[18]

The United States took the initiative in these startling developments, was at first the only country in a position to give effective help to the South Koreans, and was to continue to play a dominant role throughout the entire Korean war. Although some sixteen nations, including Great Britain, Canada, Australia, New Zealand, the Philippines, and Turkey, were ultimately to contribute military aid in some form, American forces bore the brunt of the conflict. Nevertheless it was the United Nations, fortunately free from the restraint of a Russian veto, that had accepted under the terms of its charter the challenge of Communist aggression.

The necessity for such action was clear. Unless the United Nations was prepared to answer force with counterforce, it would have revealed an impotence that would have meant the sacrifice of the principles on which it had been founded. Collective security would collapse as it had collapsed when Japan marched into Manchuria two decades earlier. Once again an aggressor, this time in Moscow rather than Tokyo, Berlin, or Rome, would have had reason to feel assured that the democratic, peace-loving nations were unable to unite in mutual defense. These considerations were the determining factor in the Security Council's deliberations, and the decision reached was an epoch-making one in world history.

President Truman's policy in calling for immediate action on the part of the United Nations and promptly sending American troops into battle in Korea was generally approved by the American people. Nothing could have more graphically demonstrated how far they had trav-

[18] Department of State, *Bulletin*, XXIII (July 31, 1950), 163–180; Beverly Smith, "The White House Story: Why We Went to War in Korea," *Saturday Evening Post*, CCXXIV (Nov. 10, 1951), 22 ff.

eled in a few momentous years along the road to collective security. The time was to come when intervention would be widely and severely criticized, both as an infringement on the congressional war-making power and as a perilous involvement outside the sphere of American national interest. The Korean war was packed with dynamite; it constantly threatened to shatter political alignments both at home and abroad. In the summer of 1950, however, the ranks were nearly closed in upholding the President and in agreeing that the challenge of Communist aggression could not possibly be allowed to go by default.[19] Even Senator Vandenberg, who had been one of the most outspoken critics of Far Eastern policy, did not hesitate to support the President's stand. "When the time came for you to act in behalf of free men and a free world," he wrote Truman on July 3, "you did so with a spectacular courage which has revived the relentless purpose of all peaceful nations to deny aggression." Senator Taft fell in line more grudgingly. "I believe the general principle of the policy is right," he stated.[20]

The Korean war was something new in the world. It involved military action, to develop on a scale hardly foreseen in midsummer of 1950, with no purpose other than to demonstrate that attack from any quarter would be met by the concerted resistance of peace-loving nations. If it was war, it remained a limited war. The ultimate political goal of the United Nations was to establish the united and peaceful Korea that had been pledged through the wartime agreement of the major powers—including Soviet Russia. This long-term goal, however, was to be sought by peaceful means. The immediate objective of the United Nations' intervention was no more than establishment of the principle that force would not be tolerated in the settlement of international disputes. In Acheson's words it was "to end the aggression, to safeguard against its renewal, and to restore peace." [21]

The war, of course, had repercussions far beyond the little peninsula on which it was being fought, far beyond even the confines of Asia. The United States and its allies accepted the North Korean attack as a Soviet test of the powers of resistance of the free world. It was feared that other such tests might be made, and that there was a very real

[19] *Public Opinion Quarterly*, XV (Spring, 1951), 170; Stebbins, *United States in World Affairs, 1950*, pp. 20–23.

[20] *Private Papers of Senator Vandenberg*, p. 543; Taft, *A Foreign Policy for Americans*, p. 106.

[21] Acheson, *Pattern of Responsibility*, 246. For attitude of the United Nations, see periodically published *United Nations Documents* and annual *Yearbook of the United Nations*.

likelihood that the Communists might plunge the entire globe into war. In December, 1950, the Joint Chiefs of Staff advised the commanders of all American troops of this dangerous situation and ordered them "to increase their readiness without creating an atmosphere of alarm." [22]

The response to the crisis on the part of the United States, aside from military action in Korea, was to mobilize its industrial resources for wartime production, build up its armed forces from 1.5 to 3.5 million men, and seek in every way to strengthen its Allies in Europe. Congress at once made supplementary funds available for these general purposes. By 1951–52, appropriations for the armed forces had risen from $12 to $41 billion, while foreign aid increased from $4.5 to $7.1 billion. [23]

Everything possible was done to strengthen the North Atlantic Treaty Organization, with the over-all direction of the integrated military forces of the member nations placed under the command of an American, in the person of General Dwight D. Eisenhower. The United States urgently called upon its European partners to increase their armaments, in conjunction with American aid, in order to provide more effective military forces on the continent. It emphatically endorsed the plan, first advanced by the Council of Europe in the autumn of 1950, for the creation of a unified European Defense Community, with a supranational army to which western Germany would contribute a number of divisions. And finally, President Truman prepared to send additional American troops to Europe in fulfillment of the nation's obligations under the terms of the North Atlantic Treaty.

The war in Korea was in the meantime becoming immeasurably complicated. In late November, 1950, on the ground that the advance of the United Nations forces into North Korea threatened vital interests in Manchuria, the Chinese Communists actively intervened. The struggle became, so the United Nations commander, General Douglas MacArthur, stated, an entirely different war. As the seesaw battle then raged up and down the narrow peninsula, both the strategy and objectives that governed American policy were brought into question at

[22] *Military Situation in the Far East: Hearings Before the Senate Armed Services and Foreign Relations Committees,* 82nd Congress, 1st Session (Washington, 1951), II, 1630, quoted in Stebbins, *United States in World Affairs, 1951,* p. 26.

[23] Stebbins, *United States in World Affairs, 1950,* pp. 252–253; *ibid., 1951,* pp. 31–32.

Herblock in the Washington *Post*, March, 1951

"We've been using more of a roundish one."

home and abroad. Political repercussions within the United States, centering about General MacArthur's demand for carrying the war into Manchuria, were paralleled by mounting controversy and dispute among the democratic Allies.[24]

The United States continued to bear the predominant burden of the war, a natural consequence of its greater resources and the availability of its manpower, and yet it was not a free agent. Military strategy had to be subordinated to the necessity of maintaining Allied unity. Nor could the Truman administration afford to disregard the pressures being exerted within the United Nations for some peaceful solution of the Korean conflict, even though the concessions proposed by other UN members sometimes went much further than American policy favored or American public opinion was willing to accept. The United States was discovering that international cooperation was not a one-way street. The American resolution to make good a stand against aggression and to refuse appeasement was interpreted in some European capitals as inviting the larger war such policies were designed to prevent.

The American people were paying the major cost of operations in Korea, and with casualties that would total some 144,000, including 25,000 dead, they were to suffer by far the greater toll in human losses except among the Koreans themselves. It was not easy to find themselves subject to the criticism and restraint of those nations in whose interest, quite as much as their own, they were making such a heavy sacrifice.

[24] See *Military Situation in the Far East: Hearings Before the Senate Armed Services and Foreign Relations Committees.*

CHAPTER 14

Mid-Century

AGAINST the background of this time of troubles, there commenced in 1950 a new chapter in that great debate over America's role in world affairs which stretched back to the earliest days of the Republic. As American overseas commitments progressively broadened, one-time isolationists questioned the very bases of the revolutionary new departure in foreign policy that was being hammered out on the anvil of Communist aggression. They did not succeed in undermining the conviction of the American people as a whole that there could be no retreat to the past, yet the doubts and misgivings they voiced tended to create new confusions as to the course the United States should follow in coping with its global responsibilities.

The debate was first set off by the demand of Senator Taft for a "re-examination" of the entire program of military aid to Europe, and was then brought even more forcefully to public attention through two important speeches by former President Hoover. "The foundation of our national policies," Hoover stated, "must be to preserve for the world this Western Hemisphere Gibraltar of Western Civilization." He argued emphatically that the Western Hemisphere did not need Europe for its defense, that it could be made self-contained in the matter of critical raw materials, and that it was still "surrounded by a great moat."

For all the implications of his position, he denied that he was advocating a return to anything that might really be called isolationism. He was ready to cooperate with such island nations as Great Britain in the Atlantic, and Japan, Formosa, the Philippines, and if possible the members of the British Commonwealth in the Pacific. Outside the continent, he was convinced, American defense should be based on air and naval power; there should be no commitment of land forces to either Europe or Asia.[1]

In subsequent speeches and writing, Taft did not seem ready to retreat as far as Hoover suggested. He was not one of those, he declared, who believed that the United States could abandon the rest of the world and rely wholly upon continental defense. The nation was engaged in a world-wide battle and must fight it on a world-wide stage. But there appeared to be something paradoxical, at least strangely confusing, about his attitude toward the commitment of land forces overseas. "Certainly our program in Europe," he was to write in *A Foreign Policy for Americans,* "seems to me far more likely to produce war with Russia than anything we have done in the East." And then he added: "I am only asking for the same policy in the Far East as in Europe." [2] Whatever his theoretical views, moreover, his continued opposition to so many of the measures designed to implement existing foreign policy seemed to deny the validity of his own thesis that the United States was engaged in a world-wide battle that had to be fought on a world-wide stage.

The attacks of the "new isolationists," which in some instances went much further than the criticism of Taft and Hoover, were met head on by the proponents of collective security within both Democratic and Republican ranks. President Truman and Secretary Acheson stressed the calamitous consequences of any retreat from the leadership that America had assumed in behalf of the free world. Acheson ridiculed Taft's demand for a "re-examination" of military aid to Europe as being something like the attitude of the farmer going out every morning and pulling up his crops to see how they were growing. He flatly rejected a policy of "sitting quivering in a storm cellar waiting for whatever fate others may wish to prepare for us." The job that the United States had to do in safeguarding peace and freedom, Acheson declared, "needs to be done cooperatively with our allies." [3]

[1] *Vital Speeches,* XVII (Jan. 1, 1951), 166, and (Feb. 15, 1951), 262–265.
[2] *Ibid.* (Jan. 15, 1951), 198–205; Robert A. Taft, *A Foreign Policy for Americans* (New York, 1951), p. 108.
[3] Department of State, *Bulletin,* XXLII (Nov. 27, 1950), 839; *ibid.,* XXIV (Jan. 1, 1951), 3–6; *ibid.,* XXV (Aug. 6, 1951), 205–206; McGeorge Bundy (ed.), *The Pattern of Responsibility—From the Record of Secretary of State Dean Acheson* (Boston, 1952), pp. 83–100.

A new Democratic voice was heard when Governor Adlai Stevenson of Illinois condemned what he described as the "re-emergence of the straight isolationist doctrine." In answer to the rhetorical questions, "Have we learned that our mission is the prevention, not just the survival of a major war? Have we discovered that there are no Gibraltars, no fortresses impregnable to death or ideas, any more?" he expressed his own conviction that there could be no return to the past.[4]

Among Republican leaders, Governor Dewey was no less forthright. "Clearly we would very soon be isolated, here in America," he said in analyzing the Hoover program. "We would be the loneliest people on earth. What would we do, an island of freedom in a Communist world, outnumbered 14 to 1, with oceans which would no longer be our protecting moat but a broad highway to our front door." [5] And from General Eisenhower, making his first report to Congress as the commander of the North Atlantic Treaty forces, came similar warnings of the vital need for cooperation with our Allies. "Western Europe is so important to our future," he declared, ". . . that we cannot afford to do less than our best in making sure that it does not go down the drain." [6]

On another level and from other than isolationist sources, foreign policy was also subject to attack. Where the United States had gone wrong in the past, some critics maintained, was in the subordination of national interest to the more expansive goals attributed to a world mission to foster liberty and peace. The American people were urged to accept more realistically the implications of a world power politics. Walter Lippmann had earlier expressed this point of view in his emphatic statement that "we must consider first and last the American national interest." It was implicit in George F. Kennan's pointed criticism of the "legalistic-moralistic" approach to world problems. Going much further, and with implications as to the "failure" of American policy that were hardly justified by the measure of success actually attained, was Hans Morgenthau of the University of Chicago: "The intoxication with moral abstractions which as a mass phenomenon started with the Spanish-American War, and which in our time has become the prevailing substitute for political thought, is indeed one of the great sources of weakness and failure in American foreign policy." [7]

[4] *Vital Speeches*, XVII (Feb. 15, 1931), 287.
[5] *Ibid.* (Mar. 1, 1951), 260.
[6] *Ibid.* (Feb. 15, 1951), 260.
[7] Walter Lippmann, *U. S. Foreign Policy: Shield of the Republic* (Boston,

These arguments, however realistic in other respects, appeared to ignore what was none the less a fact because it had idealistic overtones. The historical record clearly showed that the immediate national interest, although never forgotten, did not constitute the furthest limit in American thinking on international affairs. And in the development of foreign policy, this attitude of mind had always to be taken into consideration. The American people, that is, had repeatedly demonstrated a belief in ethical purpose that was something more than an intoxication with moral abstractions, or a rationalization of popular ambition for national power and economic advantage.

Such considerations certainly suggested that to command continuing popular support, the abandonment of isolationism and the return to Europe had to mean something more than building up armaments, spheres of influence, a new balance of power. If the immediate demands of national security constantly and rightly emphasized the necessity of developing the counterforce that would contain Soviet aggression, foreign policy had to embrace a broader goal. The American people passionately desired peace and security for themselves. They also looked to the ultimate creation of a world in which liberty and peace would be secure for all peoples—a world symbolized by the United Nations rather than a new balance of military power.[8]

Secretary Acheson, in two notable speeches in the spring of 1951, reaffirmed the ideals for which America stood in the tradition of the great statesmen of the past, from Washington to Lincoln and Theodore Roosevelt, from Jefferson to Wilson and Franklin Roosevelt:

The American people have been the leaders in a revolution that has been going on for a century and a half, a revolution by the common people. And the basic objective of American foreign policy is to make possible a world in which all peoples . . . can work, in their own way, toward a better life. . . .

We are children of freedom. We cannot be safe except in an environment of freedom. We believe in freedom as fundamentally as we believe in anything in this world. We believe in it for everyone in our country. And we don't restrict this belief to freedom for ourselves. We believe that all people

1943), p. 137; George F. Kennan, *American Diplomacy, 1900–1950* (Chicago, 1952), p. 95; Hans J. Morgenthau, "The Mainsprings of American Foreign Policy: the National Interest vs. Moral Abstractions," *American Political Science Review*, XLIV (Dec., 1950), 834.

[8] The issues merely suggested in this paragraph are historically analyzed in Robert E. Osgood's absorbing study, *Ideals and Self-Interest in America's Foreign Relations* (Chicago, 1953).

in the world are entitled to as much freedom, to develop in their own way, as we want ourselves.[9]

The debate raged on in Congress, on the public platform, and over the radio; in newspapers, pamphlets, and periodicals. The age-old prejudice against what Hoover called "the eternal malign forces of Europe" persisted in the thinking of many people. Even though the events of 1941–45 had destroyed the doctrine and the program of the old isolationism, they had not destroyed the emotions which underlay and sustained it.[10]

However, the noisy clamor of the great debate actually gave a false impression. Among responsible leaders, and on the part of the great body of the American people, there was far more agreement than disagreement on foreign policy. The idea of withdrawing from international commitments did not win any really substantial support. The United Nations and the North Atlantic Treaty continued to have strong popular backing. An overwhelming majority of the nation's newspapers completely rejected the doctrine associated with the Hoover conception of a western Gibraltar. There was no retreat on the part of farm and labor organizations, or of the business community, from their endorsement of international cooperation.[11]

Sharp differences over the extent of foreign aid were inevitable. It was impossible for anyone to know where the exact line of safety lay between expenditures for such a program and the maintenance of a stable domestic economy. There was also no certain answer to the issues raised in respect to the disposition of troops overseas, or to the question of whether the United States should place a greater reliance on air and naval power as contrasted with land forces. And what of the atomic bomb?—to which this narrative must return. Whatever was done was a calculated risk.

The presidential election of 1952 further strengthened the underlying accord on the necessity of accepting the nation's new obligations as the leader of the free world. Both party platforms upheld the promotion of collective security under the United Nations and the North

[9] On March 15, 1951, at San Francisco and on April 22, 1951, before the American Society of Newspaper Editors. Acheson, *Pattern of Responsibility*, pp. 41–42.

[10] Arthur M. Schlesinger, Jr., "The New Isolationism," *Atlantic Monthly*, CLXXXIX (May, 1952), 35.

[11] Richard P. Stebbins, *The United States in World Affairs, 1950* (New York, 1951), pp. 438–443.

Atlantic Treaty Organization. Throughout the campaign both candidates, General Eisenhower and Governor Stevenson, drove home the importance of international cooperation.

Stevenson repeatedly stressed America's world leadership: "I believe the essential direction of our foreign policy is right—building the unity and the collective strength of the free countries to prevent the expansion of Soviet domination." [12] Eisenhower constantly stressed "an integrated world policy," stated his conviction that free nations had no alternative to following the way of collective security, and said it was America's duty to help free people to stay free. "I have long insisted—and do now insist," he declared, "that isolationism in America is dead as a political issue." [13]

There were differences about the more specific approach to foreign affairs. The Democrats wholeheartedly endorsed the Truman-Acheson policy and stressed close cooperation with other peace-minded nations. The Republicans naturally felt constrained to criticize what had gone before and attempted to reconcile the divergent ideas of their internationalist and isolationist wings. This led them to call for a more "dynamic" policy and yet at the same time insist on the need for greater economy in both military expenditures and foreign aid. Moreover, while upholding international cooperation, they somewhat ambiguously gave even greater emphasis to "enlightened self-interest."

Yet in spite of these differences in the attitude of candidates and parties, the election of 1952 reaffirmed the basic purposes of the foreign policy of the previous seven years. It was still too much to say that isolationism, which was taking such an unconscionable time in dying, had been finally and permanently interred. The burdens of world leadership were too heavy to make the American people very happy about the task they had assumed. They could hardly fail to recognize, however, that the harsh realities of a world threatened by still another war were responsible for their predicament, and that there could be no escape to isolated safety.

Immediate international difficulties had not moderated during these days of the great debate. Whether in Europe or in Asia, there was no relaxing of tension, and no viable solutions appeared for the cruel problems born of a divided world. The United Nations was impor-

[12] *The New York Times,* Sept. 2, 1952.
[13] *Ibid.,* Sept. 10, 1952; Oct. 11, 1952 (editorial); Nov. 1, 1952.

tantly active on many fronts, but over any effective move to settle international disputes hung always the shadow of a Russian veto in the Security Council. In spite of Moscow's recurrent "peace offensives," there was no lifting of the heavy threat of Soviet aggression.

A ray of hope appeared in Korea, where the war had settled down to a virtual deadlock along the line of the 38th parallel. In midsummer, 1951, the Russian delegate to the United Nations opened the door to truce negotiations. Any real progress, however, was for long blocked by the obstructive tactics of the Chinese and North Korean Communists. The parleys, intermittently broken off and resumed, dragged on their weary length for month after month. And in the meantime—for another two years—the fighting went on with a steadily mounting roll of casualties.

At least some compensation for failure to solve the seemingly insoluble problems of Korea and China was the success attained in reestablishing normal relations with Japan. After intensive negotiations during the summer of 1951, representatives of the democratic powers signed at San Francisco on September 8, in spite of Russian objections, a broad and comprehensive peace treaty. Japan renounced her title to all former territories outside her main islands, assented to the trusteeship provisions which gave the United States sole authority in the Ryukyu and Bonin Islands, and accepted the international obligations of a peace-loving nation in the world community.[14]

A peace treaty did not automatically resolve all the issues centering on Japan. Although the occupation policies pursued by the United States had been generally successful in bringing about a greater democratization of Japanese society, and the new constitution with its bill of rights and renunciation of war, was a great advance, it was still to be seen how long-lasting these reforms might prove to be. Moreover, economic difficulties were very real. The end of American occupation confronted Japan with the necessity of revising her economy and finding outlets for her products to replace the loss of traditional markets, especially in China. Still, the United States enjoyed a freedom of action in its relations with Japan, where Soviet Russia had been un-

[14] State Department, *Conference for the Conclusion and Signature of the Treaty of Peace with Japan,* Publication 4392 (Washington, 1951). The treaty may also be found (as many other such documents) in Raymond Dennett and Katherine Durand (eds.), *Documents on American Foreign Relations,* XIII (Princeton, 1953), 266–67, and abridged in Ruhl J. Bartlett, *The Record of American Diplomacy* (New York, 1954), pp. 764–65.

able to block either occupation policies or a peace treaty, that stood out in sharp contrast with the situation in other parts of Asia and in Germany.[15]

One consequence of this freedom of action was the conclusion of a special Japanese-American security treaty, supplementing the general

THE JAPANESE PEACE SETTLEMENT

Areas renounced by Japan   Scale of miles   Trust Territory of the Pacific Islands (U.S. Administering Authority)

© *Council on Foreign Relations, Inc.*

peace treaty. The United States was granted the right to station American troops in Japan for the maintenance of international peace and protection of Japan against armed attack. Also, at the time of the San Francisco Conference, the United States signed a mutual defense pact with the Philippine Islands, and a tripartite defense treaty with New Zealand and Australia.[16] Although these latter agreements did not go

[15] See E. J. Lewe Van Aduard, *Japan: From Surrender to Peace* (New York, 1954).

[16] Department of State, *Bulletin,* XXV (Sept. 17, 1951), 464–465; (July 23,

so far as either the Rio de Janeiro Treaty or the North Atlantic Treaty, they nevertheless constituted far-reaching and important commitments for safeguarding the general security of the Pacific.

The treaties had been negotiated by John Foster Dulles, at this time Republican adviser to the State Department; were approved by the Senate with little opposition, and were generally applauded by the American people. The traditional willingness to act positively in the Pacific, and the desire to strengthen the security of an area lying so close to the hostile forces of both Communist Russia and Communist China, largely account for such widespread support. In the circumstances of the time, the American people were fully prepared to break through the barriers that before the war would have made the assumption of any such responsibilities impossible.

On the other side of the world, the United States continued its intensive efforts to build up and strengthen the defenses of the nations of western Europe. Congress had adopted, in October, 1951, a Mutual Security Program to take the place of the Economic Cooperation Administration, and it also provided additional funds for both military and economic assistance. Although the administration's requests were as always subject to debate, appropriations for foreign aid for the fiscal year 1953 rose to a high total of $6 billion, with primary emphasis upon the rearmament of the nations belonging to the North Atlantic Treaty Organization.[17]

Late in May, 1952, these moves were supplemented by two important political agreements: one a "peace contract" with the Bonn Government of West Germany, and the other a formal treaty establishing the European Defense Community that was signed by France, Belgium, Italy, the Netherlands, Luxembourg, and West Germany.[18] The primary purpose of the latter agreement was to provide for the projected supranational army, including the much discussed West German divisions, which was to be incorporated within the North Atlantic Treaty Organization. Although this approach to European cooperation was two years later to break down, the United States at the time strongly

---

1951), 148–149; (Aug. 27, 1951), 335. See also John Foster Dulles, "Security in the Pacific," *Foreign Affairs*, XXX (Jan., 1952), 175–187. In 1953 a further defense treaty was signed with the Republic of Korea. Bartlett, *The Record of American Diplomacy*, pp. 80–81, and in December, 1954, a comparable pact with Nationalist China. *The New York Times*, Dec. 3, 1954.

[17] Richard P. Stebbins, *The United States in World Affairs, 1952* (New York, 1953), p. 76.

[18] *Ibid.*, p. 56.

supported the EDC. Secretary Acheson characterized it as the beginnings of the realization of the ancient dream of unity among the free peoples of western Europe,[19] and at once began to exercise his influence in encouraging the treaty's ratification.

When the Eisenhower administration came into office in January, 1953, marking the return of the Republicans to power after twenty momentous years in world history, the situation with which it was confronted stood out in sharp and dramatic contrast with that which the Republicans had faced when they were last charged with the formulation of foreign policy. However the party leadership, as the presidential campaign demonstrated, had also changed with the times. If there had been in the 1920's a general readiness on the part of the Republicans to accept Harding's dictum that the United States sought no part in directing the destinies of the world, Eisenhower at once made it plain in his Inaugural Address that there would be no shirking of the global commitments already undertaken to meet the Communist menace to peace.

He was prepared to follow the main lines of policy developed by his Democratic predecessors—to support the United Nations, strengthen NATO, honor the mutual assistance pacts in the Americas and the Pacific, and uphold the principle of meeting aggression with forceful defense that had been applied in Korea. "Destiny has laid upon our country," the President stated, "the responsibility of the free world's leadership." [20]

Within a few months, one definite development took place. The long-protracted negotiations in Korea, which had so often seemed on the verge of a complete breakdown, finally led to an armistice. As signed on July 27, 1953, it provided for a military demarcation line roughly along the 38th parallel, the exchange of prisoners under the most complicated and ultimately impractical terms, and a future peace conference.[21] The conclusion of the truce was victory of a sort for the United Nations. At least temporarily, aggression had been brought to a halt. The actual fighting in Korea was over. Both President Eisenhower and Secretary of State Dulles hailed the armistice as a triumph for the principles which had led to intervention. "We have shown, in the winning of this truce," the President declared, "that the collective

[19] Department of State, *Bulletin,* XXVI (June 9, 1952), 895.
[20] *The New York Times,* Jan. 31, 1953.
[21] Department of State, *Bulletin,* XXIX (Aug. 3, 1953), 132–139.

resolve of the free world can and will meet aggression in Asia—or anywhere in the world." [22]

This statement, for all its optimistic overtones regarding the future, was basically true so far as Korea was concerned. The United Nations, largely on the initiative of the United States and with American forces carrying almost the entire burden of the actual fighting, had repelled the Communist attack and successfully protected South Korea. Yet the Communist forces had not actually been defeated. There was no assurance that the armistice would be faithfully observed, and the unification of Korea appeared as distant as ever. Intervention had been necessary—and in the long reaches of history it might prove to be one of the most decisive events of this entire period—but three years of fighting had not brought about any solution of the immensely complicated problems of eastern Asia. The future of a still divided Korea, the relationship between Communist China and the democracies, the status of Formosa, the problem of Indo-China, where the French were deeply engaged in combating native Communists, were issues still unresolved by what was no more than an uneasy stalemate along Korea's 38th parallel.

Nor did the Korean truce open up the way to settlement of the questions still in dispute in Europe. The death of Stalin on March 5, 1953, and emergence of new Soviet leadership personified by Georgi M. Malenkov, had served to intensify the existing impasse and to create more confusions in world policy.

The Eisenhower administration was committed to following the general approach to world affairs developed in the preceding years. "Our policy must be a coherent global policy," the President again stated, ". . . dedicated to making the free world secure." [23] For a time, however, the actual course taken seriously endangered the precarious unity that was the free world's first prerequisite for security. Secretary of State Dulles seemed determined to develop a new strategy that would fulfill Republican campaign promises of seizing the initiative . and meeting Russian aggression with a more positive program than containment. He talked of the "liberation" of the peoples of eastern Europe. In an effort to speed up rearmament and ratification of the treaty establishing the European Defense Community, he warned that unless there were prompt action the United States would be obliged to

[22] *The New York Times*, July 28, 1953; Aug. 6, 1953. See also Department of State, *Bulletin*, XXIX (Aug. 10, 1953), 175–176.
[23] *The New York Times*, Feb. 3, 1953.

make an "agonizing reappraisal" of its entire policy. And on January 12, 1954, he startled the nation—and even more its European allies—by stating that the National Security Council had decided to rely not upon local defenses in meeting aggression, but upon "a great capacity to retaliate instantly by means and at places of our own choosing." [24]

This suggestion that the United States might use the atomic bomb—as instant retaliation was generally interpreted—in the event of further Soviet attack in any part of the world awoke widespread alarm both within the United States and abroad. The Secretary of State undertook to amplify and interpret his original statement. In an article in *Foreign Affairs* he wrote:

The essential thing is that a potential aggressor should know in advance that he can and will be made to suffer for his aggression more than he can possibly gain by it. This calls for a system in which local defensive strength is reinforced by more mobile deterrent power. The method of doing so will vary according to the character of the various regions. . . . Local defense is important. But in such areas the main reliance must be on the power of the free community to retaliate with great force by mobile means at places of its own choice.[25]

Yet how such a policy might actually be implemented still remained very much in doubt. In a later press conference on March 16, 1954, Dulles said any action taken would be in consultation, wherever possible, with other members of the free community, and in accordance with the country's own constitutional procedures. He refused to be pinned down any more definitely. Nothing would be more futile, he stated, than "to tell the enemy in advance just where, when and how you plan to retaliate." [26] Here was obviously a threat directed against the Soviet Union, but it created more confusion among the western Allies than it apparently did among their enemies.

In making these extreme and sometimes contradictory policy statements, in which he was duly supported by President Eisenhower, the Secretary of State certainly did little to assuage the fears of European members of the free world alliance that the United States might be taking matters too much in its own hands. Public opinion abroad, especially within the ranks of the political opposition to the British and French Governments, insistently raised the question whether America

[24] *Ibid.,* Jan. 13, 1954.
[25] *Foreign Affairs,* XXXII (Apr., 1954), 353–364.
[26] *The New York Times,* Mar. 17, 1954.

was swinging toward attempted domination of the forces of democracy rather than cooperative leadership.

Dulles was abruptly recalled by such criticism to the existing realities of the world situation. The imperative necessity of reforging a weakened western unity was self-evident as the Soviet Union took shrewd advantage of every crack in the democracies' armor to foment further differences. And this became especially important when, as a result of mounting pressure from its Allies, the United States finally agreed to a new foreign ministers' conference with Great Britain, France, and Soviet Russia to explore once again the possibilities of concluding peace treaties with Austria and Germany. At this meeting, held in Berlin in February, 1954, the three western powers did succeed in presenting a united front. No progress whatsoever could be made, however, in overcoming the obstacles Soviet Russia still presented to any settlement of the basic problems involved.[27] A divided Germany remained a symbol of a divided world.

The one concrete result of the Berlin Conference, if it could be so characterized, was the agreement reached for another and larger meeting at Geneva, to which Communist China would be invited, for consideration of the problems of eastern Asia. The preliminary negotiations for the Korean peace conference stipulated in the armistice agreement had completely broken down, and new developments in Indo-China still further emphasized the urgency of trying to come to some settlement of Asiatic problems.

For seven years the French had been battling the Communist forces of the Vietminh, in rebellion against the constituted authority of Vietnam, one of three associated states of Indo-China, and their will to further resistance was rapidly weakening. The Vietminh were actively assisted by the Chinese Communists, and a new Korea appeared to be in the making. France felt that her position was virtually hopeless.

A year earlier President Eisenhower had declared that aggression in southeastern Asia, even as in Korea, was a threat to the entire community of free nations. Nevertheless American policy during the intervening months could hardly have been more confused or vacillating. Additional military and economic aid was extended to the French and Vietnam forces, but the strong opposition of both the American people and the nation's Allies effectively blocked the more active intervention

[27] Department of State, *Bulletin*, XXX (Mar. 8, 1954), 343–347.

at which administration spokesmen occasionally hinted. Then, in the face of France's evident desire to negotiate a truce, Secretary Dulles attempted on the very eve of the Geneva Conference to set up a southeastern Asia defense alliance. He was flatly rebuffed by Great Britain and had to abandon his plan. President Eisenhower thereupon sought to calm Europe's fears that the United States would block any settlement in Indo-China. With a broader reference than to conflict in this part of the world alone, he declared that while there might be little or no hope of establishing really satisfactory relations with the Communists, it might still be feasible to work out some practical way of getting along with them.[28]

In spite of these developments and the prevailing skepticism as to whether the meeting at Geneva would prove any more productive than the Berlin Conference, the foreign ministers of the interested states duly met in May, 1954, with Communist China—as in the case of the other nations—represented by her foreign minister. As the negotiations proceeded, confusion grew. It proved to be impossible to reach any agreement whatsoever on Korea, and the rapidly deteriorating military situation in Indo-China constantly overshadowed other political discussions. The continued victories of the Vietminh Communists on the battlefield, the weakness and indecision of France (highlighted by a government overturn while the conference was still in session), the opposing attitudes of the United States and Great Britain, again dangerously undermined the Allied unity that had been reforged with such difficulty at the Berlin Conference. Whereas its European partners were ready to come to terms with the Communists in Indo-China, in realistic acceptance of the situation there, the United States appeared to be mortally afraid of any move that could be construed as appeasement, or that might lead to recognition of Communist China and her admission into the United Nations.

While these issues still hung fire, Prime Minister Churchill made a hurried visit to Washington to consult with President Eisenhower. In terms of the immediate controversy, these conversations appeared largely inconclusive. The sharp divergence of views between the two countries could not be disguised. Nevertheless, Eisenhower and Churchill agreed upon a statement of common policy that strongly emphasized the basic, underlying accord existing between the United States and Great Britain. Reaffirming the principles of the Atlantic Charter, it

[28] *The New York Times,* May 4, 1954.

pledged the two nations to continue their united efforts to secure world peace.[29]

Although the Geneva Conference failed to reach any agreement on Korea, and the United States thereupon ostentatiously withdrew from the negotiations, a settlement was finally concluded in respect to Indo-China. Under the realistic guidance of Mendès-France, the dynamic new French premier, France and Vietnam accepted Vietminh authority in the northern area of Indo-China. This forced concession constituted another defeat for the free world. It was all too clear that only concerted efforts could now prevent all of southeastern Asia from following the path of China, North Korea, and northern Vietnam into the Communist camp. The United States had no alternative other than to accept the Indo-China settlement, however reluctantly, but at once renewed its efforts to create the southeastern Asia defense alliance that Secretary Dulles had unsuccessfully urged before the conference.

These efforts finally led to a conference at Manila in September which at least partially secured the new objectives of Far Eastern diplomacy. For while India and other Asiatic countries refused to participate, a collective defense treaty was concluded by eight nations—the United States, Great Britain, France, Australia, New Zealand, Pakistan, Thailand and the Philippines—for safeguarding the security of southeastern Asia. In the event of aggression within the area concerned, each of the signatory nations agreed to take action, in accordance with its constitutional processes, to meet the common danger.[30]

It nevertheless remained clear, especially in view of the attitude of such countries as India, that this primarily military agreement was at best a very limited defense against further Communist expansion. The western powers had still to recognize more explicitly the strong forces of nationalism in southeastern Asia and to understand that the temporizing with colonialism in Indo-China had not strengthened confidence in the West. A policy of anti-communism was not enough to assure the friendship and support of the Asiatic world. The United States was called upon to demonstrate in concrete terms its sympathy for the national aspirations of the peoples in these regions, and to extend to them, on a far larger scale than had been done heretofore, the economic aid that would bolster their internal resistance to the blandishments of communism.

[29] *Ibid.*, June 30, 1954.
[30] For text of treaty see *The New York Times*, Sept. 9, 1954.

As these events were taking place on the Asiatic front, there was still another shift in the kaleidoscopic scene of international events. France at long last acted upon the treaties that two years earlier had set up the European Defense Community—and its action was to reject them. The entire program of integrating West Germany into the security system represented by NATO appeared to have collapsed. The United States, which had placed such an exclusive emphasis upon the creation of EDC, had suffered a sharp diplomatic defeat.

Negotiations were at once commenced to see what could be saved from this setback. Secretary Dulles now left the initiative to the European statesmen, having learned from experience the risks of pressing any American program too strongly, and the fortunate consequence was a new series of agreements that in the face of all forebodings pointed to a fresh and promising approach toward solution of the vital issues projected by the collapse of EDC. After a preliminary conference in London at the close of September, 1954, a complex group of new conventions and treaty protocols was signed in Paris some three weeks later. They provided for the restoration of the sovereignty of West Germany—officially the Federal Republic of Germany; the creation of a new Western European Union under the aegis of the Brussels Treaty of 1948; the establishment of controls over the military forces of its member nations, including those of West Germany, and the admission of the latter nation as a full and equal partner with the existing fourteen members of the North Atlantic Treaty Organization.[31]

In a statement issued on the eve of the final signature of the various accords, Secretary Dulles declared that whereas seven weeks earlier "the western world faced a crisis of almost terrifying proportions," with all its hopes of solving the problems of inter-allied unity seemingly shattered beyond any prospect of recovery, there had once again been a rising up to meet the emergency "by what I think we can call a near miracle." The new accords, he said, marked a shining chapter in history with results that had been believed beyond possible achievement.[32]

His highly optimistic assertions were echoed by the statesmen of Great Britain, France and West Germany. It still remained to be seen, however, whether the Paris agreements would be finally ratified, and

[31] For final act of the London Conference, and the protocols and declarations of the Paris Conference, see *The New York Times*, Oct. 4 and Oct. 24, 1954. Also State Department, *London and Paris Agreements*, Publication 5659 (Washington, 1954).

[32] *The New York Times*, October 23, 1954.

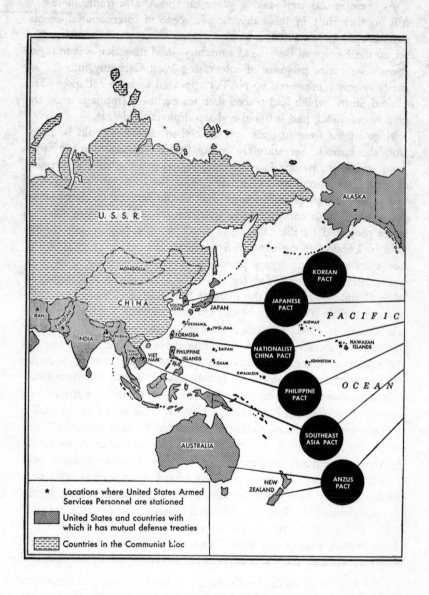

KOREAN PACT

JAPANESE PACT

NATIONALIST CHINA PACT

PHILIPPINE PACT

SOUTHEAST ASIA PACT

ANZUS PACT

★ Locations where United States Armed Services Personnel are stationed

United States and countries with which it has mutual defense treaties

Countries in the Communist bloc

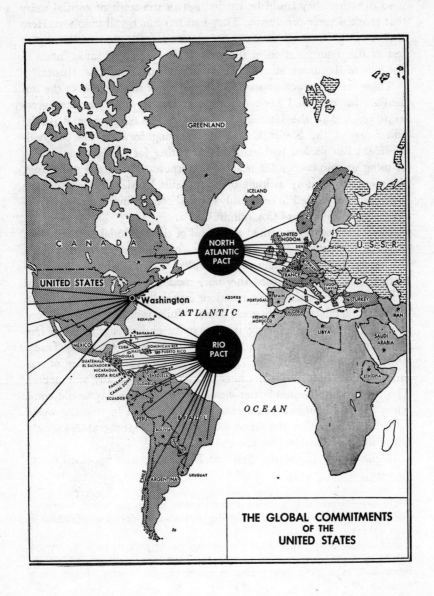

THE GLOBAL COMMITMENTS
OF THE
UNITED STATES

if so, whether they could be carried out in the spirit of cordial unity that marked their conclusion. They had left much still unsolved. Here was once again, as on so many occasions since the close of the war, a test of the determination of the free world to hold its ranks intact in the face of the unrelenting divisive pressures of Communist Russia.

There were at once hopes and fears of what might lie over the immediate international horizon. One encouraging note was the agreement reached in the United Nations, with the reluctant and partial adherence of the Soviet Union, for carrying forward the proposals President Eisenhower had made a year earlier for international action in using atomic energy for peacetime purposes. Yet at the same time, the more conciliatory attitude of Communist Russia on this and some other issues appeared to be harshly contradicted by increasingly provocative acts on the part of Communist China.

These developments caused a renewal of the perennial debate within the United States over the possibilities of peaceful coexistence in a world so sharply and dangerously divided. The Eisenhower Administration, however, reaffirmed the more moderate and restrained stand it had taken since the sharp reaction, especially abroad, to its threats of instant retaliation with great force. While insisting upon the continuing necessity of building up the unity and strength of the free world, of remaining constantly vigilant in defense, Secretary Dulles declared it was American policy to exhaust all peaceful means of sustaining international rights rather than to resort to any war action. The hope of the United States, he said, was that the day would come when the Communists would renounce their effort to rule the world by force, intimidation and fraud, but he warned that the nation should not mistake a false dawn for the real dawn.[33]

In the most sober terms President Eisenhower also appealed to the country:

Let us recognize that we owe it to ourselves and to the world to explore every possible peaceful means of settling differences before we even think of such a thing as war.

And the hard way is to have the courage to be patient, tirelessly to seek out every single avenue open to us in the hope even finally of leading the other side to a little better understanding of the honesty of our intentions. . . .[34]

[33] Address at Chicago, Nov. 29, 1954, as reported in *The New York Times*, Nov. 30, 1954.

[34] Press conference as reported in *The New York Times*, Dec. 3, 1954.

The underlying aims of American foreign policy in the 1950's had not fundamentally changed from what they had been when the Republic was founded. National security as always remained a first and basic consideration. There was still a very real concern over the promotion of trade and commerce in the interests of the nation's continuing prosperity. And there was also, as there had been throughout the history of the Republic, a strong popular conviction that American policies should be directed toward the defense of the freedom and the liberty of all people suffering under tyranny or seeking relief from foreign oppression. But if the ultimate objectives of policy—adding up to a free and secure America in a free and secure world—had not materially changed with the passing years, the conditions prevailing in the 1950's bore little relation to those existent in the early days of the Republic, or to those characterizing that era which at the opening of the twentieth century first saw the United States emerge upon the international scene as a great power.

The two global wars in which America had participated had brought about decisive shifts in the balance of international power. The rise of Soviet Russia posed a new threat to peace and freedom, holding all the world in thrall. And the United States had attained a position that made it the great protagonist in this global contest with Communist imperialism.

Yet this was not all. The development first of the atomic bomb, and then of the hydrogen bomb, had made the world over even more drastically than either past wars or the new conflict between the democratic and Communist nations. The dark menace of these incalculably destructive engines of war, possessed by Soviet Russia as well as by the United States, had a revolutionary effect upon every phase of international relations in the mid-twentieth century. Above all else, one thing appeared certain: should any major war break out, the United States could not count in the future on any margin of safety. The American people were forced to realize that war could be brought to their own shores—at once and with devastating impact. There could be no possible security except in so far as war could be avoided in every part of a world so closely integrated that what happened in Yugoslavia or Iran, in Korea or Indo-China, affected America almost as directly as events in the Western Hemisphere.

Never before had the conduct of foreign relations been so closely linked with the imperatives of military strategy, not only because of the danger of Communist imperialism in itself, but because of the threat to all civilization inherent in thermonuclear warfare. Neither a policy based on "containment" nor one threatening "retaliation" held in itself any answer to the crisis. The one foreshadowed a world of continual fears and anxiety, and the other an unimaginable war that could be as disastrous for the victor as the vanquished—if, indeed, there could possibly be any victor. Unless or until some accommodation could be found between the antagonistic purposes and ideological conflicts that divided the western democracies and the Communist powers, there could be no real hope of peaceful coexistence.

Diplomacy in these circumstances had a more vital importance than ever before in history, collective security a deeper significance, and world organization a greater urgency. The overwhelming risks of any resort to arms could not be disputed. As a consequence of its geographic position, mighty industrial resources, and armory of atomic weapons climaxed by the hydrogen bomb, the United States was confronted with an awful responsibility. The American people had for long avoided this responsibility; they could do so no longer. They faced a fateful test in the fulfillment of their inescapable obligations to employ all their resources—physical and spiritual—in a great joint endeavor to safeguard the peace and liberty of all freedom-loving people. It remained to be seen whether they could summon up and maintain the courage, the wisdom, and perhaps above all the patience to meet this test and cope successfully with a world in dire crisis rather than the peaceful world on which their great expectations were once based.

Bibliography

GENERAL

Bibliographies

In a book dealing with the rise of America to world power and the bases for the foreign policies through which it exercised such power, the sources are comparable to those of a full history of the United States. They may be found in the bibliographies of the companion volumes of this series. Within the narrower field of foreign policy itself, there are more specific bibliographical references. The standard volume, covering the period up to 1921, is Samuel F. Bemis and G. G. Griffin, *Guide to the Diplomatic History of the United States, 1775–1921* (Washington, 1935). There are also extensive references, carrying through the 1940's, in the bibliographical sections of Thomas A. Bailey, *A Diplomatic History of the American People* (rev. ed., New York, 1950). For recent years the bibliographical sections in the quarterly issues of the magazine *Foreign Affairs* (New York, 1919—) and in the annual survey of foreign policy, *The United States in World Affairs* (New York, 1931—) are also very helpful. Both of these invaluable publications are brought out by the Council on Foreign Relations. These references should be supplemented by the *Harvard Guide to American History,* compiled by Oscar Handlin, Arthur M. Schlesinger, Samuel Eliot Morison, Frederick Merk, Arthur M. Schlesinger, Jr., and Paul Herman Buck (Cambridge, Mass., 1954); the bibliographies in the other general histories listed below; and by the article lists published in the *American Historical Review* and the *Mississippi Valley Historical Review.*

Documents and Other Primary Material

Government documents are of course highly important. The end result of diplomacy is most usefully consulted in Hunter Miller's *Treaties and Other International Acts of the United States of America* (8 vols. to date, Washington, 1942–48). This may be supplemented by the State Department series, *Treaties and Other International Acts.* For presidential messages there is the standard work edited by James D. Richardson, *A Compilation of the Mes-*

sages and Papers of the Presidents. There are various editions and supplementary volumes. The papers of many Presidents, most notably for the purposes of this book those of Theodore Roosevelt, Woodrow Wilson, Herbert Hoover, and Franklin D. Roosevelt, have also been published separately.

The official diplomatic record is found in *Papers Relating to the Foreign Relations of the United States,* issued annually, with occasional special volumes, by the State Department. The lag in publication is at least partially made up through the Department of State *Bulletin,* published weekly since 1939. An invaluable if unofficial documentary record available—also since 1939—is the annual series, *Documents on American Foreign Relations,* brought out with various editors under the auspices of the World Peace Foundation (since 1953 in conjunction with the Council on Foreign Relations).

Additional diplomatic correspondence in the archives of the State Department, both published and manuscript collections of the letters of the "makers of foreign policy," documents and reports of congressional hearings, and foreign policy debates printed in the *Congressional Record,* are also highly important.

In many instances, contemporary newspaper and magazine articles provide additional source material. *The New York Times* is invaluable as a newspaper of record, printing many public documents. The *Literary Digest* and *Public Opinion* helpfully sampled popular attitudes through the 1920's. In recent years *Foreign Affairs* has often published important policy discussions, while note should also be made of the *Bulletin* of the Foreign Policy Association, together with its popular Headline pamphlets, and the *Survey* of the Institute of Pacific Relations. *Vital Speeches* contains much material that might otherwise be lost.

General Histories

Among the general histories of foreign policy, the two leading books are Samuel Flagg Bemis, *A Diplomatic History of the United States* (rev. ed., New York, 1950), and, already noted for its bibliographies, Thomas A. Bailey, *A Diplomatic History of the American People.* Arranged on a topical rather than chronological basis is Richard W. Van Alstyne, *American Diplomacy in Action* (Stanford, 1944). There is also a great deal of material in Samuel F. Bemis (ed.), *The American Secretaries of State and Their Diplomacy* (10 vols, New York, 1927–29). Useful compilations of selected documents are Ruhl J. Bartlett (ed.), *The Record of American Diplomacy* (rev. ed., New York, 1954), and Henry Steele Commager (ed.), *Documents of American History* (New York, 1950).

Among more interpretative studies are two brief but provocative books by Dexter Perkins: *The Evolution of American Foreign Policy* (New York, 1948) and *The American Approach to Foreign Policy* (Cambridge, Mass., 1952); Theodore Clark Smith's *The United States as a Factor in World History* (New York, 1941), and Walter Lippmann's very popular little volume, *U. S. Foreign Policy: Shield of the Republic* (Boston, 1943). Developments during the past half century have inspired a number of both factual and interpretative studies of this epochal period. Samuel F. Bemis has published *The United States as a World Power* (New York, 1950) and Richard W. Van Alstyne, *American Crisis Diplomacy* (Stanford, 1952) to supplement their earlier works. There are also Whitney Hart Shephardson, *The Interests of the United States as a World Power* (Claremont, Cal., 1942); Dexter Perkins, *America and Two Wars* (Boston, 1944); and the highly stimulating and provocative study by George F. Kennan, *American Diplomacy: 1900-1950* (Chicago, 1952). There are also two books on foreign policy by Allan Nevins, Nos. 55 and 56 in The Chronicles of America series: *The United States in a Chaotic World: A Chronicle of International Affairs, 1918-1933* (New Haven, 1950) and *The New Deal and World Affairs: A Chronicle of International Affairs, 1933-1945* (New Haven, 1950).

Among other comprehensive studies with a special approach indicated by their titles are Merle Curti, *Peace or War: The American Struggle, 1636-1936* (New York, 1936); James Fred Rippy, *America and the Strife of Europe* (Chicago, 1938); Charles A. Beard and G. H. E. Smith, *The Idea of National Interest* (New York, 1934); Thomas A. Bailey, *The Man in the Street, Impact of American Public Opinion on American Foreign Policy* (New York, 1948); and Gabriel A. Almond, *The American People and Foreign Policy* (New York, 1950). The trend toward seeking to evaluate rather than merely record foreign policy is reflected most interestingly in Robert E. Osgood, *Ideals and Self-Interest in America's Foreign Relations* (Chicago, 1953), a brilliant first study growing out of the work of the Center for the Study of American Foreign Policy at the University of Chicago.

Selected Regional Histories

Only a few of the many books dealing with American policy on a regional basis may be listed. Once again Samuel F. Bemis has a noteworthy contribution in *The Latin American Policy of the United States* (New York, 1943) and Dexter Perkins has summarized—and more popularly written—his several studies on the Monroe Doctrine in *Hands Off—A History of the Monroe Doctrine* (Boston, 1941). Equally useful is Graham H. Stuart, *Latin America and the United States* (New York, 1943). Among a number of books dealing more especially with the area of the Caribbean are Dana G. Munro, *The United States and the Caribbean Area* (Boston, 1934) and J. Fred Rippy, *The Caribbean Danger Zone* (New York, 1940).

A standard book on the problems of eastern Asia, still very useful, is A. Whitney Griswold, *The Far Eastern Policy of the United States* (New York, 1938). It may be supplemented by Edwin A. Falk, *From Perry to Pearl Harbor* (New York, 1943); John K. Fairbank, *The United States and China* (Cambridge, Mass., 1948), Foster Rhea Dulles, *China and America* (Princeton, 1946); and the more specialized books noted subsequently.

An excellent account of another important phase of American foreign policy is John Bartlet Brebner, Jr., *The North Atlantic Triangle: the Interplay of Canada, the United States and Great Britain* (New Haven, 1947). Along somewhat the same lines but with a more journalistic approach is Forrest Davis, *The Atlantic System* (New York, 1941).

There are of course innumerable volumes dealing with American relations with specific countries. Notable in this connection—although they have relatively little historical background—are the volumes in The American Foreign Policy Library, edited by Sumner Welles and published by the Harvard University Press.

A number of books deal in general terms with various aspects of the American "empire." In this connection should be noted the highly interesting study of Albert K. Weinberg: *Manifest Destiny: A Study of Nationalist Expansion in American History* (Baltimore, 1935). The most comprehensive account of developments since 1898, however, is Julius W. Pratt, *America's Colonial Experiment* (New York, 1950). It carries the significant subtitle, *How the United States Gained, Governed and in Part Gave Away a Colonial Empire.*

THE TRADITION OF ISOLATION, 1776–1885

The background of isolationism can only be studied through a very diverse selection of sources which would include memoirs, diaries, collections of speeches, the records of congressional debates, contemporary opinion as expressed in newspapers and magazines, and other reports of foreign policy discussions. This material is too scattered to be usefully listed, but is in part suggested in the footnotes to Chapter 1. In addition to treatment of isolationism in such sources and general histories, however, there are a number of important historical monographs which deal directly with this issue.

Among these studies, largely inspired by the debates centering about isolationism in the 1920's and 1930's, are the following: Samuel F. Bemis, "Washington's Farewell Address: A Foreign Policy of Independence," *American Historical Review,* XXXIX (Oct., 1933), 250–268; J. G. Randall, "George Washington and 'Entangling Alliances,'" *South Atlantic Quarterly,* XXX (Apr., 1931), 221–229; J. Fred Rippy and Angie Debo, "The Historical Background of the American Policy of Isolation," *Smith College Studies in History,* IX, Nos. 3 and 4 (Northampton, Apr. and July, 1924); Max Savelle, "Colonial Origins of American Diplomatic Principles," *Pacific Historical Review,* III (No. 3, 1934), 334–350; and Albert K. Weinberg, "The Historical Meaning of the American Doctrine of Isolation," *American Political Science Review,* XXXIV (Apr., 1940), 539–547. A more recent and provocative discussion is Gerald Stourzh, *Benjamin Franklin and American Foreign Policy* (Chicago, 1954).

Although largely concerned with a later period and emphasizing the strength of isolationism in the Midwest, a further group of articles should also be noted at this point. Valuable especially for its extensive bibliographical notes is Richard W. Leopold, "The Mississippi Valley and American Foreign Policy, 1890–1941," *Mississippi Valley Historical Review,* XXXVIII (Mar., 1951), 625–642. Also Ray A. Billington, "The Origins of Middle Western Isolationism," *Political Science Quarterly,* LX (Mar., 1945), 44–64; and William G. Carleton, "Isolationism and the Middle West," *Mississippi Valley Historical Review,* XXXIII (Dec., 1946), 377–390. In this connection, although its treatment of isolationism is only incidental, should be included the brilliant study of Henry Nash Smith, *Virgin Land: The American West as Symbol and Myth* (Cambridge, Mass., 1950).

Prior to the Spanish-American War the interplay of forces making for isolationism versus internationalism is perhaps most graphically illustrated in the events of the early 1820's and 1850's. Among special studies dealing with the earlier period are Edward Howland Tatum, Jr., *The United States and Europe, 1815–1823* (Berkeley, Cal., 1936); George Dangerfield, *The Era of Good Feelings* (New York, 1952); Dexter Perkins, *The Monroe Doctrine, 1823–1826* (Cambridge, Mass., 1927); and Arthur P. Whitaker, *The United States and the Independence of Latin America, 1800–1830* (Baltimore, 1941). An interesting article to which attention might also be called is Gale W. McGee, "The Monroe Doctrine—A Stopgap Measure," *Mississippi Valley Historical Review,* XXXVIII (Sept., 1951), 233–250. With more special reference to American sympathy for Greece, see Edward Mead Earle, "American Interest in the Greek Cause, 1821–27," *American Historical Review,* XXXIII (Oct., 1927), 44–63.

For the 1850's relatively few special studies are available, but there is interesting material in Merle E. Curti, *The American Peace Crusade* (Durham, N.C., 1929), and the same author's two articles: "Young America,'" *American Historical Review,* XXXII (Oct., 1926), 34–55, and "Austria and the United States, 1848–1852," *Smith College Studies in History,* XI (Northampton, Apr., 1926), 141–206. Also A. J. May, *Contemporary American Opinion of the Mid-Century Revolutions in Central Europe* (Philadelphia, 1927).

On Far Eastern aspects of American policy during these same years, apart from more general works, there is interesting material in Frederick W. Seward, *William H. Seward at Washington, as Senator and Secretary of State* (3 vols., New York, 1891); and Frederic Bancroft, *The Life of William H. Seward* (2 vols., New York, 1900). No really satisfactory biography of this statesman is available, however, and the phase of his career here under discussion is best handled by Tyler Dennett in his "Seward's Far Eastern Policy," *American Historical Review,* XXVIII (Oct., 1922), 45–62.

For the immediate post-Civil War period, see Theodore Clark Smith, "Expansion After the Civil War, 1865–71," *Political Science Quarterly,* XVI (Sept., 1901), 412–436.

IMPERIALISM AND OVERSEAS EXPANSION, 1885–1900

The diplomatic record of the stirring events at the turn of the century may be found in such official State Department publications as *Correspondence Relating to the War with Spain, Including the Philippine Expedition, and the China Relief Expedition* (3 vols., Washington, 1902), and the appropriate volumes of *Papers Relating to the Foreign Relations of the United States. Senate Document 62,* 55th Congress, 3rd Session, and *Senate Document 148,* 56th Congress, 2nd Session, also contain important papers relating to the Spanish-American War and the subsequent peace treaty. Additional material is available in the annual reports for this period of the Secretary of War, the Secretary of the Navy, and (after 1902) of the Chief of the Bureau of Insular Affairs.

The contemporary reaction to the imperialist movement is found in the debates printed in the *Congressional Record,* a great array of magazine articles, and newspaper editorials, the latter often usefully summarized in *Public Opinion* and the *Literary Digest.*

A selection of the more important articles would include in the first instance such writings of Alfred Thayer Mahan as "The United States Looks Outward," *Atlantic Monthly,* LXVI (Dec., 1890), 816–824; "Hawaii and Our Future Sea Power," *Forum,* XV (Mar., 1893), 1–11; "A Twentieth Century Outlook," *Harper's Magazine,* XCV (Sept., 1897), 521–533. They are collected with other papers in *The Interest of America in Sea Power, Present and Future* (Boston, 1897). Additional articles by Mahan are also available in his *Lessons of the War with Spain* (Boston, 1899) and *The Problem of Asia* (Boston, 1905).

Among other significant magazine contributions are Brooks Adams, "The Spanish War and the Equilibrium of the World," *Forum,* XXV (Aug., 1898), 641–651; William G. Sumner, "The Fallacy of Territorial Extension," *ibid.,* XXI (June, 1896), 414–419; James Bryce, "The Policy of Annexation for America," *ibid.,* XXIV (Dec., 1897), 385–395; J. G. Carlisle, "Our Future Policy," *Harper's Magazine,* XCVII (Oct., 1898), 720–728; Henry Cabot Lodge, "Our Blundering Foreign Policy," *Forum,* XIX (Mar., 1895), 8–17; Richard Olney, "Growth of Our Foreign Policy," *Atlantic Monthly,* LXXXV (Mar., 1900), 289–301, and "International Isolation of the United States," *ibid.,* LXXXI (May, 1898), 577–588; John R. Procter, "Isolation or Imperialism," *Forum,* XXVI (Sept., 1898), 14–26; Carl Schurz, "Manifest Destiny," *Harper's Magazine,* LXXXVIII (Oct., 1893), 737–746.

Highly interesting material is also to be found in *Selections from the Correspondence of Theodore Roosevelt and Henry Cabot Lodge* (2 vols., New York, 1925); *The Letters of Theodore Roosevelt,* ably edited by Elting E. Morison (8 vols., Cambridge, 1951–54); *America of Yesterday: As Reflected in the Journal of John Davis Long,* edited by Lawrence Mayo Shaw (Boston, 1923); and George F. Hoar, *Autobiography of Seventy Years* (2 vols., New York, 1903).

A standard diplomatic history of the period remains F. E. Chadwick, *The Relations of the United States and Spain* (3 vols., New York, 1909–11). It may be supplemented by Orestes Ferrara, *The Last Spanish War: Revelations in "Diplomacy,"* (New York, 1937); Marcus M. Wilkerson, *Public Opinion and the Spanish-American War* (Baton Rouge, 1932); and the brilliantly written if somewhat overdrawn account by Walter Millis, *The Martial Spirit* (Boston, 1931). On relations with Hawaii, one of the best accounts is to be found in Julius W. Pratt, *Expansionists of 1898* (Baltimore, 1936), but a more thorough treatment of this topic is available in S. K. Stevens, *American Expansion in Hawaii, 1842–1898* (Harrisburg, 1945). A definitive study in respect to Samoan affairs is George H. Ryden, *The*

Foreign Policy of the United States in Relation to Samoa (New Haven, 1933). A more general background treatment of Samoa, Hawaii, and the Philippines may be found in Foster Rhea Dulles, *America in the Pacific* (Boston, 1932).

Albert K. Weinberg's already cited *Manifest Destiny* (Baltimore, 1935) has important material (pp. 252–324) on imperialism, and there is a stimulating chapter in Ralph Henry Gabriel, *The Course of American Democratic Thought* (New York, 1940), pp. 339–356. Essential for an understanding of the relationship of naval and political policy is Harold and Margaret Sprout, *The Rise of American Naval Power, 1776–1918* (Princeton, 1939). Other histories include Lionel M. Gelber, *The Rise of Anglo-American Friendship: A Study in World Politics, 1898–1906* (New York, 1938); and Alfred L. P. Dennis, *Adventures in American Diplomacy, 1896–1906* (New York, 1928).

Two broader studies, interesting for their contemporary interpretation, are John H. Latané, *America as a World Power, 1897–1907* (New York, 1907); and Archibald Cary Coolidge, *The United States as a World Power* (New York, 1918).

Biographies of the actors in the drama of imperialism would include Allan Nevins, *Grover Cleveland* (New York, 1932); Charles S. Olcott, *The Life of William McKinley* (2 vols., Boston, 1916); Tyler Dennett, *John Hay: From Poetry to Politics* (New York, 1933); Henry F. Pringle, *Theodore Roosevelt* (New York, 1931); Philip C. Jessup, *Elihu Root* (2 vols., New York, 1938). While Olcott's *McKinley* is a rather uncritical account, the other books in this group are among the best political biographies—authoritative and readable—in American historical writing.

There could also be added to such a list two studies of Blaine: David S. Muzzey, *James G. Blaine—A Political Idol of Other Days* (New York, 1934); and Alice Felt Tyler, *The Foreign Policy of James G. Blaine* (Minneapolis, 1927). On the foremost exponent of expansionism, there are two very helpful books: W. D. Puleston, *Mahan* (New Haven, 1939); and William E. Livezey, *Mahan on Sea Power* (Norman, Okla., 1947). Also Allan Nevins, *Henry White—Thirty Years of American Diplomacy* (New York, 1930); and, interesting but brief, Richard W. Leopold, *Elihu Root and the Conservative Tradition* (Boston, 1954).

A few special monographs or articles should also be noted. A highly selective list would include Julius W. Pratt, "The 'Large Policy' of 1898," *Mississippi Valley Historical Review,* XIX (Sept., 1932), 219–242; Fred H. Harrington, "The Anti-Imperialist Movement in the United States, 1898–1900," *ibid.,* XXII (Sept., 1935), 211–230, and "Literary Aspects of American Anti-Imperialism, 1898–1902," *New England Quarterly,* X (Dec., 1937), 650–667; William A. Williams, "Brooks Adams and American Expansion," *ibid.,* XXV (June, 1952), 217–232; Thomas A. Bailey, "The United States and Hawaii during the Spanish-American War," *American Historical Review,* XXXVI (Apr., 1931), 552–560, and "Was the Presidential Election of 1900 a Mandate for Imperialism?" *Mississippi Valley Historical Review,* XXIV (June, 1937), 43–52.

THE UNITED STATES AS A WORLD POWER, 1900–14

The documentary sources for this period and much of the other primary material correspond to that noted for Imperialism and Overseas Expansion. This includes *Messages and Papers of the Presidents, Foreign Relations,* the *Congressional Record,* and contemporary publications.

The dominance of Theodore Roosevelt gives a special importance, in addition to his previously cited *Letters,* to *The Works of Theodore Roosevelt* (20 vols., New York, 1926), and *Theodore Roosevelt, An Autobiography* (New York, 1927). Pringle's biography should also be noted again, and John Morton Blum, *The Republican Roosevelt* (Cambridge, Mass., 1954). A number of more special studies include Tyler Dennett, *Roosevelt and the Russo-Japanese War* (New York, 1925); Thomas A. Bailey, *Theodore Roosevelt and the Japanese-American Crisis* (Stanford, 1934); Howard C. Hill, *Roosevelt and the Caribbean* (Chicago, 1927); and Gordon C. O'Gara, *Theodore Roosevelt and the Rise of the Modern Navy* (Princeton, 1945).

The biographies of Hay, Root, and White remain important, and at least two other comparable books should be added to such a list: Claude G. Bowers, *Beveridge and the Progressive Era* (Boston, 1932); and Henry F. Pringle, *The Life and Times of William Howard Taft* (2 vols., New York, 1939).

The best accounts of the inauguration of the Open Door policy are to be found in Tyler Dennett's *Americans in Eastern Asia* (New York, 1922); Alfred W. Griswold, *The Far Eastern Policy of the United States* (New York, 1938); Charles S. Campbell, Jr., *Special Business Interests and the Open Door Policy* (New Haven, 1951); and the recent and interesting biographical study of one of the foremost architects of that policy, Paul A. Varg's *Open Door Diplomat—The Life of W. W. Rockhill* (Urbana, Ill., 1952).

For further developments on the Far Eastern scene, in addition to the books on Roosevelt's policy and Griswold's history, a number of special studies may be noted. Eleanor Tupper and George E. McReynolds, *Japan in American Public Opinion* (New York, 1937), is very useful, but should be supplemented by Winston B. Thorson "American Public Opinion and the Portsmouth Peace Conference," *American Historical Review,* LIII (Apr., 1948), 439–464. Another interesting angle is developed in Outten Jones Clinard, *Japan's Influence on American Naval Power, 1897–1917* (Berkeley, 1947). Further aspects of developing conflict in this part of the world are discussed in Edward H. Zabriskie, *American-Russian Rivalry in the Far East, 1895–1914* (Philadelphia, 1946); and Pauline Tompkins, *American-Russian Relations in the Far East* (New York, 1949).

The Panama incident is given firsthand treatment in Theodore Roosevelt's own story, "How the United States Acquired the Right to Dig the Panama Canal," *Outlook,* XCIX (Oct. 7, 1911), 314–318. It is discussed more objectively in Dwight C. Miner, *The Fight for the Panama Route* (New York, 1940); while another interesting account is Gerstle Mack, *The Land Divided: A History of the Panama Canal and Other Isthmian Canal Projects*

(New York, 1944). There is a broader scope to W. H. Callcott, *The Carib-bean Policy of the United States, 1890–1920* (Baltimore, 1942).

Other significant books dealing with events of this period are the con-temporary study by Alfred T. Mahan, *The Interest of America in Inter-national Conditions* (Boston, 1910); James B. Scott's authoritative record, *The Hague Peace Conferences of 1899 and 1907* (2 vols., Baltimore, 1909); and Eugene N. Anderson, *The First Moroccan Crisis, 1904–1906* (Chicago, 1930). Critical accounts of American policy are Scott Nearing, *The Ameri-can Empire* (New York, 1921); and Scott Nearing and Joseph Freeman, *Dollar Diplomacy* (New York, 1925). A more general but interesting study is John H. Latané; *From Isolation to Leadership* (New York, 1919).

THE FIRST WORLD WAR AND AFTER, 1914–20

The literature dealing with the period of the First World War is of course voluminous. The annual editions of *Foreign Relations* are supple-mented by special volumes for the years 1914–1918: the *Lansing Papers, 1914–1920* (2 vols., Washington, 1939); and *The Paris Peace Conference* (13 vols., Washington, 1924). *Senate Document 106,* 66th Congress, 1st Session (Washington, 1919), contains the hearings on the Versailles Treaty before the Senate Foreign Relations Committee.

Among the important primary materials relating to the role of President Wilson are R. S. Baker and W. E. Dodd, *The Public Papers of Woodrow Wilson* (6 vols., New York, 1925–27); R. S. Baker, *Woodrow Wilson, Life and Letters* (8 vols., New York, 1927–39), and *Woodrow Wilson and World Settlement* (3 vols., New York, 1922). A stimulating special study is Harley Notter, *The Origins of the Foreign Policy of Woodrow Wilson* (Baltimore, 1937), and two recent books take up in detail his policy in the Far East: Tien-yi Li, *Woodrow Wilson's China Policy, 1913–1917* (New York, 1952); and Russell H. Fifield, *Woodrow Wilson and the Far East: The Diplomacy of the Shantung Question* (New York, 1952). Among the biographies, H. C. F. Bell's *Woodrow Wilson and the People* (New York, 1945), remains the best one-volume study, but a more comprehensive work is under way by Arthur S. Link, of which the first volume, *Wilson: The Road to the White House* (Princeton) appeared in 1947. There is also by the same author, a companion volume in this series, *Woodrow Wilson and the Progressive Era* (New York, 1954).

Primary material relating to Wilson's close associates includes *The Inti-mate Papers of Colonel House,* ably edited by Charles Seymour (4 vols., Boston, 1926–28); Robert Lansing's *War Memoirs* (New York, 1935), and *The Peace Negotiations: A Personal Narrative* (Boston, 1921); Josephus Daniels, *The Wilson Era: Years of War and After, 1917–23* (Chapel Hill, N. C., 1946). There is also interesting material relating to the war years in W. J. and M. B. Bryan, *The Memoirs of William Jennings Bryan* (Chicago, 1925); Burton J. Hendrick, *The Life and Letters of Walter Hines Page* (3 vols., New York, 1922–26); and *The Memoirs of Herbert Hoover: Years of Adventure, 1874–1920* (New York, 1951).

A number of useful biographies supplement such material. One of the most valuable is John A. Garraty, *Henry Cabot Lodge* (New York, 1953), which easily supersedes previous studies of the senator from Massachusetts. Others are Merle Curti, *Bryan and World Peace* (Northampton, 1931); Alex M. Arnett, *Claude Kitchin and the Wilson War Policies* (Boston, 1937); and Claudius O. Johnson, *Borah of Idaho* (New York, 1936).

A comprehensive general account of American entry into the war, with emphasis on the economic factors involved, is Charles C. Tansill, *America Goes to War* (Boston, 1938); and somewhat the same interpretation of events is given in Walter Millis' more popularly written *The Road to War—America, 1914–1917* (New York, 1935). A more conventional treatment is found in Charles Seymour, *American Diplomacy During the World War* (Baltimore, 1934), and *American Neutrality, 1914–1917* (New Haven, 1935); and Alice M. Morrissey, *The American Defense of Neutral Rights, 1914–1917* (Cambridge, Mass., 1939). A more specialized study is H. C. Peterson, *Propaganda for War: The Campaign Against American Neutrality, 1914–1917* (Norman, Okla., 1939). For further discussion of the issues involved, see the chapter on "Internationalists in War" in Eric F. Goldman, *Rendezvous with Destiny* (New York, 1952).

Perhaps the most useful one-volume account of the peacemaking—among many English and French studies—is Paul Birdsall, *Versailles Twenty Years After* (New York, 1941), but the American approach is authoritatively discussed in E. M. House and Charles Seymour, *What Really Happened at Paris* (New York, 1921); and the unique record and collection of documents in David H. Miller, *My Diary at the Conference of Paris* (21 vols., New York, 1924, available on microfilm). Extended bibliographical references to the entire literature are available in two articles appearing in the *Journal of Modern History:* Robert C. Binkley, "Ten Years of Peace Conference History," I (Dec. 1929), 607–629; and Paul Birdsall, "The Second Decade of Peace Conference History," XI (Sept., 1939), 362–378.

Two books bridging the gap between peacemaking and the American rejection of the peace, sympathetic to Wilsonian policy but critical of Wilson, are Thomas A. Bailey's *Woodrow Wilson and the Lost Peace* (New York, 1944); and *Woodrow Wilson and the Great Betrayal* (New York, 1945).

Among other accounts of the struggle over the League are Henry Cabot Lodge's own record, *The Senate and the League of Nations* (New York, 1925); Denna F. Fleming, *The United States and the League of Nations* (New York, 1932); W. Stull Holt, *Treaties Defeated by the Senate* (Baltimore, 1933); and Clarence A. Berdahl, *The Policy of the United States with Respect to the League of Nations* (New York, 1932). Another interesting study is Dexter Perkins' "Woodrow Wilson's Tour," a chapter in Daniel Aaron (ed.), *America in Crisis* (New York, 1952); a highly informative account of the original movement in support of world organization is Ruhl J. Bartlett, *The League to Enforce Peace* (Chapel Hill, N.C., 1944); and note should again be made of Garraty's *Henry Cabot Lodge* for a discerning account of its subject's role in the treaty fight.

REPUBLICAN SUPREMACY, 1921–33

The broad aspects of foreign policy during the 1920's may be followed, in addition to the customary documentary sources and general histories, in a few autobiographical records, a number of significant contemporary studies and magazine articles, and an important group of special books and monographs.

There is very little firsthand material on the foreign policy attitudes of Harding or Coolidge, apart from their messages to Congress or other public statements. This is in itself a reflection of their generally passive point of view. The record is much fuller for Hoover. His state papers have been collected in William Starr Myers (ed.), *The State Papers and Other Public Writings of Herbert Hoover* (2 vols., New York, 1934); and his *Memoirs* have also been published. The second volume, *The Cabinet and the Presidency, 1920–1933* (New York, 1952), is most useful for this period. Also very helpful are Ray L. Wilbur and Arthur M. Hyde, *The Hoover Policies* (New York, 1937); and William Starr Myers, *The Foreign Policies of Herbert Hoover, 1929–33* (New York, 1940).

There is an excellent and comprehensive biography of the first Secretary of State of this period, *Charles Evans Hughes,* by Merlo J. Pusey (2 vols., New York, 1951), and a much less satisfactory one of his successor, *Frank B. Kellogg,* by David Bryn-Jones (New York, 1937). The Stimson record is available in the invaluable collaborative autobiography, Henry L. Stimson and McGeorge Bundy, *On Active Service in Peace and War* (New York, 1948), but see also the more critical biography, Richard N. Current, *Secretary Stimson: A Study in Statecraft* (New Brunswick, 1954).

Among contemporary books, journalistic in nature and reflecting the views of the day, the most interesting are Paul Scott Mowrer, *Our Foreign Affairs* (New York, 1924); Arthur Bullard, *American Diplomacy in the Modern World* (Philadelphia, 1928); and on a more scholarly level, George Hubbard Blakeslee, *The Recent Foreign Policy of the United States* (New York, 1925). A further book with a special significance because of its author's later views is Arthur H. Vandenberg's presentation of the isolationist position in his *The Trail of a Tradition* (New York, 1926).

More important are a number of articles published in the magazine *Foreign Affairs,* established immediately after the war as a medium for the dissemination of informed and authoritative views on world politics. Full lists of these articles are published in two volumes of bibliography: *1919–1932* (New York, 1933) and *1932–42* (New York, 1945). A highly selective list would include Henry Cabot Lodge, "Foreign Relations of the United States, 1921–24," V (June, 1924), 525–539; Ogden L. Mills, "Our Foreign Policy—A Republican View," VI (July, 1928), 555–572; Franklin D. Roosevelt, "Our Foreign Policy—A Democratic View," VI (July, 1928), 573–586; and Henry L. Stimson, "Bases of American Foreign Policy During the Past Four Years," XI (April, 1933), 383–396. See also "Fundamentals in Foreign Policy," *Annals of the Academy of Political Science,* CXIV (July, 1924).

The basic source for the Washington Conference is *Senate Document 125,*

67th Congress, 2nd Session, *Conference on the Limitation of Armaments* (Washington, 1922). On its background and development, Raymond L. Buell's *The Washington Conference* (New York, 1922) remains perhaps the most satisfactory study, and its naval implications are best set forth in Harold and Margaret Sprout, *Toward a New Order of Sea Power: American Naval Policy and the World Scene, 1918-1922* (Princeton, 1940). A recent and illuminating article is J. Chal Vinson's "The Parchment Peace: The Senate Defense of the Four Power Treaty of the Washington Conference," *Mississippi Valley Historical Review,* XXXIX (Sept. 1952), 303-314.

There have been a number of accounts of the origin and negotiation of the Kellogg-Briand Anti-War Treaty—such as James T. Shotwell, *War as an Instrument of National Policy and Its Renunciation in the Pact of Paris* (New York, 1929); and David Hunter Miller, *The Peace Pact of Paris* (New York, 1928)—but they have been largely superseded by Robert H. Ferrell, *Peace in Their Time: The Origins of the Kellogg-Briand Pact* (New Haven, 1952).

Among the documentary sources for the Manchurian crisis of 1931-32 is *Senate Document 55*, 72nd Congress, 1st Session, *Conditions in Manchuria* (Washington, 1932); and the first volume of *Papers Relating to the Foreign Relations of the United States, Japan: 1931-1941* (2 vols., Washington, 1943). A firsthand account is Henry L. Stimson, *The Far Eastern Crisis: Recollections and Observations* (New York, 1936). Extensively treated in all histories dealing with American foreign policy in eastern Asia, as well as in the books on Hoover and Stimson, the most complete single monograph is Sara R. Smith, *Manchurian Crisis, 1931-32* (New York, 1948), while two interesting recent articles are Paul H. Clyde, "The Diplomacy of 'Playing No Favorites': Secretary Stimson and Manchuria, 1931," *Mississippi Valley Historical Review,* XXXV (Sept., 1948), 187-202; and Richard N. Current, "The Stimson Doctrine and the Hoover Doctrine," *American Historical Review,* LIX (Apr., 1954), 513-542.

Note should also be made of books dealing with policy toward China during this period. A general study is Foster Rhea Dulles, *China and America* (Princeton, 1946); a more specialized monograph is Dorothy Borg, *American Policy and the Chinese Revolution, 1925-1928* (New York, 1947).

The economic aspects of America's world role have an extensive bibliography of their own. Among important studies by the Bureau of Foreign and Domestic Commerce of the Department of Commerce is *The United States in the World Economy,* Economic Series No. 23 (Washington, 1943); and an authoritative general work is Raymond F. Mikesell, *United States Economic Policy and International Relations* (New York, 1952). Other books are Benamin H. Williams, *Economic Foreign Policy of the United States* (New York, 1929); National Industrial Conference Board, *Trends in the Foreign Trade of the United States* (New York, 1930); H. G. Moulton and Leo Pasvolsky, *War Debts and World Prosperity* (Washington, 1932); Cleona Lewis, *America's Stake in International Investments* (Washington, 1938); and Herbert Feis, *The Diplomacy of the Dollar: First Era 1919-1932* (Baltimore, 1950).

An interesting group of contemporary and more impressionistic books would include Francis Miller and Helen Hill, *The Giant of the Western World* (New York, 1930); Hiram Motherwell, *The Imperial Dollar* (New York, 1929); Georges Duhamel, *America: The Menace* (Boston, 1931); and Paul M. Mazur, *America Looks Abroad* (New York, 1930).

The importance of naval policy is discussed in the books by Harold and Margaret Sprout already cited. Two more general naval histories are George T. Davis, *A Navy Second to None* (New York, 1940); and Dudley W. Knox, *A History of the United States Navy* (New York, 1936). See also Donald W. Mitchell, *History of the Modern American Navy* (New York, 1946).

There is a voluminous literature on American dependencies, their history and their government. The annual reports of the Secretary of the Navy and the Secretary of the Interior are of course basically important. An early general study is William F. Willoughby, *Territories and Dependencies of the United States* (New York, 1905); there is interesting material in both William H. Hass (ed.), *The American Empire* (Chicago, 1940), and Rupert Emerson *et al., America's Pacific Dependencies* (New York, 1949); a special official report is *The United States and Non-Self-Governing Dependencies*, Department of State Publication 2812 (Washington, 1947). The most interesting of such books, however, is Julius W. Pratt, *America's Colonial Experiment* (New York, 1950). Its extensive notes provide a highly useful bibliography to the literature as a whole.

The most valuable books dealing with individual colonies or dependencies are Garel A. Grunder and William E. Livezey, *The Philippines and the United States* (Norman, Okla., 1951); Grayson L. Kirk, *Philippine Independence* (New York, 1936); V. M. Petrullo, *Puerto Rican Paradox* (New York, 1947); Joseph Barber, Jr., *Hawaii: Restless Rampart* (Indianapolis, 1941); Luther Harris Evans, *The Virgin Islands, From Naval Base to New Deal* (Ann Arbor, 1945); Earl S. Pomeroy, *Pacific Outpost, American Strategy in Guam and Micronesia* (Stanford, 1951). The latter author's article in the *Pacific Historical Review*, XVII (Feb., 1948), 43–53, "American Policy Respecting the Marshalls, Carolines and Marianas, 1898–1941," should also be noted; and G. H. Blakeslee, "The Future of American Samoa," *Foreign Affairs*, VII (Oct., 1928), 139–143.

Among the studies dealing with special phases of American policy which are of particular interest in evaluating the nation's world role are two books by Denna F. Fleming: *The United States and World Organization, 1920–33* (New York, 1938), and *The United States and the World Court* (New York, 1945); B. H. Williams, *The United States and Disarmament* (New York, 1931); Russell M. Cooper, *American Consultation in World Affairs for the Preservation of Peace* (New York, 1934); and Merze Tate, *The United States and Armaments* (Cambridge, Mass., 1948).

Attention should also be called to the annual accounts of American foreign policy that beginning with this period are published annually, with their extensive bibliographies, under the auspices of the Council on Foreign Relations. The first four volumes, with the title *Survey of American Foreign*

Relations (New York, 1928–31), cover the years 1928 to 1931 and were prepared under the direction of Charles P. Howland.

NEUTRALITY AND WAR, 1933–41

A constantly amplified wealth of material—both primary and secondary—is available for the 1930's and the events leading to American entry into the Second World War.

Among the important government documents, supplementing and carrying forward the diplomatic record as set forth in the annual *Foreign Relations* issued by the State Department, are *Japan: 1931–1941* (2 vols., Washington, 1943); *The United States and Italy, 1936–1946* (Washington, 1946); *Diplomatic Papers: The Soviet Union, 1933–1939* (Washington, 1952); and *Peace and War: United States Foreign Policy, 1931–1941* (Washington, 1943). Beginning with 1939, there is additional material in the Department of State *Bulletin*.

The annual series, *Documents on Foreign Relations,* published annually under the auspices of the World Peace Foundation, also starts with the volume for 1939.

Among congressional reports, there stand out most importantly *Pearl Harbor Attack, Hearings Before the Joint Committee on the Investigation of the Pearl Harbor Attack,* 79th Congress, 2nd Session, (39 parts, Washington, 1946); and *Senate Document 244,* 79th Congress, 2nd Session, *Investigation of the Pearl Harbor Attack. Report of the Joint Committee* (Washington, 1946).

Of the greatest significance are the *Public Papers and Addresses of Franklin D. Roosevelt,* edited with unusual skill by Samuel I. Rosenman (13 vols., New York, 1938–50). The passages dealing with foreign policy until 1941 are also available in the one-volume *Roosevelt's Foreign Policy, 1933–1941, Franklin D. Roosevelt's Unedited Speeches and Messages* (New York, 1942). There is also available for this period *F.D.R., His Personal Letters, 1928–45,* edited by Elliott Roosevelt (2 vols., New York, 1950).

A highly significant autobiographical source is *The Memoirs of Cordell Hull* (2 vols., New York, 1948). The Stimson and Bundy, *On Active Service in Peace and War,* previously noted, is extremely valuable. There is also important material in "The Morgenthau Diaries," *Colliers,* CXX (Oct. 4, 11, 18, and 25, 1947); Sumner Welles, *The Time for Decision* (New York, 1944); Robert E. Sherwood, *Roosevelt and Hopkins* (New York, 1948); and Samuel I. Rosenman, *Working with Roosevelt* (New York, 1952).

Among the useful accounts of American ambassadors abroad are Joseph E. Davies, *Mission to Moscow* (New York, 1941); Joseph C. Grew, *Ten Years in Japan* (New York, 1944), and his even more important *Turbulent Era* (2 vols., Boston, 1952); William C. Bullitt, *Report to the American People* (Boston, 1940); and *Ambassador Dodd's Diary, 1933–38,* edited by William E. Dodd, Jr., and Martha Dodd (New York, 1941). Always of immense interest are the volumes of Winston Churchill's great history—with reference to this period, *The Gathering Storm* (Boston, 1948), and *Their Finest Hour* (Boston, 1949).

There is also material from authoritative sources in both Joseph Alsop and Robert Kintner, *American White Paper: The Story of American Diplomacy and the Second World War* (New York, 1940); and Forrest Davis and Ernest K. Lindley, *How War Came* (New York, 1942).

The number of contemporary books and pamphlets dealing with the inter- ventionist-isolationist controversy is legion. Among those of special interest or significance are Hamilton Fish Armstrong, *We or They: Two Worlds in Conflict* (New York, 1936); Edwin M. Borchard and William P. Lage, *Neutrality for the United States* (New Haven, 1937); Raymond L. Buell, *Isolated America* (New York, 1940); Charles A. Beard, *Giddy Minds and Foreign Quarrels* (New York, 1936); Allen W. Dulles and Hamilton Fish Armstrong, *Can America Stay Neutral?* (New York, 1939); Edward Mead Earle, *Against This Torrent* (Princeton, 1941); Jerome Frank, *Save America First: How to Make Democracy Work* (New York, 1938); Hartley Living- ston, *Is America Afraid?* (New York, 1937); Ralph McAllister Ingersoll, *America Is Worth Fighting For* (Indianapolis, 1941); Hugh S. Johnson, *Hell-Bent for War* (Indianapolis, 1941); Anne Morrow Lindbergh, *The Wave of the Future* (New York, 1940); Nicholas J. Spykman, *America's Strategy in World Politics* (New York, 1942); Pierre Van Passen, *The Time is Now!* (New York, 1941); James P. Warburg, *Our War and Our Peace* (New York, 1941); William Allen White (ed.), *Defense for America* (New York, 1940).

The two organizations representative of isolationist and interventionist sentiment, respectively, are ably treated in Wayne S. Cole, *America First: The Battle Against Intervention—1940–41* (Madison, Wis., 1953); and Walter Johnson, *The Battle Against Isolation* (Chicago, 1944).

Sectional aspects of isolationism from the historical point of view are dis- cussed in the articles already noted: Ray A. Billington, "The Origins of Middle West Isolationism"; William G. Carleton, "Isolationism and the Middle West"; Richard W. Leopold, "The Mississippi Valley and American Foreign Policy, 1890–1941"; and also Marian D. Irish, "Foreign Policy and the South," *Journal of Politics,* X (May, 1948), 306–326.

In addition to contemporary comment in newspapers and magazines, new sources for the study of public opinion are available in the popular polls. Such reports may be found in the *Public Opinion Quarterly* and in Hadley Cantril (ed.), *Public Opinion, 1935–46* (Princeton, 1951). See also Archi- bald McLeish, *American Opinion and the War* (New York, 1942); William A. Lydgate, *What America Thinks* (New York, 1944); and among other articles, Francis S. Wickware, "What We Think About Foreign Affairs," *Harper's Magazine,* CLXXIX (Sept., 1939), 397–404.

The most comprehensive general record of developments in 1937–41 is to be found in the two monumental volumes by William L. Langer and S. Everett Gleason: *The Challenge to Isolation, 1937–1940* (New York, 1952), and *The Undeclared War, 1940–1941* (New York, 1953). They are based upon a thorough study, made possible through a grant from the Rockefeller Foundation, of a vast mass of material including State Department files, the Roosevelt papers, and such important manuscript diaries as those of Morgenthau, Berle, and Moffat. Publication was sponsored by the Council on Foreign Relations. The author's point of view is internationalist; their purpose has been to provide a "thorough analysis" of the circumstances and developments that led to American entry into the war. The two books reflect the highest standards of scholarship and are excellently organized.

A quite different account of these same events has been made by the so-called revisionist school of historians. The Roosevelt policies were first challenged in two books by Charles A. Beard: *American Foreign Policy in the Making, 1932–1940* (New Haven, 1946), and *President Roosevelt and the Coming of War, 1941* (New Haven, 1948). They contain much interesting material but are very definitely slanted to advance the author's isolationist thesis. Beard's analysis is strongly—sometimes angrily—countered by Basil Rauch in *Roosevelt: From Munich to Pearl Harbor* (New York, 1950), a book that is especially valuable for its discussion of the struggle over neutrality.

Other revisionist accounts would include George E. Morgenstern, *Pearl Harbor: the Story of the Secret War* (New York, 1947); William H. Chamberlin, *America's Second Crusade* (Chicago, 1950); and Rear Admiral Robert A. Theobald, *The Final Secret of Pearl Harbor* (New York, 1954). The most important is Charles C. Tansill, *Back Door to War—Roosevelt Foreign Policy, 1933–1941* (Chicago, 1952). This volume's extreme conclusions are not supported by the evidence presented, but it contains some valuable material and is carefully documented.

With more particular reference to war in the Pacific, the most authoritative study is Herbert Feis, *The Road to Pearl Harbor* (Princeton, 1950), while a sound but more popularly written account is found in Walter Millis, *This is Pearl! The United States and Japan—1941* (New York, 1947).

The annual survey of the Council on Foreign Relations, beginning with the issue for 1931, is entitled *The United States in World Affairs*, prepared by Walter Lippmann, William O. Scroggs, *et al.*

Among other books dealing with the special phases of contemporary foreign policy suggested by their titles are J. Fred Rippy, *South America and Hemisphere Defense* (Baton Rouge, 1941); William C. Johnstone, *The United States and Japan's New Order* (New York, 1941); Edward O. Guerrant, *Roosevelt's Good Neighbor Policy* (Albuquerque, 1950); and Grace L. Beckett, *The Reciprocal Trade Agreements Program* (New York, 1941).

THE SECOND WORLD WAR AND AFTER, 1941–53

Although this period is too recent to be viewed with any real perspective, it is not for want of available source material. The vital importance of foreign policy has led to the publication of innumerable documents, lengthy congressional hearings, and an unending stream of books and articles. The conscious effort to keep the historical record is perhaps without parallel in any previous day.

The State Department has published, among many other documentary collections, *Postwar Foreign Policy Preparations, 1939–45* (Washington,

1949); *In Quest of Peace and Security: Selected Documents on American Foreign Policy, 1941-1951* (Washington, 1951); a selection of Secretary Acheson's speeches under the title *Strengthening the Forces of Freedom* (Washington, 1950); *United States Relations with China with Special Reference to the Period 1944-1949* (Washington, 1949); *Conference for the Conclusion and Signature of the Treaty of Peace with Japan* (Washington, 1951); *Germany 1947-1949: The Story in Documents* (Washington, 1950). There is also the continuing Department of State *Bulletin* and periodic *Press Releases.*

Such material may be supplemented by *Senate Document 123*, 81st Congress, 1st Session, *A Decade of American Foreign Policy, Basic Documents, 1941-49* (Washington, 1950); the official reports of the Economic Cooperation Administration, the Mutual Defense Assistance Program, the Mutual Security Program, and the Point Four Program; and accounts of scores of congressional hearings. Of the latter there might especially be singled out *Military Assistance Program: Joint Hearings Before Committee on Foreign Relations and Committee on Armed Services*, 81st Congress, 1st Session (Washington, 1949); and *Military Situation in the Far East, Hearings Before Committee on Armed Services and Committee on Foreign Relations,* 82nd Congress, 1st Session (Washington, 1951).

Additional documents are again available in *Documents on American Foreign Relations,* the previously cited publication of the World Peace Foundation which, beginning for the year 1952, is issued under the auspices of the Council on Foreign Relations. There is also useful information, after 1947, in the annual *Major Problems of United States Foreign Policy* (Washington, 1947—) published by the Brookings Institution.

Adequate material for an analysis of the role of President Truman will not be available until publication of his planned memoirs. There is relatively little—but that little very interesting—in William Hillman, *Mr. President: The First Publication from the Personal Diaries, Papers and Revealing Interviews of Harry S. Truman* (New York, 1952). The major public statements of Secretary Acheson, including testimony before congressional committees, have been collected and most ably edited by McGeorge Bundy in *The Pattern of Responsibility—From the Record of Secretary of State Dean Acheson* (Boston, 1952). Contemporary addresses by other leading figures in and out of the administration may be found in the magazine *Vital Speeches.*

To the firsthand records of other "policy makers" already cited for the prewar period may be added such uniformly important and interesting books as *The Private Papers of Senator Vandenberg,* edited by Arthur H. Vandenberg, Jr., and J. A. Morris (Boston, 1952); *The Forrestal Diaries,* edited by Walter Millis with the collaboration of E. S. Duffield (New York, 1951); James F. Byrnes, *Speaking Frankly* (New York, 1947); Edward R. Stettinius, Jr., *Lend-Lease: Weapon for Victory* (New York, 1944), and *Roosevelt and the Russians: the Yalta Conference* (New York, 1949); William D. Leahy, *I Was There* (New York, 1950); Walter Bedell Smith, *My Three Years in Moscow* (Philadelphia, 1950); Sumner Welles, *Seven Decisions That*

Shaped History (New York, 1951); Dwight D. Eisenhower, *Crusade in Europe* (New York, 1948); and Lucius Clay, *Decision in Germany* (New York, 1950).

Again should be added the pertinent volumes of the Churchill history: *The Grand Alliance* (Boston, 1950), *The Hinge of Fate* (Boston, 1950), *Closing the Ring* (Boston, 1951), and *Triumph and Tragedy* (Boston, 1953).

Among contemporary discussions of foreign policy a number stand out through the prominence of their authors or the cogency of their ideas. A highly restricted list in the first category would include Wendell Willkie, *One World* (New York, 1943); John Foster Dulles, *War, Peace and Change* (New York, 1939), and also his *War or Peace* (New York, 1950); Henry A. Wallace, *Toward World Peace* (New York, 1948); Herbert Hoover and Hugh Gibson, *The Problems of Lasting Peace* (New York, 1943); Robert A. Taft, *A Foreign Policy for Americans* (New York, 1951); and Sumner Welles, *Where Are We Heading?* (New York, 1946).

Among the more significant books by publicists rather than political figures are Walter Lippmann, *U.S. War Aims* (Boston, 1944), *The Cold War: A Study in U.S. Foreign Policy* (New York, 1947), and *Isolation and Alliances* (Boston, 1952); Hanson W. Baldwin, *The Price of Power* (New York, 1948); Vera M. Dean, *The Four Cornerstones of Peace* (New York, 1946); Emory Reves, *The Anatomy of Peace* (New York, 1945); Hans J. Morgenthau, *In Defense of the National Interest* (New York, 1951); Norman Cousins, *Modern Man Is Obsolete* (New York, 1945), and *Steps to Peace: A Quaker View of U.S. Foreign Policy* (1951); Charles B. Marshall, *The Limits of Foreign Policy* (New York, 1954); Thomas K. Finletter, *Power and Policy: U.S. Foreign Policy and Military Power in the Hydrogen Age* (New York, 1954); George F. Kennan, *Realities of American Foreign Policy* (Princeton, 1954); and, somewhat in a category by itself for its brilliant review of conditions in Europe, Theodore White, *Fire in the Ashes* (New York, 1954).

Public opinion may be traced through the polls as summarized in the *Public Opinion Quarterly,* but it has also been made the subject of a number of special surveys. They would include Lester Markel, ed., *Public Opinion and Foreign Policy* (New York, 1949); Leonard S. Cottrell, Jr. and Sylvia Eberhart, *American Opinion on World Affairs in the Atomic Age* (Princeton, 1948); Percy W. Bidwell, *Our Foreign Policy in War and Peace: Some Regional Views* (New York, 1942), and George L. Grassmuck, *Sectional Biases in Congress on Foreign Policy* (Baltimore, 1951).

The importance of postwar relations with Soviet Russia necessitates the inclusion of a few of the more important books on this topic. Among them are John R. Deane, *The Strange Alliance: The Story of Our Efforts at Wartime Cooperation with Russia* (New York, 1947); Thomas A. Bailey, *America Faces Russia* (Ithaca, 1950), and David J. Dallin, *The Big Three: The United States, Britain, Russia* (New Haven, 1945). Especially significant are the articles by George F. Kennan included in his *American Diplomacy, 1900–1950* (Chicago, 1951).

On policy in the Far East, in addition to titles already noted, are such books as Thomas A. Bisson, *America's Far Eastern Policy* (New York,

1945); Richard H. Rovere and Arthur M. Schlesinger, Jr., *The General and the President* (New York, 1951); and the authoritative study by Herbert Feis: *The China Tangle: The American Effort in China from Pearl Harbor to the Marshall Mission* (Princeton, 1953).

Mention should be made of such special-topic books as Alvin H. Hansen, *America's Role in the World Economy* (New York, 1945); Seymour E. Harris (ed.), *Foreign Economic Policy for the United States* (Cambridge, Mass., 1948); E. F. Penrose, *Economic Planning for the Peace* (Princeton, 1953); *United States Foreign Policy: Its Organization and Control. Report of a Study Group for the Woodrow Wilson Foundation* (New York, 1952); James L. McCamy, *The Administration of American Foreign Affairs* (New York, 1950); and Graham H. Stuart, *The Department of State* (New York, 1949).

The best summary of year-by-year developments remains *The United States in World Affairs*, written from 1945 to 1949 by John C. Campbell, and since then by Richard P. Stebbins, with the aid of the research staff of the Council on Foreign Relations.

Index

Abbott, Lyman, *quoted*, 84
ABC-1 staff agreement, 194
Acheson, Dean, proposes Marshall Plan, 232, 234; on Pacific defenses, 239; negotiates North Atlantic Treaty, 242–244; seeks military appropriations, 247; on Point Four program, 248; and "total diplomacy," 249; on China policy, 252; criticized, 253, 255; upholds policies, 263, 265; and European Defense Community, 271
Adams, Brooks, 61
Adams, Henry, on Secretary of State, 18–19; and Atlantic System, 61, 62, 77
Adams, John, on American policy, 2, 3, 4, 10; on national mission, 6; advice recalled, 35
Adams, John Quincy, upholds nationalist policy, 5, 6–7; Monroe Doctrine, 8–9; as President, 9
Africa, imperialism in, 59, 248
Alaska, purchase of, 17; as American territory, 134
Albania, 184, 227
Alexander I, 5, 6
Algeciras conference, 23, 60, 77–80
Algonquin, 105
America First Committee, 200
American Asiatic Association, 63
American Banker, quoted, 47
American empire, conception of, 20, 52, 57, 69, 133
American Federation of Labor, 236
Anglo-American *rapprochement*, 34, 59–60, 61, 76, 146, 194. *See also* Great Britain

Anglo-Japanese alliance, 149
Anti-imperialism, 43–44, 52; 54–55, 58–59
Arabic, 94, 95
Arbitration treaties, as negotiated by Taft, 79–80; by Bryan, 85
Arena, quoted, 70
Armed Neutrality League, 3
"Arsenal of Democracy," 195
Arthur, Chester A., 28
Article Ten, of League of Nations covenant, 114, 121–122
Asia, *see* China, Japan, Korea
Asia Firsters, 253, 255
Atlantic Charter, 202, 209
Atlantic community, or system, 2, 62, 77, 97, 243. *See also* North Atlantic Treaty
Atlantic conference (1941), 201
Atomic bomb, 241, 281. *See also* Atomic energy
Atomic energy, 223–225, 228, 280
Atomic energy commission, 225
Australia, 257, 269, 276
Austria, 183, 229, 274
Axis powers, 172, 192

Barbary pirates, 4
Baruch, Bernard, 225
Baxter, William, *quoted*, 11
Bayard, James A., Jr., 17
Beard, Charles A., *quoted*, 140–141
Belgium, 91, 270
Benson, Admiral William S., 138
Benton, Thomas Hart, 14, 15
Berlin blockade, 240–241
Berlin conference (1954), 274, 275
Beveridge, Albert J., on imperialism,

38, 46, 47, 55; as chairman Senate Foreign Relations Committee, 83; and First World War, 103

Bipartisan foreign policy, 213, 214, 232, 249, 253

Blaine, James G., 23

Bonin Islands, 239, 268

Borah, William, and First World War, 103, 108; League of Nations, 115, 119–120; as isolationist spokesman in 1920's, 144–145; Washington Conference, 149, 152; outlawry of war, 159, 160; World Court, 171; Second World War, 186, 188, 244

Boston *Transcript*, quoted, 102

Boxer rebellion, 66

Bradley, General Omar, 252

Briand, Aristide, 159

Bricker, John, 212

Bridges, Henry Styles, 253

British Guiana, 26

Brown, Justice Henry B., 57

Brussels conference (1937), 181–182

Brussels treaty (1948), 241, 277

Bryan, William Jennings, on American growth, 19; at Trans-Mississippi conference, 37; on imperialism, 53, 54, 56; as peace advocate, 85; Secretary of State, 88–89; and *Lusitania* incident, 93; on neutrality, 98–99

Bryant, William Cullen, quoted, 10

Bryce, James, quoted, 22, 36

Buchanan, James, 16

Bulgaria, 225, 227

Burgess, John W., 30

Business Week, quoted, 180

Byrnes, James, 228, 229

Cairo conference, 211, 212–213, 250, 256

Calhoun, John C., 13

California, 14

Calles, Plutarco Elias, 155

Canada, 17, 183, 192, 223, 257

Canning, George, 8

Caribbean, early interest in, 16, 17, 23, 35, 36, 42; American control of, 59, 72–76, 80, 81, 89, 154

Carnegie, Andrew, 19, 54, 68

Carranza, Venustiano, 90

Cash-and-carry, 173, 187, 189

Cass, Lewis, 12

Castle, William R., 159

Chamberlain, Neville, 183, 184

Chapultepec, Act of, 237

Chiang Kai-shek, aided by Roosevelt, 198; at Cairo, 211; and Yalta agreements, 216; postwar aid to, 251; defeated by Chinese Communists, 251–252; and alleged "betrayal" of, 253

Chicago *Tribune*, quoted, 146, 200

China, early interest in, 14, 17; importance of trade in 1898, 47–48; Open Door policy, 62–67; Roosevelt policy toward, 70–72; Taft and dollar diplomacy, 80; and Washington conference, 150, 151; Manchuria incident, 162, 164, 177; Japanese attack on, 178–179, 181; American aid for, 198–199, 204–205; and Second World War, 205–206; at wartime conferences, 211, 214, 217; civil war in, 240, 249–252; Marshall mission to, 250; White Paper on, 252; recognition issue, 255; continuing problem of, 268; and Geneva conference, 275–276. *See also* Chinese Communists

Chinese Communists, rise to power, 249–251; American policy toward, 252–254; problem of recognition and UN membership, 255–256; intervention in Korea, 259; intervention in Indo-China, 274; at Geneva conference, 275–276; further provocations of, 280. *See also* China

Chinese Nationalists, *see* China

Christian Century, quoted, 180

Churchill, Winston, on Roosevelt peace proposals, 183; urges lend-lease, 193; meets Roosevelt, 201–202; and Atlantic Charter, 202, 209; wartime conferences, 211, 216–218; tribute to Roosevelt, 218; meets Eisenhower, 275

Churchman, quoted, 48

Clark, Champ, 29

Clark, J. Reuben, 156

Clark memorandum, 156

Clay, Henry, 7

Clay, General Lucius, 240

Clayton-Bulwer treaty, 72

Clemenceau, Georges, 109

Cleveland, Grover, on foreign policy, 20, 21; Hawaiian annexation, 25; Venezuela incident, 26–27; policy toward Cuba, 40–41; as anti-imperialist, 54

Cold war, 229, 246

Collective security, as League of Nations concept, 127, 138, 165; and Franklin D. Roosevelt, 168, 175–176; collapse in 1930's, 182, 257

Colombia, 73

Colonialism, see Imperialism

Commerce, influence on foreign policy, 1, 14, 15, 22, 32–33, 37, 43, 47–48, 49, 281; and First World War, 95–96; and Paris peace conference, 112; in 1920's, 129–133, 140; and neutrality legislation, 173–175, 186–187

Commercial and Financial Chronicle, quoted, 37

Committee to Defend America by Aiding the Allies, 200, 201

Communist China, see China

Communist imperialism, 246, 249, 281. See Soviet Russia

Communist Russia, see Soviet Russia

Congress of Industrial Organizations, 236

Connally resolution, 211

Coolidge, Calvin, and Latin American policy, 155; on America's world role, 157, 167; and Kellogg-Briand treaty, 160

Coughlin, Father Charles E., 171

Coughlinites, 200

Council of Europe, 259

Council of Foreign Ministers, 227–229

Cox, James M., 125

Crimean conference, see Yalta conference

Croly, Herbert, 83–84

Cross-channel invasion, 213

Cuba, early American interest in, 13, 16; as expansionist goal, 35, 37, 47; and Spanish-American war, 40–43; attains independence, 51; American rights in, 22, 72, 76, 133–134; revolutionary disturbances, 156

Czechoslovakia, 183–184, 188, 234–235, 236

Daniels, Josephus, 138

Danish West Indies, 17, 23, 34. See also Virgin Islands

Darwin, Charles, quoted, 30

Day, William, 45, 50

Declaration of Independence, 2

Declaration of the United Nations, 208, 209

Democratic People's Republic, 256. See also North Korea

Denmark, 190

Destroyer-naval base deal, 192–193, 195, 197, 198, 200

Dewey, Admiral George, 42, 46, 51

Dewey, Thomas, 210, 214, 242, 264

Diaz, Porfirio, 89

Disarmament, 126, 165–166, 169. See also Washington conference, Geneva disarmament conference

Dollar diplomacy, 79, 80–81, 88

Dominican Republic, 17, 23, 74, 76, 134

Dos Passos, John, quoted, 235

Dulles, John Foster, and political bipartisanship in 1944, 214; hails Korean truce, 271; sets forth new policies, 272–274; and southeastern Asia defense treaty, 275, 276; on Western European Union, 277; on policy of moderation, 280

Dumbarton Oaks conference, 213, 214, 218

Dunne, Finley Peter, 54. See also "Mr. Dooley"

Dwight, Timothy, quoted, 10

Earle, Edward Mead, 146

East Germany, 240

Economic advance, 129–131

Economic boycott, of Japan, 192, 195, 198–199, 204–205

Economic Cooperation Act of 1948, 236

Economic Cooperation Administration, 240, 270

Economic imperialism, 76, 81

Economic nationalism, 131, 170

Edwards, Jonathan, quoted, 6

Einstein, Lewis, 62

Eisenhower, Dwight D., command of NATO, 259, 264; as presidential candidate, 267; hails Korean truce, 271–272; supports Secretary Dulles, 273; and Indo-China, 274; meets Churchill, 275; on peaceful coexistence, 280

Embargo, on arms and ammunition to European belligerents, 173; movement for repeal, 185–186, 187–188; on exports to Japan, 192, 195, 198–199, 204–205. See also Neutrality legislation

Emerson, Ralph Waldo, quoted, 11

England, see Great Britain

Entangling alliances, 4, 7, 86. See also Isolationism

Ethiopia, 172, 173

European Defense Community, 259, 270–271, 272, 277

European Payments Union, 248

European Recovery Program, 232, 241, 248. See also Marshall Plan

Expansion, continental, 10; overseas, 12, 14–17, 21, 23, 31–33, 36–39, 44–49. See also Imperialism

Expansion Under New World Conditions, quoted, 31

Far East, see China, Japan, Korea, Indo-China

Federalist, quoted, 4

Fillmore, Millard, 9

Fish, Hamilton, 214

Fiske, John, 30

Five Power Treaty, 150

Food and Agricultural Organization, 213

Fordney-McCumber tariff, 132

Formosa, 252, 255, 257, 272

Forrestal, James, 220

Forum, quoted, 24, 35, 37

Four Power Treaty, 150, 151–152

Fourteen Points, 109, 112, 114, 122

France, naval war with, 4; in Mexico, 16; appeal for United States cooperation in 1863, 17; Americans' opinion of, 19; and Hawaii, 24; Atlantic system, 62; in China, 66, 70; in Caribbean, 74; Algeciras conference, 77–78; First World War, 91, 96, 97; Treaty of Guarantee with, 113, 243; Washington conference, 150; seeks assurance on collective security, 165–166; Munich crisis, 183–184; neutrality revision, 185, 187; Second World War, 190–191, 192, 213; Marshall Plan, 240; signs EDC, 270; in Indo-China, 274–276; rejects EDC, 277

Franco, General Francisco, 172

Franklin, Benjamin, quoted, 36

Frick, Henry, 147

Fulbright resolution, 211

Garner, John Nance, 186

Geneva conference (1954), on Indo-China, 274, 276

Geneva convention of International Red Cross, 18

Geneva disarmament conference, 169

Germany, Americans' opinion of, 19; in Samoa, 24; threat of rising power of, 31, 34, 59, 61, 62; in China, 66, 70; and Venezuela incident, 74; Algeciras conference, 77; First World War, 91–105; Paris peace conference, 110–114; signs Kellogg-Briand treaty, 157; occupies Rhineland, 172; supports Spanish rebels, 177; Munich crisis, 183–184; neutrality revision, 185, 188; Second World War, 187, 192, 196, 199, 202; declares war on United States, 207; final assault upon, 213; plans for occupation of, 216; becomes power vacuum, 220; occupation policies for, 229, 240–241; and peace treaty, 229, 274. See also West Germany, East Germany

Gompers, Samuel, 54

Good Neighbor policy, 154, 177

Grand Alliance, of World War II, 209, 219

Grant, Ulysses S., 17

Great Britain, United States seeks complete independence from, 2; and Monroe Doctrine, 8–9; control of Atlantic, 15; interest in Samoa, 24; and Venezuela dispute, 26–27; rapprochement with United States, 34, 59–60, 61, 76, 146; decline of power, 62; and Open Door policy, 63, 66; canal treaty, 72; and Venezuela (1902), 74; Algeciras conference, 77, 78; First World War, 91, 96, 97, 101; naval rivalry, 137–139; and Washington conference, 149, 150; Munich crisis, 183–184; neutrality revision, 185, 187; Second World War, 190, 192, 194; wartime conferences, 211, 212, 214, 216–219; control of atomic energy, 223; Korean war, 257; peace treaty, 274; accord with United States, 275–276; southeastern Asia defense pact, 276

Greece, 6–7, 201, 227, 231–232

Greenland, 35, 201

Greer, 202

Grew, Joseph C., 220

Grey, Sir Edward, 101

Guam, 22, 50, 51, 52, 134, 239

Hague conferences, 60, 82

Hague Tribunal, 171

Haiti, 23, 76, 134

Hamilton, Alexander, 3, 4

Hanna, Mark, 47, 56

Harding, Warren G., as presidential candidate, 125; declares policy as president, 126; and Washington conference, 149, 152

Harriman, Averill, 220

Harrison, Benjamin, 23, 26

Harvey, Colonel George, 124

Havana conference (1940), 191

Hawaii, early interest in, 15, 16, 17, 22, 23, 24; object of imperialist ambitions, 33, 34, 35, 37; annexation of, 43–44; as American possession, 134, 137, 239

Hawley-Smoot tariff, 132

Hay, John, on imperialism, 38; on Far Eastern policy, 60; Open Door notes and Boxer settlement, 63–67; negotiates Clayton-Bulwer treaty, 72

Hay-Herrán treaty, 73

Hemingway, Ernest, *quoted*, 118

Hippisley, Alfred E., 64, 66

Hiss, Alger, 254

Hitler, Adolf, threatening attitude of, 170, 172; Munich crisis, 183–

184; attack on Poland, 187; in Second World War, 189, 190, 192, 195, 213

Hoar, George F., 44, 52, 54, 55

Hollywood, 142

Holy Alliance, 5, 6, 7, 8, 120

Hoover, Herbert, favors Harding's election, 125–126; war debts moratorium, 131; Hawley-Smoot tariff, 132; opposes Philippine independence, 135–136; as Secretary of Commerce, 142; Latin American tour of, 156; views on foreign policy, as President, 161–162; Manchuria crisis, 163–164; disarmament, 165–166; on isolation, 168; calls for new policy, 262–263, 266

Hopkins, Harry, 218

House, Colonel Edward M., 100, 101

House Un-American Activities Committee, 254

Huerta, Victoriano, 89, 90

Hughes, Charles Evans, nominated for presidency, 100; favors Harding's election, 125–126; as Secretary of State at Washington Conference, 150; Latin American policy, 153–155; resignation, 155

Hull, Cordell, becomes Secretary of State, 168; neutrality legislation, 175, 176; on quarantine speech, 181; on isolationism, 183, 189; destroyer-naval base deal, 193; on lend-lease, 193–194; negotiations with Japan, 204–206; world organization, 209, 211; and election of 1944, 214

Hungary, 12, 225

Hydrogen bomb, 281

Iceland, 201

Ickes, Harold, 103, 197

Idealism, as force in American foreign policy, 6, 68–69, 90–91, 105–107, 118, 122–123, 158–161, 166, 264–265, 281. *See also* Moral influence, National mission

Immigration, 19–20, 143

Imperialism, in 1850's, 12, 13–16; in 1860's, 16–17; forces making for, at close of century, 21–39; upsurge in

1898, 42–57; retreat from, 57–58, 76, 133. *See also* Expansion

"Imperialism of righteousness," 48

India, 276

Indo-China, occupied by Japan, 201, 204, 205–206; postwar situation in, 252, 272; invasion and crisis, 274–275; and Geneva conference, 276

Insular cases, 56–57

International Atomic Authority, 225

International Labor Organization, 213

International Monetary Fund and International Bank for Reconstruction and Development, 213

International Trade Organization, 237

Investments, foreign, 130, 141

Iran, 227, 281

"Iron Curtain," 228

Isolationism, tradition of, 1–20; term first used by Sumner, 13; criticized by Alfred Thayer Mahan, 27, 32, 33; upheld by Henry Cabot Lodge, 35; and overseas expansion, 58; attitude of prewar Progressives, 83; and First World War, 100, 102, 104; Wilson on, 115; and League of Nations, 117, 119–120, 126–127, 128; in the 1920's, 144–149; and Herbert Hoover, 161–162, 168; policy modified at Geneva disarmament conference, 169; and World Court, 170–171; and neutrality program, 172–178, 183; final triumph of, 186; and neutrality revision, 188; and lend-lease, 194; restrains President Roosevelt, 196–200; and America First Committee, 199–200; waning force of, 208, 210–212; in election of 1944, 214–215; rejected, 220, 222; postwar debate over, 262–267

Isthmian canal, 23, 33, 69, 72. *See also* Panama Canal

Italian-Ethiopian conflict, 172, 173, 179

Italy, threatened intervention in Dominican Republic, 74; claims to Fiume, 110; at Washington conference, 150–151; signs Kellogg-Briand treaty, 157; war on Ethiopia, 172, 173; supports Spanish rebels, 177; and Munich crisis, 183; attacks

France, 191; declares war on United States, 207; and Marshall Plan, 240; dispute with Yugoslavia, 247; signs EDC, 270

Jackson, Andrew, 9

Jackson, Robert, attorney general, 197

Japan, opened up by Commodore Perry, 15; and Hawaii, 44; and Open Door policy, 66–67; friction with United States, 68; war with Russia, 70–72; and proposed internationalization of Manchuria, 80; Zimmerman note, 105; Shantung issue, 110; naval strength of, 139; at Washington conference, 149–153; signs Kellogg-Briand treaty, 157; attacks Manchuria, 162–164; in North China, 177; attacks China, 178–179; and Brussels conference, 181–182; embargo on exports to, 192, 195, 198–199, 204–205; final break with, 206–207; and Second World War, 213; and Yalta conference, 216; defeat leaves power vacuum, 220; and strategic area trusteeship, 239; occupation of, 239, 250; peace treaty with, 268

Japanese-American commercial treaty, 204

Japanese-American security treaty, 269

Jefferson, Thomas, rejects entangling alliances, 2, 4; favors trade, 3; and national mission, 6; and Monroe Doctrine, 8; scorn of Europe, 10; advice recalled, 12, 20, 127

Jessup, Philip C., 253

Jingoism, 26, 29, 49

Johnson, Andrew, 17, 18

Johnson, Hiram, 171, 188, 214, 244

Joint Chiefs of Staff, 259

Jones Act of 1916, 135

Jones, Charles W., 28

Journal of Commerce, quoted, 47

Judd, Walter H., 253

Kellogg, Frank B., 155, 159, 160

Kellogg-Briand Anti-War Treaty, 120, 157–161, 162, 163, 164, 167

Kennan, George F., 232, 264

Kipling, Rudyard, 48

Knowland, William F., 253
Knox, Frank B., 196–197
Knox, Philander C., 79, 80, 85
Konoye, Prince, 205
Korea, annexed by Japan, 71; joint occupation of, 239–240, 256; hostilities in, 256–261; truce negotiations, 268, 271–272; failure to settle division, 275, 276
Kossuth, Louis, 12
Kurile Islands, 216

Ladrone Islands, 45, 49
La Follette, Robert, opposes dollar diplomacy, 84–85; opposes entry into war, 104; as presidential candidate, 148; and Washington conference treaties, 152; opposes neutrality revision, 188, 244
La Follette, Philip, 199
Lansing, Robert, 94
Latin America, policy toward, 8–9, 26–27, 57, 67, 72–77, 80–81, 84, 88–91, 133–134, 153–157, 177, 183, 237–239. See also Monroe Doctrine, and individual countries
Lattimore, Owen, 253
Laval, Pierre, 165
League of Nations, established at peace conference, 109, 111, 113, 114; debated in United States, 115–124; defeated in Senate, 124, 125; rejected by Harding, 126; relation to naval power, 138; American attitude toward, 144, 146; membership favored by Hughes, 150; and Manchuria crisis, 163; and disarmament, 165; Roosevelt's attitude toward, 169; and Ethiopian war, 172
League to Enforce Peace, 146
Lend-lease, 192, 193–194, 198, 200
Lenroot, Irvine L., 103
Lippmann, Walter, 83, 98, 103, 153, 215, 264
Literary Digest, quoted, 37, 49, 64
Lloyd George, David, 109
Lodge, Henry Cabot, on foreign affairs, 18; as expansionist, 34–36, 39, 44–45, 47, 50; and treaty with Spain, 53; Algeciras conference, 78; League of Nations, 103, 115,

116, 119, 124; Four Power Treaty, 152
Lodge, Henry Cabot, Jr., 124 n., 160
London economic conference, 169
London naval conference, 165, 166
Long, John D., 36
Lothian, Lord, 193
Low countries, 190, 192
Lusitania, 93, 97, 99
Luxembourg, 270
Luzon, 50, 51

MacArthur, General Douglas, 259, 261
McCarran, Patrick A., 253
McCarthy, Joseph R., 253–254
McCarthyism, 254–255
Mackay, Alexander, 11
Mackinac charter, 210–211
McKinley, William, election of, 41; policy toward Cuba, 41; on Hawaiian annexation, 43; policy toward Philippines, 44, 45, 49–56; and Open Door policy, 63–64; emphasis on moral concepts, 69
Madison, James, 4, 8
Mahan, Alfred Thayer, as exponent of naval power, 23, 32–39, 137; on Venezuela incident, 27; on Hawaiian annexation, 43, 44; on Philippines, 45
Maine, 41
Malenkov, Georgi M., 272
Manchuria, and Russo-Japanese war, 70–72; proposed neutralization of, 80; crisis in 1931–32, 162–164; and Korean war, 259, 261
Mandates, established by League of Nations, 113
Manifest Destiny, 9, 12, 20, 36, 37, 43–44, 46, 127
Manila Bay, battle of, 42, 47, 49, 51
Mao Tse-tung, 255
Marshall, George C., and Marshall Plan, 232–234; mission to China, 250
Marshall Plan, 232–236, 240, 241, 244
Maximilian, Archduke of Austria, 16
Mayo, Admiral William K., 90
Mellon, Andrew, 147
Mendès-France, Pierre, 276

Mercantile imperialism, 36, 46

Mexico, 89–91, 104

Middle East, 247, 248

Milwaukee *Sentinel, quoted,* 103

Missionary enterprise, 30

"Mr. Dooley," 55, 57–58

Mitchell, General William, 134

Mobile speech, by President Wilson, 88

Modus vivendi, proposed with Japan, 206

Monroe, James, sympathy for Greece, 6, 7; formulates Monroe Doctrine, 8–9; advice recalled, 127

Monroe Doctrine, formulated, 8–9; and Napoleon III, 16; and expansionist policies, 25, 28, 84; Venezuela incident, 26–27; and Theodore Roosevelt, 74–77; in League covenant, 116, 138; Secretary Hughes' policy on, 154–155; and Franklin D. Roosevelt, 183. *See also* Rio de Janeiro treaty

Moody, William Vaughn, *quoted,* 54–55

Moral concepts—or influence—in foreign policy, 6–7, 12, 60, 66, 68–69, 85, 87–88, 92, 120–121, 127, 143, 163, 166, 264–265. *See also* Idealism, National mission

Morgan, John T., 24

Morgenthau, Hans, 264

Morocco, 23, 78

Morrow, Dwight, 155

Moscow declaration, 211

Munich conference, 183–184

Munitions trade (1914–1917), 95–96, 174

Mussolini, 170, 172, 184

Mutual Security Program, 270

Naples, Kingdom of, 5

Napoleon III, 16

Nation, quoted, 97

National Association of Manufacturers, 236

National defense (1940–1941), 190–191, 203

National mission, 1, 6, 12–13, 15, 22, 33, 48, 69, 88, 107, 281. *See also* Idealism, Moral concepts

National Security Council, 241, 273

Nation's Business, quoted, 148

Naval Policy Board, 28, 33

Naval war with France, 4

Navy, early growth of, 22, 27–29, 32–33; Theodore Roosevelt's campaign for, 67–68; Taft program, 82; Wilson program, 99, 137–139; and Washington conference, 150–151; expansion under Franklin D. Roosevelt, 191

Navy League, 139

Netherlands, 270

Netherlands East Indies, 205

Neutrality, as early policy, 3–4; and First World War, 92–105; as legislated in 1930's, 173–175, 177–178, 184–186; and Second World War, 187–189, 193–206

Neutrality legislation, 173–175, 177–178, 184–186; revised, 187–189; repealed, 203

New Deal, 168, 170, 176, 179

New Freedom, 87

New Nationalism, 83

New Republic, quoted, 103, 117, 148, 180, 188

New York *Sun, quoted,* 19, 117

New York Times, quoted, 48, 180

New Zealand, 257, 269, 276

Nicaragua, and canal project, 23, 34, 35, 37, 72; intervention in, 76, 133–134, 155; recall of troops, 156

Niebuhr, Reinhold, *quoted,* 143

Nine Power Treaty, 151, 162, 163

Norris, George W., 84, 104, 148, 171

North Africa, 60, 213, 247

North Atlantic Treaty, 242, 245, 246, 259, 266, 270

North Atlantic Treaty Organization, 246, 248, 259, 270, 271, 277

North Korea, 256–258, 276. *See also* Democratic People's Republic

Norway, 190

Nye, Gerald P., 174, 188, 214

Nye Committee, 174–175

Ogdensburg agreement, with Canada, 191–192

Ohio State Journal, *quoted,* 115

Okinawa, 239

Olds, Robert E., 159

Olney, Richard, 26–27, 86

One World, 210

Open Door policy, formulation of, 62–67; and Russo-Japanese war, 71–72; and proposed internationalization of Manchuria, 80; written into Nine Power Treaty, 151; and Manchuria crisis, 164

Oregon, 14

Organization of American States, 239

Organization for European Economic Cooperation, 248

Orlando, Vittorio Emmanuele, 109

Our Country, quoted, 30, 31

Outlawry of war, 157–161, 167

Overland Monthly, quoted, 38

Pacific ocean, American ambitions to control, 13, 14–16, 17, 23–25, 32, 37, 42, 47, 55; American position in, 134; as theater of war, 204; defenses in, 239. *See also* Imperialism, China, Japan, Strategic area trusteeship

Page, Walter Hines, 45

Pakistan, 276

Panama, 72–73, 84, 133. *See also* Panama Canal

Panama Canal, 72–73, 76, 81. *See also* Isthmian canal

Panama Canal Zone, 57, 73, 76, 133

Paris peace conference (1919), 108–114. *See also* Versailles Treaty

Peace movement, 80, 82–83. *See also* Outlawry of war

"Peace without victory," 101

Pearl Harbor, as naval station, 24, 25; attack on, 204, 206, 207

Permanent Court of Arbitration, 60, 85

Perry, Commodore Matthew C., 15

Philadelphia Record, quoted, 43

Philippine Islands, steps toward acquisition, 42–51, becomes United States possession, 51; debates over retention of, 52–58; relation to trade in China, 47–48, 51, 63; as American possession, 133, 134–135; granted freedom, 135–136; threatened by Japan, 205; in defense perimeter, 239; in Korean war, 257; signs mutual defense pact,

269; signs southeastern Asia defense pact, 276

Phony war, 189

Pierce, Franklin, 14

Point Four, 242, 248

Poland, rebellion in, 17; territorial limits of, 110; attacked by Hitler, 187; postwar status, 216, 219, 225, 229

Polls, public opinion, 178, 185, 188, 204, 212 n.

Populism, 29

Portugal, 5

Potsdam conference, 223

Preparedness movement (1915–1917), 99

Proctor, John R., *quoted*, 37

Progressives, attitude on foreign policy, 83–85, 103–104, 147–148, 176–177, 199–200

Public opinion, *see* Polls

Puerto Rico, as annexationist goal, 42, 45, 50; annexed, 51, 52; as colonial possession, 72, 76, 133

Quarantine speech, 179–181

Racial superiority, as conception underlying imperialism, 30–32

Randolph, John, 7, 8

Reciprocal trade program, *see* Trade reciprocity program

Recognition policy, toward Mexico, 89–90; toward Soviet Russia, 130–131, 177; toward Communist China, 255. *See also* Stimson Doctrine

Red Cross, 18

Reed, James, 152

Reid, Whitelaw, 78

Relief and reconstruction, 130

Reparations, in First World War, 131

Reston, James B., *quoted*, 215

Review of Reviews, quoted, 37

Rhee, Syngman, 256

Rhineland, as proposed state, 110, 113; Hitler's troops march into, 172

Rio de Janeiro Treaty, 237, 242, 270

Rockhill, William W., 63–64, 66

Roosevelt, Franklin D., on Philippine independence, 135; on Kellogg-Briand treaty, 160; becomes President, 167; nationalist phase, 168–170; and World Court, 171; attitude toward neutrality laws, 175–178; quarantine speech, 179–181; and Munich crisis, 184; seeks neutrality revision, 185–186, 187–188; during phony war, 189; redefines American policy, 191; develops program of aid to Allies, 193–199; meets Churchill, 201; orders shooting war, 202–204; policy toward Japan, 204–206; asks for declaration of war, 207; promotes peace program, 209–210; at wartime conferences, 211–212, 216–218; election of 1944, 214–215; death of, 218

Roosevelt, Theodore, as imperialist, 35–36, 39, 42, 45, 47; discouraged over attitude toward Philippines, 58; becomes President, 67; views on American foreign policy, 23, 67–69, 128, 243; policy in eastern Asia, 69–72; in Latin America, 72–77; and Algeciras conference, 77–79; and relation to Progressives, 83, 84, 85; promotes navy, 67–68, 88, 137; attitude toward First World War, 100

Roosevelt corollary to Monroe Doctrine, 74–76, 154, 156

Root, Elihu, as Secretary of State, 76, 154; supports Harding, 125; and World Court protocols, 171

Root-Takahira agreement, 71

Rumania, 225

Russia, and Monroe Doctrine, 8–9; during Civil War, 17–18; fears of at turn of century, 32, 37, 59, 61; and Boxer settlement, 66; war with Japan, 70–71; and dollar diplomacy, 80; First World War, 91; revolution in, 105; de Tocqueville prophecy on, 221. See also Soviet Russia

Russo-Japanese war, 23, 70–71, 77, 81, 216

Ryukyus, 239, 268

Saar, 110

Sakhalin, 216

Samoa, establishment of tri-partite

protectorate, 24; Cleveland policy toward, 25; control urged by Mahan, 33; and Lodge, 34; annexation of, 52; as American possession, 134, 239

San Francisco conference, 218–219

Santo Domingo, 23. See also Dominican Republic

Schuman plan, 248

Schurz, Carl, 19, 36, 54

Second New Deal, 176

Secret treaties, 109

Security Council, of United Nations, 216, 256, 257

Seward, William H., in defense of Hungarian liberty, 12; on Pacific expansion, 15–16, 37; purchase of Alaska, 17; and policy of non-intervention, 17–18

Sherwood, Robert, quoted, 189

Shotwell, James T., 159

Siegfried, André, 147

Simonds, Frank H., quoted, 146

Soulé, Pierre, 14

Southeastern Asia defense pact, 275, 276

South Korea, see Korea

Soviet Russia, recognition withheld by the United States, 130–131; American trade with, 130–131, 140; absent from Washington conference, 151; recognized, 177; and lend-lease aid, 194; invaded by Germany, 200, 201; at wartime conferences, 211, 212, 214, 216–219; rising threat of, 219–220, 223; and atomic energy, 225, 280; blocks path to peace, 227–228; and cold war, 229; rejects Marshall plan, 234; Berlin blockade, 240; increases pressure, 248, 280, 281; support for Chinese Communists, 252, 255; and Korea, 256, 258; and Japan, 268–269; United States threat of retaliation upon, 273; and Berlin conference, 274

Spain, and Holy Alliance, 5; expansionists' attitude toward, 36; American war with, 40–42, 49; treaty of peace with, 51–53; civil war in, 172–173

Spanish-American war, 40–42, 58, 67, 83

Spanish civil war, 172–173, 177, 179

Springfield *Republican, quoted,* 64

Spring-Rice, Cecil, 70

Stalin, Joseph, 131, 216, 217, 272

State Department, organization of, 142

Stevenson, Adlai E., 264, 267

Stimson, Henry L., supports Harding, 125; in Nicaragua, 155; as Secretary of State, 156; on Kellogg-Briand treaty, 161; Manchuria crisis and non-recognition doctrine, 163–164, 177; as Secretary of War, on Atlantic patrols, 196–197

Stimson Doctrine, 163–164, 177

Stockton, Robert F., 12

Stone, William J., 102, 104

Strategic area trusteeship, 239, 268

Strong, Josiah, 30, 31, 39

Submarine warfare (1914–1917), 92–95, 100–102, 104–105; (1941), 202–203

Sudetenland, 184

Sumner, Charles, 13

Sumner, William Graham, 36

Sussex, 95, 100, 102

Taft, Robert A., favors world organization, 212; opposes North Atlantic Treaty, 244; criticizes China policy, 253; on Korean war, 258; calls for "re-examination" of military aid, 262, 263

Taft, William Howard, heads Philippines commission, 54; becomes President, 79; and dollar diplomacy, 79–81, 85, 88, 154; naval program, 82

Tampico incident, 90

Tardieu, André, 61

Tariff policy, 131–132. *See also* Trade reciprocity program

Teheran conference, 211–212, 227

Thailand, 276

Tobey, Charles W., 199

Tocqueville, Alexis de, *quoted,* 221

Tojo, General, 205

Total diplomacy, 249

Tourists, 141

Tracy, Benjamin F., 28

Trade, *see* Commerce

Trade reciprocity program, 177, 237

Treaties: Anzus (Australia-New Zealand-United States) mutual defense, 269; of Brussels (1948), 241, 277; Clayton-Bulwer, 72; Five Power (1922), 150; Four Power (1922), 150, 151–152; French security (1919), 113, 243; Hay-Herrán, 73; Japanese - American commercial, 204; Japanese-American security, 269; Kellogg-Briand Anti-War, 120, 157–161, 162, 163, 164, 167; Nationalist China mutual defense, 269 n.; of Paris (1898), 51; Nine Power (1922), 151, 162, 163; North Atlantic, 242, 245, 246, 259, 270, 271, 277; Philippine mutual defense, 269; Republic of Korea mutual defense, 269 n.; of Rio de Janeiro, 237, 242, 270; southeastern Asia defense, 275, 276; of Versailles, 11, 114–115

Triple Alliance, 78

Triple Entente, 78

Truman, Harry S., becomes President, 218; and San Francisco conference, 218–219; and Truman Doctrine, 231; and Marshall plan, 235; on economic policy, 237; Berlin air lift, 241; re-election, 242; North Atlantic Treaty, 242, 245; sends Marshall to China, 250; and Korean crisis, 256, 257–258; troops to Europe, 259; supports general policy, 263

Truman Doctrine, 231–232, 236, 244

Trusteeship, *see* Strategic area trusteeship

Turkey, 231, 232, 257

Twain, Mark, 54

Tydings-McDuffie Act, 135

Tyler, John, 9

United Nations, Declaration of, 209; early steps toward organization, 213–214, 216; creation of, 218–219; program for control of atomic energy, 223–225; in Iran and Greece, 227; as "town meeting of the world," 228; and Truman Doctrine, 231, 232; strategic area trusteeship, 239; popular support for, 246, 266; Communist China membership in, 255–256, 275; and Korean war, 256–258, 261, 271–272; and Soviet veto, 267–268

United Nations Relief and Rehabilitation Administration, 213, 234

United States Information program, 254

U.S.S.R., see Soviet Russia

Van Buren, Martin, 9

Vandenberg, Arthur H., as isolationist, 145, 198; attitude changed by Pearl Harbor, 207; supports internationalism, 210, 215, 219; fearful of Russia, 228; and Truman Doctrine, 232; on Marshall plan, 235; resolution for regional agreements, 241–242; supports North Atlantic Treaty, 244; and Korean war, 258

Vandenberg resolution, 241–242

Venezuela, 26–27, 29, 74

Vera Cruz incident, 90

Versailles Treaty, terms of, 111, 114–115; rejected by senate, 124, 125; La Follette calls for revision, 148; Hitler demands revision, 172. See also League of Nations

Vichy France, 201

Vietminh, 274, 275

Vietnam, 274, 276

Virgin Islands, 57, 133. See also Danish West Indies

Voice of America, 254

Vorys, John M., 185

Walker, Isaac P., 12

Wallace, Henry A., 228

Wall Street Journal, quoted, 47

War debts, 130, 131, 132, 174, 193

War of 1812, 4, 5

Washington, George, advice on foreign policy, 2; Farewell Address, 3–4; advice recalled, 12, 13, 17–18, 20, 35, 38, 86, 127

Washington Conference for the Limitation of Armaments, 139, 149–153, 164

Washington Post, quoted, 38, 43

Washington Star, quoted, 26

"Watchful waiting," 89

Webster, Daniel, 7, 8, 11

Welles, Sumner, 181, 189

Western European Union, 241, 277

West Germany, 240, 270, 277

Wheeler, Burton K., 198

White, Henry, 42, 45, 77

White, William Allen, quoted, 57, 83; and Committee to Defend America, 200–201

"White Man's Burden," 48

White Paper, on China, 252

Whitman, Walt, quoted, 11–12

Whitthorne, Washington C., 28

Willkie, Wendell, 197, 210

Wilson, Woodrow, becomes President, 87; ideas on foreign policy, 87–88, 168; Latin American policy, 88–91, 154; and neutral rights, 92–95; influenced by financial interests, 96; and preparedness, 99; election of 1916, 100; seeks to avoid war, 100–102; asks for declaration of war, 105–107; goes to Paris, 108; at peace conference, 108–114; struggle over League, 115–127, 209, 211; and United States leadership, 128; attitude toward navy, 138, 243

World Court, 144, 171–172

World's Work, quoted, 57

Yalta conference, 214, 216–218, 225

"Young America," 12

Yugoslavia, 201, 227, 247, 281

Zimmerman note, 104–105

harper ✦ torchbooks

HUMANITIES AND SOCIAL SCIENCES

American Studies: General

LOUIS D. BRANDEIS: Other People's Money, and How the Bankers Use It. ‡ Ed. with an Intro. by Richard M. Abrams   TB/3081
THOMAS C. COCHRAN: The Inner Revolution. Essays on the Social Sciences in History   TB/1140
HENRY STEELE COMMAGER, Ed.: The Struggle for Racial Equality   TB/1300
EDWARD S. CORWIN: American Constitutional History. Essays edited by Alpheus T. Mason and Gerald Garvey △   TB/1136
CARL N. DEGLER, Ed.: Pivotal Interpretations of American History   Vol. I TB/1240; Vol. II TB/1241
A. HUNTER DUPREE: Science in the Federal Government: A History of Policies and Activities to 1940 TB/573
A. S. EISENSTADT, Ed.: The Craft of American History: Recent Essays in American Historical Writing
Vol. I TB/1255; Vol. II TB/1256
CHARLOTTE P. GILMAN: Women and Economics: A Study of the Economic Relation between Men and Women as a Factor in Social Evolution. ‡ Ed. with an Introduction by Carl N. Degler   TB/3073
OSCAR HANDLIN, Ed.: This Was America: As Recorded by European Travelers in the Eighteenth, Nineteenth and Twentieth Centuries. Illus.   TB/1119
MARCUS LEE HANSEN: The Atlantic Migration: 1607-1860. Edited by Arthur M. Schlesinger   TB/1052
MARCUS LEE HANSEN: The Immigrant in American History.   TB/1120
JOHN HIGHAM, Ed.: The Reconstruction of American History △   TB/1068
ROBERT H. JACKSON: The Supreme Court in the American System of Government   TB/1106
JOHN F. KENNEDY: A Nation of Immigrants. △ Illus.
TB/1118
LEONARD W. LEVY, Ed.: American Constitutional Law: Historical Essays   TB/1285
LEONARD W. LEVY, Ed.: Judicial Review and the Supreme Court   TB/1296
LEONARD W. LEVY: The Law of the Commonwealth and Chief Justice Shaw   TB/1309
HENRY F. MAY: Protestant Churches and Industrial America. New Intro. by the Author   TB/1334
RALPH BARTON PERRY: Puritanism and Democracy
TB/1138
ARNOLD ROSE: The Negro in America   TB/3048
MAURICE R. STEIN: The Eclipse of Community. An Interpretation of American Studies   TB/1128
W. LLOYD WARNER and Associates: Democracy in Jonesville: A Study in Quality and Inequality ¶ TB/1129
W. LLOYD WARNER: Social Class in America: The Evaluation of Status   TB/1013

American Studies: Colonial

BERNARD BAILYN, Ed.: Apologia of Robert Keayne: Self-Portrait of a Puritan Merchant   TB/1201
BERNARD BAILYN: The New England Merchants in the Seventeenth Century   TB/1149
JOSEPH CHARLES: The Origins of the American Party System   TB/1049
HENRY STEELE COMMAGER & ELMO GIORDANETTI, Eds.: Was America a Mistake? An Eighteenth Century Controversy   TB/1329
CHARLES GIBSON: Spain in America †   TB/3077
LAWRENCE H. GIPSON: The Coming of the Revolution: 1763-1775. † Illus.   TB/3007
LEONARD W. LEVY: Freedom of Speech and Press in Early American History: Legacy of Suppression TB/1109
PERRY MILLER: Errand Into the Wilderness   TB/1139
PERRY MILLER & T. H. JOHNSON, Eds.: The Puritans: A Sourcebook of Their Writings
Vol. I TB/1093; Vol. II TB/1094
EDMUND S. MORGAN, Ed.: The Diary of Michael Wigglesworth, 1653-1657: The Conscience of a Puritan
TB/1228
EDMUND S. MORGAN: The Puritan Family: Religion and Domestic Relations in Seventeenth-Century New England   TB/1227
RICHARD B. MORRIS: Government and Labor in Early America   TB/1244
KENNETH B. MURDOCK: Literature and Theology in Colonial New England   TB/99
WALLACE NOTESTEIN: The English People on the Eve of Colonization: 1603-1630. † Illus.   TB/3006
JOHN P. ROCHE: Origins of American Political Thought: Selected Readings   TB/1301
JOHN SMITH: Captain John Smith's America: Selections from His Writings. Ed. with Intro. by John Lankford
TB/3078
LOUIS B. WRIGHT: The Cultural Life of the American Colonies: 1607-1763. † Illus.   TB/3005

American Studies: From the Revolution to 1860

JOHN R. ALDEN: The American Revolution: 1775-1783. † Illus.   TB/3011
MAX BELOFF, Ed.: The Debate on the American Revolution, 1761-1783: A Sourcebook △   TB/1225
RAY A. BILLINGTON: The Far Western Frontier: 1830-1860. † Illus.   TB/3012
EDMUND BURKE: On the American Revolution: Selected Speeches and Letters. ‡ Edited by Elliott Robert Barkan   TB/3068
WHITNEY R. CROSS: The Burned-Over District: The Social and Intellectual History of Enthusiastic Religion in Western New York, 1800-1850 △   TB/1242
GEORGE DANGERFIELD: The Awakening of American Nationalism: 1815-1828. † Illus.   TB/3061

---

† The New American Nation Series, edited by Henry Steele Commager and Richard B. Morris.
‡ American Perspectives series, edited by Bernard Wishy and William E. Leuchtenburg.
* The Rise of Modern Europe series, edited by William L. Langer.
** History of Europe series, edited by J. H. Plumb.
¶ Researches in the Social, Cultural and Behavioral Sciences, edited by Benjamin Nelson.
§ The Library of Religion and Culture, edited by Benjamin Nelson.
Σ Harper Modern Science Series, edited by James R. Newman.
º Not for sale in Canada.
△ Not for sale in the U. K.

1

CLEMENT EATON: The Freedom-of-Thought Struggle in the Old South. *Revised and Enlarged*. *Illus*. TB/1150
CLEMENT EATON: The Growth of Southern Civilization: 1790-1860. † *Illus*. TB/3040
LOUIS FILLER: The Crusade Against Slavery: 1830-1860. † *Illus*. TB/3029
DIXON RYAN FOX: The Decline of Aristocracy in the Politics of New York: 1801-1840. ‡ *Edited by Robert V. Remini* TB/3064
WILLIAM W. FREEHLING, Ed.: The Nullification Era: *A Documentary Record* ‡ TB/3079
FELIX GILBERT: The Beginnings of American Foreign Policy: *To the Farewell Address* TB/1200
FRANCIS GRIERSON: The Valley of Shadows: *The Coming of the Civil War in Lincoln's Midwest: A Contemporary Account* TB/1246
FRANCIS J. GRUND: Aristocracy in America: *Social Class in the Formative Years of the New Nation* TB/1001
ALEXANDER HAMILTON: The Reports of Alexander Hamilton. ‡ *Edited by Jacob E. Cooke* TB/3060
THOMAS JEFFERSON: Notes on the State of Virginia. ‡ *Edited by Thomas P. Abernethy* TB/3052
JAMES MADISON: The Forging of American Federalism: *Selected Writings of James Madison. Edited by Saul K. Padover* TB/1226
BERNARD MAYO: Myths and Men: *Patrick Henry, George Washington, Thomas Jefferson* TB/1108
JOHN C. MILLER: Alexander Hamilton and the Growth of the New Nation TB/3057
RICHARD B. MORRIS, Ed.: The Era of the American Revolution TB/1180
R. B. NYE: The Cultural Life of the New Nation: 1776-1801. † *Illus*. TB/3026
JAMES PARTON: The Presidency of Andrew Jackson. *From Vol. III of the Life of Andrew Jackson*. ‡ *Ed. with an Intro. by Robert V. Remini* TB/3080
FRANCIS S. PHILBRICK: The Rise of the West, 1754-1830. † *Illus*. TB/3067
TIMOTHY L. SMITH: Revivalism and Social Reform: *American Protestantism on the Eve of the Civil War* TB/1229
ALBION W. TOURGÉE: A Fool's Errand. ‡ *Ed. by George Fredrickson* TB/3074
A. F. TYLER: Freedom's Ferment: *Phases of American Social History from the Revolution to the Outbreak of the Civil War*. 31 illus. TB/1074
GLYNDON G. VAN DEUSEN: The Jacksonian Era: 1828-1848. † *Illus*. TB/3028
LOUIS B. WRIGHT: Culture on the Moving Frontier TB/1053

American Studies: The Civil War to 1900

W. R. BROCK: An American Crisis: Congress and Reconstruction, 1865-67 º △ TB/1283
THOMAS C. COCHRAN & WILLIAM MILLER: The Age of Enterprise: *A Social History of Industrial America* TB/1054
W. A. DUNNING: Essays on the Civil War and Reconstruction. *Introduction by David Donald* TB/1181
W. A. DUNNING: Reconstruction, Political and Economic: 1865-1877 TB/1073
HAROLD U. FAULKNER: Politics, Reform and Expansion: 1890-1900. † *Illus*. TB/3020
HELEN HUNT JACKSON: A Century of Dishonor: *The Early Crusade for Indian Reform*. ‡ *Edited by Andrew F. Rolle* TB/3063
ALBERT D. KIRWAN: Revolt of the Rednecks: *Mississippi Politics, 1876-1925* TB/1199
ROBERT GREEN MC CLOSKEY: American Conservatism in the Age of Enterprise: 1865-1910 TB/1137
ARTHUR MANN: Yankee Reformers in the Urban Age: *Social Reform in Boston, 1880-1900* TB/1247
WHITELAW REID: After the War: *A Tour of the Southern States, 1865-1866*. ‡ *Edited by C. Vann Woodward* TB/3066

CHARLES H. SHINN: Mining Camps: *A Study in American Frontier Government*. ‡ *Edited by Rodman W. Paul* TB/3062
VERNON LANE WHARTON: The Negro in Mississippi: 1865-1890 TB/1178

American Studies: 1900 to the Present

RAY STANNARD BAKER: Following the Color Line: *American Negro Citizenship in Progressive Era*. ‡ *Illus*. *Edited by Dewey W. Grantham, Jr*. TB/3053
RANDOLPH S. BOURNE: War and the Intellectuals: *Collected Essays, 1915-1919*. ‡ *Edited by Carl Resek* TB/3043
A. RUSSELL BUCHANAN: The United States and World War II. † *Illus*. Vol. I TB/3044; Vol. II TB/3045
ABRAHAM CAHAN: The Rise of David Levinsky: *a documentary novel of social mobility in early twentieth century America. Intro. by John Higham* TB/1028
THOMAS C. COCHRAN: The American Business System: *A Historical Perspective, 1900-1955* TB/1080
FOSTER RHEA DULLES: America's Rise to World Power: 1898-1954. † *Illus*. TB/3021
JOHN D. HICKS: Republican Ascendancy: 1921-1933. † *Illus*. TB/3041
SIDNEY HOOK: Reason, Social Myths, and Democracy TB/1237
ROBERT HUNTER: Poverty: *Social Conscience in the Progressive Era*. ‡ *Edited by Peter d'A. Jones* TB/3065
WILLIAM L. LANGER & S. EVERETT GLEASON: The Challenge to Isolation: *The World Crisis of 1937-1940 and American Foreign Policy*
  Vol. I TB/3054; Vol. II TB/3055
WILLIAM E. LEUCHTENBURG: Franklin D. Roosevelt and the New Deal: 1932-1940. † *Illus*. TB/3025
ARTHUR S. LINK: Woodrow Wilson and the Progressive Era: 1910-1917. † *Illus*. TB/3023
GEORGE E. MOWRY: The Era of Theodore Roosevelt and the Birth of Modern America: 1900-1912. † *Illus*. TB/3022
RUSSEL B. NYE: Midwestern Progressive Politics: *A Historical Study of Its Origins and Development, 1870-1958* TB/1202
WILLIAM PRESTON, JR.: Aliens and Dissenters: *Federal Suppression of Radicals, 1903-1933* TB/1287
WALTER RAUSCHENBUSCH: Christianity and the Social Crisis. ‡ *Edited by Robert D. Cross* TB/3059
JACOB RIIS: The Making of an American. ‡ *Edited by Roy Lubove* TB/3070
PHILIP SELZNICK: TVA and the Grass Roots: *A Study in the Sociology of Formal Organization* TB/1230
IDA M. TARBELL: The History of the Standard Oil Company: *Briefer Version*. ‡ *Edited by David M. Chalmers* TB/3071
GEORGE B. TINDALL, Ed.: A Populist Reader ‡ TB/3069
TWELVE SOUTHERNERS: I'll Take My Stand: *The South and the Agrarian Tradition. Intro. by Louis D. Rubin, Jr., Biographical Essays by Virginia Rock* TB/1072

Anthropology

JACQUES BARZUN: Race: *A Study in Superstition. Revised Edition* TB/1172
JOSEPH B. CASAGRANDE, Ed.: In the Company of Man: *Twenty Portraits of Anthropological Informants. Illus*. TB/3047
W. E. LE GROS CLARK: The Antecedents of Man: *Intro. to Evolution of the Primates*. º △ *Illus*. TB/559
CORA DU BOIS: The People of Alor. *New Preface by the author. Illus*. Vol. I TB/1042; Vol. II TB/1043
RAYMOND FIRTH, Ed.: Man and Culture: *An Evaluation of the Work of Bronislaw Malinowski* ¶ º △ TB/1133
DAVID LANDY: Tropical Childhood: *Cultural Transmission and Learning in a Puerto Rican Village* ¶ TB/1235

L. S. B. LEAKEY: Adam's Ancestors: *The Evolution of Man and His Culture.* △ *Illus.*   TB/1019

EDWARD BURNETT TYLOR: Religion in Primitive Culture. *Part II of "Primitive Culture."* § Intro. by Paul Radin   TB/34

W. LLOYD WARNER: A Black Civilization: *A Study of an Australian Tribe.* ¶ *Illus.*   TB/3056

Art and Art History

WALTER LOWRIE: Art in the Early Church. *Revised Edition. 452 illus.*   TB/124

EMILE MÂLE: The Gothic Image: *Religious Art in France of the Thirteenth Century.* § △ *190 illus.*   TB/44

MILLARD MEISS: Painting in Florence and Siena after the Black Death: *The Arts, Religion and Society in the Mid-Fourteenth Century. 169 illus.*   TB/1148

ERICH NEUMANN: The Archetypal World of Henry Moore. △ *107 illus.*   TB/2020

DORA & ERWIN PANOFSKY: Pandora's Box: *The Changing Aspects of a Mythical Symbol. Revised Edition. Illus.*   TB/2021

ERWIN PANOFSKY: Studies in Iconology: *Humanistic Themes in the Art of the Renaissance.* △ *180 illustrations*   TB/1077

ALEXANDRE PIANKOFF: The Shrines of Tut-Ankh-Amon. *Edited by N. Rambova. 117 illus.*   TB/2011

JEAN SEZNEC: The Survival of the Pagan Gods: *The Mythological Tradition and Its Place in Renaissance Humanism and Art. 108 illustrations*   TB/2004

OTTO VON SIMSON: The Gothic Cathedral: *Origins of Gothic Architecture and the Medieval Concept of Order.* △ *58 illus.*   TB/2018

HEINRICH ZIMMER: Myth and Symbols in Indian Art and Civilization. *70 illustrations*   TB/2005

Business, Economics & Economic History

REINHARD BENDIX: Work and Authority in Industry: *Ideologies of Management in the Course of Industrialization*   TB/3035

GILBERT BURCK & EDITORS OF FORTUNE: The Computer Age: *And Its Potential for Management*   TB/1179

THOMAS C. COCHRAN: The American Business System: *A Historical Perspective, 1900-1955*   TB/1080

THOMAS C. COCHRAN: The Inner Revolution: *Essays on the Social Sciences in History* △   TB/1140

THOMAS C. COCHRAN & WILLIAM MILLER: The Age of Enterprise: *A Social History of Industrial America* TB/1054

ROBERT DAHL & CHARLES E. LINDBLOM: Politics, Economics, and Welfare: *Planning and Politico-Economic Systems Resolved into Basic Social Processes*   TB/3037

PETER F. DRUCKER: The New Society: *The Anatomy of Industrial Order* △   TB/1082

EDITORS OF FORTUNE: America in the Sixties: *The Economy and the Society*   TB/1015

ROBERT L. HEILBRONER: The Great Ascent: *The Struggle for Economic Development in Our Time*   TB/3030

ROBERT L. HEILBRONER: The Limits of American Capitalism   TB/1305

FRANK H. KNIGHT: The Economic Organization   TB/1214

FRANK H. KNIGHT: Risk, Uncertainty and Profit   TB/1215

ABBA P. LERNER: Everybody's Business: *Current Assumptions in Economics and Public Policy*   TB/3051

ROBERT GREEN MC CLOSKEY: American Conservatism in the Age of Enterprise, 1865-1910 △   TB/1137

PAUL MANTOUX: The Industrial Revolution in the Eighteenth Century: *The Beginnings of the Modern Factory System in England* ○ △   TB/1079

WILLIAM MILLER, Ed.: Men in Business: *Essays on the Historical Role of the Entrepreneur*   TB/1081

RICHARD B. MORRIS: Government and Labor in Early America △   TB/1244

HERBERT SIMON: The Shape of Automation: *For Men and Management*   TB/1245

PERRIN STRYKER: The Character of the Executive: *Eleven Studies in Managerial Qualities*   TB/1041

Education

JACQUES BARZUN: The House of Intellect △   TB/1051

RICHARD M. JONES, Ed.: Contemporary Educational Psychology: *Selected Readings*   TB/1292

CLARK KERR: The Uses of the University   TB/1264

JOHN U. NEF: Cultural Foundations of Industrial Civilization △   TB/1024

Historiography & Philosophy of History

JACOB BURCKHARDT: On History and Historians. △ *Introduction by H. R. Trevor-Roper*   TB/1216

WILHELM DILTHEY: Pattern and Meaning in History: *Thoughts on History and Society.* ○ △ *Edited with an Introduction by H. P. Rickman*   TB/1075

J. H. HEXTER: Reappraisals in History: *New Views on History & Society in Early Modern Europe* △ TB/1100

H. STUART HUGHES: History as Art and as Science: *Twin Vistas on the Past*   TB/1207

RAYMOND KLIBANSKY & H. J. PATON, Eds.: Philosophy and History: *The Ernst Cassirer Festschrift. Illus.*   TB/1115

ARNALDO MOMIGLIANO: Studies in Historiography ○ △   TB/1283

GEORGE H. NADEL, Ed.: Studies in the Philosophy of History: *Selected Essays from History and Theory*   TB/1208

JOSE ORTEGA Y GASSET: The Modern Theme. *Introduction by Jose Ferrater Mora*   TB/1038

KARL R. POPPER: The Open Society and Its Enemies △
    Vol. I: *The Spell of Plato*   TB/1101
    Vol. II: *The High Tide of Prophecy: Hegel, Marx and the Aftermath*   TB/1102

KARL R. POPPER: The Poverty of Historicism ○ △   TB/1126

G. J. RENIER: History: *Its Purpose and Method* △ TB/1209

W. H. WALSH: Philosophy of History: *An Introduction* △   TB/1020

History: General

WOLFGANG FRANKE: China and the West. *Trans by R. A. Wilson*   TB/1326

L. CARRINGTON GOODRICH: A Short History of the Chinese People. △ *Illus.*   TB/3015

DAN N. JACOBS & HANS H. BAERWALD: Chinese Communism: *Selected Documents*   TB/3031

BERNARD LEWIS: The Arabs in History △   TB/1029

BERNARD LEWIS: The Middle East and the West ○ △   TB/1274

History: Ancient

A. ANDREWES: The Greek Tyrants △   TB/1103

ADOLF ERMAN, Ed. The Ancient Egyptians: *A Sourcebook of Their Writings. New material and Introduction by William Kelly Simpson*   TB/1233

MICHAEL GRANT: Ancient History ○ △   TB/1190

SAMUEL NOAH KRAMER: Sumerian Mythology   TB/1055

NAPHTALI LEWIS & MEYER REINHOLD, Eds.: Roman Civilization. *Sourcebook I: The Republic*   TB/1231

NAPHTALI LEWIS & MEYER REINHOLD, Eds.: Roman Civilization. *Sourcebook II: The Empire*   TB/1232

History: Medieval

P. BOISSONNADE: Life and Work in Medieval Europe: *The Evolution of the Medieval Economy, the 5th to the 15th Century.* ○ △ *Preface by Lynn White, Jr.* TB/1141

HELEN CAM: England before Elizabeth △   TB/1026

NORMAN COHN: The Pursuit of the Millennium: *Revolutionary Messianism in Medieval and Reformation Europe* △   TB/1037

G. G. COULTON: Medieval Village, Manor, and Monastery
TB/1022

CHRISTOPHER DAWSON, Ed.: Mission to Asia: *Narratives and Letters of the Franciscan Missionaries in Mongolia and China in the 13th and 14th Centuries* △
TB/315

HEINRICH FICHTENAU: The Carolingian Empire: *The Age of Charlemagne* △
TB/1142

GALBERT OF BRUGES: The Murder of Charles the Good. *Trans. with Intro. by James Bruce Ross*
TB/1311

F. L. GANSHOF: Feudalism △
TB/1058

DENO GEANAKOPLOS: Byzantine East and Latin West: *Two Worlds of Christendom in the Middle Ages and Renaissance*
TB/1265

EDWARD GIBBON: The Triumph of Christendom in the Roman Empire *(Chaps. XV-XX of "Decline and Fall," J. B. Bury edition).* § △ *Illus.*
TB/46

W. O. HASSALL, Ed.: Medieval England: *As Viewed by Contemporaries* △
TB/1205

DENYS HAY: Europe: The Emergence of an Idea TB/1275

DENYS HAY: The Medieval Centuries ○ △
TB/1192

J. M. HUSSEY: The Byzantine World △
TB/1057

ROBERT LATOUCHE: The Birth of Western Economy: *Economic Aspects of the Dark Ages.* ○ △ *Intro. by Philip Grierson*
TB/1290

FERDINAND LOT: The End of the Ancient World and the Beginnings of the Middle Ages. *Introduction by Glanville Downey*
TB/1044

ACHILLE LUCHAIRE: Social France at the Time of Philip Augustus. *New Intro. by John W. Baldwin*
TB/1314

MARSILIUS OF PADUA: The Defender of the Peace. *Trans. with Intro. by Alan Gewirth*
TB/1310

G. MOLLAT: The Popes at Avignon: 1305-1378 △ TB/308

CHARLES PETIT-DUTAILLIS: The Feudal Monarchy in France and England: *From the Tenth to the Thirteenth Century* ○ △
TB/1165

HENRI PIRENNE: Early Democracies in the Low Countries: *Urban Society and Political Conflict in the Middle Ages and the Renaissance. Introduction by John H. Mundy*
TB/1110

STEVEN RUNCIMAN: A History of the Crusades. △
Volume I: *The First Crusade and the Foundation of the Kingdom of Jerusalem. Illus.*
TB/1143
Volume II: *The Kingdom of Jerusalem and the Frankish East, 1100-1187. Illus.*
TB/1243
Volume III: *The Kingdom of Acre and the Later Crusades*
TB/1298

SULPICIUS SEVERUS et al.: The Western Fathers: *Being the Lives of Martin of Tours, Ambrose, Augustine of Hippo, Honoratus of Arles and Germanus of Auxerre.* △ *Edited and trans. by F. O. Hoare* TB/309

J. M. WALLACE-HADRILL: The Barbarian West: *The Early Middle Ages, A.D. 400-1000* △
TB/1061

History: Renaissance & Reformation

JACOB BURCKHARDT: The Civilization of the Renaissance in Italy. △ *Intro. by Benjamin Nelson & Charles Trinkaus. Illus.* Vol. I TB/40; Vol. II TB/41

JOHN CALVIN & JACOPO SADOLETO: A Reformation Debate. *Edited by John C. Olin*
TB/1239

ERNST CASSIRER: The Individual and the Cosmos in Renaissance Philosophy. △ *Translated with an Introduction by Mario Domandi*
TB/1097

FEDERICO CHABOD: Machiavelli and the Renaissance △
TB/1193

EDWARD P. CHEYNEY: The Dawn of a New Era, 1250-1453. * *Illus.*
TB/3002

G. CONSTANT: The Reformation in England: *The English Schism, Henry VIII, 1509-1547* △
TB/314

R. TREVOR DAVIES: The Golden Century of Spain, 1501-1621 ○ △
TB/1194

G. R. ELTON: Reformation Europe, 1517-1559 ** ○ △
TB/1270

DESIDERIUS ERASMUS: Christian Humanism and the Reformation: *Selected Writings. Edited and translated by John C. Olin*
TB/1166

WALLACE K. FERGUSON et al.: Facets of the Renaissance
TB/1098

WALLACE K. FERGUSON et al.: The Renaissance: *Six Essays. Illus.*
TB/1084

JOHN NEVILLE FIGGIS: The Divine Right of Kings. *Introduction by G. R. Elton*
TB/1191

JOHN NEVILLE FIGGIS: Political Thought from Gerson to Grotius: 1414-1625: *Seven Studies. Introduction by Garrett Mattingly*
TB/1032

MYRON P. GILMORE: The World of Humanism, 1453-1517. * *Illus.*
TB/3003

FRANCESCO GUICCIARDINI: Maxims and Reflections of a Renaissance Statesman *(Ricordi). Trans. by Mario Domandi. Intro. by Nicolai Rubinstein*
TB/1160

J. H. HEXTER: More's Utopia: *The Biography of an Idea. New Epilogue by the Author*
TB/1195

HAJO HOLBORN: Ulrich von Hutten and the German Reformation
TB/1238

JOHAN HUIZINGA: Erasmus and the Age of Reformation. △ *Illus.*
TB/19

JOEL HURSTFIELD: The Elizabethan Nation △ TB/1312

JOEL HURSTFIELD, Ed.: The Reformation Crisis △ TB/1267

ULRICH VON HUTTEN et al.: On the Eve of the Reformation: *"Letters of Obscure Men." Introduction by Hajo Holborn*
TB/1124

PAUL O. KRISTELLER: Renaissance Thought: *The Classic, Scholastic, and Humanist Strains*
TB/1048

PAUL O. KRISTELLER: Renaissance Thought II: *Papers on Humanism and the Arts*
TB/1163

NICCOLÒ MACHIAVELLI: History of Florence and of the Affairs of Italy: *from the earliest times to the death of Lorenzo the Magnificent.* △ *Introduction by Felix Gilbert*
TB/1027

ALFRED VON MARTIN: Sociology of the Renaissance. *Introduction by Wallace K. Ferguson*
TB/1099

GARRETT MATTINGLY et al.: Renaissance Profiles. △ *Edited by J. H. Plumb*
TB/1162

MILLARD MEISS: Painting in Florence and Siena after the Black Death: *The Arts, Religion and Society in the Mid-Fourteenth Century.* △ *169 illus.*
TB/1148

J. E. NEALE: The Age of Catherine de Medici ○ △ TB/1085

ERWIN PANOFSKY: Studies in Iconology: *Humanistic Themes in the Art of the Renaissance.* △ *180 illustrations*
TB/1077

J. H. PARRY: The Establishment of the European Hegemony: 1415-1715: *Trade and Exploration in the Age of the Renaissance* △
TB/1045

BUONACCORSO PITTI & GREGORIO DATI: Two Memoirs of Renaissance Florence: *The Diaries of Buonaccorso Pitti and Gregorio Dati. Ed. with an Intro. by Gene Brucker. Trans. by Julia Martines*
TB/1333

J. H. PLUMB: The Italian Renaissance: *A Concise Survey of Its History and Culture* △
TB/1161

A. F. POLLARD: Henry VIII. ○ △ *Introduction by A. G. Dickens*
TB/1249

A. F. POLLARD: Wolsey. ○ △ *Introduction by A. G. Dickens*
TB/1248

CECIL ROTH: The Jews in the Renaissance. *Illus.* TB/834

A. L. ROWSE: The Expansion of Elizabethan England. ○ △ *Illus.*
TB/1220

GORDON RUPP: Luther's Progress to the Diet of Worms ○ △
TB/120

FERDINAND SCHEVILL: The Medici. *Illus.* TB/1010

FERDINAND SCHEVILL: Medieval and Renaissance Florence. *Illus.* Volume I: *Medieval Florence* TB/1090
Volume II: *The Coming of Humanism and the Age of the Medici*
TB/1091

R. H. TAWNEY: The Agrarian Problem in the Sixteenth Century. *New Intro. by Lawrence Stone* TB/1315

G. M. TREVELYAN: England in the Age of Wycliffe, 1368-1520 ○ △
TB/1112

VESPASIANO: Renaissance Princes, Popes, and Prelates: *The Vespasiano Memoirs: Lives of Illustrious Men of the XVth Century. Intro. by Myron P. Gilmore* TB/1111

History: Modern European

FREDERICK B. ARTZ: Reaction and Revolution, 1815-1832. * *Illus.* TB/3034

MAX BELOFF: The Age of Absolutism, 1660-1815 △ TB/1062

ROBERT C. BINKLEY: Realism and Nationalism, 1852-1871. * *Illus.* TB/3038

EUGENE C. BLACK, Ed.: European Political History, 1815-1870: *Aspects of Liberalism* TB/1331

ASA BRIGGS: The Making of Modern England, 1784-1867: *The Age of Improvement* ○ △ TB/1203

CRANE BRINTON: A Decade of Revolution, 1789-1799. * *Illus.* TB/3018

D. W. BROGAN: The Development of Modern France. ○ △ Volume I: *From the Fall of the Empire to the Dreyfus Affair* TB/1184
Volume II: *The Shadow of War, World War I, Between the Two Wars. New Introduction by the Author* TB/1185

J. BRONOWSKI & BRUCE MAZLISH: The Western Intellectual Tradition: *From Leonardo to Hegel* △ TB/3001

GEOFFREY BRUUN: Europe and the French Imperium, 1799-1814. * *Illus.* TB/3033

ALAN BULLOCK: Hitler, A Study in Tyranny. ○ △ *Illus.* TB/1123

E. H. CARR: German-Soviet Relations Between the Two World Wars, 1919-1939 TB/1278

E. H. CARR: International Relations Between the Two World Wars, 1919-1939 ○ △ TB/1279

E. H. CARR: The Twenty Years' Crisis, 1919-1939: *An Introduction to the Study of International Relations* ○ △ TB/1122

GORDON A. CRAIG: From Bismarck to Adenauer: *Aspects of German Statecraft. Revised Edition* TB/1171

DENIS DIDEROT: The Encyclopedia: *Selections. Ed. and trans. by Stephen Gendzier* TB/1299

WALTER L. DORN: Competition for Empire, 1740-1763. * *Illus.* TB/3032

FRANKLIN L. FORD: Robe and Sword: *The Regrouping of the French Aristocracy after Louis XIV* TB/1217

CARL J. FRIEDRICH: The Age of the Baroque, 1610-1660. * *Illus.* TB/3004

RENÉ FUELOEP-MILLER: The Mind and Face of Bolshevism: *An Examination of Cultural Life in Soviet Russia. New Epilogue by the Author* TB/1188

M. DOROTHY GEORGE: London Life in the Eighteenth Century △ TB/1182

LEO GERSHOY: From Despotism to Revolution, 1763-1789. * *Illus.* TB/3017

C. C. GILLISPIE: Genesis and Geology: *The Decades before Darwin* § TB/51

ALBERT GOODWIN, Ed.: The European Nobility in the Eighteenth Century △ TB/1313

ALBERT GOODWIN: The French Revolution △ TB/1064

ALBERT GUÉRARD: France in the Classical Age: *The Life and Death of an Ideal* △ TB/1183

CARLTON J. H. HAYES: A Generation of Materialism, 1871-1900. * *Illus.* TB/3039

J. H. HEXTER: Reappraisals in History: *New Views on History and Society in Early Modern Europe* △ TB/1100

STANLEY HOFFMANN et al.: In Search of France: *The Economy, Society and Political System in the Twentieth Century* TB/1219

A. R. HUMPHREYS: The Augustan World: *Society, Thought, & Letters in 18th Century England* ○ △ TB/1105

DAN N. JACOBS, Ed.: The New Communist Manifesto and Related Documents. *Third edition, revised* TB/1078

LIONEL KOCHAN: The Struggle for Germany: 1914-45 TB/1304

HANS KOHN: The Mind of Germany: *The Education of a Nation* △ TB/1204

HANS KOHN, Ed.: The Mind of Modern Russia: *Historical and Political Thought of Russia's Great Age* TB/1065

WALTER LAQUEUR & GEORGE L. MOSSE, Eds.: Education and Social Structure in the 20th Century. ○ △ *Vol. 6 of the Journal of Contemporary History* TB/1339

WALTER LAQUEUR & GEORGE L. MOSSE, Eds.: International Fascism, 1920-1945. ○ △ *Volume 1 of Journal of Contemporary History* TB/1276

WALTER LAQUEUR & GEORGE L. MOSSE, Eds.: The Left-Wing Intellectuals between the Wars 1919-1939. ○ △ *Volume 2 of Journal of Contemporary History* TB/1286

WALTER LAQUEUR & GEORGE L. MOSSE, Eds.: Literature and Politics in the 20th Century. ○ △ *Vol. 5 of the Journal of Contemporary History* TB/1328

WALTER LAQUEUR & GEORGE L. MOSSE, Eds.: The New History: *Trends in Historical Research and Writing since World War II.* ○ △ *Vol. 4 of the Journal of Contemporary History* TB/1327

WALTER LAQUEUR & GEORGE L. MOSSE, Eds.: 1914: *The Coming of the First World War.* ○ △ *Volume 3 of Journal of Contemporary History* TB/1306

FRANK E. MANUEL: The Prophets of Paris: *Turgot, Condorcet, Saint-Simon, Fourier, and Comte* TB/1218

KINGSLEY MARTIN: French Liberal Thought in the Eighteenth Century: *A Study of Political Ideas from Bayle to Condorcet* TB/1114

ROBERT K. MERTON: Science, Technology and Society in Seventeenth Century England ¶ *New Intro. by the Author* TB/1324

L. B. NAMIER: Facing East: *Essays on Germany, the Balkans, and Russia in the 20th Century* △ TB/1280

L. B. NAMIER: Personalities and Powers: *Selected Essays* △ TB/1186

L. B. NAMIER: Vanished Supremacies: *Essays on European History, 1812-1918* ○ TB/1088

NAPOLEON III: Napoleonic Ideas: *Des Idées Napoléoniennes, par le Prince Napoléon-Louis Bonaparte. Ed. by Brison D. Gooch* TB/1336

FRANZ NEUMANN: Behemoth: *The Structure and Practice of National Socialism, 1933-1944* TB/1289

FREDERICK L. NUSSBAUM: The Triumph of Science and Reason, 1660-1685. * *Illus.* TB/3009

DAVID OGG: Europe of the Ancien Régime, 1715-1783 ** ○ △ TB/1271

JOHN PLAMENATZ: German Marxism and Russian Communism. ○ △ *New Preface by the Author* TB/1189

RAYMOND W. POSTGATE, Ed.: Revolution from 1789 to 1906: *Selected Documents* TB/1063

PENFIELD ROBERTS: The Quest for Security, 1715-1740. * *Illus.* TB/3016

PRISCILLA ROBERTSON: Revolutions of 1848: *A Social History* TB/1025

GEORGE RUDÉ: Revolutionary Europe, 1783-1815 ** ○ △ TB/1272

LOUIS, DUC DE SAINT-SIMON: Versailles, The Court, and Louis XIV. ○ △ *Introductory Note by Peter Gay* TB/1250

HUGH SETON-WATSON: Eastern Europe Between the Wars, 1918-1941 TB/1330

ALBERT SOREL: Europe Under the Old Regime. *Translated by Francis H. Herrick* TB/1121

N. N. SUKHANOV: The Russian Revolution, 1917: *Eyewitness Account.* △ *Edited by Joel Carmichael* Vol. I TB/1066; Vol. II TB/1067

A. J. P. TAYLOR: From Napoleon to Lenin: *Historical Essays* ○ △ TB/1268

A. J. P. TAYLOR: The Habsburg Monarchy, 1809-1918: *A History of the Austrian Empire and Austria-Hungary* ○ △ TB/1187

G. M. TREVELYAN: British History in the Nineteenth Century and After: 1782-1919. ○ △ *Second Edition* TB/1251

H. R. TREVOR-ROPER: Historical Essays ○ △   TB/1269
ELIZABETH WISKEMANN: Europe of the Dictators, 1919-1945 ** ○ △   TB/1273
JOHN B. WOLF: The Emergence of the Great Powers, 1685-1715. * Illus.   TB/3010
JOHN B. WOLF: France: 1814-1919: The Rise of a Liberal-Democratic Society   TB/3019

Intellectual History & History of Ideas

HERSCHEL BAKER: The Image of Man: A Study of the Idea of Human Dignity in Classical Antiquity, the Middle Ages, and the Renaissance   TB/1047
R. R. BOLGAR: The Classical Heritage and Its Beneficiaries: From the Carolingian Age to the End of the Renaissance △   TB/1125
RANDOLPH S. BOURNE: War and the Intellectuals: Collected Essays, 1915-1919. △ ‡ Edited by Carl Resek   TB/3043
J. BRONOWSKI & BRUCE MAZLISH: The Western Intellectual Tradition: From Leonardo to Hegel △   TB/3001
ERNST CASSIRER: The Individual and the Cosmos in Renaissance Philosophy. △ Translated with an Introduction by Mario Domandi   TB/1097
NORMAN COHN: The Pursuit of the Millennium: Revolutionary Messianism in Medieval and Reformation Europe △   TB/1037
C. C. GILLISPIE: Genesis and Geology: The Decades before Darwin §   TB/51
G. RACHEL LEVY: Religious Conceptions of the Stone Age and Their Influence upon European Thought. △ Illus. Introduction by Henri Frankfort   TB/106
ARTHUR O. LOVEJOY: The Great Chain of Being: A Study of the History of an Idea   TB/1009
FRANK E. MANUEL: The Prophets of Paris: Turgot, Condorcet, Saint-Simon, Fourier, and Comte △   TB/1218
PERRY MILLER & T. H. JOHNSON, Editors: The Puritans: A Sourcebook of Their Writings
   Vol. I TB/1093; Vol. II TB/1094
RALPH BARTON PERRY: The Thought and Character of William James: Briefer Version   TB/1156
GEORG SIMMEL et al.: Essays on Sociology, Philosophy, and Aesthetics. ¶ Edited by Kurt H. Wolff   TB/1234
BRUNO SNELL: The Discovery of the Mind: The Greek Origins of European Thought △   TB/1018
PAGET TOYNBEE: Dante Alighieri: His Life and Works. Edited with Intro. by Charles S. Singleton △   TB/1206
W. WARREN WAGAR, Ed.: European Intellectual History since Darwin and Marx   TB/1297
PHILIP P. WIENER: Evolution and the Founders of Pragmatism. △ Foreword by John Dewey   TB/1212
BASIL WILLEY: Nineteenth Century Studies: Coleridge to Matthew Arnold ○ △   TB/1261
BASIL WILLEY: More Nineteenth Century Studies: A Group of Honest Doubters ○ △   TB/1262

Law

EDWARD S. CORWIN: American Constitutional History: Essays edited by Alpheus T. Mason & Gerald Garvey   TB/1136
ROBERT H. JACKSON: The Supreme Court in the American System of Government   TB/1106
LEONARD W. LEVY, Ed.: American Constitutional Law: Historical Essays   TB/1285
LEONARD W. LEVY: Freedom of Speech and Press in Early American History: Legacy of Suppression   TB/1109
LEONARD W. LEVY, Ed.: Judicial Review and the Supreme Court   TB/1296
LEONARD W. LEVY: The Law of the Commonwealth and Chief Justice Shaw   TB/1309
RICHARD B. MORRIS: Fair Trial: Fourteen Who Stood Accused, from Anne Hutchinson to Alger Hiss. New Preface by the Author.   TB/1335

Literature, Poetry, The Novel & Criticism

JAMES BAIRD: Ishmael: The Art of Melville in the Contexts of International Primitivism   TB/1023
JACQUES BARZUN: The House of Intellect △   TB/1051
W. J. BATE: From Classic to Romantic: Premises of Taste in Eighteenth Century England   TB/1036
RACHEL BESPALOFF: On the Iliad   TB/2006
JAMES BOSWELL: The Life of Dr. Johnson & The Journal of a Tour to the Hebrides with Samuel Johnson LL.D.: Selections. ○ △ Edited by F. V. Morley. Illus. by Ernest Shepard   TB/1254
ERNST R. CURTIUS: European Literature and the Latin Middle Ages △   TB/2015
ADOLF ERMAN, Ed.: The Ancient Egyptians: A Sourcebook of Their Writings. New Material and Introduction by William Kelly Simpson   TB/1233
ALFRED HARBAGE: As They Liked It: A Study of Shakespeare's Moral Artistry   TB/1035
STANLEY R. HOPPER, Ed : Spiritual Problems in Contemporary Literature §   TB/21
A. R. HUMPHREYS: The Augustan World: Society, Thought and Letters in 18th Century England ○ △   TB/1105
ARNOLD KETTLE: An Introduction to the English Novel. △
   Volume I: Defoe to George Eliot   TB/1011
   Volume II: Henry James to the Present   TB/1012
RICHMOND LATTIMORE: The Poetry of Greek Tragedy △   TB/1257
J. B. LEISHMAN: The Monarch of Wit: An Analytical and Comparative Study of the Poetry of John Donne ○ △   TB/1258
J. B. LEISHMAN: Themes and Variations in Shakespeare's Sonnets ○ △   TB/1259
ROGER SHERMAN LOOMIS: The Development of Arthurian Romance △   TB/1167
JOHN STUART MILL: On Bentham and Coleridge. △ Introduction by F. R. Leavis   TB/1070
KENNETH B. MURDOCK: Literature and Theology in Colonial New England   TB/99
SAMUEL PEPYS: The Diary of Samuel Pepys. ○ Edited by O. F. Morshead. Illus. by Ernest Shepard   TB/1007
ST.-JOHN PERSE: Seamarks   TB/2002
V. DE S. PINTO: Crisis in English Poetry, 1880-1940 ○   TB/1260
ROBERT PREYER, Ed.: Victorian Literature   TB/1302
GEORGE SANTAYANA: Interpretations of Poetry and Religion §   TB/9
C. K. STEAD: The New Poetic: Yeats to Eliot △   TB/1263
HEINRICH STRAUMANN: American Literature in the Twentieth Century. △ Third Edition, Revised   TB/1168
PAGET TOYNBEE: Dante Alighieri: His Life and Works. Edited with Intro. by Charles S. Singleton   TB/1206
DOROTHY VAN GHENT: The English Novel: Form and Function   TB/1050
BASIL WILLEY: Nineteenth Century Studies: Coleridge to Matthew Arnold △   TB/1261
BASIL WILLEY: More Nineteenth Century Studies: A Group of Honest Doubters ○ △   TB/1262
RAYMOND WILLIAMS: Culture and Society, 1780-1950 ○ △   TB/1252
RAYMOND WILLIAMS: The Long Revolution. ○ △ Revised Edition   TB/1253
MORTON DAUWEN ZABEL, Editor: Literary Opinion in America   Vol. I TB/3013; Vol. II TB/3014

Myth, Symbol & Folklore

MIRCEA ELIADE: Cosmos and History: The Myth of the Eternal Return § △   TB/2050
MIRCEA ELIADE: Rites and Symbols of Initiation: The Mysteries of Birth and Rebirth § △   TB/1236
THEODOR H. GASTER: Thespis: Ritual, Myth and Drama in the Ancient Near East △   TB/1281

C. G. JUNG & C. KERÉNYI: Essays on a Science of Mythology: *The Myths of the Divine Child and the Divine Maiden* TB/2014

DORA & ERWIN PANOFSKY: Pandora's Box: *The Changing Aspects of a Mythical Symbol.* △ *Revised edition. Illus.* TB/2021

ERWIN PANOFSKY: Studies in Iconology: *Humanistic Themes in the Art of the Renaissance.* △ *180 illustrations* TB/1077

JEAN SEZNEC: The Survival of the Pagan Gods: *The Mythological Tradition and its Place in Renaissance Humanism and Art.* △ *108 illustrations* TB/2004

HELLMUT WILHELM: Change: *Eight Lectures on the I Ching* △ TB/2019

HEINRICH ZIMMER: Myths and Symbols in Indian Art and Civilization. △ *70 illustrations* TB/2005

Philosophy

G. E. M. ANSCOMBE: An Introduction to Wittgenstein's Tractatus. ○ △ *Second Edition, Revised* TB/1210

HENRI BERGSON: Time and Free Will: *An Essay on the Immediate Data of Consciousness* ○ △ TB/1021

H. J. BLACKHAM: Six Existentialist Thinkers: *Kierkegaard, Nietzsche, Jaspers, Marcel, Heidegger, Sartre* ○ △ TB/1002

CRANE BRINTON: Nietzsche. *New Preface, Bibliography and Epilogue by the Author* TB/1197

MARTIN BUBER: The Knowledge of Man. △ *Ed. with an Intro. by Maurice Friedman. Trans. by Maurice Friedman and Ronald Gregor Smith* TB/135

ERNST CASSIRER: The Individual and the Cosmos in Renaissance Philosophy. △ *Translated with an Introduction by Mario Domandi* TB/1097

ERNST CASSIRER: Rousseau, Kant and Goethe. *Introduction by Peter Gay* TB/1092

FREDERICK COPLESTON: Medieval Philosophy ○ △ TB/376

F. M. CORNFORD: Principium Sapientiae: *A Study of the Origins of Greek Philosophical Thought. Edited by W. K. C. Guthrie* TB/1213

F. M. CORNFORD: From Religion to Philosophy: *A Study in the Origins of Western Speculation* § TB/20

WILFRID DESAN: The Tragic Finale: *An Essay on the Philosophy of Jean-Paul Sartre* TB/1030

A. P. D'ENTRÈVES: Natural Law: *An Historical Survey* △ TB/1223

MARVIN FARBER: The Aims of Phenomenology: *The Motives, Methods, and Impact of Husserl's Thought* TB/1291

MARVIN FARBER: Phenomenology and Existence: *Towards a Philosophy within Nature* TB/1295

HERBERT FINGARETTE: The Self in Transformation: *Psychoanalysis, Philosophy and the Life of the Spirit* ¶ TB/1177

PAUL FRIEDLÄNDER: Plato: *An Introduction* △ TB/2017

J. GLENN GRAY: The Warriors: *Reflections on Men in Battle. Intro. by Hannah Arendt* TB/1294

WILLIAM CHASE GREENE: Moira: *Fate, Good, and Evil in Greek Thought* TB/1104

W. K. C. GUTHRIE: The Greek Philosophers: *From Thales to Aristotle* ○ △ TB/1008

G. W. F. HEGEL: The Phenomenology of Mind ○ △ TB/1303

F. H. HEINEMANN: Existentialism and the Modern Predicament △ TB/28

ISAAC HUSIK: A History of Medieval Jewish Philosophy JP/3

EDMUND HUSSERL: Phenomenology and the Crisis of Philosophy. *Translated with an Introduction by Quentin Lauer* TB/1170

IMMANUEL KANT: The Doctrine of Virtue, *being Part II of the Metaphysic of Morals. Trans. with Notes & Intro. by Mary J. Gregor. Foreword by H. J. Paton* TB/110

IMMANUEL KANT: Groundwork of the Metaphysic of Morals. *Trans. & analyzed by H. J. Paton* TB/1159

IMMANUEL KANT: Lectures on Ethics. § △ *Introduction by Lewis W. Beck* TB/105

IMMANUEL KANT: Religion Within the Limits of Reason Alone. § *Intro. by T. M. Greene & J. Silber* TB/67

QUENTIN LAUER: Phenomenology: *Its Genesis and Prospect* TB/1169

MAURICE MANDELBAUM: The Problem of Historical Knowledge: *An Answer to Relativism. New Preface by the Author* TB/1338

GABRIEL MARCEL: Being and Having: *An Existential Diary.* △ *Intro. by James Collins* TB/310

GEORGE A. MORGAN: What Nietzsche Means TB/1198

H. J. PATON: The Categorical Imperative: *A Study in Kant's Moral Philosophy* △ TB/1325

PHILO, SAADYA GAON, & JEHUDA HALEVI: Three Jewish Philosophers. *Ed. by Hans Lewy, Alexander Altmann, & Isaak Heinemann* TB/813

MICHAEL POLANYI: Personal Knowledge: *Towards a Post-Critical Philosophy* △ TB/1158

WILLARD VAN ORMAN QUINE: Elementary Logic: *Revised Edition* TB/577

WILLARD VAN ORMAN QUINE: From a Logical Point of View: *Logico-Philosophical Essays* TB/566

BERTRAND RUSSELL et al.: The Philosophy of Bertrand Russell. *Edited by Paul Arthur Schilpp*
Vol. I TB/1095; Vol. II TB/1096

L. S. STEBBING: A Modern Introduction to Logic △ TB/538

ALFRED NORTH WHITEHEAD: Process and Reality: *An Essay in Cosmology* △ TB/1033

PHILIP P. WIENER: Evolution and the Founders of Pragmatism. *Foreword by John Dewey* TB/1212

WILHELM WINDELBAND: A History of Philosophy
Vol. I: *Greek, Roman, Medieval* TB/38
Vol. II: *Renaissance, Enlightenment, Modern* TB/39

LUDWIG WITTGENSTEIN: The Blue and Brown Books ○ TB/1211

Political Science & Government

JEREMY BENTHAM: The Handbook of Political Fallacies: *Introduction by Crane Brinton* TB/1069

C. E. BLACK: The Dynamics of Modernization: *A Study in Comparative History* TB/1321

KENNETH E. BOULDING: Conflict and Defense: *A General Theory* TB/3024

CRANE BRINTON: English Political Thought in the Nineteenth Century TB/1071

ROBERT CONQUEST: Power and Policy in the USSR: *The Study of Soviet Dynastics* △ TB/1307

EDWARD S. CORWIN: American Constitutional History: *Essays edited by Alpheus T. Mason and Gerald Garvey* TB/1136

ROBERT DAHL & CHARLES E. LINDBLOM: Politics, Economics, and Welfare: *Planning and Politico-Economic Systems Resolved into Basic Social Processes* TB/3037

JOHN NEVILLE FIGGIS: The Divine Right of Kings. *Introduction by G. R. Elton* TB/1191

JOHN NEVILLE FIGGIS: Political Thought from Gerson to Grotius: 1414-1625: *Seven Studies. Introduction by Garrett Mattingly* TB/1032

F. L. GANSHOF: Feudalism △ TB/1058

G. P. GOOCH: English Democratic Ideas in the Seventeenth Century TB/1006

J. H. HEXTER: More's Utopia: *The Biography of an Idea. New Epilogue by the Author* TB/1195

SIDNEY HOOK: Reason, Social Myths and Democracy △ TB/1237

ROBERT H. JACKSON: The Supreme Court in the American System of Government △ TB/1106

DAN N. JACOBS, Ed.: The New Communist Manifesto and *Related Documents. Third Edition, Revised* TB/1078

DAN N. JACOBS & HANS BAERWALD, Eds.: Chinese Communism: *Selected Documents* TB/3031

7

HANS KOHN: Political Ideologies of the 20th Century
TB/1277
ROY C. MACRIDIS, Ed.: Political Parties: *Contemporary Trends and Ideas* TB/1322
ROBERT GREEN MC CLOSKEY: American Conservatism in the Age of Enterprise, 1865-1910 TB/1137
KINGSLEY MARTIN: French Liberal Thought in the Eighteenth Century: *Political Ideas from Bayle to Condorcet* △ TB/1114
ROBERTO MICHELS: First Lectures in Political Sociology. *Edited by Alfred de Grazia* ¶ ° TB/1224
JOHN STUART MILL: On Bentham and Coleridge. △ *Introduction by F. R. Leavis* TB/1070
BARRINGTON MOORE, JR.: Political Power and Social Theory: *Seven Studies* ¶ TB/1221
BARRINGTON MOORE, JR.: Soviet Politics—The Dilemma of Power: *The Role of Ideas in Social Change* ¶
TB/1222
BARRINGTON MOORE, JR.: Terror and Progress—USSR: *Some Sources of Change and Stability in the Soviet Dictatorship* ¶ TB/1266
JOHN B. MORRALL: Political Thought in Medieval Times △ TB/1076
JOHN PLAMENATZ: German Marxism and Russian Communism. ° △ *New Preface by the Author* TB/1189
KARL R. POPPER: The Open Society and Its Enemies △
Vol. I: *The Spell of Plato* TB/1101
Vol. II: *The High Tide of Prophecy: Hegel, Marx and the Aftermath* TB/1102
JOHN P. ROCHE, Ed.: American Political Thought: *From Jefferson to Progressivism* TB/1332
HENRI DE SAINT-SIMON: Social Organization, The Science of Man, and Other Writings. *Edited and Translated by Felix Markham* TB/1152
CHARLES I. SCHOTTLAND, Ed.: The Welfare State TB/1323
JOSEPH A. SCHUMPETER: Capitalism, Socialism and Democracy △ TB/3008
BENJAMIN I. SCHWARTZ: Chinese Communism and the Rise of Mao TB/1308
CHARLES H. SHINN: Mining Camps: *A Study in American Frontier Government.* ‡ *Edited by Rodman W. Paul* TB/3062
PETER WOLL, Ed.: Public Administration and Policy: *Selected Essays* TB/1284

Psychology

ALFRED ADLER: The Individual Psychology of Alfred Adler. △ *Edited by Heinz L. and Rowena R. Ansbacher* TB/1154
ALFRED ADLER: Problems of Neurosis. *Introduction by Heinz L. Ansbacher* TB/1145
ARTHUR BURTON & ROBERT E. HARRIS, Eds.: Clinical Studies of Personality
Vol. I TB/3075; Vol. II TB/3076
HADLEY CANTRIL: The Invasion from Mars: *A Study in the Psychology of Panic* ¶ TB/1282
HERBERT FINGARETTE: The Self in Transformation: *Psychoanalysis, Philosophy and the Life of the Spirit* ¶
TB/1177
SIGMUND FREUD: On Creativity and the Unconscious: *Papers on the Psychology of Art, Literature, Love, Religion.* § *Intro. by Benjamin Nelson* TB/45
C. JUDSON HERRICK: The Evolution of Human Nature
TB/545
WILLIAM JAMES: Psychology: *The Briefer Course.* *Edited with an Intro. by Gordon Allport* TB/1034
C. G. JUNG: Psychological Reflections △ TB/2001
C. G. JUNG: Symbols of Transformation: *An Analysis of the Prelude to a Case of Schizophrenia.* △ *Illus.*
Vol. I TB/2009; Vol. II TB/2010
C. G. JUNG & C. KERÉNYI: Essays on a Science of Mythology: *The Myths of the Divine Child and the Divine Maiden* TB/2014

KARL MENNINGER: Theory of Psychoanalytic Technique
TB/1144
ERICH NEUMANN: Amor and Psyche: *The Psychic Development of the Feminine* △ TB/2012
ERICH NEUMANN: The Archetypal World of Henry Moore. △ *107 illus.* TB/2020
ERICH NEUMANN: The Origins and History of Consciousness △ Vol. I *Illus.* TB/2007; Vol. II TB/2008
RALPH BARTON PERRY: The Thought and Character of William James: *Briefer Version* TB/1156
JOHN H. SCHAAR: Escape from Authority: *The Perspectives of Erich Fromm* TB/1155
MUZAFER SHERIF: The Psychology of Social Norms
TB/3072

Sociology

JACQUES BARZUN: Race: *A Study in Superstition. Revised Edition* TB/1172
BERNARD BERELSON, Ed.: The Behavioral Sciences Today TB/1127
ABRAHAM CAHAN: The Rise of David Levinsky: *A documentary novel of social mobility in early twentieth century America. Intro. by John Higham* TB/1028
KENNETH B. CLARK: Dark Ghetto: *Dilemmas of Social Power. Foreword by Gunnar Myrdal* TB/1317
LEWIS A. COSER, Ed.: Political Sociology TB/1293
ALLISON DAVIS & JOHN DOLLARD: Children of Bondage: *The Personality Development of Negro Youth in the Urban South* ¶ TB/3049
ST. CLAIR DRAKE & HORACE R. CAYTON: Black Metropolis: *A Study of Negro Life in a Northern City.* △ *Revised and Enlarged. Intro. by Everett C. Hughes*
Vol. I TB/1086; Vol. II TB/1087
EMILE DURKHEIM et al.: Essays on Sociology and Philosophy: *With Analyses of Durkheim's Life and Work.* ¶ *Edited by Kurt H. Wolff* TB/1151
LEON FESTINGER, HENRY W. RIECKEN & STANLEY SCHACHTER: When Prophecy Fails: *A Social and Psychological Account of a Modern Group that Predicted the Destruction of the World* ¶ TB/1132
ALVIN W. GOULDNER: Wildcat Strike: *A Study in Worker-Management Relationships* ¶ TB/1176
CÉSAR GRAÑA: Modernity and Its Discontents: *French Society and the French Man of Letters in the Nineteenth Century* ¶ TB/1318
FRANCIS J. GRUND: Aristocracy in America: *Social Class in the Formative Years of the New Nation* △ TB/1001
KURT LEWIN: Field Theory in Social Science: *Selected Theoretical Papers.* ¶ △ *Edited with a Foreword by Dorwin Cartwright* TB/1135
R. M. MAC IVER: Social Causation TB/1153
ROBERT K. MERTON, LEONARD BROOM, LEONARD S. COTTRELL, JR., Editors: Sociology Today: *Problems and Prospects* ¶ Vol. I TB/1173; Vol. II TB/1174
ROBERTO MICHELS: First Lectures in Political Sociology. *Edited by Alfred de Grazia* ¶ ° TB/1224
BARRINGTON MOORE, JR.: Political Power and Social Theory: *Seven Studies* ¶ TB/1221
BARRINGTON MOORE, JR.: Soviet Politics—The Dilemma of Power: *The Role of Ideas in Social Change* ¶
TB/1222
TALCOTT PARSONS & EDWARD A. SHILS, Editors: Toward a General Theory of Action: *Theoretical Foundations for the Social Sciences* TB/1083
ARNOLD ROSE: The Negro in America: *The Condensed Version of Gunnar Myrdal's An American Dilemma*
TB/3048
GEORGE ROSEN: Madness in Society: *Chapters in the Historical Sociology of Mental Illness.* ¶ *Preface by Benjamin Nelson* TB/1337
KURT SAMUELSSON: Religion and Economic Action: *A Critique of Max Weber's The Protestant Ethic and the Spirit of Capitalism.* ¶ ° *Trans. by E. G. French. Ed. with Intro. by D. C. Coleman* TB/1131

PHILIP SELZNICK: TVA and the Grass Roots: *A Study in the Sociology of Formal Organization*   TB/1230

GEORG SIMMEL et al.: Essays on Sociology, Philosophy, and Aesthetics. ¶ *Edited by Kurt H. Wolff*   TB/1234

HERBERT SIMON: The Shape of Automation: *For Men and Management* △   TB/1245

PITIRIM A. SOROKIN: Contemporary Sociological Theories. *Through the First Quarter of the 20th Century* TB/3046

MAURICE R. STEIN: The Eclipse of Community: *An Interpretation of American Studies*   TB/1128

WILLIAM I. THOMAS: The Unadjusted Girl: *With Cases and Standpoint for Behavior Analysis.* ¶ *New Intro. by Michael Parenti*   TB/1319

EDWARD A. TIRYAKIAN, Ed.: Sociological Theory, Values and Sociocultural Change: *Essays in Honor of Pitirim A. Sorokin* ¶ △ ○   TB/1316

FERDINAND TÖNNIES: Community and Society: *Gemeinschaft und Gesellschaft. Translated and edited by Charles P. Loomis*   TB/1116

W. LLOYD WARNER & Associates: Democracy in Jonesville: *A Study in Quality and Inequality*   TB/1129

W. LLOYD WARNER: Social Class in America: *The Evaluation of Status*   TB/1013

RELIGION

Ancient & Classical

J. H. BREASTED: Development of Religion and Thought in Ancient Egypt. *Intro. by John A. Wilson*   TB/57

HENRI FRANKFORT: Ancient Egyptian Religion: *An Interpretation*   TB/77

G. RACHEL LEVY: Religious Conceptions of the Stone Age and their Influence upon European Thought. △ *Illus. Introduction by Henri Frankfort*   TB/106

MARTIN P. NILSSON: Greek Folk Religion. *Foreword by Arthur Darby Nock*   TB/78

ALEXANDRE PIANKOFF: The Shrines of Tut-Ankh-Amon. △ *Edited by N. Rambova. 117 illus.*   TB/2011

ERWIN ROHDE: Psyche: *The Cult of Souls and Belief in Immortality Among the Greeks.* △ *Intro. by W. K. C. Guthrie*   Vol. I TB/140; Vol. II TB/141

H. J. ROSE: Religion in Greece and Rome △   TB/55

Biblical Thought & Literature

W. F. ALBRIGHT: The Biblical Period from Abraham to Ezra   TB/102

C. K. BARRETT, Ed.: The New Testament Background: *Selected Documents* △   TB/86

C. H. DODD: The Authority of the Bible △   TB/43

M. S. ENSLIN: Christian Beginnings △   TB/5

M. S. ENSLIN: The Literature of the Christian Movement △   TB/6

JOHN GRAY: Archaeology and the Old Testament World. △ *Illus.*   TB/127

JAMES MUILENBURG: The Way of Israel: *Biblical Faith and Ethics* △   TB/133

H. H. ROWLEY: The Growth of the Old Testament △   TB/107

GEORGE ADAM SMITH: The Historical Geography of the Holy Land. ○ △ *Revised and reset*   TB/138

D. WINTON THOMAS, Ed.: Documents from Old Testament Times △   TB/85

WALTHER ZIMMERLI: The Law and the Prophets: *A Study of the Meaning of the Old Testament* △   TB/144

The Judaic Tradition

LEO BAECK: Judaism and Christianity. *Trans. with Intro. by Walter Kaufmann*   TB/823

SALO W. BARON: Modern Nationalism and Religion   TB/818

MARTIN BUBER: Eclipse of God: *Studies in the Relation Between Religion and Philosophy* △   TB/12

MARTIN BUBER: For the Sake of Heaven   TB/801

MARTIN BUBER: Hasidism and Modern Man. △ *Ed. and Trans. by Maurice Friedman*   TB/839

MARTIN BUBER: The Knowledge of Man. △ *Edited with an Introduction by Maurice Friedman. Translated by Maurice Friedman and Ronald Gregor Smith* TB/135

MARTIN BUBER: Moses: *The Revelation and the Covenant* △   TB/837

MARTIN BUBER: The Origin and Meaning of Hasidism △   TB/835

MARTIN BUBER: Pointing the Way. △ *Introduction by Maurice S. Friedman*   TB/103

MARTIN BUBER: The Prophetic Faith   TB/73

MARTIN BUBER: Two Types of Faith: *the interpenetration of Judaism and Christianity* ○ △   TB/75

ERNST LUDWIG EHRLICH: A Concise History of Israel: *From the Earliest Times to the Destruction of the Temple in A.D. 70* ○ △   TB/128

MAURICE S. FRIEDMAN: Martin Buber: *The Life of Dialogue* △   TB/64

GENESIS: The NJV Translation   TB/836

SOLOMON GRAYZEL: A History of the Contemporary Jews   TB/816

WILL HERBERG: Judaism and Modern Man   TB/810

ARTHUR HERTZBERG: The Zionist Idea   TB/817

ABRAHAM J. HESCHEL: God in Search of Man: *A Philosophy of Judaism*   TB/807

ISAAC HUSIK: A History of Medieval Jewish Philosophy   TB/803

JACOB R. MARCUS: The Jew in the Medieval World TB/814

MAX L. MARGOLIS & ALEXANDER MARX: A History of the Jewish People   TB/806

T. J. MEEK: Hebrew Origins   TB/69

JAMES PARKES: The Conflict of the Church and the Synagogue: *The Jews and Early Christianity*   TB/821

PHILO, SAADYA GAON, & JEHUDA HALEVI: Three Jewish Philosophers. *Ed. by Hans Lewey, Alexander Altmann, & Isaak Heinemann*   TB/813

CECIL ROTH: A History of the Marranos   TB/812

CECIL ROTH: The Jews in the Renaissance. *Illus.* TB/834

HERMAN L. STRACK: Introduction to the Talmud and Midrash   TB/808

JOSHUA TRACHTENBERG: The Devil and the Jews: *The Medieval Conception of the Jew and its Relation to Modern Anti-Semitism*   TB/822

Christianity: General

ROLAND H. BAINTON: Christendom: *A Short History of Christianity and its Impact on Western Civilization.* △ *Illus.*   Vol. I TB/131; Vol. II TB/132

Christianity: Origins & Early Development

AUGUSTINE: An Augustine Synthesis. △ *Edited by Erich Przywara*   TB/335

W. D. DAVIES: Paul and Rabbinic Judaism: *Some Rabbinic Elements in Pauline Theology. New Intro. by the Author* △ ○   TB/146

ADOLF DEISSMANN: Paul: *A Study in Social and Religious History*   TB/15

EDWARD GIBBON: The Triumph of Christendom in the Roman Empire (Chaps. XV-XX of "Decline and Fall," J. B. Bury edition). § △ *Illus.*   TB/46

EDGAR J. GOODSPEED: A Life of Jesus   TB/1

ROBERT M. GRANT: Gnosticism and Early Christianity. △ *Revised Edition*   TB/136

ADOLF HARNACK: The Mission and Expansion of Christianity in the First Three Centuries. *Introduction by Jaroslav Pelikan*   TB/92

R. K. HARRISON: The Dead Sea Scrolls : *An Introduction* ○ △   TB/84

EDWIN HATCH: The Influence of Greek Ideas on Christianity. § △ *Introduction and Bibliography by Frederick C. Grant*   TB/18

GERHART B. LADNER: The Idea of Reform: *Its Impact on Christian Thought and Action in the Age of the Fathers* TB/149

ARTHUR DARBY NOCK: Early Gentile Christianity and Its Hellenistic Background TB/111

ARTHUR DARBY NOCK: St. Paul º △ TB/104

ORIGEN: On First Principles. △ *Edited by G. W. Butterworth. Introduction by Henri de Lubac* TB/311

JAMES PARKES: The Conflict of the Church and the Synagogue: *The Jews and Early Christianity* TB/821

SULPICIUS SEVERUS et al.: The Western Fathers: *Being the Lives of Martin of Tours, Ambrose, Augustine of Hippo, Honoratus of Arles and Germanus of Auxerre.* △ *Edited and translated by F. R. Hoare* TB/309

JOHANNES WEISS: Earliest Christianity: *A History of the Period A.D. 30-150. Introduction and Bibliography by Frederick C. Grant* Volume I TB/53
Volume II TB/54

Christianity: The Middle Ages and The Reformation

ANSELM OF CANTERBURY: Truth, Freedom and Evil: *Three Philosophical Dialogues. Ed., trans., and Intro. by Jasper Hopkins & Herbert Richardson* TB/317

JOHN CALVIN & JACOPO SADOLETO: A Reformation Debate. *Edited by John C. Olin* TB/1239

G. CONSTANT: The Reformation in England: *The English Schism, Henry VIII, 1509-1547* △ TB/314

CHRISTOPHER DAWSON, Ed.: Mission to Asia: *Narratives and Letters of the Franciscan Missionaries in Mongolia and China in the 13th and 14th Centuries* △ TB/315

JOHANNES ECKHART: Meister Eckhart: *A Modern Translation by R. B. Blakney* TB/8

DESIDERIUS ERASMUS: Christian Humanism and the Reformation: *Selected Writings. Edited and translated by John C. Olin* TB/1166

ÉTIENNE GILSON: Dante and Philosophy △ TB/1089

WILLIAM HALLER: The Rise of Puritanism △ TB/22

HAJO HOLBORN: Ulrich von Hutten and the German Reformation TB/1238

JOHAN HUIZINGA: Erasmus and the Age of Reformation. △ *Illus.* TB/19

A. C. MC GIFFERT: Protestant Thought Before Kant △ *Preface by Jaroslav Pelikan* TB/93

JOHN T. MC NEILL: Makers of the Christian Tradition: *From Alfred the Great to Schleiermacher* △ TB/121

G. MOLLAT: The Popes at Avignon, 1305-1378 △ TB/308

GORDON RUPP: Luther's Progress to the Diet of Worms º △ TB/120

Christianity: The Protestant Tradition

KARL BARTH: Church Dogmatics: *A Selection* △ TB/95

KARL BARTH: Dogmatics in Outline △ TB/56

KARL BARTH: The Word of God and the Word of Man TB/13

RUDOLF BULTMANN et al: Translating Theology into the Modern Age: *Historical, Systematic and Pastoral Reflections on Theology and the Church in the Contemporary Situation. Volume 2 of Journal for Theology and the Church, edited by Robert W. Funk in association with Gerhard Ebeling* TB/252

WHITNEY R. CROSS: The Burned-Over District: *The Social and Intellectual History of Enthusiastic Religion in Western New York, 1800-1850* △ TB/1242

NELS F. S. FERRÉ: Swedish Contributions to Modern Theology. *New Preface by the Author. Additional chapter by William A. Johnson* TB/147

ERNST KÄSEMANN, et al.: Distinctive Protestant and Catholic Themes Reconsidered. *Volume 3 of Journal for Theology and the Church, edited by Robert W. Funk in association with Gerhard Ebeling* TB/253

SOREN KIERKEGAARD: On Authority and Revelation: *The Book on Adler. Translated by Walter Lowrie. Intro. by Frederick Sontag* TB/139

SOREN KIERKEGAARD: Crisis in the Life of an Actress *and Other Essays on Drama.* △ *Trans. with Intro. by Stephen D. Crites* TB/145

SOREN KIERKEGAARD: Edifying Discourses. *Edited with an Introduction by Paul Holmer* TB/32

SOREN KIERKEGAARD: The Journals of Kierkegaard. º △ *Ed. with Intro. by Alexander Dru* TB/52

SOREN KIERKEGAARD: The Point of View for My Work as an Author: *A Report to History.* § *Preface by Benjamin Nelson* TB/88

SOREN KIERKEGAARD: The Present Age. § △ *Translated and edited by Alexander Dru. Introduction by Walter Kaufmann* TB/94

SOREN KIERKEGAARD: Purity of Heart △ TB/4

SOREN KIERKEGAARD: Repetition: *An Essay in Experimental Psychology.* △ *Translated with Introduction & Notes by Walter Lowrie* TB/117

SOREN KIERKEGAARD: Works of Love: *Some Christian Reflections in the Form of Discourses* △ TB/122

WALTER LOWRIE: Kierkegaard: *A Life* Vol. I TB/89
Vol. II TB/90

JOHN MACQUARRIE: The Scope of Demythologizing: *Bultmann and His Critics* △ TB/134

PERRY MILLER & T. H. JOHNSON, Editors: The Puritans: *A Sourcebook of Their Writings* Vol. I TB/1093
Vol. II TB/1094

WOLFHART PANNENBERG, et al.: History and Hermeneutic. *Volume 4 of Journal for Theology and the Church, edited by Robert W. Funk in association with Gerhard Ebeling* TB/254

JAMES M. ROBINSON et al.: The Bultmann School of Biblical Interpretation: New Directions? *Volume 1 of Journal for Theology and the Church, edited by Robert W. Funk in association with Gerhard Ebeling* TB/251

F. SCHLEIERMACHER: The Christian Faith. △ *Introduction by Richard R. Niebuhr* Vol. I TB/108
Vol. II TB/109

F. SCHLEIERMACHER: On Religion: *Speeches to Its Cultured Despisers. Intro. by Rudolf Otto* TB/36

TIMOTHY L. SMITH: Revivalism and Social Reform: *American Protestantism on the Eve of the Civil War* TB/1229

PAUL TILLICH: Dynamics of Faith △ TB/42

PAUL TILLICH: Morality and Beyond TB/142

EVELYN UNDERHILL: Worship △ TB/10

Christianity: The Roman and Eastern Traditions

DOM CUTHBERT BUTLER: Western Mysticism: *The Teaching of Augustine, Gregory and Bernard on Contemplation and the Contemplative Life* § º △ TB/312

A. ROBERT CAPONIGRI, Ed.: Modern Catholic Thinkers I: *God and Man* △ TB/306

A. ROBERT CAPONIGRI, Ed.: Modern Catholic Thinkers II: *The Church and the Political Order* △ TB/307

THOMAS CORBISHLEY, S.J.: Roman Catholicism △ TB/112

CHRISTOPHER DAWSON: The Historic Reality of Christian Culture TB/305

G. P. FEDOTOV: The Russian Religious Mind: *Kievan Christianity, the 10th to the 13th centuries* TB/370

ÉTIENNE GILSON: The Spirit of Thomism TB/313

GABRIEL MARCEL: Being and Having: *An Existential Diary.* △ *Introduction by James Collins* TB/310

GABRIEL MARCEL: Homo Viator: *Introduction to a Metaphysic of Hope* TB/397

FRANCIS DE SALES: Introduction to the Devout Life. *Trans. by John K. Ryan* TB/316

GUSTAVE WEIGEL, S. J.: Catholic Theology in Dialogue TB/301

10

Oriental Religions: Far Eastern, Near Eastern

TOR ANDRAE: Mohammed: *The Man and His Faith* △
TB/62
EDWARD CONZE: Buddhism: *Its Essence and Develop-ment.* ° △ *Foreword by Arthur Waley* TB/58
EDWARD CONZE et al., Editors: Buddhist Texts Through the Ages △ TB/113
ANANDA COOMARASWAMY: Buddha and the Gospel of Buddhism. △ *Illus.* TB/119
H. G. CREEL: Confucius and the Chinese Way TB/63
FRANKLIN EDGERTON, Trans. & Ed.: The Bhagavad Gita TB/115
SWAMI NIKHILANANDA, Trans. & Ed.: The Upanishads: *A One-Volume Abridgment* △ TB/114
HELLMUT WILHELM: Change: *Eight Lectures on the I Ching* △ TB/2019

Philosophy of Religion

NICOLAS BERDYAEV: The Beginning and the End § △ TB/14
NICOLAS BERDYAEV: Christian Existentialism: *A Berd-yaev Synthesis.* △ *Ed. by Donald A. Lowrie* TB/130
NICOLAS BERDYAEV: The Destiny of Man △ TB/61
RUDOLF BULTMANN: History and Eschatology: *The Pres-ence of Eternity* ° TB/91
RUDOLF BULTMANN AND FIVE CRITICS: Kerygma and Myth: *A Theological Debate* △ TB/80
RUDOLF BULTMANN and KARL KUNDSIN: Form Criticism: *Two Essays on New Testament Research.* △ *Trans-lated by Frederick C. Grant* TB/96
MIRCEA ELIADE: Myths, Dreams, and Mysteries: *The En-counter between Contemporary Faiths and Archaic Realities* § △ ° TB/1320
MIRCEA ELIADE: The Sacred and the Profane TB/81
LUDWIG FEUERBACH: The Essence of Christianity. § *In-troduction by Karl Barth. Foreword by H. Richard Niebuhr* TB/11
ÉTIENNE GILSON: The Spirit of Thomism TB/313
ADOLF HARNACK: What is Christianity? § △ *Introduction by Rudolf Bultmann* TB/17
FRIEDRICH HEGEL: On Christianity: *Early Theological Writings. Ed. by R. Kroner and T. M. Knox* TB/79
KARL HEIM: Christian Faith and Natural Science △ TB/16
IMMANUEL KANT: Religion Within the Limits of Reason Alone. § *Intro. by T. M. Greene & J. Silber* TB/67
K. E. KIRK: The Vision of God: *The Christian Doctrine of the Summum Bonum* § △ TB/137
JOHN MACQUARRIE: An Existentialist Theology: *A Com-parison of Heidegger and Bultmann.* ° △ *Preface by Rudolf Bultmann* TB/125
PAUL RAMSEY, Ed.: Faith and Ethics: *The Theology of H. Richard Niebuhr* TB/129
EUGEN ROSENSTOCK-HUESSY: The Christian Future *or the Modern Mind Outrun. Intro. by Harold Stahmer* TB/143
PIERRE TEILHARD DE CHARDIN: The Divine Milieu ° △ TB/384
PIERRE TEILHARD DE CHARDIN: The Phenomenon of Man ° △ TB/383

Religion, Culture & Society

JOSEPH L. BLAU, Ed.: Cornerstones of Religious Freedom in America: *Selected Basic Documents, Court De-cisions and Public Statements. Revised and Enlarged Edition* TB/118
WILLIAM A. CLEBSCH & CHARLES R. JAEKLE: Pastoral Care in Historical Perspective: *An Essay with Exhibits. New Preface by the Authors* TB/148
C. C. GILLISPIE: Genesis and Geology: *The Decades be-fore Darwin* § TB/51
KYLE HASELDEN: The Racial Problem in Christian Per-spective TB/116

WALTER KAUFMANN, Ed.: Religion from Tolstoy to Camus: *Basic Writings on Religious Truth and Morals. Enlarged Edition* TB/123
KENNETH B. MURDOCK: Literature and Theology in Colonial New England TB/99
H. RICHARD NIEBUHR: Christ and Culture △ TB/3
H. RICHARD NIEBUHR: The Kingdom of God in America TB/49
R. B. PERRY: Puritanism and Democracy TB/1138
PAUL PFUETZE: Self, Society, Existence: *Human Nature and Dialogue in the Thought of George Herbert Mead and Martin Buber* TB/1059
WALTER RAUSCHENBUSCH: Christianity and the Social Crisis. ‡ *Edited by Robert D. Cross* TB/3059
KURT SAMUELSSON: Religion and Economic Action: *A Critique of Max Weber's The Protestant Ethic and the Spirit of Capitalism* ¶ ° △ *Trans. by E. G. French. Ed. with Intro. by D. C. Coleman* TB/1131
TIMOTHY L. SMITH: Revivalism and Social Reform: *Amer-ican Protestantism on the Eve of the Civil War* △ TB/1229

NATURAL SCIENCES AND MATHEMATICS

Biological Sciences

CHARLOTTE AUERBACH: The Science of Genetics Σ △ TB/568
JOHN TYLER BONNER: The Ideas of Biology. Σ △ *Illus.* TB/570
A. J. CAIN: Animal Species and their Evolution. △ *Illus.* TB/519
W. E. LE GROS CLARK: The Antecedents of Man: *An Intro-duction to Evolution of the Primates.* ° △ *Illus.* TB/559
W. H. DOWDESWELL: Animal Ecology. △ *Illus.* TB/543
W. H. DOWDESWELL: The Mechanism of Evolution. △ *Illus.* TB/527
R. W. GERARD: Unresting Cells. *Illus.* TB/541
J. E. MORTON: Molluscs: *An Introduction to Their Form and Functions. Illus.* TB/529
P. M. SHEPPARD: Natural Selection and Heredity. △ *Illus.* TB/528
EDMUND W. SINNOTT: Cell and Psyche: *The Biology of Purpose* TB/546
C. H. WADDINGTON: The Nature of Life: *The Main Prob-lems and Trends in Modern Biology* △ TB/580

Chemistry

J. R. PARTINGTON: A Short History of Chemistry. △ *Illus.* TB/522

Communication Theory

J. R. PIERCE: Symbols, Signals and Noise: *The Nature and Process of Communication* △ TB/574

Geography

R. E. COKER: This Great and Wide Sea: *An Introduction to Oceanography and Marine Biology. Illus.* TB/551
F. K. HARE: The Restless Atmosphere △ TB/560

History of Science

MARIE BOAS: The Scientific Renaissance, 1450-1630 ° △ TB/583
W. DAMPIER, Ed.: Readings in the Literature of Science. *Illus.* TB/512
A. HUNTER DUPREE: Science in the Federal Government: *A History of Policies and Activities to 1940* △ TB/573
ALEXANDRE KOYRÉ: From the Closed World to the Infinite Universe: *Copernicus, Kepler, Galileo, Newton, etc.* △ TB/31

A. G. VAN MELSEN: From Atomos to Atom: *A History of the Concept Atom* TB/517

STEPHEN TOULMIN & JUNE GOODFIELD: The Architecture of Matter: *Physics, Chemistry & Physiology of Matter, Both Animate & Inanimate, As it Evolved Since the Beginning of Science* º △ TB/584

STEPHEN TOULMIN & JUNE GOODFIELD: The Discovery of Time º △ TB/585

Mathematics

E. W. BETH: The Foundations of Mathematics: *A Study in the Philosophy of Science* △ TB/581

S. KÖRNER: The Philosophy of Mathematics: *An Introduction* △ TB/547

GEORGE E. OWEN: Fundamentals of Scientific Mathematics TB/569

WILLARD VAN ORMAN QUINE: Mathematical Logic TB/558

FREDERICK WAISMANN: Introduction to Mathematical Thinking. *Foreword by Karl Menger* TB/511

Philosophy of Science

R. B. BRAITHWAITE: Scientific Explanation TB/515

J. BRONOWSKI: Science and Human Values. △ *Revised and Enlarged Edition* TB/505

ALBERT EINSTEIN et al.: Albert Einstein: Philosopher-Scientist. *Edited by Paul A. Schilpp* Vol. I TB/502
Vol. II TB/503

WERNER HEISENBERG: Physics and Philosophy: *The Revolution in Modern Science* △ TB/549

KARL R. POPPER: Logic of Scientific Discovery △ TB/576

STEPHEN TOULMIN: Foresight and Understanding: *An Enquiry into the Aims of Science.* △ *Foreword by Jacques Barzun* TB/564

STEPHEN TOULMIN: The Philosophy of Science: *An Introduction* △ TB/513

Physics and Cosmology

JOHN E. ALLEN: Aerodynamics: *A Space Age Survey* △ TB/582

P. W. BRIDGMAN: Nature of Thermodynamics TB/537

C. V. DURELL: Readable Relativity. △ *Foreword by Freeman J. Dyson* TB/530

ARTHUR EDDINGTON: Space, Time and Gravitation: *An Outline of the General Relativity Theory* TB/510

GEORGE GAMOW: Biography of Physics Σ △ TB/567

STEPHEN TOULMIN & JUNE GOODFIELD: The Fabric of the Heavens: *The Development of Astronomy and Dynamics.* △ *Illus.* TB/579